Charlotte Riddell's City Novels and Victorian Business

In spite of the popularity she enjoyed during her lifetime, Charlotte Riddell (1832–1906) has received little attention from scholars. Silvana Colella makes a strong case for the relevance of Riddell's novels as narrative experiments that shed new light on the troubled experience of Victorian capitalism. Drawing on her impressive knowledge of commerce and finance, Riddell produced several novels that narrate the fate of individuals – manufacturers, accountants, entrepreneurs, City men and their female companions – who pursue the liberal dream of self-determination in the unstable world of London business. Colella situates novels such as *Too Much Alone, George Geith, The Race for Wealth, Austin Friars* and *The Senior Partner* in the broader cultural context, examining business manuals, commercial biographies and essays to highlight Victorian constructions of the business ideal and the changing cultural status of the City of London. Combining historicist and formalist readings, Colella charts the progression of Riddell's imaginative commitment to the business world, focusing on the author's gendered awareness of the promises and disenchantments associated with the changing dynamics of capitalist modernisation. Her book enriches our understanding of Victorian business culture, the literary history of capitalism, and the intersections of gender, genre and economics.

Silvana Colella is Professor of English Literature at the University of Macerata, Italy.

Charlotte Riddell's City Novels and Victorian Business

Narrating Capitalism

Silvana Colella

Routledge
Taylor & Francis Group

LONDON AND NEW YORK

First published 2016 by Routledge

2 Park Square, Milton Park, Abingdon, Oxfordshire OX14 4RN
52 Vanderbilt Avenue, New York, NY 10017

Routledge is an imprint of the Taylor & Francis Group, an informa business

First issued in paperback 2018

Library of Congress Cataloging-in-Publication Data
A catalog record for this book has been requested

ISBN: 978-1-4724-5473-7 (hbk)
ISBN: 978-0-367-14047-2 (pbk)

Typeset in Times New Roman
by Apex CoVantage LLC

A Francesca e Silvia

Contents

Acknowledgements

It is a pleasure to acknowledge the help I have received over the years during which this book has taken shape. I am deeply grateful to Deirdre d'Albertis who first pointed me towards Charlotte Riddell's works: her suggestion is the genesis of this project. My thinking owes much to Nancy Henry with whom I have discussed Riddell's life and works on several occasions, I wish to thank her for her thought-provoking questions and for sharing her ideas and material with me. Susan Morgan persuaded me, over dinner in Rome, that what I thought was a vague project already had a structure; Martin Kayman's friendship and kind encouragements were crucial to the completion of this work; the many conversations I had with Andrew King, while working through the final chapters, have been invaluable – I am very grateful to them all.

Parts of this book were presented to various audiences in the United States and Britain; I have benefitted greatly from the lively intellectual exchanges and incredibly supportive atmosphere of INCS conferences. A most sincere *grazie* to Gordon Bigelow, Chris Vanden Bossche, Helen Black, Brian Cooper, Mary Jean Corbett, Dino Felluga, Keith Hanley, Claudia Klaver, Christine Krueger, Greg Kucich, Barbara Leckie, Theresa Mangum, Deborah Denenholz Morse, Margueritte Murphy, Linda Peterson, George Robb, Kristin Samuelian, Marc Schoenfield, Claire Simmons, Richard Stein, Rebecca Stern, David Wayne Thomas, Alex Weltlaufer, Sharon Weltman and Susan Zlotnick. Writing this book would have been a much more solitary adventure without the support of this warm and vibrant community of scholars.

The University of Macerata warrants special thanks for providing travel funding even in times of severe budget cuts. My colleagues and friends in the Dipartimento di studi umanistici, Marina Camboni, Valerio De Angelis, Tatiana Petrovich Njegosh and Giuseppe Nori, have been most generous with their time during my research leave. I also owe enduring debts to Gill Philip, Anna Lukianowicz and Dominic Stewart, who have clarified innumerable linguistic questions. They have made me feel more at ease in the foreign tongue. Many thanks are due to Sally Washington, Luisa Villa, Renato Rizzoli, Dawn Kutner and Sheila Fitzjerald for providing companionship, conviviality and sound life advice throughout the years in which this book was in the making.

I have had the opportunity to carry out research in many institutions including: the British Library, the Houghton Library at Harvard University, the Henry Ransom Centre at the University of Austin, Texas, the Gabinetto Viesseux in Florence, the Biblioteca Paolo Baffi at the Bank of Italy and the Centro Studi Americani in Rome. At each I was helped by friendly and knowledgeable staff who went out of their way to offer assistance. Portions of this book appeared in articles published in *RaVoN* and *Victorian Periodicals Review* and I would like to thank the editors of those journals for permission to reprint the material here.

On a more personal note, deeper thanks go to my husband for his continuing support, enthusiasm, generosity, intellectual curiosity and formidable knowledge of all matters economic and financial. My very resourceful daughters could not have been more patient, understanding and encouraging: to them the book is dedicated, *con amore*.

Introduction

> A *casual* character, so to speak, is natural to the most intense words: externally, even, they will interest the 'after world' more for having interested the present world; they must have a life of *some* place and *some* time before they can have one of all space and all time.
>
> Walter Bagehot, 'Mr. Macaulay', 1856

In 1855, Charlotte Eliza Cowan (1832–1906) (later Riddell) left the country of her birth, Ireland, and moved to London. Like the male protagonists of most of her business novels, she had limited financial means and was in pursuit of the liberal dream of self-determination. Her talents were literary. The burgeoning market for fiction provided the arena where they were tested. Ten years later, nine novels were in print; three of them had a distinct and unusual focus on the City of London, the centre of trade and finance, where the author resided with her husband, Joseph Hadley Riddell, a moderately successful businessman. With the publication of *George Geith of Fen Court* in 1864, Riddell reaped financial and symbolic rewards. To the hefty sum of 800 pounds, paid by Tinsley Brothers for the purchase of the manuscript, corresponded a marked increase in symbolic capital. Journals and newspapers alike followed Riddell's career with growing interest and curiosity, even though assessments of her works were not unanimously positive. In the Gale digital archive of nineteenth-century British newspapers, *George Geith* returns 2,327 hits, while *Little Dorrit* occurs 1,828 times. Hit counting is a blunt instrument to measure popularity. Yet it gives us a rough sense of the cultural penetration of Riddell's novel. In September 1866, when the celebrated author of *George Geith* experienced a bout of bad health, the news (for news it was) was reported with some trepidation in a variety of provincial newspapers: the *Caledonian Mercury*; the *Leeds Mercury*; the *Manchester Courier and Lancashire General*; the *Bath Chronicle and Weekly Gazette*; the *Lancaster Gazette* and the *Stirling Observer* among others. As for the metropolitan press, the *Morning Post* was most appreciative of nearly every City novel Riddell produced. A tad less enthusiastic, the *Graphic* too supported her career with positive reviews throughout. When Riddell's popularity was on the wane and her novels no longer commanded high prices, newspapers still welcomed her stories.

In the 1880s and 1890s she published in the *Citizen*, the *Manchester Courier*, the *Weekly Irish Time*, the *Illustrated London News* and the *Swindon Advertiser*. From December 1902 to January 1903, the *Lincolnshire Echo* serialised a new novel by Mrs. J.H. Riddell, *Fair Abbotsmead*, of which there is no trace in the bibliographical records, scant as they are, of Riddell's output.[1] Established journals such as the *Saturday Review* or the *Athenaeum* tended to criticise her experiments. Being vigilant was their prerogative; authors of the calibre of Dickens or Trollope were not immune from criticism. The reviewers questioned, now and then, the accuracy of Riddell's representations and took issue with her plot lines for being too intricate or with the morals of her stories for being too loose. The unique blending of financial and literary writing which constitutes the trademark of her novelistic art was often frowned upon by reviewers whose task it was to patrol the borders of the literary, as Poovey has argued.[2] Still, even the most adversative readers, puzzled by Riddell's 'fearful and wonderful knowledge of matters financial',[3] identified the City novel as her specialty. She was primarily the novelist of the City of London. Her reputation was aided not hampered by the relative eccentricity of her thematic choice.

Riddell's success story is one of rise and fall, like many similar tales in the annals of Victorian fiction. What makes it worthy of closer scrutiny is the sharp divergence between then and now. Her media identity in the nineteenth century hinged on the novels of commerce and City life she wrote from the early 1860s well into the 1880s, among which *George Geith* was undoubtedly the most successful. What posterity has selectively remembered are not the business-centred City novels, but Riddell's secondary line of production: ghost stories and supernatural tales. These stories have been reprinted in modern editions.[4] Her novels, on the other hand, with the exception of *A Struggle for Fame* (1883), still remain dormant in the obscure storehouses of what Aleida Assmann calls 'passive cultural memory'.[5] Why this should be so is difficult to say. One hypothesis is that Riddell's ghost stories fit aesthetic categorisations more neatly than do her novels. These stories are easily classifiable as a popular form of literature which does not make grand claims, stays within prescribed bounds and is moderately innovative.[6] More arduous is to classify Riddell's bolder novelistic experiments. Are they literature or journalism, as some Victorian reviewers wondered? Do they err too much on the side of the factual or are they fictional misrepresentations of a reality no 'lady' could presume to know well?[7] A female novelist, who confidently appropriated fields of life marked as masculine, narrating the uses and ruses of credit instruments alongside the subtleties of human affections, was bound to raise persistent questions. Yet it is significant that, despite much questioning, the mid-Victorian field of literary production was capacious or tolerant enough to accommodate Riddell's renegotiations of aesthetic and gender boundaries.

The 'After World'

Posterity has been less welcoming. The recovery work carried out by feminist critics since the 1980s has left Riddell's City novels untouched, possibly because her questers are men rather than women of business. As a feminist precursor Riddell has appeared unconvincing. Given the centrality of economic issues in her novels, given the segment of historical reality Riddell chose to narrate (the City, the business world), it is somewhat surprising that her novels have not featured more prominently in literary criticism which addresses the complex relationship between economics and Victorian fiction. Economic criticism (old and new) tends to privilege canonical authors and sacralised texts.[8] When the bar is raised to include a broader spectrum of literary expressions, then Riddell's novels become more visible as they do in Tamara Wagner's *Financial Speculation in Victorian Fiction*, in Rebecca Stern's *Home Economics*, in Nancy Henry's essays and in Ranald Michie's *Guilty Money*.[9] This is not to imply that no attention has been paid to Riddell as a novelist: Linda Peterson, Patricia Srebrnik, and Margaret Kelleher have written illuminating articles.[10] Nonetheless, the author who more systematically than her fellow novelists welcomed the challenge of narrating capitalism remains mostly unread and underexamined today, as if the ubiquity of economic concerns in her fiction were too literal or too blatant to be of interest.

What might explain this neglect is the misalignment between the pro-capitalist sentiment, which finds expression in Riddell's novels, and the prevalently Marxist orientation of much twentieth-century literary criticism. While this kind of critical thinking is certainly valuable and has produced innovative and stimulating analyses of nineteenth-century fiction, it has also confirmed one prevailing historical narrative: 'It remains a common view', Kathleen Blake notes in *Pleasures of Benthamism*, 'that most great Victorian writers joined in a "counter-revolution" against a new industrial age'.[11] To a large extent they did. Harangues against financial speculation, for instance, are a staple of British realism. Devising ways to deal with the embarrassment of riches, the vulgarity of material interests, the disruptive potential of 'filthy lucre' is one of the most prominent vocations of nineteenth-century fiction, as Elsie Michie's *The Vulgar Question of Money* brilliantly illustrates.[12] Yet, Blake contends, 'there are closer affinities than are commonly acknowledged between Utilitarians and political economists and other writers of the period – Dickens, Carlyle, Trollope, Eliot, Gaskell, and Tagore'.[13] This commonality becomes noticeable when the 'radical' reformist bent of 'the bourgeois tradition of industrial market culture', the tradition comprising liberalism, Benthamism and capitalism, is underscored. Reformist rather than dismal, 'favourable to freedom, and levelling vis-à-vis gender and class',[14] this tradition was a powerful force in the culture of the period. In Victorian literary and cultural studies, however, the opposition to bourgeois, liberal, capitalist values has carried more weight and authority. As Christine MacLeod observes, 'We are more familiar with the voices of those who deplored industrialization's harmful effects than of those who welcomed its benefits and hymned its achievements'.[15] Her own study of the popular worship of 'heroes of invention' goes a long way towards remedying this 'unbalanced picture', restoring to visibility what she defines as 'one nineteenth-century "tradition" that has not survived'.[16]

Heeding Blake's and MacLeod's suggestion that we should attend more closely to the cultures of the market in Victorian England, my book aims to bring

Riddell's long-forgotten business novels under the spotlight of 'active memory'.[17] Two reasons can be adduced to justify this decision. Firstly, the discrepancy between extensive popularity 'then' and almost complete invisibility 'now' is too blatant to be ignored. It raises questions about the reception of literary works and the different 'frames of attention, valuation and use'[18] which make them meaningful or not. Why were Victorian audiences captivated by Riddell's understanding of what life looked like in the new, rampant environment of scantily regulated nineteenth-century capitalism? What were the contexts that authorised her works and contributed to determining their significance? How was her fiction received? What features pleased readers and critics, what thematic choices or stylistic whims displeased them? These questions were the springboard of my analyses. To them the chapters that follow will offer some answers. Secondly, that a woman writer should carve a niche for herself in the crowded market for fiction by weaving stories which hinge upon business pursuits and the work-oriented life of City men is remarkable in light of both gender and literary conventions. In 1884 one indignant female reader wrote to the *Pall Mall Gazette* lamenting the fact that Riddell had not been included in the list of female writers worthy of inheriting 'the mantle of the great, immortal Brontë': 'I must protest against the positivist Walhalla of our Optimist Critic on English literature in Tuesday's issue', she objects, 'It is, then, on Mrs Oliphant only that has descended the mantle of the great, the immortal Brontë? Heaven forbid! . . . Did not a woman write *George Geith*! Such an exquisite delineation of city life as no man's pen has ever attained to?'[19] Whether criticised or applauded, Riddell's focus on men, the City of London and economic activities appeared unique. What writing about City life entailed, in terms of revising and adapting novelistic conventions, will be examined in the chapters included in the second part of this book. One aspect, however, is worth anticipating. In *The Imagination of Class*, Dan Bivona and Roger Henkle claim that the 'great "plot," the central narrative paradigm of male bourgeois life . . . the story of the man rising in the business world, whetting himself on competition, defining his subjectivity by the competitive process itself' is very rarely told in Victorian England. This story, they continue,

> is being told in actual lives all over England; it is the grist for books such as Samuel Smiles's popular *Self-Help* (1859). But it is rarely the epistemic text of cultural expressions; the middle-class man on the make almost never becomes the protagonist. This is the denied element in the representation of the middle-class male. This is the contradiction in the bourgeois capitalist ideology of mid-Victorian England.[20]

The great plot of male bourgeois life constitutes the central narrative paradigm of Riddell's City novels. Though some of her protagonists are highborn, their stories become significant once they set foot in the City and acquire the middle-class status of men on the make, rising and falling in the business world. For Riddell, this 'epistemic text' is the norm, not the exception. More adamantly than other Victorian authors, she offers readers paradigmatic tales of individual self-assertion in the highly unstable sphere of business, where capitalist competition and the acquisitive urge are neither invisible nor denied. How does Riddell's realism accommodate the representation of work? How do her novels deal with the nether regions where money is actually made, things are produced, transactions executed, and the ordinary details of the life of the market matter a great deal? The documentary effect of Riddell's novels is pronounced; they set out to be illustrations of modern realities which, in her perception, were imperfectly understood by her contemporaries. One does not have to take their truth claim at face value. But it is important not to neglect the epistemological claims of her realism, the kind of knowledge these novels wished to transmit and the affective work they performed. As Harry Shaw states, 'Realism supposes that, in our encounter with reality, we can produce new and more adequate knowledge'.[21] This supposition plays no negligible role in the way Riddell's novels are shaped. The plot of development is their backbone, but the style of narration, the rhetorical strategies, the forms of direct address frequently deployed, all contribute to rendering Riddell's reflections on the historical reality of her time complex and sometimes ambivalent interpretations of the experience of commercial and financial modernity.

Modes of Reading

The question of how to attend to the forgotten, how to read the works of understudied women writers, is nuanced; the relation these works entertain with the great tradition 'may be hazy, epigonal or simply absent', writes Pamela Gilbert: 'Viewed in an evolutionary narrative they may appear to lack clear parentage or to be barren of progeny. The tastes they reflect are often not easily accessible to readers now'.[22] It is therefore all the more important to devise a mode of reading that 'fully respect[s] the complexity of our subject', as Gilbert suggests.[23] For this purpose, a mixed method, one that seeks to combine formalism and historicism, or to explain salient formal features through the work of historical contextualisation, seems most appropriate. I apply to Riddell's texts the kind of close reading usually reserved to 'elite' works with their consolidated pedigree of sophistication. I take Riddell's novels seriously as formal experiments with Victorian social and psychological realism, considering the layered and uneven texture of her writing as deeply interconnected with the unconventional topics, the specialist themes, that most engaged her attention. Rather than glossing over those features of her style (direct reader addresses; an excessively moralising narrator; plots too thin or too thick; scenes only loosely related to the progression of the story, for instance) which seem to contravene what literary critics are trained to perceive as aesthetic quality, I interrogate them in the light of both historical, contextual evidence and of narrative and critical theories. What purpose did those features serve, if any? What vision did they help convey? How were they perceived by Victorian readers? Taking these novels seriously also entails paying attention to Victorian theories of reading, to the models professional readers – the reviewers – deployed in order to assess not the absolute value of a given work of fiction, but its ability to affect the mind of readers, hold their interest, move them or elicit their indignation.[24] After all, what Victorian readers thought and wrote about Riddell's City novels surpasses in quantitative terms what twentieth- and twenty-first-century critics have produced – which amounts to a handful of excellent articles and book chapters. Riddell's realist take on commerce and finance, her pro-business rhetoric, the paradigmatic stories of self-help she narrates certainly captured the attention of her contemporaries. My book is partly an attempt to understand how Riddell spoke to them and how the novels she wrote interpret and re-imagine their troubled modernity. To paraphrase Bagehot, her words had a 'life of *some* place and *some* time' which ought to be recovered.[25]

The act of recovering begs at least one question: how are retrieved texts relevant today? More specifically, what do Riddell's novels add to our understanding of the literary history of capitalism? Can the past they helped to configure be correlated to present concerns? As Nancy Henry notes, in recent economic criticism there is a tendency to see in Victorian literature 'an opportunity to trace the pre-conditions of the globalization we are experiencing now'; the study of the past is often explained 'through references to the economic present'.[26] The path I have followed tends to privilege contextualisation and historicism – in other words, the light Riddell's novels shed on their present. This is a necessary step in any recovery project. However, the way I read and interpret these novels is also present-oriented. It could not be otherwise. I zoom in on one feature of Riddell's fiction that resonates with today's preoccupations: the problematic question of work-life balance, which she explored in novel after novel imagining the private sphere as inextricably linked to the world of business and the life of the market. The appeal of her novels today has a lot to do with the way in which they narrate the complications of living in a capitalist world, where opportunities are many and economic uncertainty a persistent spectre. This insistence on uncertainty made her fiction appear mostly gloomy to Victorian critics. Today it can be reframed as far-sighted. There are also aspects of Riddell's take on capitalism which can best be apprehended when discontinuities are underscored. For example, literary and cultural critics tend to assign to finance and speculation a prominent position in their descriptions of Victorian capitalism, thus projecting an image of the economy, dominated by abstract, impersonal forces, which pre-figures our global financial present.[27] The work of historians helps to recalibrate this narrative. In the British tradition, historians have argued, 'personal' or 'family' capitalism was incredibly resilient.[28] The process of financialisation was certainly underway in the second half of the nineteenth century, but the economy, as Riddell understood it, was not necessarily synonymous with impersonality, with intangible and abstract mechanisms for coining money from money, with large, anonymous corporations and inscrutable forces. Rather, it was still a world in which goods were produced and exchanged, small partnerships not big companies were the preferred form of enterprise, and even in the City mercantile activities had not been supplanted by financial engineering.[29] In the Victorian business subculture, discussed in Chapter 1, momentous changes – the dangerous appeal of financial speculation and the insurgence of white-collar crime in particular – did not go unnoticed. Authors of business advice manuals, commercial biographies and memoirs, however, were also keenly interested in investigating and regulating the daily life of ordinary men of business for whom the drudgery and the excitement of an existence devoted to business activities, the precarious balance between work and life, the stress and anxieties germane to those pursuits were more problematic than the abstract power of financial markets or of fictitious capital. Riddell's novels tap into this cultural reservoir of beliefs, ideas, attitudes, norms and sentiments. The significance of her stories can best be apprehended when this frame of attention is reactivated.

Capitalism and Modernity

What aspects of nineteenth-century capitalism were integral parts of Riddell's world? Her father, James Cowan, was a manufacturer, proprietor of the Barns Cotton Mills in Carrickfergus, in what is now Northern Ireland. Active in the local community, he was appointed High Sheriff of county Antrim in 1848. Her mother, Ellen Kilshaw, was the daughter of a Liverpool merchant who suffered great losses in the early 1820s in consequence of an ill-advised partnership. Ellen was in the habit of corresponding with Margaret Fuller's parents, whom she had met while travelling in America with her brother. In a letter addressed to Timothy Fuller she chronicled in some detail the tale of commercial woes that were afflicting her family:

> Papa's misfortunes were aggravated; he became acquainted with a gentleman of the name of Breed, who was reported to be very rich, he sought papa, being unacquainted (as we afterwards found was his nature) with the manner of transacting business in this country: a most respectable gentleman wished papa to enter into partnership with him, and he should have six hundred a year secured to him, whatever might be the profit of the business; when Mr. B. heard it, he said if papa would enter with him, he [Mr B.] would secure one thousand a year to him; papa could not hesitate between the two offers, considering his large family, and from that day he dates all his subsequent difficulties, he was completely deceived in the character of the above named gentleman, speculation were entered into, which he did not approve, differences of opinion continually arose, and thousands were lost, one decisive quarrel terminated their transactions and papa found himself enmeshed in some debt.[30]

The letter continues in a similar vein for a few more paragraphs; Ellen provides specific information about poor investments, the falling prices of perishable merchandise bought by her father, the extent of financial losses and her brother's efforts to be pro-active in the midst of a disastrous crisis, adding at one point: 'You may be surprised at my knowing as much about mercantile affairs, but papa and John found it a relief to their minds, to communicate with us, and I was too dearly interested to forget any particulars'. The particulars of economic vicissitudes clearly impressed themselves on the mind of this anxious middle-class lady, who, in a letter to Mrs. Fuller, sidestepped delicacy to admit quite adamantly that monetary preoccupations haunted her life: 'early in the morning, last thing at night I think of money, but my dear friend you must not suppose me mercenary'.[31] Ellen Kilshaw was later to experience a new season of misfortunes when her husband died, his property 'passed into other hands' and only a 'small jointure' was left to provide for the widow and her daughter, Charlotte.[32] The pressure of economic need must have played no marginal role in the decision to move to London and to turn Charlotte's passion for writing into a source of income.

Industrial and commercial activities, memories of calamitous ruins, the experience of precariousness: this is the 'personal' capitalism with which Riddell was arguably acquainted even before she relocated to London and married a City man, Joseph Hadley Riddell. His various occupations in the City had little to do with either banking or the Stock Exchange. The Census data pin him down as 'civil engineer', 'boiler manufacturer', 'hot water engineer' and 'agent to patent American stove merchant' – in other words, he was one of the many small traders who continued to operate in the City well into the 1880s.[33] Riddell described her husband as 'courageous and hopeful, gifted with indomitable energy . . . endowed with marvellous persistence and perseverance; modestly conscious of talents which ought to have made their mark, he, when, a mere lad, began his long quest after fortune, one single favour from whom he was never destined to receive',[34] a description which echoes many similar portraits of struggling men in her fiction. Her heroes are mainly small capitalists, not spectacular financiers such as Merdle in *Little Dorrit* or Melmotte in *The Way We Live Now*. In the light of the biographical context, this is perhaps unsurprising. Considering the literary tradition, with its fascination for larger-than-life figures of speculators, Riddell's take on the City is unconventional. She does not deny the hold of speculation on the minds of her contemporaries. Some of her novels –*The Race for Wealth* (1866), *The Senior Partner* (1882) and *Mitre Court* (1885) – contain powerful invectives against this 'mania' and the legislative reforms that facilitated its spread. But what goes under the term 'real economy' ('the part of the economy that is concerned with actually producing goods and services, as opposed to the part of the economy that is concerned with buying and selling on the financial markets')[35] seemed to her a vastly more fascinating and challenging field even for a novelist. In an important respect, narrating capitalism meant taking stock of how the real economy was interwoven with the fabric of bourgeois life.

It also meant coming to terms with the modern condition. In the most common view of 'modernity', the term refers to a new type of society, to the institutional arrangements and intellectual milieu that emerged from a sequence of major transformations affecting Europe and North America and culminating in the industrial and political revolutions of the late eighteenth and early nineteenth centuries. As Peter Wagner maintains, 'modernity was associated with the open horizon of the future, with unending progress towards a better human condition brought about by a radically novel and unique institutional arrangement'.[36] Specific to modernity is its commitment to freedom, to the principle of individual and collective self-determination and to the belief in rational mastery, understood as increased rational control over society, nature and the self. Wagner also specifies that the ways in which modernity was experienced 'differed considerably between societies'; the interpretations given to the experiences of modernity 'were contested from the beginning and continued being revised in light of further experiences with their consequences'.[37] In Riddell's novels the experience of economic modernity (the market society, capitalism) is primary, whereas the political project recedes into the background. In the self-understanding of both characters and narrators, aware of themselves as modern, the present is one of constantly accelerating change. This dynamism has a twofold effect: on the one hand the experience of modernity is configured as one of plurality and of possibility; on the other, the destructiveness of capitalist modernisation, or the 'tragedy of development' as Marshall Berman calls it referring to Goethe's *Faust*,[38] comes to the fore, increasingly so in the novels of the 1880s. The utopian streak of modernity, its promise of autonomy and progress, orients the ideological outlook of such novels as *Too Much Alone* (1860), *City and Suburb* (1861), *George Geith* (1864), *The Race for Wealth* (1866) and *Austin Friars* (1870), though all of them contain tragic elements typically related to the impact of economic modernity on the private sphere. From the mid 1870s onwards, Riddell's vision darkens and her fascination with the City takes on negative connotations. *Mortomely's Estate* (1874) is a novel of bankruptcy in which Riddell reworks her own experience of financial collapse, after the liquidation of her husband's business in 1871. The trauma of this crisis casts a long shadow on the liberal utopia of self-determination, as the tragedy of loss is told in terms that emphasise the battle of one individual against persecutory institutional powers. With *The Senior Partner* and *Mitre Court*, the experience of commercial and financial modernity comes to be associated with lost illusions; the individuals operating in the City are either antiquated and stubbornly nostalgic merchants or youthful newcomers for whom no promise of progress holds true. Both novels can be read as Riddell's interpretations of the sense of decline or stagnation that was widespread in *fin-de-siècle* culture and society.

While Riddell's fiction might be said to be a product of commercial and financial modernity, it is also a producer of it. It is through an active engagement with their historical present that her novels produce forms of subjectivity, models of conduct, and memories of momentous transformations which contribute to shaping the narratives of modernity. Salient in this respect is her understanding of gender issues. In the City novels, the sphere of work exists in relation to the market, on the one hand, and to home, domestic life, private affections (sometimes straying into the improper), on the other. The novels analysed in this book offer several variations on this tripartite structure. Riddell even presented her unusual choice of the City theme as the result of domestic affections. In the 1890s, when the celebrity author – preferably depicted at home surrounded by familiar objects – was a relatively new invention of the popular press,[39] Riddell was interviewed by Raymond Blathwayt for the *Pall Mall Gazette* and by Helen Black for the *Lady's Pictorial*. Prompted by the former to explain what had induced her to take up the City theme, 'so unlikely a subject for a woman to handle well or technically', Riddell reverted to personal, biographical reasons. It is worth quoting this interview at some length, since Riddell's direct testimonies about her art are few and far between.

> I married a City man, a civil engineer, and we used to live in Scots-yard, in the very picturesque old house in which my hero 'Austin Friars' was born. All the pathos of the City, the pathos in the lives of struggling men entered into my soul, and I felt I must write, strongly as my publisher objected to my choice of subject, which he said was one no woman could handle well . . . In fact, I was and still am heartily in love with the City . . . I always find that when a City man once begins my novels he reads the whole of them, and many business people in the country write to me about them. I fancy I must have a certain sympathy with City men, their lives and hopes and struggles, for they have always spoken to me very freely about their affairs, and so to a great extent I have learnt a great deal from them. I have been sharply criticised, especially by the *Saturday*, but my City matters are always right . . .Yes I suppose I do know more about the City and City ways than most women; but do you not think that nowadays ladies seem to take an absolute pride in not knowing or caring about City matters . . . there is quite an incapacity in a woman for all that lies East of Temple Bar.[40]

A mixture of defiance and traditionalism colours this retrospective view: defiance vis-à-vis a hostile publishing environment ('All my publishers would look upon my writing as a joke at first') as well as prejudicial expectations about masculine and feminine types of knowledge ('I know more about the City . . . than most women'); traditionalism when it comes to defending aesthetic choices on the basis of personal or family relationships. Riddell presents herself as a wife who finds the world in which her husband is active vastly more interesting than the sphere allotted to women, but does not seem to have much faith in the ability of other women to share her knowledge and interests.

Yet, as Patricia Srebrnik has suggested, Riddell's novels address a segment of the middle classes composed of men and women; they do not merely 'chronicle the lives of social and professional groups whose activities were rarely described in detail in Victorian fiction,' Srebrnick argues, they also discuss 'those activities from the point of view of middle- and lower-middle class wives and working women'.[41] Though the heroes of self-help are mostly men, their female companions play substantial roles in the unfolding of the stories Riddell narrates. Typically, these heroines desire a share of the active life their husbands lead, as Lina and Beryl do in *Too Much Alone* and *George Geith* respectively. Some of them even view the City with rapt eyes, as a space of almost unlimited possibilities, but they do not cross the threshold of the home. When they do, as in *Austin Friars*, for instance, the plot returns them to domestic roles. In other words, the modernity these novels portray travels at two different speeds, fast-paced in the sphere of business, where opportunities for self-fashioning abound, but slow-moving on the domestic stage where the only deviation from stasis is the temptation of adultery. This uneven development generates a particular kind of plot: forward-looking, hopeful and dynamic on the one hand, sensationalistic and tragic on the other. Riddell does not advocate explicitly a broadening of the sphere of influence and action reserved to women. What she does, instead, is to dwell on dissatisfaction, unfulfilled desires, unhappy marriages and the long shadow of a domestic, private world that lags behind the more dynamic and exciting ambits of capitalist activities, be they industrial or commercial. Riddell insists on the indivisibility of private and public, work and home; the interaction between the two is the central axis around which her stories revolve. If what she knew of City men inspired her City novels, how she imagined the predicaments of women on the cusp of the old and the new is of equal interest. Riddell herself was deeply involved in the running of her husband's business; she negotiated with creditors and took care of the constant flow of correspondence, all the while performing her own duties as novelist and, for seven years, as editor of the *St James's Magazine.* In a suit brought against her husband, in the hectic months preceding his bankruptcy, a creditor described her as 'an experienced woman of business'.[42] Some of her heroines find themselves in analogous situations: they help with business decisions (Mary Matson in *Too Much Alone*), write commercial letters (Beryl in *George Geith*), deal with rough creditors and accountants (Dolly in *Mortomley's Estate*), or co-run a business partnership (Yorke in *Austin Friars*). Their participation in the life of the market may be indirect, but it defines their modern world. A growing body of scholarship, in recent years, has drawn attention to the complex interactions between gender and economic ideas and practices: Susan Zlotnick's analyses of male and female literary responses to the industrial revolution; Deanna Kreisel's explorations of the rhetorical interconnections between images of feminised sexuality and Victorian anxieties about capitalist development; Jill Rappoport's study of 'giving women' and the lateral transactions in which they were involved; the various types of 'Economic Women', both real and fictional, analysed in the collection of essays edited by Lana Dalley and Jill Rappoport are all good cases in point.[43] Charlotte Riddell's position 'as a woman writing about finance more authoritatively than her male contemporaries', Nancy Henry argues, 'might make her an example of how masculine and feminine spheres of influence were not as separate as they have seemed'.[44] What Riddell's City novels bring into sharp focus is the pervasiveness of economic concerns in the lives of both men and women, regardless of their different structural position vis-à-vis the gendered division of labour. Her most brazen representation of female economic agency and self-interest is to be found in *A Struggle for Fame* (1883), as I argue in the Epilogue. This semi-autobiographical *Künslterroman* replicates the progressive plot of development and self-help that constitutes the central narrative paradigmatic in Riddell's City novels: the subject embodying undiluted economic individualism, however, is a woman, not a man. Like Trollope's *Autobiography*, published in the same year, *A Struggle for Fame* is, in some ways, a retrospective narrative of self-determination, a fictional re-ordering of the battle for success that maximises the virtues of individual striving, and minimises the power of market forces to determine the direction of one's life. It is a fitting tale with which to conclude this book.

Plan of the Study

Charlotte Riddell's City Novels and Victorian Business: Narrating Capitalism is primarily a work of literary criticism. The main objective is to provide interpretations of Riddell's novels in relation to the cultural, social, economic and legal contexts in which they were produced and consumed. Contexts, of course, are constructed rather than reconstructed; as Robert Hume writes 'we are building the best simulacrum we can from such "traces" as remain'.[45] Partial as this enterprise might be, it gives us a baseline from which to start. My selection of contexts has been determined by the overarching themes of Riddell's fiction: business and the City. Part I contains two chapters devoted respectively to Victorian business culture and to the City of London as a literary subject. Authors of business advice manuals were fond of quoting the Latin word *negotium* when explaining the meaning of 'business' to their readership: 'Its Latin equivalent, *negotium* (*nego otium*) denotes self-denial of ease for the sake of an object to be attained. In a more restricted sense, the word business signifies those pursuits which involve buying and selling or bargaining in some way'.[46] The denial of ease was in more than one sense a defining feature of business pursuits as they were discussed in the pages of the periodical press, in business handbooks, memoirs and biographies. In the sample of texts analysed in Chapter 1, business is viewed as a modern vocation still lacking the prestige of more traditional callings; a problematic and demanding life-script, exacting a high price in terms of mental and bodily health; and a national glory celebrated in orotund rhetoric in one particular genre of writing, commercial biographies. My analyses underscore how business and the life of its devotees were codified in different types of writing. Samuel Smiles's *Self-Help* (1859) illustrates only one strand in a more varied spectrum of representations. The emphasis on overwork and on the excessive demands of business, negligible in Smiles's vertiginous list of successful paragons, crops up frequently in advice manuals and memoirs, complicating the national myth of commercial glories. Riddell's fiction was deeply attuned to contemporaneous discourses about the pains and gains of business, discourses with which other novelists were less willing to engage. Though it may appear paradoxical, the proximity of Riddell's texts to the 'tangential rumour, the everyday, transient writing that never acquires the status of an oeuvre, or is immediately lost'[47] helps to define the uniqueness of her contribution.

Chapter 2, 'The Golden City and the Spectral', turns to a set of texts, by Charles Dickens, John Hollingshead, George Augustus Sala and David Morier Evans, originally published as journalistic pieces and later collected in volume form. The aim of this chapter is to explore how the symbolic boundaries of the City of London were redrawn in the middle decades of the nineteenth century, when the City was undergoing momentous transformations. The title of the chapter alludes to the metaphorical identities – golden and spectral – articulated by different observers to emblematise either the glorious power and grand mission of this 'citadel' of British 'greatness' (as Patterson viewed it)[48] or its dark, Gothicised, criminal underbelly, and the spectrality of its 'paper' inhabitants (as Hollingshead and Sala depicted them).[49] I argue that the City was a 'fact' which required much fictionalising to be rendered knowable. The sketch form was the preferred frame through which these authors made sense of the City. Unlike Riddell, who opted for the long duration of the novel form, the writers who in the 1850s and 1860s described, narrated and elucidated the City to a public of curious outsiders, invested in brevity, in the quick tempo and mini-closures of the sketch. Their snapshots project a prevalently dystopian vision of the Square Mile, depicted as a depopulated necropolis (Dickens), a 'City of Unlimited Paper' (Hollingshead), and a zombie-like enclave of lingering 'spectres' (Sala). In Garret Ziegler's interpretation, these representations helped to clear a symbolic space for the advent of the abstract City of financial labour, by erasing the traces of 'lived experience'.[50] However, as I contend with reference to Sala's and Hollingshead's sketches, their vocal denunciations of financial speculation and white-collar crime were rooted in anti-democratic sentiment, expressed through a marked attitude of scorn towards the crowd of small traders, clerks, and employees still living and working in the City. The final section focuses on David Morier Evans's works, examining in particular the tension between the local and the global, the blending of documentary and imaginative writing and the personal tone he adopts to translate the mysteries of the City into intimate narratives told from the perspective of an insider.

The second part of the book, 'Narrating Capitalism', is structured chronologically. In addition to in-depth analyses of the novels, each chapter contains further discussions of relevant contextual material, useful to elucidate the specific themes addressed in each novel. Chapter 3, 'Glorious Uncertainty: *Too Much Alone*', analyses Riddell's first narrative foray into the world of commerce and finance. *Too Much Alone* (1860) is both a business novel and a novel of adultery. Focusing on how the text configures the emotional regimes of capitalism, this chapter examines Riddell's representation of improper desires and capricious feelings in relation to what she sees as endemic in commercial society: not fraud, but insecurity and uncertainty, whether glorious or dreary. The experience of uncertainty, I argue, provides the point of intersection between the two narrative strands. Explicitly addressed to business people, the novel offers a lesson in sentimental education, guiding readers to tolerate the uncertain repackaged as an intense emotional experience. The chapter introduces and discusses the most distinctive feature of Riddell's urban realism: her dual focus on business and domesticity, work and home. The tensions and problems of one are the tensions and problems of the other. Riddell's style of narration, with its balancing of expression and prohibition, its propensity to embalm ambiguity in long sentences, carries part of the educational message. In Riddell's understanding of mid-Victorian capitalism uncertainty is inspiring and progressive as well as disheartening and unsettling. Hence the tendency of this novel to value characters who learn to cope with all sorts of unstable situations, including adulterous desire.

Chapter 4, 'Novel Experiments: *City and Suburb*', draws on narrative theory to examine direct reader addresses, the use of distancing and engaging narrative strategies and the function of counterfactuals in the representation of urban life. Two storylines are intersected in this novel: one is predicated on a strict causal logic, the other is imbued with a sense of randomness or what Riddell calls the 'unexpectedness of occurrences'.[51] While distancing strategies prevail in the way the main plot line, hinging on Alan Ruthven's progress, is narrated, immersive strategies are deployed with reference to the story of Hugh Elyot and Ina Trenham, both characters associated with an ethos of cosmopolitan tolerance. The novel is also divided between the vindication of business as a modern vocation, open to all, and the condemnation of vulgarity and materialism. Realism and social satire are deployed to diversify the geography of the story world: the suburbs, where wealthy merchants live, are conveniently constrained by the satirical frame, while the cosmopolitan City retains the fuzzy contours of a virtual world rife with possibilities. My contention is that the high frequency of reader addresses and narratorial interventions is related to these internal tensions: the narrator Riddell imagines is hyper-active in her efforts to hold the story together and to exert a measure of semantic control on divergent narrative impulses.

George Geith, the story of a clergyman who becomes an accountant in the City, proved vastly more successful than Riddell's previous City novels. Chapter 5 discusses the critical reception of this novel and offers an explanation for its popularity, contingent upon two factors: Riddell's frequent appeals to the countryside ideal, popular at mid-century, and the successful balancing acts performed in the text. It is no coincidence that a novel in which accounting defines the sphere of business should be structured around a principle of balance. This chapter analyses the rhetorical and narrative strategies which contribute to rendering *George Geith* a paradigmatic tale of order and harmony. The cautious compromises and reassuring solutions imagined in this novel are the result of a careful balancing of contrasting elements: the country and the city, business and leisure, money and prestige, even speculation and morality appear neatly harmonised in the symbolic economy of the narrative. Accounting is not just a theme, but also a trope in the novel. A double-entry model of assessment anchors meanings in this text: problematic issues related to the topical question of the morality of the market are entered twice in the novel's moral ledger so that the debit and credit side even each other out. That Riddell's contemporaries found her compromises more convincing than the conflicts she had explored in previous novels suggests how deeply felt was the demand for fictional resolutions of the contradictions of modernity.

The Race for Wealth (1866), analysed in Chapter 6, does not replicate the model of aesthetic harmony formalised in *George Geith*. The novel revolves around a highly controversial topic – the business of food and drink adulteration – hotly debated in the 1860s. In the absence of effective legislation, food adulteration was a blatant example of tolerated commercial misconduct at mid-century. Riddell exploits and amplifies the ambivalence of this situation. My reading draws on the insights of Frederic Jameson's *The Antinomies of Realism* (2013) to explore the tension between plot and scene, arguing that Riddell's rendering of both commercial and domestic frauds (adultery) is inquisitive rather than anxious. The novel probes moral limits. This probing is achieved in the 'realm of affect' (as Jameson defines it) rather than plot; it is a question of how things are described, as opposed to what narrative destiny prescribes. I discuss the novel's imaginative investment in the impure and the messy, which can be detected at various levels: in the choice of subject matter (adulteration and adultery) as well as in the style of telling. The attraction of the impure works against the certainties of melodramatic binaries, producing a different sort of realism from the one tested in *George Geith* to much public acclaim.

Chapter 7, 'A Liberal Education: *Austin Friars*', focuses on the intersections between Riddell's novel and liberalism. From 1867 until 1874, during the 'golden age of liberal reform',[52] Riddell was editor and proprietor of the *St. James's Magazine*. Under her editorship, the magazine paid increased attention to the political and cultural project of liberalism. The novel she published soon after starting her career as editor, *Austin Friars*, revolves around three 'embodiments' of liberalism, to use Hadley's metaphor:[53] the woman of business, the self-cultivating male individual, and the liberal intersubjectivity of the commercial sphere. While all Riddell's novels resonate with concepts and beliefs associated with classical economic liberalism, *Austin Friars* more specifically engages with the procedures of liberalisation and the pedagogy of self-cultivation. To some extent, *Austin Friars* is a reformed City novel: it extends the textual franchise to the representation of female liberal agency (though not in triumphant terms); it focuses on the process of self-development that produces the ideal citizen, endowed with a capaciousness of vision, and it describes in meticulous detail how in the commercial sphere transcending self-interest might yield efficient results. Declared an immoral book by the *Saturday Review*, the novel was also criticised for the excess of technical financial knowledge exhibited in its pages. The business plot is structured around the exchange of bills and the transfer of credit; the emphasis falls on how to behave when the quality of credit deteriorates. With respect to this, the moral of the novel is not confusing: appeals to cooperation and tolerant judgment are scattered throughout the narrative; offering instead of withholding help is described as an economically rational decision. Liberal education and financial education overlap. That they do so in a novel so committed to redeeming the *faux pas* of a woman whose commercial as well as erotic knowledge is well above average, further testify to the liberalising tenor of this tale of commerce and love.

Chapter 8, 'Rewriting the Crisis: *Mortomley's Estate*', addresses the question of bankruptcy in Victorian England. *Mortomley's Estate* is one of Riddell's most polemical novels; her attacks against the new system of administration licensed by the 1869 Bankruptcy Act are vocal and frequent. The novel is also a re-enactment of the trauma of financial ruin that Riddell and her husband had experienced in 1871. In this chapter, I argue that *Mortomley's Estate* is a very atypical novel of bankruptcy: Riddell favours a hyper-technical reading of ruin which goes against the grain of well-established literary conventions. The paradigm of the fortunate fall is questioned, the household clearance scene (a staple in literary renderings of bankruptcy) is extended over many chapters, the figure of the bankrupt is notable for his absence and the role of women is amplified. Riddell's divergence from tradition can be seen as a way of reckoning with the emotional impact of failure; its long-term effects are registered through a form of 'traumatic realism' which evokes distress in the suspension of, or deviation from, consolidated models of representation. The novel is also a story of resilience, structured as a heroic battle between one 'small' individual (the bankrupt's wife, Dolly) and legal and financial systems of power. The fantasy of compensation conveyed through this story offers the kind of justice that the law avows to protect, but does not seem automatically to guarantee. The chapter concludes with a brief discussion of the comic one-volume novel *Frank Sinclair's Wife* (1873) and the ghost stories that Riddell went on to write under the increased pressure to earn money. The ghost of bankruptcy intermittently haunts these texts.

The novels Riddell wrote in the 1880s, *The Senior Partner* and *Mitre Court*, are dealt with in Chapter 9. A mood of disillusion prevails in both texts; they share an anxious focus on economic decline and a similar interest in intergenerational conflicts within family firms. The aspirations of youthful protagonists recede into the background, while heavy Victorian fathers come to the fore, emblems of an antiquated model of economic subjectivity which the novels preserve and, at the same time, expose as a myth that no longer holds much value. In terms of formal features, the main difference with previous novels is a veering away from 'narration' towards 'observation,' observation of character, in particular, with a marked preference for obsolete literary figures. The eccentric miser in *Mitre Court* and the extremely parsimonious merchant in *The Senior Partner* are reminiscent of a much earlier stage in the development of capitalism when primary accumulation and monopolistic advantages sustained the mercantile fortunes of the nation. While *The Senior Partner* focuses on the problems of intergenerational succession within a small family firm, *Mitre Court* resonates with late Victorian concerns about cultural heritage and the 'preservation' rather than 'restoration' of old buildings. Riddell adopts a preservationist stance, most noticeable in the attempt to protect both historical landmarks and old forms of economic subjectivity, psychological as well as material architectures whose heritage value is memorialised in her writing. This caring attitude towards the past, however, is in tension with the critical, even corrosive perspective of the disenchanted late nineteenth-century narrator, resulting in a somewhat uneasy cohabitation of the residual, empathic affectivity of realism and the more deterministic streak of incipient naturalism. Questioning the belief in progress, *The Senior Partner* and *Mitre Court* zoom in on the frustrated aspirations of a young generation of City players for whom the world of capitalist competition is an incubus of determinism.

Reversing this interpretation of decline, *A Struggle for Fame* (1883) narrates the vicissitudes of Glenarva Westley and Bernard Kelly, both of Irish origin, in the competitive milieu of the mid-nineteenth-century market for books. In the Epilogue, I argue that in this novel Riddell revises the progressive plot of development, the great plot of male bourgeois life, placing a woman at the centre. More specifically, Riddell imagines a dual trajectory which differentiates between chance and freedom along gender lines: Bernard Kelly will attain success aided by a striking series of fortuitous circumstances that test the limits of realistic verisimilitude; Glenarva's adventures in the marketplace, on the other hand, are configured as the prototypical expression of undiluted self-help and virtuous individual striving. Glenarva's open confrontation with market forces, unassisted by fortune, is Riddell's final tribute to the ideals and the myths that, until the 1870s, had sustained her imaginative engagement with the City and the world of business. In November 2014, at the Dublin Book Festival, a small independent Irish publisher, Tramp Press, launched the first title of their Recovered Voices series: Charlotte Riddell's *A Struggle for Fame*. The decision to republish Riddell's *Künstleroman* is both a welcome indication that her works are finally gaining in acknowledgement and a confirmation of the legacy of indifference towards Riddell's novels of the City. By forging a return path, this book hopes to provide new frames of attention within which the significance of her commitment to narrating capitalism can be reassessed.

Notes

1 See Michael Flower, 'The Charlotte Riddell Website', http://www.charlotteriddell. co.uk, last accessed 12 March 2015; the entry 'Charlotte Riddell' in *Orlando: Women's Writing in the British Isle from the Beginnings to the Present*, http://orlando.cambridge. org/ last accessed May 2014; Andrew Maunder, 'Charlotte Eliza Lawson Riddell', in *Nineteenth-Century British Women Writers*, ed. Abigail Bloom (London: Aldywch Press, 2000), pp. 323–7; Janet Todd ed., *British Women Writers: A Critical Reference Guide* (New York: Continuum, 1989), pp. 568–70 and Charlotte Mitchell, 'Riddell, Charlotte Eliza Lawson (1832–1906)', *Oxford Dictionary of National Biography*, http://www.oxforddnb.com/view/article/35748?docPos=3 last accessed 5 April 2015.
2 Mary Poovey, *Genres of the Credit Economy: Mediating Value in Eighteenth-and Nineteenth-Century Britain* (Chicago: The University of Chicago Press, 2008), chapter 5.
3 [John Ashcroft Noble], 'New Novels', *The Academy* 709 (5 December 1885), p. 372.
4 See E.F. Bleiler, ed., *The Collected Ghost Stories of Mrs. J.H. Riddell* (New York: Dover Publications, 1977). Riddell's stories have also appeared in anthologies, see, for example, Peter Haining, ed., *The Mammoth Book of Haunted House Stories* (New York: Carrol & Graf, 2000) and A. Susan Williams, ed., *The Penguin Book of Classic Fantasy by Women* (Harmondsworth: Penguin, 1995).
5 Aleida Assmann, 'Canon and Archive', in *Cultural and Memory Studies. An Interdisciplinary Handbook*, ed. Astrid Erll and Ansgar Nünning (Berlin: Walter de Gruyter, 2008), p. 102. *A Struggle for Fame* is now available in a new edition (Dublin: Tramp Press, 2014).
6 As Bleiler notes, 'the ideas in Mrs. Riddell's ghost stories were not novel; they were shared by most of her contemporaries who wrote such fiction' see Bleiler, 'Mrs. Riddell, Mid-Victorian Ghosts, and Christmas Annuals', in *The Collected Ghost Stories*, p. xvii.
7 As the *Saturday Review* observed, with reference to Riddell's 1870 novel *Austin Friars*, the 'facility with which she handles commercial slang is remarkable in a lady'. See 'Austin Friars', *The Saturday Review* 29, no. 762 (4 June 1870), p. 758.
8 Mark Osteen and Martha Woodmansee distinguish between a 'first wave of economic criticism, which appeared during the late 1970s and early 1980s' and a second wave of scholarship that investigates 'the relations among literature, culture and economics'; the latter is characterized by its proximity to the methods and assumptions of both New Historicism and Cultural Studies. See Mark Osteen and Martha Woodmansee, 'Taking Account of the New Economic Criticism: An Historical Introduction', in *The New Economic Criticism: Studies at the Intersection of Literature and Economics* (London: Routledge, 1999), p. 3.
9 See Tamara S. Wagner, *Financial Speculation in Victorian Fiction: Plotting Money and the Novel Genre, 1815–1901* (Columbus: The Ohio State University Press, 2010);

Rebecca Stern, *Home Economics: Domestic Frauds in Victorian England* (Colum-
bus: The Ohio State University Press, 2008); Nancy Henry, '"Ladies do it?": Victorian
Women Investors in Fact and Fiction', in *Victorian Literature and Finance*, ed. Francis
O'Gorman (Oxford: Oxford UP, 2007), pp. 111–34 and 'Charlotte Riddell: Novelist of
"the City"', in *Economic Women: Essays on Desire and Dispossession in Nineteenth-
Century British Culture*, ed. Lana L. Dalley and Jill Rappoport (Columbus: The Ohio
State University Press, 2013), pp. 193–205, and Ranald C. Michie, *Guilty Money: The
City of London in Victorian and Edwardian Culture, 1815–1914* (London: Pickering &
Chatto, 2009). Michie's work contains synopses of a vast range of lesser-known novels
that feature City scenes.
10 Linda Peterson, 'Challenging Brontëan Myths of Authorship: Charlotte Riddell and
A Struggle for Fame (1883)', in *Becoming a Woman of Letters: Myths of Authorship
and Facts of the Victorian Market* (Princeton: Princeton University Press, 2009),
pp. 151–70; Margaret Kelleher, 'Charlotte Riddell's *A Struggle for Fame*: The Field
of Women's Literary Production', *Colby Literary Quarterly* 36, no. 2 (June 2000),
pp. 116–31 and Patricia Srebrnik, 'Mrs. Riddell and the Reviewers: A Case Study in
Victorian Popular Fiction', *Women's Studies* 23, no.1 (1994), pp. 69–84.
11 Kathleen Blake, *Pleasures of Benthamism: Victorian Literature, Utility, Political
Economy* (Oxford: Oxford University Press, 2009), p. 27.
12 See Christopher Herbert, 'Filthy Lucre: Victorian Ideas of Money', *Victorian Studies*
44, no. 2 (Winter 2002), pp. 185–213 and Elsie B. Michie, *The Vulgar Question of
Money: Heiresses, Materialism, and the Novel of Manners from Jane Austen to Henry
James* (Baltimore: The Johns Hopkins University Press, 2011).
13 Blake, p. 224.
14 Ibid.
15 Christine MacLeod, *Heroes of Invention: Technology, Liberalism and British Identity,
1750–1914* (Cambridge: Cambridge University Press, 2007), p. 10.
16 MacLeod, p. 6.
17 Assmann, p. 99.
18 Ibid., p. 98.
19 'Occasional Notes', *The Pall Mall Gazette*, 24 April 1884, p. 2.
20 Daniel Bivona and Roger B. Henkle, *The Imagination of Class: Masculinity and the
Victorian Urban Poor* (Columbus: Ohio State University Press, 2006), p. 13.
21 Harry E. Shaw, *Narrating Reality: Austen, Scott, Eliot* (Ithaca: Cornell University
Press, 1999), p. 33.
22 Pamela Gilbert, 'Ouida and the Canon: Recovering, Reconsidering, and Revisioning
the Popular', in *Ouida and Victorian Popular Culture*, ed. Andrew King and Jane Jordan (Aldershot: Ashgate, 2013), p. 39.
23 Ibid.
24 On the physiological underpinnings of Victorian novel theory see Nicholas Dames,
*The Physiology of the Novel: Reading, Neural Science, and the Form of Victorian Fic-
tion* (Oxford: Oxford University Press, 2007).
25 Walter Bagehot, 'Mr. Macaulay', 1856, in *The Collected Works of Walter Bagehot*,
vol. 1, *The Literary Essays*, ed. Norman St John-Stevas (London: The Economist,
1965), p. 403.
26 Nancy Henry, '2008 and All That: Economics and Victorian Literature', *Victorian Literature and Culture* 43 (2015), p. 218.
27 In *Genres of the Credit Economy*, Poovey concentrates on financial crises; Anna Kornbluh, in *Realizing Capital: Financial and Psychic Economies in Victorian Form* (New
York: Fordham University Press, 2014) emphasises the notion of 'fictitious capital';
in *From Dickens to* Dracula*: Gothic, Economics, and Victorian Fiction* (Cambridge:
Cambridge University Press, 2005), Gail Turley Houston focuses on the panics and
anxieties generated by the process of 'bankerization'; the stock-market graph is the
modern form of abstraction analysed by Audrey Jaffe in *The Affective Life of the*

Average Man: The Victorian Novel and the Stock-Market Graph (Columbus: Ohio University Press, 2010); for Tamara Wagner, 'the Victorian novel was significantly shaped by financial speculation' (p. 2). As Aeron Hunt rightly observes in *Personal Business: Character and Commerce in Victorian Literature and Culture* (Charlottesville: University of Virginia Press, 2014), 'when literary critics come to put descriptive flesh onto the broad conceptual and historical outline of "Victorian capitalism," the business world they depict often feels like a very impersonal place'; this emphasis on abstraction is linked to theoretical accounts of economic modernization, 'from Marx's analysis of class relations, fetishism, and alienation, to Weber's discussion of rationalization, specialization, and bureaucratization' (p. 24); however, as Hunt's book perceptively illustrates, there are many ways in which Victorian business and capitalism 'invoked and engaged the personal' (p. 15).

28 See Alfred Chandler, *Scale and Scope: the Dynamics of Industrial Capitalism* (Cambridge, MA: Belknap Press, 1990); Mary B. Rose, 'The family firm in British business, 1780–1914', in *Business Enterprise in Modern Britain: From the Eighteenth Century to the Twentieth* Century, ed. Maurice W. Kirby and Mary B. Rose (London: Routledge, 1994), pp. 61–87; Jonathan Brown and Mary B. Rose eds, *Entrepreneurship, Networks, and Modern Business* (Manchester: Manchester University Press, 1993) and Andrea Colli, *The History of Family Business, 1750–2000* (Cambridge: Cambridge University Press, 2003).
29 See Michael Ball and David Sunderland, *An Economic History of London, 1800–1914* (London: Routledge, 2001), p. 359 and Michie, *Guilty Money*.
30 Letter to Timothy Fuller, 1821, in Margaret Fuller Family Papers, 1662–1970 (MS Am 1086), vol.2, p. 63, Houghton Library, Harvard University.
31 Letter to Mrs. Fuller, 24 July 1819, vol. 2, p. 38.
32 Helen C. Black, 'Mrs. Riddell' in *Notable Women Authors of the Day* (London: Maclaren and Company, 1906), p. 16.
33 Census 1851; 1861 (RG 9/795); 1871 (RG10/1340), The National Archives, London.
34 Black, p. 18–19.
35 See *Longman Business English Dictionary* (Harlow: Pearson Longman, 2007).
36 Peter Wagner, *Modernity as Experience and Interpretation: A New Sociology of Modernity* (Cambridge: Polity Press, 2008), p. 1.
37 Ibid., p. 4.
38 Marshal Berman, *All that is Solid Melts into Air: the Experience of Modernity* (London: Penguin, 1988), p. 40.
39 See Ann R. Hawkins and Maura Ives, eds. *Women Writers and the Artifacts of Celebrity in the Long Nineteenth Century* (Farnham: Ashgate, 2012).
40 [Raymond Blathwayt], 'Lady Novelists – A Chat with Mrs. J.H. Riddell', *Pall Mall Gazette*, 18 February 1890, p. 3.
41 Srebrnik, p. 76.
42 Riddell v. Riddell and Smith. R133 (1871). British National Archives C16/747.
43 See Susan Zlotnick, *Women, Writing, and the Industrial Revolution* (Baltimore: The Johns Hopkins University Press, 1998); Deanna K. Kreisel, *Economic Woman: Demand, Gender and Narrative Closure in Eliot and Hardy* (Toronto: University of Toronto Press, 2012); Jill Rappoport, *Giving Women: Alliance and Exchange in Victorian Culture* (Oxford: Oxford University Press, 2012); and Dalley and Rappoport, *Economic Women*.
44 Henry, 'Charlotte Riddell', p. 205.
45 Robert D. Hume, *Reconstructing Contexts: the Aims and Principles of Archeo-Historicism* (Oxford: Oxford University press, 1999), pp. 1–2.
46 Samuel Robert Wells, *How to Do Business: A Pocket Manual of Practical affairs, and a Guide to Success in Life* (New York and London: Fowler and Wells Publishers, 1857), p. 9.
47 Michel Foucault, *The Archeology of Knowledge* (London: Routledge, 2008), p. 153.

48 [Robert Hogarth Patterson], 'The City of Gold', *Blackwood's Edinburgh Magazine* 96, no. 587 (September 1864), p. 367.

49 John Hollingshead, *Under Bow Bells: A City Book for All Readers* (London: Groombridge and Sons, 1859); George Augustus Sala, *Gaslight and Daylight: With Some London Scenes They Shine Upon* (London: Chapman & Hall, 1859).

50 Garret Ziegler, 'The City of London, Real and Unreal', *Victorian Studies* 49, no. 3, (Spring 2007), pp. 431–55.

51 Charlotte Riddell, *City and Suburb*, 1861, (London: Hutchinson& Co., n.d.), p. 187.

52 Jonathan Parry, *The Rise and Fall of Liberal Government In Victorian Britain* (New Haven: Yale University Press, 1993), p. 224.

53 Elaine Hadley, *Living Liberalism: Practical Citizenship in Mid-Victorian Britain* (Chicago: The University of Chicago press, 2010).

Part I

Victorian Business and the City of London

1 'The Wisdom of Business'

Victorian Constructions of the Business Ideal

> ... but for the wisdom of business, wherein man's life is most conversant, there
> be no books of it, except some few scattered advertisements, that have no propor-
> tion to the magnitude of this subject. For if books were written of this ... I doubt
> not but learned men with mean experience would far excel men of long experience
> without learning, and outshoot them in their own bow.
>
> Francis Bacon, *The Advancement of Learning*, 1605

Business and trade, commercial and industrial activities, financial speculation and
money making, the drudgery of work and the predicaments of City men and their
female companions: Charlotte Riddell's novels ascribe special significance to this
admittedly mundane microcosm. In her understanding, the prose of life revolves
around work. Novels too, she claims, if they wish to touch the right chords, ought
to take stock of the intricacies of the work-life balance – a subject of never-ending
fascination for this writer who, in her own life, had to face financial insecurity, the
bankruptcy of her husband, debts or obligations to his relatives, and popularity
dwindling into marginality. Though framed in the humdrum and beset by economic uncertainty, the imagined world of capitalist modernity that Riddell places
at the centre of her City novels holds many attractions, foremost among them
the promise of self-determination that drives her characters to action. The initial
resistance she encountered among potential publishers did not deter her from pursuing the idea that, given the primacy of business in the life of her contemporaries, business should be represented in the realm of fiction in starker, if not truer,
colours. And this is what her novels set out to do: business people, the narrator
states in *Too Much Alone* (1860), 'like to have their feelings, causes of action, and
modes of thought put into words. A novel about business, about their hopes, anxieties, joys, and troubles throws a new mental light across the pages of their life.'[1]

   How Riddell imagines, reinvents and narrates the business world and the life
of its devotees will be properly dealt with in the chapters to come. The aim of
this introductory chapter is to provide a framework in relation to which Riddell's
thematic focus can be historicised and contextualised. Her novels are part of a
larger cultural reservoir, a diverse set of ideas, beliefs and narratives, which gave
shape and meaning to what Harold Perkins calls the 'entrepreneurial ideal'.[2] My

analyses concentrate not so much on what constitutes or should constitute its unique features, but on the discourses that contributed to the rationalisation and problematisation of the business vocation as a peculiarly modern, work-oriented and very demanding life-script. I shall look at a variety of texts – essays and articles published in the periodical press, business advice manuals and memoirs, biographies of notable merchants – in which the social and cultural significance of business is negotiated, norms and values are reinforced, examples of good practice are celebrated, greed and other related vices are opportunely chastised, and the 'man of business' emerges as a cultural presence and an object of critical scrutiny.

The nineteenth-century archive of business writing and writing about business is vast, though literary and cultural critics have been rather indifferent to it.[3] My selection criteria depend on three factors: firstly, since the 'man of business' is Riddell's favourite type of character, I have given precedence to texts which, in various ways, explore the contours of his identity and desires; secondly, since one of the explicit functions Riddell's City novels perform is to confer a higher degree of cultural legitimacy upon business pursuits, I have focused on texts which pose the question of symbolic prestige or the lack of it, whether directly or not; finally, I have broadened my sample to include well-known, popular publications, such as Samuel Smiles's *Self-Help,* as well as lesser-known interventions in the attempt to do justice to the variety of opinions, myths and narratives which contributed to delimiting 'business' as an object of discourse. The interpretation of this fairly representative, but still fractional, sample of texts has the main purpose of delineating configurations of historical meanings, with an emphasis on how discussions about business, men of business and their predicaments were received in the popular press.

In *Genres of the Credit Economy*, Mary Poovey analyses the problems that pertain to the transition from 'textual interpretation' to 'historical description', arguing for the importance of attending closely to 'the function to which texts were put by past readers'.[4] Though this approach 'will not enable modern readers to recover the *meanings* a text once had', focusing on functions which are contingent upon '*genre, discipline* and *institutional position*' helps to understand what insights were likely to be 'grasped' or 'shared' by past readers.[5] In this chapter, I consider different types of texts and their related functions. Offering advice is the pragmatic aim of business manuals: they respond to the need for professional guidance in a field of work which encompassed a vast array of positions and was always threatened by the allure of unfettered materialism. Manuals and guidebooks attempt to regulate business conduct mainly through cautionary tales. Performing acts of celebration is the self-appointed task of commercial biographies: they forge business 'monuments'[6] out of individual exemplars of success. Their function is to commemorate the very idea of progress, turning individual achievements into testimonials of national glory. Of course, there is no sharp distinction between cautionary and celebratory narratives, but the idea of business they project varies depending on where the emphasis falls: the oscillation between 'pains' and 'gains' is ultimately what defines business as a problematic life-script.

'The Metaphysics of Business'

In the first volume of *George Geith of Fen Court* (1864), the authorial narrator steps forward to justify the novelty of her approach. Business, she claims, has not yet found its bard:

> Every class has found some writer to tell its tale, but I can remember no book which has ever described a shopkeeper as a man, or ventured into that debatable middle land, where talent and energy are struggling from morning to night in dingy offices, in dark warehouses, unknown to the world's eyes, solely because business has never learnt to be self-conscious.[7]

This lack of self-consciousness is not the only impediment she identifies; hostile prejudices and the sneering attitude of the upper classes towards trade are also enlisted as cultural habits which have prevented business from accruing the symbolic consecration it deserves. Targeting these preconceptions openly, the narrator exclaims: ' "Come down to our level, ye sneerers," shouts business, "Come from chambers of pleasure, from couches of ease, from servants, equipages, and bankers' balances to our level, where we fight it out till we see if you despise us still" '.[8] Derision, antipathy, aristocratic contempt, lack of self-reflection: in Riddell's understanding business is a distinctly underexposed, underexamined cultural and social object. That the 'backbone' of national progress, 'beneficial to millions and millions'[9] of people, should be so devalued appears to her as a glaring contradiction. To what extent did Riddell's contemporaries share her diagnosis of the symbolic malaise of business?

There is abundant literary evidence that business – as a vocational trajectory and a life-script – lacked a legitimating frame of reference or the symbolic prestige accorded to older, more traditional callings. It was a modern vocation, democratically open to many, but looked upon with circumspection for its proximity to 'the vulgar question of money'.[10] In the complex cultural negotiations through which the much-contested materialism of the age was at the same time critiqued and accepted, business pursuits were greeted with varying degrees of suspicion. It is not difficult to find in mid-Victorian novels distinct echoes of what McKendrick calls 'literary and educational luddism'[11] and Martin J. Weiner defines as 'a cultural *cordone sanitaire* encircling the forces of economic development – technology, industry, commerce'.[12] Scholars have amply documented the anti-industrial, anti-business bias of much Victorian literature, often overtly critical of the dirty game of making money.[13] Kathleen Blake finds traces of this legacy even in the field of Victorian studies, which, she argues, exhibits a 'leaning towards ideology critique, whether right or left, largely oppositional to Utilitarian, capitalist, liberal, bourgeois values'.[14] In the 1980s, when the nostalgia for 'Victorian values' ranked high on the conservative political agenda, historians were debating the role played by cultural influences in stultifying the entrepreneurial imperative. The 'decline of the industrial spirit', Weiner famously contended, was culturally induced; a literary tradition of entrenched anti-industrialism, the hegemony of what he terms the 'Southern metaphor'[15] (the pastoral vision of Englishness) and the resilience of gentry values contributed substantially to discouraging a whole generation of Britons from embarking upon a business career. The hypothesis of a culturally induced economic decline has been contested on many sides either emphasising that the very notion of decline is misleading and inaccurate or regarding cultural influences as a lot less powerful than Weiner had assumed. As Rubinstein states, the cultural thesis 'fails to present a persuasive nexus to account for the transmission of cultural values into economic behaviour and performance'.[16] For James Raven, it is highly uncertain that 'after 1850 either management recruitment or entry into business became more restrictive. A case can be made for the handsome reward of modern captains of industry and for a greater encouragement of business activities'.[17] Furthermore, he adds, a broader, more inclusive sample of cultural and literary 'expressions' should be considered: 'The danger of concentrating upon the 'garden of England' myth is that it undervalues the positive artistic response to industrial development'.[18]

The genealogy of the culture-versus-industry debate can be traced back to the nineteenth century. In the pages of the periodical press the question of the 'dignity' of business, or the lack of it, gradually emerges as a central concern when commentators embark upon the task of elucidating what business is and does. The articles I am considering in this section share a common focus on business as a way of life, as a defining template for the biography of ordinary men whose experience of commercial modernity is deemed worthy of serious reflection.[19] I have given precedence to texts which tackle the question of what business does, how its demands, rituals, and ideals shape the life script of its votaries. There are of course some themes which crop up regularly over many decades: business habits; fortunes made in business; retiring from business; exemplary commercial lives; the philosophy of business; the poetry and romance of the City; business and literary pursuits; commercial travellers and their adventures. Running through this diverse set of themes is the cultural awareness that, for all its topicality, the idea of business stands in need of elucidation to render it less inscrutable and to correct common errors, mistaken assumptions, or prejudices. It is not difficult to detect an insistence on business sacraments, on rules of conduct which may not guarantee grace or success but certainly define a standard of normality set against both the unpredictable vagaries of the market and the predictable objections of business detractors.

Among these objections, William Hazlitt's famous comments about 'ordinary business' being incompatible with 'imagination' or 'thought' are often singled out, explicitly or not, as points of contention. For Hazlitt, the 'want of imagination' is the 'great requisite . . . for the prosperous management of ordinary business'.[20] For many other Victorian commentators, the divorce between contemplative and active pursuits is not only an inaccurate representation of reality but a bad piece of advice, as it tends to encourage a narrow and distorted model of *vita activa*. The article 'Union of Literary and Business Habits' is a good case in point.[21] The author sets out to demonstrate that 'by the mixing of the pleasures of knowledge and taste with the ordinary duties of business, a great addition may be made to the current happiness of life.'[22] As a practical illustration, he refers to the career of a manufacturer who, by cultivating a taste for poetry, ensured for himself an enjoyable life even after his business had been relinquished. The problematic moment in the life of a man of business, the time when he is most likely to '[fall] to pieces', coincides with the 'abstraction from business'; it is arduous to renounce the fullness of a life of action, but 'literary interests' can be helpful in smoothing the transition.[23] Hazlitt's categories are the two poles around which the argument revolves, but it is action, tinged with poetry, that stands out as most conducive to happiness.

Considering how often the dichotomy Hazlitt formalised is invoked and disputed, one could argue that his essay provided a framework within which to pin down the characteristics of business (variously defined) by keeping open the question of its relation to the sphere of thought and contemplation. In other words, a certain 'longing for the high'[24] colours these interventions in defence of the business vocation, which is proved valuable not in itself but in relation to the loftier domain of intellectual achievements. Remarkable in this respect is an article published in the *Saturday Review*, 'Literature and Business', which defends the superior quality of 'literature' (in its broadest meaning) produced 'in the intervals of business', arguing that business guarantees the best training in the ability of 'putting one's self in relation to other minds'.[25] A generous knowledge of life, habits of precision, and 'a rare sanity of mind and style' are the assets that a man of business brings to literary pursuits. The author states: 'The man of business who writes, being disciplined to common sense, is little likely to fall into that over-elaboration of trifles, that subtlety of the schools, and that indulgence of his own fantastic humours which belongs to the recluse author'.[26] Therefore, the author concludes, Samuel Bailey of Sheffield, a banker and man of letters, is a more polished writer than Thomas Carlyle: 'Had Mr. Carlyle been a man of affairs as well as a man of letters, his splendid genius might probably have found deliverance from its besetting infirmities and most mischievous aberrations'.[27]

Vindicating business as the type of experience that best prepares men for literary endeavours may appear as an indirect, devious route towards the goal of cultural legitimacy. But the point is that this goal becomes explicit only later in the century. In the 1840s, 1850s, and 1860s, the issue of the 'dignity of business' emerges between the lines as a continuous but implicit concern among those who choose to discuss modern conceptions of business and do so with an eye to its symbolic reputation. It is noteworthy that in the 1840s, the term of comparison is not the gentlemanly ideal but rather 'labour' or more specifically the 'moral discourses of labour', which Patrick Joyce defines as the 'attempt by workers to address work and economic life in a humane and just way'.[28] The man of business is compared to the labourer, for instance, when the issue of work–life balance is brought to the fore. The equilibrium between leisure and work, deemed necessary for all sorts of workers, appears wanting in the life of over-anxious men of business: 'Now, the man of business, although he may not exert his muscular system in any great degree, is under exactly the same regulations as the ordinary labourer. The nervous system, which he chiefly exerts in his calling, also requires frequent alternations of labour and rest'.[29] The claims of labour, a subject of much discussion in the 1830s and 1840s, provide inspiration for the assertion not so much of the claims of business as of the need to contain its encroachment upon the private sphere. Likewise, the idea of a reciprocity of interests between labour and capital, which Joyce identifies as a central element in the 'rhetoric of "the people"'[30] during the 1840s and 1850s, is invoked to mitigate the disruptive effects of individual acquisitiveness. As the author of an article grandly entitled 'The Metaphysics of Business' explains:

> We thoroughly believe that, in time, such great bodies of people will feel and act more as only a large kind of families, and enjoy almost, if not altogether, in common the fruits of the general industry, finding that thereby they realise greater enjoyments than are to be obtained by each standing upon his individual acquisitiveness.[31]

The vice of competitiveness and human greed, denounced in operative discourse, is not translated into a virtue when observed from the perspective of business; rather, the emphasis falls on the same rhetoric employed by Richard Cobden, for instance, who defended commerce as 'something like the spirit of history, infusing "culture" with purpose and direction in the great utopian project of improving mankind'.[32] The interest in literary pursuits and intellectual cultivation, the importance of 'intervals' or leisure and the idea of a reciprocity of interests in interconnected social groups delineate a picture of business framed by civilizing motives which derives its consecration from an open confrontation not with gentry values but with the political and cultural discourses of 'the people'.

In the 1870s, a more reflective approach to the question of the dignity of business can be detected in several articles. In 'A Captain of Industry', the author initially asks 'why the man whose business it is to quietly organize crowds for purposes of production has less place in our sympathy than the man who organizes crowds for purposes of violence'.[33] The answer to this question contains an extended demonstration that 'real business fairness' and 'magnanimity'[34] are certainly compatible with the attainment of wealth. As is customary in many articles, the writer bases his opinions on real-life examples, confuting prejudices with biographical facts and raising the latter to the status of cultural paradigms. Alfred Crespi, writing for the *New Monthly Magazine* in 1875, devotes several pages to the discussion of 'class prejudices' which misguide young men in their choice of a career: 'A really sensible man with the welfare of his children at heart', he warns, 'ought not to allow himself to be blinded by the supposed dignity of one calling to the prejudice of another'.[35] His comparison between trades and professions is intended to extol the advantages of the former ('Trades encourage independence and self-reliance. A profession often makes a man servile and dependent')[36] and more generally to counteract erroneous notions of honour and prestige which affect vocational choices. The most orotund apology of business in the late 1870s appears in a series of long articles, by 'Launcelot Cross', published in the *New Monthly Magazine*. What distinguishes these interventions is the rhetoric adopted:

it is opulent in its show of erudition, copiously referencing the classics, from Homer to Plutarch. Further, it is grandiose in its use of prosopopeia whereby business comes to acquire a 'soul' and a 'skeleton:

> It is now time to examine the constitution and sentient principle of Business: to look closely into the thing itself. It is a complex mechanism, but as we have already said it possesses organic unity: it is, in fact, a true representation of the paragon of animals, man himself; and under that form, a combination of the concrete and the ethereal, we shall consider it.[37]

Cross indulges in apodictic declarations, writing that the 'essence of all History is the History of Business' and that 'Business is the saving intellectual spring . . . it generates an affection for all the graces and potentialities of social life'.[38] The author transforms the rather prosaic catalogue of business habits into a decalog of quasi-divine accomplishments, presenting the 'Man of Business' as an 'absolute': 'In heaven there is an affluence of beauty and joy, and he endeavours to produce their shadow on earth'.[39]

In the same years, but in more muffled tones, James M'Crea asserts the centrality and dignity of business by a simple appeal to royalty. 'The Queen as a Woman of Business' and 'The Prince as a Man of Business', both published in *Time* (1879), provide a series of snapshots of the daily round of business that even 'her Majesty's shoulders' have to bear: 'Though the English Monarch be the crowning ornament of the Constitution, personally associated more with ideas of dignity and splendor than of toil, it is a grievous mistake to suppose that the lot of British Royalty is, has been, or can be exempt from labour'.[40] M'Crea reminds his readers that the 'toils of Monarchy' require the same kind of methodical application needed in other, humbler spheres, offering a fairly precise account of how the sovereign's work is apportioned on a daily and weekly basis. These articles understand business in a broad sense as synonymous with work, but they also promote a peculiar vision of business habits in a royal garb that adds a touch of courtly glamour to very practical virtues. In line with these contributions that seek to elevate the symbolic prestige of business are also articles discussing literary misrepresentations. In the *Nineteenth Century*, Henry Jones writes,

> Of course there is no lack of business-men in our modern plays; rather, of one certain type of business-man, hereafter to be examined, there is an inordinate profusion. Indeed, this particular individual, under various aliases and constantly changing his trade, may be said in one sense to have been the great prop and mainstay of English comedy for some twenty years past . . . Ordinarily the man of business is simply a peg to hang jokes upon. He invariably drops his H's and puts in superfluous aspirates . . . the want of all sincerity and searchingness in the portrait must be apparent to any intelligent person who will take the trouble to read a modern comedy where an English tradesman is depicted and then compare it to the average English tradesman who can be met with behind any counter in town or country.[41]

The writer's demand for more truthfulness and sincerity highlights a distance between referent and representation perceived as symptomatic of broader cultural issues. The anti-business snobbery of literary caricatures is only one example of a persistent tendency in English society to discourage business talent. As H.E. Morgan claims, 'There is no more startling fact in the actual condition of this country than that a people whose greatness was made by business . . . should deliberately and traditionally teach boys and young men of those classes from which we may expect higher intelligence and inherited ability to despise business'.[42] Ardently criticising this 'feudal sentiment', Morgan argues for the urgent necessity to bring the university and business 'into organised touch', launching an 'educational campaign . . . to raise the standard in which business is regarded'.[43] Morgan puts the blame on the educational system—public schools and universities—looking at Germany as an alternative model of successful integration of business and rank.

This by no means exhaustive overview of the cultural conversation around business has highlighted a set of concerns that overlap with Riddell's vision. In the opinion of several writers and journalists, business pursuits, in which a large segment of the population was actively engaged, appear in need of some type of cultural recognition, the kind of recognition that the periodical press, alert to the demands and the purchasing power of its middle-class readers, was willing to offer. This does not imply that indignant denunciations of the ills of business were rare. On the contrary, they appear with regularity especially when prompted by dramatic events – the Railway mania in the 1850s, recurrent commercial panics, or momentous changes in the legislative framework. But it is important to remember that outrage and contempt were not the only responses. 'We are more familiar with the voices of those who deplored industrialization's harmful effects' – observes Christine Macleod – 'than of those who welcomed its benefits and hymned its achievements . . . lack of attention to the latter has produced an unbalanced picture of nineteenth-century popular culture, which is only starting to be remedied'.[44] That Riddell, at the beginning of her career, should decide to invest in the imaginative potential of business heroes and the City of London is to her credit. Her engagement went against the grain of commonly held assumptions about women writers' areas of expertise, which certainly included pecuniary matters but not the more specific professional knowledge of commerce, industry and finance that she exhibits in her texts. Placed in relationship with popular culture, however, her novels resonate with interests, preoccupations and myths about modern economic heroism eliciting a high degree of public attention – which goes some way towards explaining the type of popularity she enjoyed. How Riddell uses the formal resources of fiction to explore the emotional regimes of capitalism and the contradictory demands placed on the Victorian man of business defines the specificity of her approach, as I will explain in my analysis of her novels.

There is also another kind of business discourse that ought to be taken into account – a discourse framed by explicitly didactic, pragmatic goals and shaped by the need to contain greed and ambition, while at the same time encouraging the healthy pursuit of profits. Conduct-of-life literature, by its very nature, tends to be normative and procedural, which does not mean, however, that it is blind to contradictions. The texts I will now turn to help clarify what kinds of tensions were more difficult to rationalise, what standards of normality were ideally devised and what protocols suggested in the attempt to reconcile a generation of businessmen or bourgeois workers to the intrinsic uncertainty and precariousness of their chosen career. The self-appointed task of advice manuals is to guide, to steer in the right direction and, at the same time, to issue repeated warnings not just against temptations but also against the very normality they seek to stabilise. The focus of many authors on the (ab)normality of overwork is noticeable in this respect. Commercial biographies, on the other hand, serve primarily a celebratory function, often announced in the appended paratexts. What they celebrate are both individual examples of success and the economic progress of the nation. In some cases, the form of commemoration this type of writing produces is based on a simple stratagem: the iterated enumeration of examples arranged according to the same pattern. Samuel Smiles adopts this format in *Self-Help*. In its 'objective infinity'[45] the potentially endless, unconcluded form of the list conveys a sense of abundance and openness, keeping alive the hope that emulation might actually work.

Mammon and Manhood

In the year of the Great Exhibition, when the self-congratulatory mood of the British middle classes was reaching its peak,[46] the Young Men's Christian Association offered three prizes of 50, 30 and 20 guineas for the best essays written on the topic 'The Evils of the Present System of Business, and the Difficulty they present to the Attainment and Development of Personal Piety, with Suggestions for their Removal'. Forty-six essays were submitted. *Business As It Is, And As It Might Be* (1854), by Jospeh Lyndall, won the first prize and was published three years later under the auspices of the Association. Lyndall responds to the call with all the vigorous zeal of an argumentative mind, familiar with the ins and outs of 'the present system of business'.[47] The first evils trumpeted in his essay, however, are not, as one might expect, dishonesty, commercial cheating, overtrading or other blatant examples of immorality. Rather, the author starts off with a direct indictment of overwork: 'the effect of late business hours' on the 'general mass'[48] of people is disastrous, he argues; 'over-application' or the 'total absorption of the mind in the cares of business'[49] is equally detrimental; lack of physical exercise produces 'sickness' in the counting-house;[50] and 'excessive competition' encourages a variety of 'serious evils'.[51] In other words, a life devoted to business is a life of overwork, with all its attendant ills. The celebration of British glories, of entrepreneurship and inventiveness, technological advancements and human ingenuity, paraded in Samuel Smiles's bestseller *Self-Help*, reflects the mood of hopeful optimism captured in the very idea of the Crystal Palace. Lyndall's prize-winning but obscure treatise attends more closely to an undercurrent of concerns about the costs and pains of the country's success story. Fatigue, exhaustion, stress, overwork and sickness are likely to beset the life of the unheroic man of business that most authors of advice manuals, unlike Samuel Smiles, have in mind. Lowering the bar several notches down, these authors do not see a vertiginous list of commercial or industrial grandees who have left their mark in the history of economic progress. They see an assemblage of anonymous bourgeois workers most of them 'blundering into an occupation'[52] with few chances of happiness or of ever gaining anything more than a modest income. How-to-do manuals have a paradoxical moral obligation: to encourage individual talent, setting for it the ambitious goal of success, and to discourage excessive ambition, to warn readers against the many snares and ruses of a business life, deflating the myth of success they otherwise promote. American and English authors go about dispensing precious life advice in slightly different ways. The latter incline towards a tragic view of what business does, the former are less reticent in sponsoring its many potentialities.

Edwin Freedly's *A Practical Treatise on Business, with an Inquiry into the Chances of Success and Causes of Failure* (1853), which sold over 10,000 copies in the US within a few months of publication, circulated in England in an abridged version brought out by Routledge. The book is a collection of quotations, long extracts from journal articles and original observations through which the 'wisdom of business' is condensed. Freedly's upbeat tone is unmistakable: 'Business is a source of happiness in several ways. Its pursuit engages, invigorates, and enlarges the mind; its usefulness promotes self-respect; its results, if successful, increase the power of doing what the head conceives and the heart desires'.[53] Unlike English authors, always cautious in gauging the potential for happiness of business pursuits, Freedley articulates a thoroughly optimistic narrative in which business is declared compatible 'with the highest degree of moral culture and intellectual ability'[54] and getting money is not stigmatised: 'Men of business! Get money. Get an abundance of it, but get it honourably. Elevate your business. Remember that the more elevated the business character, the more easy it will be to get money'.[55] Even the highly controversial figure of the speculator commands some admiration in this book: 'There is a certain quantum of the spirit of the wild and eager and hazardous adventure ever in the community,' Freedly contends, 'and it *will* seek exercise and gratification in some form or other . . . Men therefore *will* speculate'.[56] Freedley's position is eccentric in the British context, both for his frank acceptance of the desire for money and for his depiction of business life as the shortest way to happiness, provided that the individual in question is endowed with the necessary attributes for success – 'industry, 'arrangement', 'calculation', 'prudence', 'punctuality' and 'perseverance'.[57] There is little variance across the spectrum of texts I have considered when it comes to the catalogue of correct attributes that aspiring men of business ought to possess. What varies is the intensity of the belief in the ability of youthful talent to toe the line and to bear the hardships of work and competition.

Other American writers, notably clergymen, do not entirely share Freedly's buoyant view. They emphasise the social utility of trade, commerce, and financial activities in the modern world but also the pressures, anxieties, and frequent failures experienced by those involved in these pursuits. These drawbacks are then justified by pointing toward a superior end: the progress and advancement of a whole community that relies on businessmen to increase its prosperity. The

essays collected in *The Man of Business, Considered in Six Aspects* (1864) purport to offer a guide for young men who are about to enter the 'boundless' field of
business – a field that is rapidly encroaching upon 'the comparative tranquillity
of professional life'.[58] These essays project a view of business as hegemonic: in
the near future, men of all description will be transformed into businessmen. The
hegemony of business verges on the grandiose when the discussion focuses on the
position, influence and duties of men of business:

> They have the power to create a panic, to honour or dishonour a nation every
> day. They can give their city and country a good name all over the earth, or
> they can carry bankruptcy over a wide domain. There is no earthly power
> which is felt so quickly and so widely as the power that moves the circulat-
> ing medium . . . Ready money is ready power; and the men who have all the
> money of a nation in their hands must be an important class.[59]

In their position as 'trustees for humanity',[60] men of business are burdened with
a tremendous responsibility, so much so that even the most successful among
them, who never recoil before their appointed duty, bear on their body the physical marks of distress: a 'pale forehead', an 'anxious look', a 'wiry frame'.[61] The
celebration of the power of businessmen 'to make or unmake a nation'[62] is here
intimately related to a discourse of honourable suffering: businessmen work hard,
their load is heavy, many of them 'bear their burdens manfully' but often 'the
intellect is taxed to an extent of which few dream'.[63] Hence the need for instructive and inspiring handbooks that might teach youthful readers how to endure a
calling which, despite its public flair, exacts a high price in terms of psychological
and physical health. The businessmen of tomorrow must be moulded according
to a model of male subjectivity – 'a higher type of manhood'[64] – which appreciates in equal degree the will to succeed and the ability to endure a state of constant anxiety, the traditional virtues of industry, inventiveness and punctuality,
and the nerve to bear 'the mighty oppressive hand of the giant Business'[65] under
which many neophytes succumb. 'To be successful and happy', we are constantly
reminded, 'costs something'.[66] Not surprisingly, most of the essays collected in
The Man of Business are devoted to the investigation of appropriate strategies for
dealing with the disappointments, the drudgery, the uneasiness and the countless
worries strewn along the rather cheerless path to success. These strategies range
from an emphasis on the 'counter-attractions'[67] or 'safe pleasures'[68] offered by
self-learning and the pursuit of knowledge, to the commendation of an active,
energetic family life as an antidote to the peculiar *hybris* of the overreaching businessman. This insistence on the regulation – rationalisation – of leisure time, and
on the satisfaction to be derived from it, is dialectically related to the difficulty of
ever fully rationalising the uncertainties and inherent paradoxes of the business
world.

   The paradox of money, for instance, is a problematic issue in these essays. Making money is, on the one hand, the obvious goal of any business activity; but, on
the other, it is not sanctioned as a fully legitimate object of male desire: 'Mammon

and Manhood are incompatible' as the author of *Worth and Wealth* bluntly states.[69] Classed under the rubric of 'temptations', the wish to make money is construed simultaneously as a powerful incentive to individual exertion ('especially for those who began with nothing')[70] and a dangerous Moloch to whom many a businessman has sacrificed 'all that is dignified in his nature, happy in his condition, or hopeful in his prospects'.[71] The subtle distinction between the legitimate wish to improve one's condition through honest toil and the deplorable determination to become rich is hard to negotiate even for the 'distinguished' American clergymen who, in this book, preach a militant version of entrepreneurial Christianity. They differentiate between lawful and unlawful business practices, between a noble dedication to and an excessive absorption into one's own occupation, between lofty and petty aims; but, in the end, blatant self-interest or the pursuit of gain can never be willed away from the scene of business. It can only be tentatively rationalised by a careful balancing of rewards and punishments: the man 'who plunges into the midst of bustling contests for gain without hesitation and without alarm'[72] is doomed to a life of disappointments and failures. Only by sublimating the 'lust of gain' can the businessman act as trustworthy mediator between the individual and the community in such a way as 'to benefit the world'.[73]

On the whole, the American perspective, with its insistence on the added value for the whole community of the hard but noble work of individual businessmen, articulates a positive ideal of the '*many-sided* man'[74] better equipped to face the challenges of industrial and financial modernity. That these challenges also include a good dose of individual suffering is not detrimental to the cultural and social prestige of the whole class of businessmen whose power these essays are so keen to acclaim. In England, on the other hand, a more guarded attitude can be detected in texts which admonish readers of all ages against the destructive potential of a disproportionate dedication to business. The anonymous author of *A Business Life* (1861) is driven to put pen to paper by the wish to 'save many of his fellow men, and young tradesman especially, from the fearful anxieties he has suffered'.[75] He captures the attention of his potential readers by describing the scene of writing – he jots down his memoir while commuting to work, by train, in what little time he can spare from his all-absorbing occupation – and by refusing to reveal his identity, claiming that the chronicle of his experience might jeopardise his future career. As contemporary reviewers noticed, the record this author presents has all the 'freshness' of experience and none of the 'stereotyped phrases' used by his predecessors.[76] His jaded account of what a business life implies addresses the same issues – entering into business, speculation and overtrading, business attitudes, domestic life – that are discussed in more neutral terms by other authors.[77] He addresses these issues, however, from the paradoxical perspective of 'a first-class man of business' making large sums of money 'by [his] legitimate avocation' who perceives his unquestionable talents as a 'kind of fatality':

> It has been for many years a kind of fatality with me that I must be in a constant state of excitement, anxiety and speculation. My mind is so constituted

that no common, ordinary business could possibly content me ... To scheme, plan, to contrive is my peculiar forte; tact I possess to considerable extent; and any employment of the mental power, where ingenuity is called for, although it may be collaterally, is my happiness.[78]

That this happiness should be depicted as fatal depends no doubt on the particular field in which his talents are spent – the field of speculation whose symbolic legitimacy was quite shaky in the 1860s. The divergence between individual talents and their application, however, is also related to what appears as an inherently dysfunctional environment: in the 'house of glass'[79] where businesses are conducted the 'depravity' rather than 'goodness' of human nature dictates the rules. Therefore, the much-debated question of when and how a young man should enter into business is settled not as a problem of timing but as a question of lost innocence: no one should be trusted in business 'until the ways of the world, the tricks of the world, and the depravity of human nature, have been so thoroughly driven into him that he suspects a trick at every turn, and, although he has the address to act as if he had the most implicit confidence in the goodness of human nature ... yet takes care to run no risk'.[80] In this respect, no happiness, no peace of mind can ever be warranted by a business life. Nor can success ever be adequately uncoupled from its opposite, since failure – as this memoir clearly shows – is often determined by an abuse of the very same qualities or individual talents that lead to success. Hence the particular urgency of the plea that this anonymous London tradesman articulates: his experience is proffered as an admonishment to all those who, like him, are driven by restlessness to overreach themselves. The sense of urgency is frequently conveyed in direct addresses to the reader – 'you' – imagined as a young son, a husband-to-be, or a father, always about to make a mistake and take the wrong turn.

The predicaments of the (British) male subject admitted into the 'house of glass' have little to do with the insufficient social prestige of his occupation vis-à-vis other, more gentlemanly pursuits. They have a lot more to do, instead, with the difficulty of balancing the creative and the destructive potential of one's own 'peculiar forte'. The 'inventive faculties',[81] the ability to scheme and plan, the profit-seeking urge are an integral part of the business ideal, but they are likely to turn into a negative asset whenever the wish to succeed oversteps the imaginary boundary separating an 'undue devotion to business' from a 'healthful' dedication to it, as the author of *High-Pressure Business Life*, Henry Smith, asserts.[82] Knowing when and where to draw the line is never easy for the individual caught in the 'vortex of business',[83] where time is speed, work becomes overwork and success (or survival) means adapting to the ever accelerating rhythm of life prompted by competition.

The business man of today lives in a perpetual atmosphere of excitement, hurrying towards his days at railway speed, and conducting all his business at that high-pressure rate which has been already referred to ... This business mania grows with what it feeds on, and its intensity is always, therefore, commensurate with its success.[84]

Smith devotes much attention to the pathologies, the physical and moral 'evils' endemic to a business life. 'There are no gains without pains',[85] he likes to reiterate, but in his medical understanding of the relationship between business and life the meaning of pain is purged of any reference to manly suffering or to the Christian belief that pain is in the hands of God.[86] He uses medical language and arguments to demonstrate that the distortion of life towards work is the main pathology and that such a distortion is inbuilt in the business ideal. The devotees of business, in other words, do not seem to have much of a choice: 'Men in business will maintain, and with some show of reason, that unless they adapted the same methods that other people did, they would be unable to compete with them in the commercial struggle that perpetually goes on'.[87] Identifying in this vicious circle the main cause of the modern, urban malaise affecting an increasing number of people, Smith draws a bleak portrait of the business world: here the 'dementia of overwork'[88] is the norm (and likely to remain so for a long time), a stressful, high-pressure existence is the *sine qua non* of success, and the 'spindle-shanked, lean, lank, miserable dyspeptic looking beings'[89] who carry on the business of the world are anything but happy. Smith compiles a long list of physical and mental ailments that await the man of business 'with the certainty and force of an avenging Nemesis'[90]: they range from indigestion and constipation to 'softening and insanity', 'exhaustion of nervous power' and eventually 'want of virile power'.[91] Like other observers before and after him, Smith inveighs against Mammon, the idol to whom all chances of happiness are sacrificed, but this moral crusade is only a residual element in his discourse. More relevant is Smith's insistence on the distortions produced by overworking and on the need to achieve a different understanding of the work-life balance. Although his inflated view of the dire consequences of the business mania – nothing less than the 'destruction of society'[92] seems to be in store – is apocalyptic, his depiction of the ailing body and softened mind of stressed out men stands in sharp contrast to the gospel of work as a bulwark of masculinity, old and new.

As Herbert Sussman maintains, the 'definition of manhood as self-discipline, as the ability to control male energy and to deploy this power not for sexual but for productive purposes was clearly specific to bourgeois men'.[93] What Smith's analysis suggests is that productive purposes can backfire: work does not provide an unproblematic outlet for the sublimation of male sexual energy. Indeed, the more productivity is enhanced as the main public duty of the male subject and the more subjects compete to achieve this end, the more 'enfeebled and diseased'[94] the male population grows. Smith's businessmen are caught in a no-win situation – not only are mammon and manhood incompatible, but the dominant idea of work is itself self-defeating. *High-Pressure Business Life* could be read as one further testimony of the anti-industrial, anti-entrepreneurial orientation of much nineteenth-century English culture. After all, there is a good deal of medical (rather than literary) luddism in Smith's construction of the business ideal. His arguments, however – like some of the arguments put forward in *A Business Life* and to a lesser extent *The Man of Business* – are also interesting for a different reason: they are motivated by the need to probe the new reality of work, with all its implications, in a world in which business, despite much literary hostility, has become dominant. Smith's preoccupations convey uneasiness not about business *per se* but about what appears as the only sanctioned way of understanding productivity, performance, and the relationship between work and life.

In the guidebooks and essays I have mentioned so far, the culture of business is questioned from within because of the imbalances, the paradoxes, the distortions that are inscribed in the very ideal these authors are trying to reassess and in some cases to celebrate. Their perspective is not informed by the same 'antipathy to infant industrialism'[95] that Carlyle, Arnold, Ruskin, Dickens and other male critics of the period had articulated. Nor is it motivated by what Weiner dubs the 'counter-revolution of values'[96] based upon a profound distaste for the vulgarity of industrial capitalism. Rather, these texts criticise the specific modalities according to which commercial modernity is regulated: the excessive demands of business in relation to life, the costs and pains of success, the unwritten rules of the 'house of glass' – in short, the formula for anxiety and unhappiness that seems to be germane to the business ideal. The insiders' view of the business world is not marred by tensions related to insufficient prestige or lack of symbolic legitimization; it is predicated upon a frank acceptance of the importance of business pursuits and simultaneously on a more or less explicit recognition that the hegemony of business entails a model of male subjectivity which many perceive as unendurable. There is a substantial distinction between Matthew Arnold's indictment of the way of life, habits, manners, and even thoughts of middle-class businessmen[97] and Smith's concern with the 'dementia of overwork'. Looking at texts which do not have a high-cultural status but are addressed to a public of impassive insiders – who badly need counselling rather than refinement – permits us to gain a different understanding of the cultural tensions underlying the British repudiation of industrial modernity. What emerges in these texts is a kind of counter-discourse poised midway between a straightforward acceptance of the business ideal and a denunciation of its fatal logic; a discourse that exposes the unnerving private side of the business vocation and the tensions built into the normative masculinity of the man of business. The characterisation of Riddell's male protagonists – Maurice Storn in *Too Much Alone* (1860), Alan Ruthven in *City and Suburb* (1861), Lawrence Barbour in *The Race for Wealth* (1866) – is more aligned with this counter-discourse than it is with fictional representations of businessmen and financiers – Bounderby, Dombey, Merdle, Melmotte, Lopez, Bulstrode (to name the most famous examples) – as emblems of greed, hypocrisy, criminal conduct and an exorbitant will to power.

The tensions explored in business manuals and memoirs are less visible in commercial biographies. When the focus is on success stories recounted from an ex-post perspective, the pains of business tend to be subsumed into a broader narrative of national progress and gains.[98] Repeatedly, authors lament the scarcity of books that illustrate the mercantile lives of eminent men of business or traders. At the beginning of the century, in 1808, the *Athenaeum* solicited the production of mercantile biographies in an article that openly defended their national utility: 'we have to regret', the author states, 'that the biography of a certain description of men, eminent in this country should yet remain a desideratum in our national literature. England may certainly be considered as the greatest commercial country in the world; and it would be very desirable to be put in possession of facts and anecdotes illustrative of the character of her merchants'.[99] Though mercantile biographies might be displeasing to the 'fastidious taste' of literary men, the author concludes, the 'character of the merchant is an object of national importance',[100] which should be explored with greater zeal. Fifty years later, the same complaint is echoed by biographers who present their work as a much-needed, long-awaited literary and educational supplement to the commercial advancement of the country.

The Wesleyan minister, William Arthur, author of *The Successful Merchant: Sketches of the Life of Mr. Samuel Budgett* (1852), introduces his biographical study with lengthy reflections on what he perceives as a lack of reciprocal understanding between 'literary men', for whom 'commerce is a dirty thing',[101] and the 'most numerous and energetic class of the community': 'For business, as a class, literature has done little. They can lay their hands on a few books that are not likely to estrange them from their avocation just in proportion as they charm them . . . Thus many business men dread books, just as literary men dread business. The two things have been at enmity'.[102] To bridge this communicative gap or to overcome this enmity, Arthur redefines the epic scope of commercial biographies. He claims that when his predecessors have taken up 'a commercial man' they have systematically 'dropped business as a leaden thing, a dead weight, that would sink the book'.[103] An increased dose of realism and 'more attention to practical life' is the antidote Arthur recommends against the tendency to overlook the specific particulars that make a mercantile life worth memorialising. In other words, the proper way to celebrate commercial 'monuments' (as he likes to describe the achievements of merchants) is by providing meticulous literary records of how those monuments came to be erected, what bargaining skills were involved, what kind of transactions executed, what decisions made in times of uncertainty. The demand for more realism is at one with the commemorative function: only when the specific history of the bargaining and trading behind each business monument is appropriately narrated and explained, will the public significance of those monuments be extolled. In Arthur's reflections on the genre of commercial biography, the commemorative function is directly linked to the creation of usable, portable memories – records of transactions, commercial deeds, bargains – to which aspiring young traders can revert for much-needed guidance. His biography of Samuel Budgett is accordingly constructed along a dual axis: on the one hand, a string of episodes and anecdotes that showcase Budgett's shrewdness in bargaining; on the other, a profusion of commentaries, admonishments and exhortations that echo some of the concerns voiced in business advice manuals. For instance, Budgett's 'excessive love of a good bargain'[104] is simultaneously celebrated as an innate characteristic of the 'born merchant', already perceivable in the child's keen interest in money, and denounced as a temptation that youthful apprentices should learn to resist. Budgett's 'rigid bargain-making did not arise from a love of money, from selfish ambition, from indifference to the interests of others', Arthur explains, 'It arose solely from his natural passion for successful trade'.[105] Several episodes in this account illustrate how the merchant built his fortune by skilfully calculating potential profits and losses especially in the smallest of transactions. This ability is the business virtue that Arthur is most keen to eulogise. Redefined as an 'impulse to convert to gain that which others would let run to loss', or as a 'marvellous love of traffic',[106] self-interest acquires an aura of purity and heroic connotations:

> He would buy as scarcely any other man could buy; he would sell as scarcely any other man could sell. He was an athletes [sic] on the arena of trade, and rejoiced to bear off the prize. He was a soldier on the battle-field of bargains, and conquered he would not be. His power over the minds of others was immense, his insight into their character piercing, his address in managing his own case masterly, and, above all his purpose so inflexible that no regard to delicacy or to appearance would for a moment beguile him from his object. He would accomplish a first-rate transaction, be the difficulty what it might.[107]

That this peculiarity of the successful merchant might be deemed a 'defect' or might convey an 'unfavourable impression'[108] of the business character is openly acknowledged by Arthur who elaborates his mercantile portrait bearing in mind the lessons of realism, as Aeron Hunt has argued.[109] Arthur draws from those lessons the idea that flaws are admissible: 'Let the critics have it as they will', he exclaims, 'nothing is so natural in a man as contradictions';[110] ideal 'fictitious heroes' may verge on the statuesque, but real and realistic ones 'are very far from being a rigidly symmetrical race'.[111] A good dose of what the *Chambers's Edinburgh Journal* called 'pulpit discourses' is interspersed with the biographical narrative in a way that Victorian reviewers found tedious and redundant. They responded positively to the realistic bent of the factual story, but dismissed as superfluous the 'homilies' and 'vain repetitions' of the moralising biographer.[112] The tale of progress from relative poverty to success and respectability, as the *Tait's Edinburgh Magazine* observed, was meaningful *per se* and needed no further elucidation to be made exemplary.[113] What professional readers expected of commercial biographies, in other words, was a confirmation of the veracity of the narrative of progress, unencumbered by the moralising apparatus of excessive admonitions and religious fervour. Just as the memoir of the anonymous London tradesman was praised for its freshness, so too *The Successful Merchant* was valued as a practical *vade mecum* for the young man of business and criticised for the tendency to stray into the rhetoric of pulpit discourse. The realistic mode of representation provides the standard in relation to which business memoirs and commercial biographies are assessed, which is hardly surprising considering that these texts presented themselves and were received as belonging to the broad category of literature. Though not preeminently fictional, these accounts shared with many novels the master trope of the *Bildung* or, in Bakhtin's words, the 'image of *man growing* in *national-historical time*'.[114] The cultural centrality of this paradigm structures not only the texts themselves, but also the critics' appraisal of their significance and usefulness for the general public. Just as novelists, including Riddell, were taken to task when the sermonising proclivities of narrators appeared disproportionate, so too biographers and memorialists were chided for adorning their story with unwarranted and tedious morals added on to the main plot. Whether factual or fictional, the plot of individual advancement, *Bildung* and progress was in more ways than one the master trope of modernity.[115]

In *Self-Help; with Illustrations of Character and Conduct* (1859), Samuel Smiles amasses a vast array of cases, drawn from different historical periods and professional ambits; they all confirm the truth of self-help and perseverance as well as the validity of the model of *Bildung* (as self-culture) multiplied in a variety of examples. As the *Fraser's Magazine* remarked: "One of the greatest merits of the work lies in the proofs with which it overflows that the most important results achieved in life are generally obtained through the simplest means and the exercise of ordinary qualities – in showing that what man has done and been, that many man do and be".[116] With 20,000 copies sold within few years of publication and over 55,000 copies disseminated worldwide after the second edition came out in 1866, *Self-Help* undoubtedly hit the right note. The sheer quantity of illustrations piled up in the pages of this book, the overflow of evidence Smiles is able to muster, satisfies the need for ennobling exemplars of industrial heroism voiced by many writers. This abundance is also a quantitative proof that certifies the transition from the 'one' to the 'many', from the individual paragon to the collective pattern. Progress and self-improvement, as the book's iterative mode demonstrates, are multipliable. Indeed, the second edition, which contains only minor revisions to the text, adds a long series of new names to what is ideally an open-ended catalogue of anecdotes and illustrations, a potentially infinite list. It is significant, however, that the chapter entitled 'Men of Business' is the one in which the iteration of examples or sketches is less pronounced, and the few names selected as illustrative, from Napoleon to the Duke of Wellington, are notable for not belonging to the sphere of trade proper. Though Smiles, like other writers, begins this chapter by contesting Hazlitt's derogatory representation of the man of business, the tone he adopts is cautious: 'It must be admitted, that Trade tries character perhaps more severely than any other pursuit in life. It puts to the severest tests honesty, self-denial, justice, and truthfulness'.[117] The business community of England, he reassures his readers, 'is still sound at heart' but instances of 'flagrant dishonesty' are many: 'there are tradesmen who adulterate, contractors who "scamp", manufacturers who give us shoddy instead of wool, "dressing" instead of cotton, cast-iron tools instead of steel, needles without eyes, razors made only "to sell", and swindled fabrics in many shapes'.[118] These he considers 'exceptional cases' though they constitute a counter-pattern of negative instances – 'the Sadleirs, Dean Pauls, and Redpaths' – which interrupts the show of positivity the book as a whole celebrates. Even for a fine purveyor of popular myths such as Samuel Smiles, the sphere of business and trade is problematic and not easily amenable to the narrative of national success stylised in his catalogue of names and deeds.

A writer who with greater conviction attempted to disengage trade from its dubious reputation is Henry Fox Bourne, author of *The Romance of Trade* (1876).

His appeal to romance and to the chivalrous history of commerce, banking and business occurs at a time when the belief in economic progress was beginning to be challenged by slow growth, increased international competition and a growing, anxious sense that decline was looming ahead.[119] In this context, Fox Bourne's account of glorious conquests and adventures in the annals of trade functions as a hopeful connotator of continuity, reminding readers that examples of past greatness still have their use. Some nostalgia colours his vision, but the sense of loss is held in tension with a belief in the energies still at work in the troubled present:

> There is, for the most part, less of striking personal incident in the lives of modern English merchants than in those of their predecessors. A few familiar stories of beggarboys who have risen to be millionaires, by steady perseverance and quick perception of the ways in which to make best use of the chances open to them, illustrate the careers of thousands of great merchants. There is plenty of romance still in ledgers and office-stools, cheque-books and cash-boxes; but there is more variety and charm in the history of the heroes of such lately-born commerce as we find in England's great American offshoot than generally occurs in the recent trading annals of our own country.[120]

The historical and transnational scope of Fox Bourne's collection of business portraits, which includes English, Italian, Dutch, American and Indian figures and covers a temporal span of five centuries, brings home a point frequently made by apologists of commerce: the cosmopolitan constitution of the 'brotherhood' of commerce, sustained by both material and symbolic bonds across national borders.[121] Bourne's romantic take on trade extends even to such 'commercial follies' as 'Manias and Panics' introduced in chapter 11: 'so many famous manias, the direct consequences of which have been only panics and ruin to thousands, have, indirectly, been of great value, not only as warnings to posterity, but in actually opening up new and very helpful paths to trade'.[122] Establishing lines of continuity between old-world commerce and the contemporary scene, Fox Bourne uses the biographical form to prop up the shaky myth of progress to which he subscribes, even if his backward looking stance inevitably locates heroism in the past.

By the mid-1880s, the celebration of business stars had become formulaic and clichéd, as the 'storybook heroes'[123] romantically evoked in *Fortunes Made in Business* (1884) exemplify. Hunt has argued that Victorian business biographies tended to 'personalize' the economic scene at a time 'when British commercial culture appeared increasingly *im*personal and complex to many contemporary observers'.[124] Over time, however, as this personalization became more conventional and 'de-individualized', authors 'worked to surround their businessmen with a heightened aura of charisma that personalized their success to an extreme degree'.[125] The charismatic model of economic man, Hunt continues, 'established a powerful practical fantasy that countered more mechanistic models of economic subjectivity and addressed concerns that economic life was dominated by systems, institutions and forces unaligned with discernible personal and social agents'.[126] Undoubtedly, the emphasis on individual striving acquires a glamorous halo in the various stories recounted in *Fortunes Made in Business*. However, as the title clearly indicates, it is the very idea of fortune making that carries special significance, particularly at a time when the main preoccupation of contemporary observers was the sharply declining rate of profits, as the *Athenaeum* noticed. 'This book appears at an opportune time', the reviewer argues, 'Depression has, it is said, overtaken some of the principal industries of the country . . . the masters complain that their profits have an unhappy tendency to approximate to a minimum, even when there is any profit at all'. In this critical situation, 'the recital of such tales as are here told might fairly be expected to have a consolatory and stimulating effect'.[127] By the end of the century, the personalised story of success could be deemed 'consolatory' and 'stimulating' insofar as it moved to the foreground a representation of business as the privileged arena where fortunes were and could still be made. Both the *Athenaeum* and the *Saturday Review*, in two articles which discuss at some length the merits and demerits of *Fortunes Made in Business*, fastidiously differentiate between those who earned their fortunes in the business sphere (and deserve the admiration of readers) and those who distinguished themselves in politics, for instance, and should not, therefore, have been included in this canon of commercial and industrial grandees. As these comments suggests, the prestige of business pursuits was not a matter of dispute. Against a backdrop of decreasing returns and economic decline, the symbolic as well as material profits of business are proudly reassessed as a national patrimony which can and should be differentiated from other traditions. The stories of Isaac Holden, the inventor of the lucifer match, or R. C. Lister a 'successful and ingenious manufacturer', remembered in *Fortunes Made in Business*, are singled out in both review articles as particularly instructive and significant, while the trajectory of the Gladstone family appears out of line with the overarching scope of this collection: 'It would try Mr. Gladstone's marvellous powers of language to show by what processes the reputation of either himself or his late colleague had either originated or been enhanced by business' observed the *Saturday Review*.[128] The same rhetoric of heroism structures the tales of both business and political characters in this book; they are all enveloped in an aura of glamour and charisma. Yet, for late-Victorian reviewers distinction pertains to business proper and to the story of individual striving, inventiveness and money making that they endorse with renewed enthusiasm. Furthermore, the hyperbolic representations – the digressions into Arthurian legends, the plays of Shakespeare or the *Arabian Nights* – whereby some writers construct the charisma of their heroes are dismissed as so much 'padding' by reviewers who remain critical of fictive overstatements or 'inconsequent nonsense',[129] inviting readers to mistrust them. For example, the unnamed author of 'Romance of Invention' appeals to the popularity of romance heroes, from Don Quixote to Robinson Crusoe, to introduce his topic, arguing that, even if literary or legendary characters are not historical figures, 'we give about as good credence to these tales as we do to many articles of faith'. He also encourages readers to embrace the romance of today: 'We want our readers to contemplate the giants, dragons, magicians, and enchantments which are to be met in this daily life of England in the nineteenth century, and what manner of men those must be who combat with them'.[130] It is questionable, however, whether such exhortations to blur the distinction between romance and the real world had much mileage.[131] The *Athenaeum* had no hesitations in exposing this chapter as an example of 'extremely illiterate composition', the kind of 'trash' that cheapened the value of the collection.[132] Once again reviewers enforced the realistic rule, remaining suspicious of hyperboles just as they were of excessive sermonising.

The lionising strategies adopted in *Fortunes Made in Business* served more than one purpose: to counteract the perceived decline of trade with a fresh emphasis on fortunes made heroically, to remind readers that this recent heritage had its own intrinsic value and to augment the stature of industrial or commercial heroes of the recent past through the enchantment of charisma. The celebration of charismatic figures is clearly in contrast with earlier depictions of the man of business as a suffering, overworked individual caught into the vortex of business. This chapter has underlined the tensions and paradoxes frequently registered by business writers, the ideals they sought to promote, the norms they devised, and the critical reception some of them received, which was grounded on the same demand for realism that guided reviewers in their assessment of novels. Samuel Smiles's *Self-Help* is arguably the most famous mid-Victorian intervention in the discussion around business; it has long been considered illustrative of a broader cultural orientation. However, as this chapter has argued, the ways in which the discursive object 'business' was constructed were more varied. As an ideological construct, 'economic man' was multifaceted. Smiles's impressive string of persevering and successful characters encapsulates one side of the story. Other writers took a different angle, moving to the foreground the distortions of business and the problematic flipside of a vocation that seemed to entail a great deal of unhappiness. Victorian observers were also concerned with the question of the dignity of business that surfaces time and again in the periodical press. Celebratory and cautionary modes of representation are deployed in different genres of writing, or within the same text, suggesting that the balance between positive and negative assessments of the business ideal was continuously recalibrated. On the whole, as Riddell's novels also show, being in business was perceived as a very mixed blessing.

Exaggerated Representations?

In this overwhelmingly masculine cohort of voices, does Riddell's contribution stand out as unique or exceptional? Amanda Anderson has persuasively discussed the 'temptations of aggrandized agency' and 'the logic of exceptionalism'[133] that, she argues, transpire in the analyses of feminist critics, especially those who, in the 1980s, were engaged in the kind of recovery work which, albeit 'hagiographic', did change the cultural history of the Victorian period. 'It is inevitable that feminists would want to bring heroic or otherwise prominent women within the annals of history', Anderson admits, but since 'agency and critical reflection are insufficiently or confusedly theorized' the tendency to produce 'exaggerated representations' of feminine critical consciousness is pronounced.[134] However, one could argue that the attribution of aggrandized agency is not only a feminist slip. The same logic of exceptionalism can be detected in critical assessments of canonised Victorian authors, whose novels are valued precisely for proffering exceptionally complex, multi-layered and refined aesthetic responses to, or critical interpretations of, the world in which they were produced and the dynamics of power specific to it – responses or interpretations that vary according to the different theoretical categories deployed in the analysis of texts. Aggrandizing seems to be an effect of the critical game, more or less self-consciously pursued, as Mary Poovey intimates in her critique of 'highly professionalized textual interpretations' (including her own) that risk to generate ahistorical insights, validating as 'universal subject position' the critic's own 'experience of a text'.[135] The tension between formalism and historicism is a conundrum of literary studies in general. It becomes an even thornier issue when the object of investigation is an author, such as Riddell, whose works had popular appeal, were valued as accomplished aesthetic products in their own time (though with some reservations), but have never qualified as eligible for admission into the tradition of literary history according to the criteria of 'greatness' that posterity has devised, including the revisionary criteria formulated by feminist critics. Should one adopt a historicist approach which maximises the cultural value of popular appeal, while minimising issues of form and style? What is the use of formalism when dealing with novels that are neither formulaic nor exceptionally unique or polished? In general, the form of Riddell's novels could be characterised as informal – a way of shaping and structuring experience that tolerates a measure of disorder and is imbued with a sense of arbitrariness and contingency. Nonetheless, this book argues that the relationship her novels entertain with the contemporary reality they were immersed in can best be apprehended by looking closely at, and taking seriously, the formal solutions, the experiments, the styles of narration, the plots she crafted and the deviations from Victorian aesthetic canons that reviewers infallibly noted. To see form in action, plot-driven models of reading are insufficient; how stories are told counts a great deal, as it did for Victorian critics who applied the same standards of judgment to a wide range of novels, including the ones we have forgotten. These standards were not transparent nor were they free from ideological preconceptions. But, as Nicholas Dames claims in *The Physiology of the Novel*, the Victorian models or 'theories' of reading that inspired much review writing of the period are an important cultural mediation to understand what effects fictional forms were expected to have on readers. Reflecting on the recovery work of feminist scholars, Pamela Gilbert observes:

> As literary critics, many of us were trained to look for writers we can read into the tradition recognized as 'great' under new criticism – that is, the one that culminated in early twentieth century modernism, that validated realism, continuity, complexity, universality and contemplative interiority. But Victorian popular modes often were not framed within those values. They were frequently based on melodramatic oppositions, episodic set pieces,

stark contrasts, the pleasure of contemporary (and fleeting references) and emotional responsiveness in the moment. These are not qualities prized by literary critics, though they are still prized by television writers and opera fans . . . we need a method of reading appropriate to the object – especially when that object is 'popular' fiction.[136]

In Gilbert's assessment the central question is how to approach values histori-cally, how to read critically bearing in mind the 'qualities' prised by Victorian pro-fessional and non-professional readers, how to recover not just texts but also their affiliations to models of taste 'that are not easily accessible to readers now'.[137] My interpretations of Riddell's novels seek to follow this path, which implies taking into account those aspects of her style which are most discordant with the paradigms of 'greatness' that ensure or facilitate entry into the tradition of literary history. Before attending to Riddell's forgotten novels, however, another layer of equally forgotten texts and statements had to be unearthed in order to situate her fiction within a broader context of cultural expressions which contributed to the creation of models of value, validating certain kinds of narratives, shaping readers' expectations and orienting their tastes. Thus, to revert to my initial ques-tion (how 'exceptional' was Riddell's contribution to Victorian constructions of the business ideal?), one tentative answer would be that uniqueness is a function of proximity and connections as well as of critical distance. In other words, to gauge Riddell's creative contribution it is important not to disregard how deeply in accordance with widely circulating discourses her focus on business actually was, despite what the narrators of her novels like to reiterate. True, other Victo-rian novelists were not as committed to business as she was; but the plot of the self-made man of business, who suffers anxieties and uncertainties, is tempted in many ways, experiences the ups and downs of the life of the market, with vary-ing degrees of stoicism and pride, and is celebrated for his virtues, heroism and charisma was a fiction reproduced, cherished and critiqued in many texts and dif-ferent genres of writing, though not in the majority of canonical novels, as Dan Bivona and Roger Henkle have noted.

Riddell does not rewrite the meaning of business along proto-feminist lines;[138] she accepts the cultural and social template that assigns to men the jurisdiction of business pursuits, even if some of her heroines long for the opportunity to join their male counterparts in the struggles for wealth. In this respect, her fic-tion offers little scope to the temptations of aggrandized agency; but it brings sexual difference forcefully into the picture. Her City novels echo many of the concerns that were being regularly discussed in the pages of the periodical press, or in books addressed specifically to the business community: from the lack of prestige to the heavy demands imposed on men of business, from the paradox of money to the celebration of individual striving and self-determination that her protagonists share with the subjects of commercial biographies and memoirs. But the experience of commercial and financial modernity these novels narrate is gen-der marked. The intertwined trajectories of men and women, not equally situated vis-à-vis the opportunities that the business world or the City has to offer, are, for this author, what best represents the reality of Victorian business. The 'wisdom of business' according to Riddell revolves around the complex interaction between work and home, masculine aspirations and female desires. Whether this vision is overdetermined by the genre of writing in which Riddell chooses to express herself (fiction and novels specialise in the domestic, private side of life), or whether it is the result of critical detachment from both discursive and material realities is a moot point. Less debatable is that the unexceptional normality of business interests and activities, to which Riddell's imagination is drawn, was a prominent and problematic dimension of bourgeois life and one which has not received the kind of critical attention devoted to other aspects of the social, cultural and intellectual world of the middle classes. That we may find Riddell's vision 'exceptional' is contingent upon the acts of forgetting through which literary and cultural histories selectively remember.

Notes

1 Charlotte Riddell, *Too Much Alone*, 1860, (London: Hutchinson, n.d.), p. 30.
2 Harold Perkins, *Origins of Modern English Society* (London: Ark Paperbacks 1985), p. 221. 'The entrepreneur, according to the ideal, was the lynchpin of society. Although labour was the source of all wealth, it was capital which called it forth and set it in operation. The entrepreneur was the impresario, the creative force, the initiator of the economic cycle' (Ibid., p. 222).
3 A point made by Christine Macleod (pp. 9–14) and more recently by Aeron Hunt, *Personal*, p. 14.
4 Poovey, *Genres*, p. 339 and p. 345.
5 Ibid., p. 345.
6 See William Arthur, *The Successful Merchant: Sketches of the Life of Mr. Samuel Budgett, Late of Kingswood Hill* (New York: Carlton & Porter, 1857), p. 18. The book was first published in England in 1852 (London: Hamilton, Adam and Co., 1852). Quotations from Arthur's biography, in this chapter, refer to the American edition.
7 Charlotte Riddell, *George Geith*, 1864, (London: Hutchinson, n.d.), p. 123.
8 Ibid., p. 74.
9 Ibid., pp. 123–4.
10 See Michie, *The Vulgar Question*.
11 Neil McKendrick, '"Gentleman and Players" revisited: the gentlemanly ideal, the business ideal and the professional ideal in English literary culture', in *Business Life and Public Policy*, ed. N. McKendrick and R.B. Outwhite (Cambridge: Cambridge University Press, 1986), p. 102.
12 Martin J, Wiener, *English Culture and the Decline of the Industrial Spirit, 1850–1980* (Harmondsworth: Penguin, 1985), p. ix.
13 See John McVeagh, *Tradefull Merchants: The Portrayal of the Capitalist in Literature* (London: Routledge, 1981); Norman Russell, *The Novelists and Mammon: Literary Responses to the World of Commerce in the Nineteenth Century* (Oxford: Clarendon Press, 1986); Arthur Pollard, ed. *The Representation of Business in English Literature* (London: IAE, 2000); Wagner, *Financial Speculation* and Zlotnick.
14 Blake, p. 26.
15 Weiner, p. 42.
16 W.D. Rubinstein, 'Cultural Explanations for Britain's Economic Decline: How True?' in *British Culture and Economic Decline*, ed. Collins, Bruce and Keith Robbins (London: Weidenfeld and Nicolson 1990), p. 61.

17 James Raven, 'British History and Enterprise Culture, *Past and Present* 123 (May 1989), p. 173.
18 Raven, p. 173.
19 Women of business are hardly ever mentioned, and when they are, they tend to be portrayed in a comic vein. See, for example, 'Women of Business', *The Tait's Edinburgh Magazine* 1, no. 9 (October 1834), pp. 596–7 and Mrs. Adolphe Smith, 'An American Woman of Business', *The Tinsley's Magazine* 29 (November 1881), pp. 490–93. The idea that women of the middle class should take up more active employments is put forward in some articles – see 'Paying Daughters', *The National Magazine* 2, no.7 (May 1857), p. 31 – but opting for a business life is not considered a realistic option.
20 William Hazlitt, *Table Talk, Second Series* (New York: Wiley and Putnam, 1846), p. 117.
21 'Union of Literary and Business Habits', *The Chambers's Edinburgh Journal* 229 (June 1836), pp. 163–4.
22 Ibid., p. 163.
23 Ibid., p. 164.
24 In *The London Journal, 1845–83: Periodicals, Production and Gender* (Aldershot: Ashgate, 2004), Andrew King discusses this type of longing with reference to the category he terms the 'parergic': 'It is a system whereby texts are based on originals that are invested with greater symbolic capital and authority' (p. 57).
25 'Literature and Business', *The Saturday Review* 29, no. 745 (5 February 1870), p. 77. Arthur Helps's work, *Essays Written in the Intervals of Business* (London: William Pickering, 1843) is clearly echoed in this article. For Aeron Hunt 'Helps's mode of reading injected an element of psychological depth into the representations of business and business character' (Hunt, *Personal*, p. 65).
26 'Literature and Business', p. 177.
27 Ibid.
28 Patrick Joyce, *Visions of the People: Industrial England and the Question of Class* (Cambridge: Cambridge University Press, 1991), p. 112.
29 'Business and Leisure', *The Chambers's Edinburgh Journal* 375 (6 April 1839), p. 81.
30 Patrick Joyce, *Democratic Subjects: The Self and the Social in Nineteenth-Century England* (Cambridge: Cambridge University Press, 1991), p. 170.
31 'The Metaphysics of Business', *The Chambers's Edinburgh Journal* 74 (31 May 1845), p. 338.
32 Joyce, *Democratic Subjects*, p. 170.
33 H.A. Page, 'A Captain of Industry', *Good Words* 13 (January 1872), p. 490.
34 Ibid., p. 492.
35 Alfred Crespi, 'Trades and Professions', *The New Monthly Magazine* 7, no. 48 (June 1879), p. 647.
36 Ibid., p. 650.
37 Launcelot Cross, 'Leaves from Life. No. IV, Business', *The New Monthly Magazine* 90 (June 1879), p. 641.
38 Launcelot Cross, 'Leaves from Life. No. V. Business – (continued)', *The New Monthly Magazine* 116 (July 1879), p. 776 and p. 774.
39 Launcelot Cross, 'The Man of Business – Absolute', *The New Monthly Magazine* 117 (January 1880), pp. 611–12. As I argue more extensively in the next section of this chapter, Crespi's and Cross's interventions mirror a pattern of idealisation of the man of business (merchant, inventor, industrialist or entrepreneur) that emerges in popular culture as a response to what was then known as the 'depression of trade' which many feared would jeopardise irrevocably the economic progress of the nation.
40 James M'Crea, 'The Queen as a Woman of Business', *Time* 1 (April 1879), p. 40. See also M'Crea, 'The Prince as a Man of Business', *Time* 1 (May 1879), pp. 153–8.

41 [Henry Jones], 'Religion and the Stage', *Nineteenth Century* 17, no. 95 (January 1885), pp. 156–7.
42 H.E. Morgan, 'The Dignity of Business', *Review of Reviews* 47, no. 277 (January 1913), p. 21.
43 Ibid., p. 23. See also H.E. Morgan, 'The Dignity of Business. Creating a Common Meeting Ground', *Review of Reviews* 47, no. 278 (February 1913), pp. 137–40.
44 MacLeod, p. 10.
45 See Umberto Eco, *La vertigine della lista* (Milano: Bompiani, 2009), p. 17.
46 'As every child in England knew', writes Thomas Richard, 'the innovation of the Great Exhibition was that it announced the long-awaited arrival of the millennium of prosperity. The country may still have been on the threshold of abundance, but now that abundance, far from being a distant fruit of generations of diligent labor, seemed more tangible than it ever had been before'; see Richards, *The Commodity Culture of Victorian England: Advertising and Spectacle, 1851–1914* (Stanford: Stanford University Press, 1990), p. 66. On the global import of this millennial dream see Paul Young, *Globalization and the Great Exhibition: The Victorian New World Order* (Basingstoke: Palgrave, 2009).
47 Joseph Lyndall, *Business: As it Is, and As It Might Be* (London: Walton and Maberly, 1854), p. 1.
48 Ibid., p. 4.
49 Ibid., p. 6.
50 Ibid., p. 12.
51 Ibid., p. 24.
52 Wells, *How to do Business*, p. 36.
53 Edwin T. Freedley, *A Practical Treatise on Business, with an inquiry into the chances of success and causes of failure* (London: George Routledge and Co, 1853), p. 2.
54 Ibid., p. 7.
55 Ibid., p. 46.
56 Ibid., p. 118.
57 Ibid., p. 25.
58 James W. Alexander and others, *The Man of Business Considered in Six Aspects. A Book for Young Men* (1864) (Edinburgh: William P. Nimmo, 1872), p. vi and p. iii. These essays were originally published by Randolph, New York, in 1857.
59 Ibid., p. 57.
60 Ibid., p. 70.
61 Ibid., p. 59.
62 Ibid., p. 60.
63 Ibid., p. 59.
64 Ibid., p. 150.
65 Ibid., p. 20.
66 Ibid., p. 21.
67 Ibid., p. 32.
68 Ibid., p. 29.
69 Freeman Hunt, *Worth and Wealth. A Collection of Maxims, Morals and Miscellanies for Merchants and Men of Business* (New York: Stringer and Townsend, 1856), p. 151. Freedley's and Hunt's miscellaneous treatises were the most prominent guidebooks for young men before the Civil War. See Richard Weiss, *The American Myth of Success: From Horatio Alger to Norman Vincent Pealie* (Urbana: University of Illinois Press, 1988).
70 Alexander, p. 112.
71 Ibid., p. 133.
72 Ibid., p. 107.
73 Ibid., p. 163.

74 Ibid., p. 160.
75 Anon. *Business Life: Experiences of a London Tradesman with practical advice and directions for avoiding many of the evils connected with our present commercial system and state of society* (London: Houlston and Wright, 1861), p. xi.
76 'The Experience of a London Tradesman', *London Review* 2, no. 38 (23 March 1861), p. 335.
77 See, for instance Rev. J. Baldwin Brown, *The Young Man's Entrance upon Life and Commencement of Business* (London: John F. Shaw, 1855) and W.R. Grey, *Business Manners and Business Matters or Friendly Hints on Every-Day Affairs* (London: William Kent & Co., 1862).
78 Anon., *Business Life*, p. 100.
79 In London, 'every commercial black act is as carefully registered, and the author as well known, as our household words. To carry on a business successfully in London, you must remember that you live in a house of glass, and you must take care that you do not act which is contrary to sound commercial principles' (Ibid., p. 195).
80 Ibid., p. 31.
81 Ibid., p. 100.
82 Henry Smith MD, *High-Pressure Business Life, its Evils, Physical and Moral* (London: J.A. Brook and Co., 1876), p. 14.
83 Ibid., p. 40.
84 Ibid., p. 23.
85 Ibid., p. 13.
86 See Lucy Bending, *The Representation of Bodily Pain in Late Nineteenth Century English Culture* (Oxford: Oxford University Press, 2000).
87 Smith, p. 70.
88 Ibid., p. 60.
89 Ibid., p. 47.
90 Ibid., p. 63.
91 Ibid., p. 61 and p. 67.
92 Ibid., p. 14.
93 Herbert, Sussman, *Victorian Masculinities: Manhood and Masculine Poetics in Early Victorian Literature and Art* (Cambridge: Cambridge University Press, 1995), p. 11.
94 Smith, p. 79.
95 Zlotnick, p. 14.
96 Wiener, p. 27.
97 It is worth quoting Arnold's famous passage: 'Culture says: "Consider these people, then, their way of life, their habits, their manners, the very tones of their voice: look at them attentively; observe the literature they read, the things which give them pleasure, the words which come forth out of their mouths, the thoughts which make the furniture of their minds; would any amount of wealth be worth having with the condition that one was to become just like these people by having it?"' Matthew Arnold, *Culture and Anarchy and Other Writings*, ed. Stefan Collini, (Cambridge: Cambridge University Press, 1993), p. 65.
98 See for instance H.R. Fox Bourne, *English Merchants: Memoirs in Illustration of the Progress of British Commerce*, 2 vols. (London: Richard Bentley, 1866) and, by the same author, *Famous London Merchants: A Book for Boys* (London: James Hogg & Son 1869).
99 'On Mercantile Biography', *The Athenaeum* 24 (December 1808), p. 495.
100 Ibid.
101 Arthur, p. 31.
102 Ibid., p. 32.
103 Ibid., p. 27.
104 Ibid., p. 54.

105   Ibid., p. 83.
106   Ibid., pp. 45–6 and p. 47.
107   Ibid., p. 65.
108   Ibid., p. 65.
109   See Hunt, *Personal*, p. 97.
110   Arthur, 63.
111   Ibid., p. 62.
112   'The Successful Merchant', *The Chamber's Edinburgh Journal* 429 (20 March 1852), p. 190.
113   The reviewer specifically criticises Arthur for 'he is constantly breaking the threads of his narrative by tedious homilies of his own, or, still more tedious, dwelling upon and expounding facts and circumstances which were so manifest as to require no moral', see 'The Successful Merchant', *The Tait's Edinburgh Magazine* 19, no. 219 (20 March 1852), p. 190.
114   M.M. Bakhtin, 'The *Bildungsroman* and Its Significance in the History of Realism: Toward a Historical Typology of the Novel' in *Speech Genres and Other Late Essays*, trans. Vern W. McGee (Austin: University of Texas Press, 1986), p. 25.
115   See Franco Moretti, *The Way of the World: The* Bildungsroman *in European Culture* (London: Verso, 1996).
116   'Self-Help', *Fraser's Magazine for Town and Country* 61, no. 366 (June 1860), p. 778.
117   Samuel Smiles, *Self-Help With Illustrations of Character, Conduct, and Perseverance* (Oxford: Oxford University Press, 2002), p. 238.
118   Ibid., p. 239.
119   See for instance the analyses of the social historian Thomas Hey Sweet Escott, *England: Its People, Polity and Pursuits* (1879) (London: Cassell, 1881). In Chapter 8 I discuss in greater detail the perception of imminent economic and social decline that was widespread in the last two decades of the nineteenth century.
120   Henry Fox Bourne, *The Romance of Trade* (London: Cassell, Petter, Galpin & Co, 1876), p. 347.
121   See, for instance, Patterson, 'The City of Gold', pp. 367–384.
122   Bourne, *Romance of Trade*, p. 293.
123   Hunt, *Personal*, p. 101.
124   Ibid., p. 112.
125   Ibid.
126   Ibid., p. 115.
127   'Fortunes Made in Business', *The Athenaeum* 2944 (March 1884), p. 401.
128   'Fortunes Made in Business', *The Saturday Review* 57, no. 1488 (13 May 1884), p. 581.
129   'Fortunes', *Athenaeum*, p. 402.
130   *Fortunes Made in Business, Biographical and Anecdotic from the Recent History of Industry and Commerce, by Various Writers*, 2 vols. (London: Sampson Low, Marston, Searle & Rivington, 1884), vol. 1, p. 190.
131   Aeron Hunt suggests that they did. She argues that, in the chapter 'Romance of invention', the writer self-consciously reflects on questions that concern the nature of our belief in fiction, questions that 'mirror those posed by literary theorists' (Hunt, *Personal*, p. 117): 'Ruminating on its deployment of fiction, *Fortunes Made in Business* suggests that no divide exists between the textual forms of romance and the real world, because romance is a principle of life in contemporary Britain' (Ibid). Hunts concludes that: 'as fictions can deliver a deeper truth than a historical or scientific account of the real, far from fearing the fictionalization of lives and the replacement of realist character truths by romance conventions and charismatic exorbitance, readers should embrace the process. To recognize fiction – to 'entertain a doubt whether

Crusoe was really born in Yorkshire' – and to still 'go on practically giving faith to all the main story' makes the reader a worthy participant in building the romance of contemporary British business' (Ibid, p. 119).

132 'Fortunes', *Athenaeum*, p. 402.
133 Amanda Anderson, *The Way We Argue Now: A Study in the Culture of Theory* (Princeton, Princeton University Press, 2006), p. 46 and p. 47.
134 Ibid., p. 56.
135 Poovey self-critically cites her own reading of *David Copperfield* in *Uneven Developments* as an example of the discrepancy between 'formalist method' and 'historicist ambition' (Poovey, *Genres*, p. 343).
136 Gilbert, p. 40.
137 Ibid., p. 39.
138 In *A Woman's Thoughts about Women* (1858), Dinah Mulock Craik devotes many pages to the discussion of the benefits to be reaped from the diffusion of correct business attitudes among women of all classes. Craik's conduct-book for female singles, while paying lip service to Victorian ideologies of womanhood, values entrepreneurship, competition, economic independence and the invigorating possibilities of the marketplace as desirable and respectable ideals for women as well as men.

2 The Golden City and the Spectral

I have seen the West End, the parks, the fine squares, but I love the City far better. The City seems so much more in earnest: its business, its rush, its roar, are such serious things, sights and sounds. The City is getting its living – the West End but enjoying its pleasure. At the West End you may be amused, but in the City you are deeply excited.

Charlotte Brontë, *Villette*, 1853

Human experience is gleaned and its sharing, organised, meanings are conceived, absorbed and negotiated, around *places*. And it is in places and of places that human urges and desires are born, live in hope to be satisfied, risk frustration and are being – more often than not – frustrated.

Zygmunt Bauman, *City of Fears, City of Hopes*, 2003

'In the City of London – to the east of Gracechurch Street, on the wrong side of the Monument, between the Mint and Pish Street Hill, and the River and the India House, lies a little tract of over-built and over-populated town, a *terra incognita* to all save those who reside or rent offices in the neighbourhood: may I be permitted to introduce my readers to it?'[1] With these words Riddell inaugurates the series of novels which, a few years later, would make her famous as 'the novelist of the City and of Middlesex'.[2] Topographical accuracy, as Marie-Laure Ryan argues, is an efficient 'immersive' strategy whereby realism draws readers into the text: 'Through the instantaneous character of the act of reference, the use of a place name teletransports the readers to the corresponding location . . . The most immersive toponyms are the names of real places'.[3] Like Balzac, to whom she was sometimes compared, Riddell establishes the setting all at once at the beginning of every novel, using toponyms to pin down the geographical coordinates of the story-world within the perimeter of the Square Mile and its immediate surroundings. Not only business, but more specifically the City of London is Riddell's specialty. This part of the metropolis is both a physical, material space and a symbolic one, charged with conflicting connotations. Selecting the City setting affects the way in which urban experience is narrated. The primacy of work, for example, can hardly be overlooked. It dominates the life of Riddell's characters as it arguably dominated the life of her readers. Economic concerns too are pushed to the fore, more starkly than in much fiction of the period. Finally, the pervasiveness of financial insecurity, spilling over into the realm of affections, tests the limits of realism. Replete with seemingly unmediated references to a complex extratextual reality – the City – Riddell's novels offer fictional paradigms for understanding that historical reality,[4] paradigms at once pseudo-documentary (telling the truth about business and the City is the novels' *raison d'être*) and self-reflective (musing upon the stories they are telling ranks high in the ideological agenda of Riddell's narrators). The chapters to come will investigate how each novel thinks through form and how the City and capitalism more broadly are codified within a realistic frame. To do that, however, another set of frames must be considered first, for the City was a 'fact' that required much fictionalising to be rendered knowable.

Throughout their history, cities have been 'sites of most rapid change', as Bauman argues; as a rule, the 'city-born change caught the living . . . unawares and unprepared'.[5] These two interlinked facets, change and surprise, certainly characterise mid-Victorian representations of the City of London. In the 1860s and 1870s, the City was synonymous with change, incessant transformation, and impermanence. Its architectural and urbanistic features were being drastically redesigned, as old houses and buildings were knocked down to make room for new, functional edifices that proclaimed the global power of the City in the very novelty of their grandiose façades.[6] Similarly, at a more intangible level, the City was identified with fast and capricious capitalism, with fortunes rapidly made and promptly lost, with the transience of the present perceived with much anxiety by economic actors in thrall to the highs and lows of the market. The glaring misconduct of some of them, amply documented in the press, adds another twist to the popular image of the City of London as the site where capitalist modernisation unfolded in extreme forms. The hub of international trade and finance, celebrated as the heart of British global power, was also the home of white-collar crime and fraudulent schemes which repeatedly exposed the public of investors to the spectre of ruin.[7] The prevailing cultural narrative of the City of London, in the years when Riddell turned her attention to it, was a tale of two Cities: power and glory on the one hand, crime and disillusionment on the other; the invisible complexity of financial operations and the visible reality of crime, indignantly registered by financial journalists and novelists alike. The golden City and the spectral mutually defined each other. The imaginative path Riddell pursued to navigate between these extremes entails a decided reinvestment in the lynchpin of realism: the serious imitation of everyday life (even of life in the City) captured in the 'fillers' which, as Moretti observes, offer '*the kind of narrative pleasure compatible with the new regularity of bourgeois life*'.[8] The business of imagining regularity is laborious in Riddell's prose; it involves recalibrating the relationship between realism and sensationalism (*Too Much Alone*); adjusting narration to stabilise the inherent instability of fast capitalism (*George Geith*); or, alternatively, embracing the disordered capaciousness of the novel form to confront the murky side of business with unusual frankness (*The Race for Wealth*). Given the extremes of virtue and vice, glory and shame that contemporaneous representations of the City tended to privilege, it is perhaps less surprising that regularity should become such a formal challenge.

This chapter discusses the representational modes that mid-Victorian writers and journalists deployed when describing, narrating or elucidating the City for the general public.[9] The work of transmuting the City into a legible narrative was performed primarily through the framing provided by the sketch form; this framing often entailed an act of distancing carried out through the use of irony, sarcasm, scorn (the target of which was not just finance) or, in Dickens's case, affable narratorial detachment. Explaining the City to outsiders also involved devising imaginative strategies to personalise the world of capital and finance. For Charles Dickens, George Augustus Sala and John Hollingshead, who contributed several sketches and short essays to *Household Words* and *All Year Round*, the City is a rich repository of stories of human ambition and greed, a ghostly reality which inspires mournful reflections and a symbol of the paper flimsiness of the credit economy. For David Morier Evans, City correspondent and author of monumental volumes which chronicled the manias and panics of the 1840s and 1850s, the City is a 'world within itself',[10] intricate and fascinating, best revealed to the uninitiated through a representational style which mingles facts and fiction, references to contemporary events and imaginative narratives. Unlike Riddell, these authors write the City through the compact frame and quick tempo of the short form, composing sketches or brief narratives that hinge on the single episode, the contained moment of revelation, or the illustrative local example. Only translated as brevity, can the complexity of the City be narrated. Short forms, rapid strokes and mini-closures provide at least a momentary glimpse of the significance of the whole.

Opting for the prolonged duration of the novel form was Riddell's innovation. 'It seems strange as one thinks of it', wrote Anne Thackeray (later Ritchie) in a review of *Too Much Alone* and *George Geith*, 'that before these books came out no one ever thought of writing about city life'.[11] The genre of the City novel that Riddell inaugurated in the early 1860s lives on today in the many types of fiction – from financial thrillers and fictional memoirs of traders, to crime stories and documentary novels set in the City – which capitalise on the melodrama of the financial district.[12] These stories cover very different experiences from the ones Riddell articulates in her novels; they are frequently presented as redemption narratives, written from the ex post perspective of repentant City rogues, disillusioned traders, or jaded and tough City girls. The infamous reputation of the City and of Wall Street as theatres of unfettered avarice and financial excess has intensified especially in the aftermath of the 2008 crash. But when Riddell invited her readers to explore what she calls a '*terra incognita*' and to follow the trajectories of more or less youthful City men with great expectations, the physical and mental space she evoked was not yet entirely defined by the abstract, impersonal and partly unintelligible mechanisms and machinations of financial engineering. Algorithms are today's villains, as Harris's thriller *The Fear Index* testifies.[13] For Riddell, trade, industry and to a lesser extent financial speculation are all activities located firmly in the City and its surroundings; the running of small businesses or partnerships is the kind of economic enterprise she preferably portrays, while large corporations only appear on the horizon in the 1880s, and when they do, they are not necessarily impersonal. In other words, to understand in historical terms the City that Riddell recreates, one needs to take a step back from habitual descriptions of Victorian capitalism as already 'financialised' and therefore abstract and impersonal.[14] As Hunt writes: 'variations on the theme of abstraction, complexity, and impersonality structure many of the assumptions in literary criticism and cultural studies of the period, crowding out of the picture the personalized experiences and interpersonal relationships that persist'.[15] The point is not just to broaden the picture by including the personal, but to consider financialisation as a process (not a given) that preoccupied Victorian observers to a great extent, though not to the exclusion of other concerns.

In the texts analysed in this chapter and in Riddell's novels, the City is always in the process of becoming; it elicits literary interest insofar as it appears as a particular type of transient reality, a reality, however, that could boast a millennial tradition of solid prominence in the history of the nation, as Riddell takes pleasure in reminding her readers. As the epicentre of change and modernisation, the City provoked different types of reaction. The financial journalist, Robert Hogarth Patterson, writing for the *Blackwood's Edinburgh Magazine* in 1864, depicted the 'City of gold' as the 'citadel of our greatness': 'it is no exaggeration to say' – he added – 'that the progress of mankind is mirrored in the operations of this monetary metropolis'.[16] A small place with a global mission, the golden City was the dynamic working space of a new class of men 'who [went] about their business with liveliness and zest',[17] keeping healthy and young in the exciting pursuit of profit. When Charles Dickens's uncommercial traveller surveyed this precinct of Mammon, the citadel appeared in a different light: its street deserted, it churches empty and its activities silently at rest – a ghostly town, in the perception of Dickens and George Augustus Sala; a deadly, insubstantial paper City in John Hollingshead's favourite metaphor. In between the golden and the spectral City, lies a range of connotations which it is worth exploring further.

The Other City

Over the course of many decades, via several twists and turns, the City of London developed into a global financial centre. Historians have documented this process in detail. Kynaston charts the move towards financialisation almost year by year, looking at a variety of records and constructing a rich, dense narrative that defies oversimplifications. Ultimately, Kynaston observes, 'what abided – day after day, week after week, year after year – was not so much the larger environment as the actual grinding routine: the voluminous ledgers, the salient account books, the endless, pernickety correspondence. *There* lies the true, inner, inscrutable history of the City'[18] – a history, I would add, with which Riddell's novels are inextricably connected. Michael Ball and David Sunderland have demonstrated to what extent the Victorian City was not, or not prevalently, 'a place for high finance':

> The nineteenth-century City contained thriving businesses in commercial trade and also some manufacturing enterprises – the two would often merge together under one proprietor. Overall, according to the 1891 census, such enterprises constituted up to two-thirds of the firms operating in the City. They included manufacturing chemists and 435 commercial brokers dealing in such commodities as tea, cotton and ivory. Textile and clothing businesses – merchants, warehouses and manufacturers – added another 652 firms. There were 207 'makers' of a wide variety of goods including chronometers and revolving-shutters; and 602 manufacturers – making things as un-City-like as sausage machines, springs and sheep dips. A further 2,461 merchants could be added dealing in a wide variety of goods. The list is as long as it is varied and illustrates the dangers of simply seeing the City as a place for high finance.[19]

As these numbers reveal, the types of business conducted in the City were primarily those which 'had an appeal of some sort to the senses', as Bagehot put it: mercantile activities, physical trade and manufacturing.[20] Of course, this is not to deny the many intersections between such undertakings and the financial operations normally involved in the running of businesses. But, as Ranald Michie argues, 'finance did not dominate' the activities of the City: 'By the middle of the nineteenth century the City of London . . . was still primarily a commercial centre with trade and shipping being the most important act undertaken there . . . the City of London as a financial centre was taking shape in addition to the City of London as a commercial centre, not instead of it'.[21]

In 1867, Benjamin Scott, author of *A Statistical Vindication of the City of London,* described trade as the 'specialty' of the City: 'It is the commerce of London – its traffic with foreign and distant parts, its interchange of commodities with every quarter of the globe, which makes the City what it is – the busiest, most enterprising and most wealthy emporium of either ancient or modern times'.[22] In his account, it is the mercantile component that makes this part of London 'stand alone', 'second to no district of the Metropolis, no City or Town of the Empire',[23] even if the 1861 Census had insinuated fears that a quickly depopulating Square Mile would soon lose its prominence. Some 30 years later, the exchange and production of goods on a grand scale still defined the spirit of the place; for Charles. C. Turner the City is both 'the chief abode of the great god Money' and a 'great commercial maw' swallowing and digesting 'the world's tribute': 'Bound for London, speeding under steam and sail from the far Antipodes and the sweltering tropics, from north and east and west, in infinite variety, comes the produce of every land and sea. But, swallowed up in the great city's prosaic greyness, the wonder and romance of this vast commerce are seldom appreciated. Yet they are worth a thought'.[24] Indeed, these wonders are worth more than a passing thought. Turner's description expands into a rapt account of the activities carried out in

'Commercial Sale Rooms'. Specialising in different types of merchandise, these Rooms deal in enormous quantities of goods. 'It is safe to assume', reflects Turner, 'that the average citizen who is not connected with Exchange life has no conception of its importance, its great interest, or of the huge army of somewhat modest and exclusive men devoted to it'.[25] At the beginning of the twentieth century, the importance of the mercantile component remained almost unchallenged, though elaborate descriptions seemed necessary to reinforce its symbolic value and to pay tribute to the 'army' of 'modest' men earning their living in the City.

Riddell's novels could be adduced as further evidence that in the imagination and perceptions of Victorian observers finance had not yet supplanted the City's more traditional functions. She writes of chemical manufacturers (*Too Much Alone*), inventors and engineers (*City and Suburb*), accountants (*George Geith*), merchants (*The Senior Partner*) and producers of adulterated food (*The Race for Wealth*) as if the City were preeminently their turf, their grazing ground, while financiers, speculators and the future they represent are encroaching upon the scene destabilising it. I emphasise this not to suggest that her fiction provides a polished mirror in which to see an accurate reflection of the old City about to be obliterated by the new. Rather, my point is that the not yet financialised environment she imagines, the City of industrial and commercial undertakings, is perceived as existing in an uneasy relationship with the City to come; to use Koselleck's categories, the 'horizon of expectation' affects the way in which the 'space of experience' is articulated.[26] Like other Victorian novelists, Riddell typically sets her stories slightly back in time; the present she narrates is already the past of her readers and its 'pathos' is contingent upon the very precarious temporal existence of the now, always imperilled by the rapidity with which transformations occur, or the future impinges on the present. This configuration, this imaginative truth of the City, characterises Riddell's vision. The *longue durée* of her novels ensures that the 'space of experience' is enlarged, expanded and rendered significant, rather than being reduced to the episodic and the fleeting. To understand in what ways her writing differs from, or is analogous to, contemporary City narratives, I turn now to a set of texts which were mostly published in popular periodicals and later collected in volume form. To the best of my knowledge, the City novel, as Riddell conceived it, was not a genre of writing that other authors before her had practiced. As a subject of literary musings, the City had of course inspired various writers; but in the 1850s and 1860s the short form was the frame privileged by those who, like Riddell, considered the City deserving of attention.

The City of Unlimited Paper

George Augustus Sala uses the conceit of spectrality to hammer home the unpalatable truth of white-collar crime, a phenomenon that was provoking much indignation in the early 1850s. His sketch, 'City Spectres' (1852), parades a shabby assemblage of 'gaunt men, with haggard countenances and seedy habiliments'[27] who linger in the vicinity of the Royal Exchange, Capel Court or Lombard Street. They haunt the imagination of this writer as ghostly reminders of the unfinished

business of crime. Sala pictures them returning upon the scene of their past misde-
meanours, but not to repent or amend the wrongs done, as some ghosts would do
in Victorian supernatural tales. The gothicised atmosphere thus evoked projects a
dark image of the City, a place that owes its spectrality to the high frequency of
crime and to the quickness with which wealth turns into dust when speculation
gains the upper hand. Most noticeable, however, is the fastidious attention Sala
pays to the 'habiliments' that signal the spectres' uncertain class collocation:

> See him once, and forget him if you can. His countenance is woebegone: his
> hat is battered in the crown, torn in the brim, worn away in the forepart, by
> constant pulling off; napless long since; but rendered factitiously lustrous by
> the matutinal application of a wet brush; his satin stock — black once, brown
> now — fastened at the back with a vicious wrench and a rusty buckle: his
> sorry body-coat (Spectres never wear frock-coats), tesselated on the collar
> and elbows with cracked grease-spots; torn at the pockets with continuous
> thrusting-in of papers; dotted white with the tombstones of dead buttons: his
> shrinking, withered, shame-faced trousers: his boots (not Bluchers, but nearly
> always Wellingtons) cracked at the sides and gone at the heel, the connection
> still preserved by the aid of a red-hot poker and gutta percha. I know all about
> that Ghost. He passed to the world of spectres in 1825. He must have been
> that head clerk in the great banking firm of Sir John Jebber, Jefferson, and Co.
> which speculated somewhat too greedily.[28]

For all its ghostliness, this figure is a very tangible, particularised emblem of
shabby respectability turned sour. Neither unquestionably bourgeois nor blatantly
working-class, the clothes that cover the spectral body of the head clerk retain
only a vague semblance of decorum; they are material signifiers of the frustrated,
thwarted desire for upward mobility that drove this spectre and his fellow ghostly
clerks towards the false promises of speculation. What haunts the imagination
of the observer – the eye lingering with a perverse kind of realistic *jouissance*
on every crack, dead button, rip and grease-spot – is not just misconduct but the
inadmissible aspirations behind it, the effrontery of clerks who aim higher at their
own peril. Speculation interferes with the tripartite structure of the class system,
encouraging lower-middle-class individuals to push the boundaries, to jostle for a
larger share of the national wealth, to become protagonists in the City rather than
simple cogs in a mechanism run by others. The spectre of upward and downward
mobility is the truly recalcitrant presence in the City Sala represents; criminal
behaviour is its corollary. 'There is attraction of repulsion', Dickens was later
to write with reference to City churchyards;[29] the same structure of feeling, the
same attraction towards the repulsive detail, animates Sala's descriptions. Disgust
works as a distancing strategy vis-à-vis both the corrupted morals of clerks and
their highly suspicious ambitions.

Like Sala, John Hollingshead, who contributed vignettes and sketches of City
life to *Household Words* in the late 1850s, translates the City into images of negative volatility. In one of these sketches, the central conceit is the insubstantiality of

paper and puppets. 'The City of Unlimited Paper' harks back to early nineteenth-century diatribes – Cobbet's *Paper against Gold* (1828) springs to mind – but it does not replicate their radicalism. Rather, as I argue, the indictment of paper derives its vehemence from the repulsion that both the grand spectacle of criminal finance and the small, miserable charade of petit bourgeois capitalism provoke. The sketch begins with a dystopic vision of the paper City and its inhabitants; it then evolves into a panoramic view of bogus companies, with allegorical names ('The House of Collaps Brothers', 'the firm of Messrs. Ignes, Fatui and Company')[30] and ramifications all over the world, responsible for turning the 'New Babylon' into a grave for 'sunken capital' and fallen people.

> Within a certain circle of which Bow Church is the centre, lie the ruins of a great paper city. Its rulers – solid and substantial as they appear to the eye – are made of paper. They ride in paper carriages, they marry paper wives, and unto them are born paper children; their food is paper, their thoughts are paper. They buy paper and they sell paper; they borrow paper and they lend paper – a paper that shrinks and withers in the grasp like leaves of the sensitive plants.[31]

Eating and breathing paper, the denizens of the City lead a life of regular crime and infrequent punishment. Improbable companies rise to the pinnacle of commerce and go belly up in an instant; obscure, manipulative clerks embezzle the money of more or less honest partners; railway lines always remain hypothetical and the City is a rather despicable stage where 'puppets' – old and new – hold sway. In Hollingshead's vignettes, the City inspires sarcasm, a degree of scorn for the corruptibility of human beings, trapped between mediocrity and vice, and a mild interest in the unglamorous existence of small traders. In the only piece presented as a 'descriptive record of my actual experience',[32] the author surveys the spectacle of the City 'from the trifling elevation of a few hundred feet'.[33] What he sees is 'one mass of undistinguishable equality', of anonymous human beings ('black dots') compared to repulsive insects, 'the most miserable beetles that ever crawled down a gutter'.[34] 'Unequal and vastly different they may be to each other', the writer notices from his position of aloofness, 'with all their outer and their inner trappings – their wealth and their poverty; their meekness and their severity . . . but, to me, they appear only as a set of amusing puppets acting a play'.[35] The negative uniformity of 'unlimited paper', the 'undistinguishable equality' of City puppets, the miserable littleness of 'black dots', the crawling animalism of 'beetles': Hollingshead's vocabulary is reminiscent of a resilient tradition of anti-democratic sentiment. The microcosm he observes, far from being an abstract city of paper, is a concrete environment with distinct social connotations: it is a stage where lower-middle-class heroes and villains play their parts. The grey lives of white collars provide abundant material for reflection. In Hollingshead's sketches the passionate denunciation of frauds and white-collar crime is interspersed with a 'parodic discourse of littleness'[36] that is at best ambivalent about the ill-defined, derivative and suspicious aspirations of a new breed of petty bourgeois workers dwelling in the City.

In the second half of the nineteenth century, the City residential population declined sharply: of the 129,000 residents recorded in the 1851 Census, only 75,000 remained in 1871. In *The Uncommercial Traveller*, Dickens prematurely dubbed the Square Mile 'The City of the Absent'. In fact, as Kynaston explains, residential numbers fell over a period of 20 or so years and this gradual decrease, mainly caused by the growing market value of real estate, was accompanied by a significant change in the social composition of the population: 'many of those living in the City were retailers, and small-scale producers (such as watchmakers and tailors), who tended to use their homes partly as a place to live, partly as working premises'; the mid-Victorian City was home to 'a plethora of small-scale family firms performing a bewildering variety of functions'.[37] Hollingshead's sketches acknowledge the presence of this population, albeit grudgingly: he refers to them as 'a band of hungry traders', a 'motley tribe of small capitalists who are ever looking for a profitable investment',[38] a small army of predatory dealers among whom, as the beleaguered narrator of 'Good-Will' laments, 'I am parcelled out'.[39] Guilty money and frauds provide the overarching theme of the vignettes collected in *Under Bow Bells*, but interwoven with this standardised representation of the evil powers at work in the City is a more detailed, sometimes sympathetic, mostly hostile narrative about men and women whose life and identity are entirely defined by their petty occupations: 'puppet clerks' in dingy offices ('My lost Home'); would-be secretaries stressed out by unfair competition ('Wanted, A Secretary'); fatigued waiters overwhelmed by imperious orders of food ('Too Weak for the Place'); small traders with a smattering of gentility and a strong desire to speak with dukes ('The Afflicted Duke of Spindles'); elderly, retired clerks hanging on to their painful memories of work ('The End of Fordyce Brothers'); disabled young employees mistrusted by their seniors ('Poor Tom – a City Weed') and men of leisure who stoop to business, find it revolting and smelly, but enjoy the pleasure of money ('My Two Partners').

Under Bow Bells starts off with a metaphorical depiction of the City of paper and ends with a warning about 'new puppets' replacing old ones. Paper and puppets signify emptiness, corrupted moral standards and the deterioration of society in a way that is intended to inspire indignation. However, most of the sketches and short stories portray a more detailed small world, a city within the City, whose inhabitants move uneasily between the temptations of crime and the drudgery of work, between dishonesty as a shortcut to wealth and the dullness of unrewarded probity. Hollingshead pins the blame on ambitious clerks. In 'The End of Fordyce, Brothers', a story fairly representative of the tone of the whole collection, the deceitful Michael Armstrong rises from the post of junior clerk to that of private secretary by flaunting impeccable business manners and a stern dedication to work. The senior partners take his correct behaviour at face value, whereas the employees, including the narrator, soon realise that 'everything he did was the result of deep, quick, keen, and selfish calculation'.[40] Affecting deafness, Armstrong obtains valuable commercial information not meant for his ears, which he exploits for illegitimate speculative purposes. Eventually his crimes are discovered and he commits suicide.

Narrated from the perspective of a loyal clerk who, in his old age, likes to return to the sequestered nook where the house of Fordyce once stood, the story pits probity and loyalty against ambition and avarice, but only to raise the disturbing possibility that good, honest clerks are indistinguishable from calculating, insincere ones, as both types perform their ordinary and dull routines according to the strictest business etiquette. Armstrong's 'remarkable business aptitude, his care and industry, his manners, and probably his supposed infirmity . . . had a natural influence and met with adequate reward'.[41] Trusting appearances, the senior partners promote the wrong clerk with disastrous results. In the grey area of poorly remunerated and tedious clerical occupations, on which the ordinary running of business houses depends, not only is the legitimate desire to better one's position indistinguishable from excessive ambition, but the efficient, correct performance of one's duty is not to be trusted as an indication of the worker's worth. For the army of 'modest people' working in the City, day after day, there seems to be little hope of redemption. Hollingshead has some sympathy for the losers and thrashes those who try to win – harshly if their means are illegitimate and condescendingly if they ever achieve anything.

Insignificant as they might be, the lower-middle-class people working in the City of paper are perceived as a threat by Hollingshead – and not only by him. Bagehot, for instance, in *Lombard Street* (1873), conjures up the image of a 'dirty crowd of little men' when explaining how the 'increasingly democratic structure of English commerce' works.[42] He admits that the entry of new agents, physiological to the dynamic world of trade, has negative repercussions on commercial morality. The 'little men' who want business fast have neither the culture nor the ease of the City aristocracy. Unscrupulous in testing the limits of legitimacy, they are the first ones to panic in times of crisis. However, 'these defects and others in the democratic structure of commerce are compensated by one great excellence', Bagehot avers, 'No country of great hereditary trade, no European country at least, was ever so little "sleepy", to use the only fit word, as England; no other was ever so prompt at once to seize new advantages'.[43] This promptness does not characterise men of 'large wealth' who tend to consider every change of circumstance a 'bore', Bagehot argues. The best exponents of the 'propensity to variation' are the new men, unpolished and rough, who cannot afford to stay still:

> But a new man, who has his way to make in the world, knows that such changes are his opportunities; he is always on the look-out for them, and always heeds them when he finds them. The rough and vulgar structure of English commerce is the secret of its life; for it contains 'the propensity to variation', which, in the social as in the animal kingdom, is the principle of progress.[44]

Bagehot does not deny that the 'democratic structure' of the 'delicate' system he describes in *Lombard Street* entails some risk, but he supports a more inclusive view of the society of actors playing on the City stage than the one Hollingshead had been able or willing to imagine.

As the historian John Bailey maintains, these new men, and the members of the lower middle class in particular, 'were in the front line of engagement with modernity. Its men and women were both agents and casualties of modem mobility in its many forms and disjunctions. They were at the forefront in the democratisation of self-fashioning and the exploration of options of identity, both actualized and lived out in the head'.[45] Hollingshead reacts defensively to this engagement with modernity, denigrating his characters' desire for social mobility and their timid attempts at self-fashioning frequently thwarted by villains from their own ranks. The focus on this social group adds an interesting twist to the customary image of the City where imponderable and dubious transactions predominate. The flipside of grand finance is an unglamorous scene brimming with potential malefactors ready to claim their right to trade, as threatening in their littleness as any colossal financial adventurer. Hollingshead's vignettes depict a dual City: one, self-referential (paper breeds paper) abstract and artificial; the other, literal, prosaic and menacing. The indictment of paper, speculation and greed derives part of its energy from the fear of social mobility and 'undistinguishable equality' that finds a displaced expression in Hollingshead's mocking sketches of clerks, small traders, and petty employees. In other words, the attack on finance capitalism is motivated by status anxiety and anti-democratic fears. Preoccupations with the negative magic of money run parallel to the scornful discourse of littleness through which Hollingshead represents the City of the present and of the living.

In 'The City of London, Real and Unreal' Garrett Ziegler argues that mid-Victorian journalism documented and 'propelled' the transition from the 'experiential' to the 'financial' City: the deletion of 'the concrete, particular, lived space of the City', noticeable in mid-Victorian urban sketches and City narratives, helped 'produce "the modern form of abstraction" that characterizes the finance capitalism that came to be centered in the City'.[46] As Ziegler concludes, 'In order to build the economy of the future . . . it was necessary for the Victorians to kill the lived space of the City, to turn it into a ghost town, a wilderness of shades and speculation'.[47] Undoubtedly, the spectral, paper City that Sala and Hollingshead envisage seems to anticipate the depersonalisation associated with finance capitalism. However, as Hollingshead's very concrete and particular crowd of local residents testifies, there remains a distressing, experiential dimension that is not elided nor 'killed' in these texts. The experience of work is still a lived experience even in the spectral City and it is not written off as residual. Hollingshead dwells on it, troubled by the unclassifiable nature of a 'dirty crowd of little men' (to use Bagehot's expression) who did not have a coherent class identification, were socially unstable, and stubbornly desired the undesirable: prosperity and respectability. The metaphorical centrality of 'spectres', 'paper' and 'puppets' is in tension with the even more prominent presence of 'little men' and 'hungry traders' with half-decent occupations and suspicious ambitions. Prefiguring the abstract City was not the only cultural work Sala's and Hollingshead's texts performed. Containing and chastising the desires of these City dwellers appears as an even more pressing concern. The form of the sketch is especially apt at conveying a sense of stasis in the midst of changefulness, as Amanpal Garcha has argued:

'sketches self-consciously advertise their partial, fragmentary status, and they assert the value of temporal stasis and "authentic" stylistic consistency'.[48] Captured in a series of unrelated snapshots, the fragmented, 'lived experience' of Hollingshead's City dwellers is sketched rather than plotted; it is frozen in a temporal frame that denies any idea of progress. The stasis is both formal and ideological: for the 'black dots' or 'puppets', observed with varying degrees of pity and scorn, there is no imaginable progress.

The anti-democratic sentiment feeding Hollingshead's invectives against financialisation has gone remarkably unnoticed in recent interpretations of his journalism. Admittedly, 'The City of Unlimited Paper' lends itself rather well to support descriptions of the nineteenth-century economy as in various ways fictitious. Referencing only this sketch, Anna Kornbluh mentions Hollingshead's vision of a 'zombie-land of "hideous nightmares"',[49] but overlooks the reverse of the picture; in *Realism, Photography and Nineteenth-Century Fiction*, Daniel Novak again selects the same article to substantiate his claim that 'paper money itself was figured as a form of fiction';[50] for Adam Hansen, likewise, Hollingshead's 'utterly insubstantial' City '[c]omposed of flimsy deals and arrangements' is more remarkable than the mobile city of small traders;[51] while Ziegeler, who looks at other sketches as well, concludes: 'The emptying City of Evans and Dickens has now, in Hollingshead's essay, run its course. It is reduced to a necropolis, its bones picked over by the most marginal and invisible of people, its center a hole of vanishing money'.[52] One is tempted to ask, who is doing the emptying, whether the Victorians themselves or the critics who disregard the other City and its 'invisible' people. Of course, the credit economy was perceived as flimsy, insubstantial and in many ways untrustworthy – and 'The City of Unlimited Paper' is a prime illustration of this. But underneath these perceptions of the City, lies another stratum of popular worries which have to do with social mobility, precarious class identities and the scramble for wealth that the availability of speculative schemes made even more acute. Hollingshead defensively represents the attempts of the petit bourgeoisie to participate in this game, ridiculing them with the same vigour marshalled to condemn fictitious paper. Rather than dead or erased, the crowd of 'small men' was a social group that 'failed to disappear' both in Hollingshead's sketches and in the economic history of Britain and Europe: 'The long nineteenth century', Crossick and Haupt argue, 'was a period in which small enterprise, and with it its petit-bourgeois owners, failed to disappear in the way expected by those who have seen it as ill-suited to the needs of an industrial society in which large-scale capital, large bureaucratic institutions, and the antagonism of labour and capital came to prevail'.[53]

Although most of Riddell's business heroes belong to upper-class families, typically impoverished by the irresponsible squandering of previous generations, the position they occupy in the City is that of small entrepreneurs nursing legitimate ambitions and a strong desire to be independent. Like Bagehot, Riddell values the 'democratic structure of English commerce', which her novels plot in story after story, exploring the intimate repercussions of capitalist competition and the quest for profit. She is not immune to the 'attraction of repulsion' exemplified in

Hollingshead's sketches, as *The Race for Wealth*, for instance, illustrates. None-theless, the dynamism these novels relentlessly imagine, the varieties of 'lived experience' Riddell's City encompasses within its precincts and the range of social identities explored stand in stark contrast to the stasis of puppets and the impersonality of paper. Rather than killing the lived space of the City and propel-ling its transformation into a metonymy of finance capitalism, Riddell's novels seek to re-signify that space by shifting attention to the intricate nexus of private and public concerns. The many realities of Victorian capitalism, as historians have demonstrated, even in the changing City landscape of the mid-nineteenth century, did not just give way to high finance. They persisted as important constituents of an environment with which the average Victorian was arguably more famil-iar than with the operations of the Stock Exchange, as Hollingshead's popular sketches and Riddell's novels suggest though with different ideological orienta-tions. Personal or family capitalism, the running of small businesses or partner-ships remained for a long time the central structure of the British economy, as Rose, Payne and Taylor aver.[54] The type of abstraction that Ziegler sums up as 'making money without making anything'[55] gained prominence as the century drew to a close but even in the City it did not supplant other activities.

This might help explain why Riddell's City is neither golden nor spectral, nei-ther grandiose nor prematurely ghostly; or, to put it differently, why in its 'attempt to deal with a historical world'[56] her realism conjures the image of a crowded urban space alive with potentialities that the novel form allows to explore in greater detail. Unless one is willing to emend and complicate the historical description of capitalism as always already financialised, abstract and impersonal, it is hard to understand what kind of claim Riddell's realism makes. As Shaw writes, 'Lit-erary realism always carries with it an ontological claim. It does not attempt to represent the world "directly". It does claim to tell us what our world is really like'.[57] In forging connections between the various components of a world seen as historical, Riddell's realism places the reader in a different kind of relation-ship with the imagined City of her times – one that is not overdetermined by the worrying signs of what Kornbluh calls 'finance's propulsive futurity'.[58] Riddell's novels were certainly not blind to the contradictions of the liberal dream they still promote and to the predicaments of those invisible people, the diurnal inhabitants of the City, whom Sala, Hollingshead and Dickens metamorphose into ghosts, with a certain scornful relish. Riddell's pro-business, pro-capitalist stance does not exclude critical attacks on new legislative instruments (the Limited Liability Act) and institutions (joint stock companies) which facilitated the development of finance capitalism. But her picture is multi-faceted and it certainly prioritises the contradictory desires of the living over the muted reasons of half-dead spectres.

The City of the Absent

The 'City of the Absent' that Dickens described in the sketch of the same name was a statistically documented reality. The 1861 Census confirmed the downward turn of the City's demographic curve. It is interesting to note, however, that this evidence was not received with the authority of an unquestionable truth. Benjamin Scott had no hesitation in declaring it downright 'fallacious'.[59] His *Statistical Vindication* rests on the conviction that what the Census should have quantified as the true, authentic population inhabiting the City was the diurnal and 'ever-increasing throng of its frequenters'[60] who spent a substantial part of their life in all the different branches of employment located in the City. The *Athenaeum* was ready to endorse this view, attributing to the 'throng' of commuters the status of 'citizens in the full sense of the word'.[61] Disputing the official, statistical answer to the question 'Where do people *live*?' Scott speculates:

> What is population? Who are inhabitants? Where do people live? The changes may be rung upon these terms to any tune that may best harmonize with the views of fallacy-mongers. People may be truly said to *live* where, by their active avocations, they obtain the means by which they subsist. Says Shylock, and is he not right? "You take my *life*, when you take the means whereby I live." Charles Lamb says somewhere, referring to his desk at the India House, "I derive *life* from this dead board." . . . Where do people *live*? If it were asked, "where do people snore?" than the correct answer would certainly be, "where they sleep".[62]

Scott's assumption is that 'living' means working rather than sleeping; in other words people properly inhabit the space where they earn a living, where they 'put forth their energies . . . tax their brains, and . . . devote themselves wholly to the real and exclusive business of their lives'.[63] Though not residing in the Square Mile, 'the army of people moving on the City every morning *belongs to the City*'.[64] As Scott claims in words that are reminiscent of Riddell's rhetoric: 'Their thoughts, hopes, cares and anxieties are concentrated in the City of London'.[65] Significantly, he appeals to the authority of Shakespeare and Lamb to support his unorthodox view. Literature is recruited to confute the wrong impression produced by numbers and statistics: there is 'life' in work, and there is an ever-growing population whose lived experience is defined by the work they do in the City. This truth may be more literary than mathematical, but Scott presents it as a fact, upbraiding the mendacious representations of the desolate, 'deserted and degraded City'[66] that circulated in the popular press. As Scott's *Statistical Vindication* suggests, defining what counts as 'lived experience' in the City of London was a matter of some dispute. Official records disclaimed the importance of the 'daylight' City; literary sketches made much of the gothic hues of the 'gaslight' City; Scott, like Riddell, holds on to the very modern truth that life revolves around work. Dickens deletes the presence of workers – absent, invisible – but not the traces of work, trade and commodities.

In *The Uncommercial Traveller* (1860), the absent and the dead seem to have replaced citizens and commuters. The trope of the City as necropolis is central; churchyards, tombs and invisible corpses yield an irresistible, melancholic charm. Indulging in an eerie fantasy of pre-mourning, the uncommercial traveller imagines himself as 'the Last Man', overlooking a scene evacuated by the living.

Like the Census officers who went about collecting data in the middle of the night, Dickens's traveller visits the Square Mile only 'after business-hours', or on Saturdays and Sundays, thus foreclosing the possibility of ever coming face to face with its diurnal, more lively bustle. Yet, even while registering or producing absence, Dickens's sketches dwell on the traces of mercantile life still lingering in the air, when the streets are deserted, the churches empty and trade is a mute presence perceived indirectly through the persistent aroma of commodities:

But, in other cases, rot and mildew and dead citizens formed the uppermost scent, while, infused into it in a dreamy way not at all displeasing, was the staple character of the neighbourhood. In the churches about Mark-lane, for example, there was a dry whiff of wheat; and I accidentally struck an airy sample of barley out of an aged hassock in one of them. From Rood-lane to Tower-street, and thereabouts, there was often a subtle flavour of wine; sometimes of tea. One church near Mincing-lane smelt like a druggist's drawer. Behind the monument, the service had a flavor of damaged oranges, which, a little further down towards the river, tempered into herrings, and gradually toned into a cosmopolitan blast of fish.

('City of London Churches')[67]

In 'City of London Churches' the olfactory modality predominates. The traveller sees absence and senses presence. Wherever he goes, commercial odours hit his nostrils. Inside one church, he is overwhelmed by a 'strong kind of invisible snuff' making its way 'up my nose, in my eyes, and down my throat': 'the snuff seems to be made of the decay of matting, wood, cloth, stone, iron, earth, and something else. Is the something else the decay of dead citizens in the vaults below? As sure as Death it is!'[68] This composite smell is the odour of time – time that goes by leaving invisible but perceptible traces of the work of decomposition. The churches that Dickens admires are 'Monuments of another age',[69] as fascinating in their littleness as the Pyramids of Egypt or the buildings of the Eternal City. They speak of a time when the City of London was London and the ghostly, modern City had not yet emerged. However, this nostalgic attitude is offset by the not unpleasant intrusion of the myriad odours emitted by trade: the lingering aroma of wheat, wine, oranges and other commodities exchanged in the modern City is an olfactory reminder of the presence of the living, identified with activities that little have to do with the abstractions of finance. Dickens insists on the melancholic atmosphere of a deserted urban space where dead citizens are more numerous than local residents. But he does not erase the traces of the other City. Rather, they are evoked through olfactory descriptions which emphasise their persistence. Each neighbourhood is connoted by a distinct odour, the result of commodities being produced or exchanged on a grand scale. Even while insisting on absence or imagining the depersonalisation of financial labour, Dickens relies on a sensory mode whose specific 'representational value' resides in its capacity 'for recalling and re-presenting experience thanks to the strong memory-triggering potential of smells'.[70]

The flipside of the deserted City is the odorous, material reality of trade – aestheticised in the 'cosmopolitan blast' that the uncommercial traveller cannot but notice, despite his best efforts to observe emptiness, absence and stasis.

In 'The City of the Absent' once again the trope of the necropolis prevails. Churchyards are the secluded spots that the narrator is pleased to haunt after business hours, finding in them odd revenants of a pre-industrial past: 'an old man and an old woman . . . making hay' or 'charity children' intent upon innocent wooing.[71] Yet even churchyards are described in close proximity to shops and small firms: the narrator follows these signs of active life to detect the presence of hidden-away churchyards. 'You do not come upon these churchyards violently; there are shapes of transition in the neighbourhood. An antiquated news shop, or barber's shop, apparently bereft of customers in the earlier days of George the Third, would warn me to look out for one. A very quiet court, in combination with an unaccountable dyer's and scourer's, would prepare me for a churchyard'.[72] The City of the absent exists in relation to the City of the living, it can be discovered only by taking due notice of the rather humble, quaintly passé kinds of trade Dickens sentimentalises. Indeed, proceeding from the spectral space of death (the churchyard of 'Saint Ghastly Grim') to the 'hushed resorts of business', the uncommercial traveller imagines even the activities of 'mighty Lombard-street' as tangible, concrete and pleasantly innocuous:

> Pausing in the alleys behind the closed Banks of mighty Lombard-street, it gives one as good as a rich feeling to think of the broad counters with a rim along the edge, made for telling money out on, the scales for weighing precious metals, the ponderous ledgers, and, above all, the bright copper shovels for shovelling gold. When I draw money it never seems so much money as when it is shovelled at me out of a bright copper shovel.[73]

This antiquated image of solid money shovelled over the counter seems an ironic reversal of the insubstantiality of paper, or even a denial of the magnitude of the financial transactions negotiated in Lombard Street. Dickens focuses intensely on the present when he wonders: 'Where are all the people who on busy working-days pervade these scenes?' but he sets the clock slightly back when imagining the daily routines of work. Not only is money represented in the bullion form of coins and precious metals, but the 'banker's clerk', who vanishes after business hours, is humanised and singularised in the exercise of his proper function as the anonymous hero of a romantic love plot: 'The waste-paper baskets of these closed counting-houses would let me into many hints of business matters if I had the exploration of them, and what secrets of the hearts should I discover on the "pads" of the young clerks – the sheets of cartridge-paper and blotting-paper interposed between their writing and their desks!'[74] The trope of the necropolis gradually gives way to a sentimental representation of City life: banking, for instance, comes to be epitomised by the sound of gold coins 'musically pouring out of the shovel' and the City streets, 'dry as they look', are transmogrified into 'courts of Love Omnipotent'.[75] Dickens's sketches too tell a dual tale: on the one hand, they reproduce images of desolation and emptiness propelling, as Ziegler suggests, the depersonalisation of the City; on the other, they hang on to a vision of City life dominated by the material traces of commerce (the lingering smells of commodities) and framed, in absentia, by the diurnal activities of modest workers suffused with a touch of romance.

Hollingshead's and Dickens's sketches respond to momentous changes occurring in the City prefiguring to some extent its future developments. Hollingshead incriminates speculation in general. His texts, however, as I have argued, also target a more particularised and less spectacular underworld of imaginary City residents and commuters whose material aspirations seem to stand in need of some kind of containment. The prosaic lives of lower-middle-class people have a potential for social disruption that Hollingshead finds as worrying as the forgeries and frauds of notorious swindlers. Dickens refrains from evoking the spectre of crime, opting for snapshots of the City at rest. He redefines its cultural status, first of all, by selecting tokens of permanence – old, venerable churches – in the midst of a confusing and ever changing scenario. Secondly, he capitalises on the referential backwardness of the olfactory to convey, beyond the vision of a depopulated City, the sensory presence of trade and commodities. It is this world of perishable goods and warehouses, rather than the unscented sphere of high finance, that Dickens evokes as the material weekday complement of the deserted City. He evokes this world, however, in absentia, and at a safe distance from its unsentimental and mundane existence.[76] In all the texts I have considered, distancing strategies prevail in the tones and modulations of the various narrative voices: irony and sarcasm (Sala), defensive scorn (Hollingshead) and the leisurely detachment of an on-looker sauntering down the City streets only when its inhabitants are nowhere to be seen. Framed in these sketches is the still life of the City on the cusp of the new, its fleeting present depicted as a quasi-dystopian nightmare or as a quaintly regressive dream of rest – quite a contrast with Lucy Snow's enthusiastic vision of the deep excitement associated with the 'business', the 'rush' and 'roar' of the City.[77] Like Brontë, Riddell favours the City in action, the messiness of its non-deserted streets and the business life of its present inhabitants. She narrates extensively what other Victorian authors preferred to sketch. Novels of course are better predisposed to deal with progress through multiple plots, multiple characters and the ease of a long narration. Foregoing brevity, Riddell invests in progress, though the experiments she conducted, the variations on the City theme she imagined, and the balancing of immersive and distancing narrative strategies in her texts all suggest that progress remained an embattled ideal.

A Paradise of Delight

David Morier Evans is perhaps the most authoritative and knowledgeable interpreter of 'City men and City manners' among the writers considered in this chapter. He compiled several prodigiously documented volumes which examine the manias and panics of the late 1840s and 1850s.[78] More relevant to my argument are his less monumental works intended for a larger readership, *City Men and*

City Manners: The City; or The Physiology of London Business with Sketches on 'Change, and at the Other Coffee Houses (1852), first issued in 1845 under a slightly different title, and *Speculative Notes and Notes on Speculation* (1864) a collection of sketches and articles previously published in various journals. These works offer snapshots of City life and extended reflections on the intricate workings of commerce and finance for the instruction of the general public. The tension between the local and the global, between national and international concerns is addressed in ways that are compatible with the model of cosmopolitan realism theorised by Tanya Agathocleous in *Urban Realism and the Cosmopolitan Imagination:* 'realist literature and cosmopolitanism' – she writes – 'came together in certain texts because both involved a desire for a sense of unity that might mitigate their post-Enlightenment scepticism'.[79] In Evans's texts, however, the desire for a sense of unity, or more specifically for a coherent vision of peaceful order (despite the unsettling primacy of speculation) is cognate with the need to assuage fears occasioned by the inherent instability of the architecture of credit.

City Men and City Manners zooms in systematically on the daily operations of different groups of market players performing on the City stage. Sketch-like scenes, brief descriptions of City types, minor anecdotes and major musings are assimilated into a unifying perspective through the affable, worldly voice of Evans's journalistic persona. Alternating between a rhetoric of suspicion and one of conviviality, Evans cordons off the unhealthy, problematic identity of the financial City (pivoting on the dubious operations of Stock Exchange), from the less compromised, more traditional model of the City as the hub of mercantile activities located in the pleasantly cosmopolitan 'walks' of the newly renovated Royal Exchange. The different modulations of the narratorial voice, mistrustful and apprehensive in one case, jocose and reassuring in the other, rhetorically effect a separation that was increasingly difficult to realise.

For instance, discussing 'time bargains' Evans pits the precariousness of 'foreign bonds' against the reliability of 'British stocks' and adopts moralistic terms to indicate the promiscuity of the former: 'these carry the marks of their shame and disgrace in the shape of arrear on coupons overdue for several years'.[80] His misgivings about volatile foreign assets, however, are counterbalanced by the vision of conviviality and cosmopolitan tolerance projected in his sketch on the Royal Exchange, the open temple of mercantile affairs where different national interests are said to interact on the basis of 'the equitable principle of reciprocity': 'if there is a place where all are equal – he claims – and the distinction of wealth is unknown, it is on 'Change. The small jostle with the great, heedless of right or might, and the concerns of the one weigh as heavily as those of the other'.[81] An analogous sense of global communion and shared interests prevails in Evans's descriptions of the activities of the international coffee-houses – the Jamaica, the Baltic, the Jerusalem, the North and South America – each house scanning in detail the condition of one specific area of the world, but all tending to promote a peaceful understanding of commercial interrelatedness. However, when Evans tackles the contentious issue of recurrent panics, the harmonious balancing of local and global perspectives gives way to a starker contrast between 'us' and 'them', between English and foreign interests. He commends the role of the British press in denouncing foreign schemes and frauds, suggesting that the commercial brotherhood of nations is a chimera in times of crisis: 'Without the assistance of the daily press' – he writes – 'the enormous wealth, out of which the English public have been in many instances no better than swindled, would have been suffered to improve and support foreign nations in luxury and idleness, without the least chance of receiving a moderate rate of interest for their principal'.[82]

City Men and City Manners encourages readers to acknowledge the increasingly global dimension of the City, but also to look with circumspection upon foreign securities, schemes and speculators. In *Speculative Notes and Notes on Speculation* (1864), the City of global finance has become an integral component of Evans's observed or imagined world and his narratorial stance changes accordingly. The more global is the scenario he illustrates, the more personal and intimate the tone of his sketches becomes. Speculation is undoubtedly the 'ruling passion' of the day, as the author clarifies at the onset of his discussion, and the City is well on its way to becoming a global financial centre connected to the rest of the world by a network of invisible ramifications. Yet the more extensive is the reach of finance, the more circumscribed becomes the perspective of the observer. Immersed in a public space where personal and professional relationships often seem to overlap, the narrator adopts a mode of speech that openly counteracts the impersonality of the market. Whether entertaining readers with fond memories of his childhood in the City, or instructing them on the intricacies of finance, he relies on personal experience and knowledge to render the abstract dimension of City life more individualised and legible.

The stories he chooses to recount frequently involve 'friends' and acquaintances. The City may extend its powerful influence impersonally all over the globe, but the microcosm that Evans inhabits seems a relatively small community of familiar faces. In 'Review of Some Extraordinary Operations', for instance, the situation is convivial: the narrator dines with two unnamed friends and delights in sharing with the reader their respective stories of profits made or lost and anxieties endured. 'The Ruling Passion Strong in Death', a cautionary tale about the 'dread infatuation attending a speculative career', narrates the unfortunate fall of 'my poor friend Perez Y—'.[83] What makes this predictable tale rather peculiar is Evans's personal touch. The speculative career of 'poor Perez' is only sketchily described, whilst the narrative concentrates on the ties of friendship linking the reporter to the unfortunate speculator. Upon receiving news of Perez's illness, the narrator seeks him out and makes sure that he is well taken care of. The death-bed scene appropriately winds up a story that mingles financial advice and compassion, public and private sentiments. In 'What is and What is not an Investment?' the author starts off with a discussion of the 'rubbish market' (stocks and shares of little value) and proceeds to make his point by relating the story of yet another friend who made a handsome profit by not neglecting the 'trifles' in the rubbish market. The distinction between investment and speculation is blurred in this episode and the narrator ends up congratulating his friend upon the favourable turn of the wheel of fortune that allowed him 'to liquidate numerous small pressing liabilities'.[84] The sympathy manifested for the small speculator who waits patiently and is finally rewarded conveys the moral of the story: it might be difficult to understand precisely what an investment is, but it is not hard to sympathise with friends assisted by fortune when they most need it.

As Poovey claims, Evans borrows features of imaginative writing to translate the mysteries and abstractions of finance for the lay reader in a way that is meant to be reassuring.[85] There is also another rhetorical strategy at work. Evans's sketches balance the general and the particular, the principles and the examples, by emphasising the private as well as public dimension of City life. The small crowd of friends paraded in this book – whether or not a fiction devised to illustrate specific points – is the fulcrum of narrative interest. In relation to these often unnamed people, Evans defines his own position as observer and reporter, a position predicated not on detachment but on a kind of affectionate proximity to the world of small and big operators who are directly involved in the life of the market. When these operators are well-known public figures, such as the American financier George Peabody, Evans personalises their story by concocting a 'dream-vision' that offers readers a glimpse of the private sentiments and anxieties felt by the financier in the midst of a crisis of remarkable proportions. Although not a friend of Evans's, Peabody gets included in the field of observation as a character in a dream: the public career of the famous financier is turned into an intimate affair, the feelings, perceptions and fears that might have coloured his experience of the crisis occupy centre stage. In Evans's account, the 'City of the Absent' comes alive with the stories and anecdotes of those who inhabit this world during the day: they may lead a life of work, but this experience is not necessarily alienating or divested of meaning. Evans's perspective encourages readers to perceive the City as a small community of interconnected individuals whose experiences provide not only powerful illustrations of general concepts, but also salient examples of interpersonal relationships based on sympathy and friendship.

In two semi-autobiographical sketches, Evans confers upon the City the singular prestige of a *lieu de mémoire*, a place imbued with 'shades of the past'[86] and invested with the affective significance of personal memories. Born and brought up 'within a stone's throw of the great national establishment as the Bank is sometimes called',[87] Evans is pleased to share with readers the memories of his infancy, casting himself in the role of the prudent man of business who has worked his way up:

> I have left the chrysalis state. I have been working and have worked upwards. I have worked into the heart's core of the City of London. Steadiness in conduct, and punctuality in the performance of my engagements, has thrown me into strange channels. If not a Whittington at the very outset, I have not forgotten his story, problematic though it is in some details, and, following his example, have made available for beneficial purposes my leisure hours.[88]

The professional status of financial journalists, as Parsons explains, was inherently 'shaky': they were often regarded as an 'inferior breed' inhabiting an unregulated business world where the distinction between information and vested interest was blurred.[89] In fact, Evans does not define his status and role within the City in relation to the work of other journalists or correspondents. Rather, he reframes his identity as that of a businessman who finds great pleasure in the exercise of his own vocation:

> What I used to think an intolerable bore – what a great number of other people still think an intolerable bore – a City life, is to me now a paradise of delight, and I move through its shifting scenes and its circles, much in the old-fashioned manner of a horse in a mill, who rarely leaves the centre of his operations save to take his rest and his corn . . .The only close stickers to the collar like myself are the money brokers of the present day . . . and I mean those who are real money brokers . . . whose very looks and appearance are capital itself, and whose simple word for L 100.00 would be taken quite as readily as their signature on their cheque.[90]

To turn the infernal City of manias and speculation into an almost intimate paradise of unsuspected pleasures two rhetorical strategies are deployed: a post-Wordsworthian idealisation of childhood, with the Royal Exchange replacing mother nature as the *locus amoenus* of infantile rambles ('what portion of the Royal Exchange was I unacquainted with?');[91] and a displaced identification with bankers, brokers and businessmen, leading actors on the City stage. Like the money brokers whose word is worth thousands of pounds, the City-born journalist haunts the 'nooks and corners surrounding the Royal Exchange, Birchin Lane, and other various outlets and inlets', like them he is a 'go-between' gathering commercial intelligence.[92] The acquisition of information rather than money is his goal, but in other respects Evans's position in the City is presented as analogous to that of merchants, financiers and brokers who determine the life of the market. He proudly establishes his own credentials as City man by expatiating on his proximity to those who really counts: 'I am directly interested in the state and fluctuation of the rate of discount, in the position and change of various investments and enterprises', he writes, 'I am therefore thrown into association with the leading bankers, the chief discount establishments, the principal money and stock brokers; in short with almost anyone who has anything to do with capital or finance'.[93] Based on both personal recollections and professional experiences, Evans's knowledge of the City seems to know no limits. Dangerous and attractive in equal degree, the world of capital and finance is brought home to readers in ways that render its mysteries appealing. The condemnation of speculative ventures exists side by side with the admiration for the workings of a complex system which, as Evans clearly saw, was destined to dominate the economic life of the country. When the Square Mile finally comes to be identified with finance, the personalised perspective of the observer intervenes to compensate for the impersonal, immaterial and esoteric character of the global City.

    The sketches and narratives analysed in this chapter contributed to re-drawing the symbolic boundaries of the City of London at a time when the transition towards increased financialisation was raising fears and apprehensions. Speaking as an insider, admitted to the inner circle of power, but also as a critical observer, Evans's journalistic persona is uniquely positioned to offer an account which oscillates between admiration and critique, affection and estrangement. His professional knowledge as well as his personal, biographical experiences are flaunted as credentials which qualify him as a particular type of chronicler or 'sketcher' – 'a City-bred boy – a true son of Cockaigne'[94] rubbing elbows with the highest and the lowest in the recent annals of the City. In the late 1850s, Riddell was an Irish immigrant and a newcomer to the City where she resided, for a while, with her husband. She was neither an insider nor an outsider. For newcomers, Bauman writes, 'nothing in the city is "natural"; nothing is taken for granted'.[95] For Riddell too, perhaps, strangeness and surprise engendered a new way of looking at things. In a matter of a few years, she became a keen interpreter of the City, the business world and its maladies. What stories did she tell? How did she speak to her readers? The next chapter focuses on her first City novel, *Too Much Alone*, arguing that educating readers in the uses of uncertainty is the realistic *enjeu* of this text, carried out through a skilful adaptation of the sensationalistic device of adultery.

Notes

1 *Too Much Alone*, p. 1.
2 See Stewart M. Ellis, 'Mrs J. H. Riddell, the Novelist of the City and of Middlesex', in *Wilkie Collins, Le Fanu and Others* (London: Constable 1934).
3 Marie-Laure Ryan, *Narrative as Virtual Reality: Immersion and Interactivity in Literature and Electronic Media* (Baltimore: The Johns Hopkins University Press, 2001), pp. 128–9.
4 As Harry Shaw argues, 'The narrative apparatus of realism involves us in emotional and cognitive activities that allow us to experience what it would be like to come to grips with the way history moves. Contemplation of the already achieved typicality of figures is not the primary mode in which we experience realistic representation. An evolving participation in a set of mental processes that promises to help us grasp the typical determinants of a historical situation is' (p. 35). It is in this sense that the realistic paradigms I refer to here are to be understood.
5 Zygmunt Bauman, *City of Fears, City of Hope* (London: Goldsmith, 2003), p. 3.
6 The renovation of City architecture was already underway in the 1840s, when banking establishments, such as the London and Westminster Bank, and insurance companies 'changed the face of the early-Victorian City, erecting a series of grandiose headquarters, usually in the grand Italian manner'; the new Royal Exchange completed in 1844 'altered the very hub of the City', see David Kynaston, *The City of London. A World of its Own 1815–1890* (London: Pimlico, 1996), p. 139. In the 1860s a new wave of alterations took place: traditional landmarks were pulled down and replaced with purpose-built office blocks. Kynaston mentions the old Flower Pot Tavern 'immortalised by Lamb' as one such landmark that passed 'into the historical ether' (p. 244). On the 'kaleidoscopic rate of change taking place on the streets of London' in the 1860s see also Lynda Nead, *Victorian Babylon: People, Streets and Images in Nineteenth-Century London* (New Haven: Yale University Press, 2005), p. 29.
7 See George Robb, *White-Collar Crime in Modern England: Financial Fraud and Business Morality, 1845–1929* (Cambridge: Cambridge University press, 1992) and G.R. Searle, *Morality and the Market in Victorian England* (Oxford: Oxford University Press, 1998), chapter 5.

8   Franco Moretti, *The Bourgeois Between History and Literature* (London: Verso, 2013), p. 81.
9   The City makes its appearance in novels too, of course, though never in a prominent position. In the sample of texts analysed in this chapter, the City is not only the preferred setting, but also, a microcosm that needs to be explained, understood and critiqued, for its uniqueness is both evident and hard to grasp. In other words, these texts share with Riddell's novels a specific focus on the Square Mile.
10 David Morier Evans, *City Men and City Manners: The City, or, The Physiology of London Business; with Sketches on 'Change, and at the Coffee Houses* (London: Groombridhe & Sons, 1852), p. 1.
11 Anne Thackeray, 'Heroines and their Grandmothers', *The Cornhill Magazine* 11, no. 65 (May 1865), p. 634.
12 See for example: Geraint Anderson, *City Boy: Beer and Loathing in the Square Mile* (London: Headline, 2010) and *Just Business* (London: Headline, 2011); Justine Cartwright, *Other People's Money* (London: Bloomsbury, 2011); David Charters, *No Tears: Tales from the Square Mile* (London: Elliott and Thompson, 2010); Cyrus Moore, *City of Thieves* (London: Sphere, 2009); Alex Preston, *This Bleeding City* (London: Faber & Faber, 2011); Henry Sutton, *Get Me Out of Here* (London: Harvey Secker, 2010); Suzana S., *Confessions of a City Girl* (London: Virgin Books, 2009) and Venetia Thompson, *Gross Misconduct: My Year of Excess in the City* (London: Pocket Books 2010).
13 Robert Harris, *The Fear Index* (London: Hutchinson, 2011).
14 A recent formulation of the unreality of Victorian capitalism is to be found on the first page of Anna Kornbluh's *Realizing Capital*: 'Beside the worldly difficulties of *acquiring* capital . . . stand the philosophical difficulties of *realizing* capital, securing the status of "real" for something evidently ethereal. Ambitious naïfs and their generous friends – and every other player in the mid-Victorian economy – found themselves beset by these difficulties of the real as a result of the ascendance of capital propelled by "financialization," the transition to an economy in which the speculative begetting of money from money supersedes the industrial production and consumption of goods' (p. 1). See also Patrick Brantlinger, *Fictions of State: Culture and Credit in Britain, 1694–1994* (Ithaca: Cornell University Press, 1996), pp. 1–47; and Houston, *From Dickens to* Dracula.
15 Hunt, *Personal*, p. 24.
16 Patterson, p. 367.
17 Ibid., p. 368.
18 Kynaston, p. 247.
19 Ball and Sunderland, p. 359.
20 'In most kinds of business there is an appeal of some sort to the senses: there are goods in ships or machines; even in banking there is much physical money to be counted. But the Stock Exchange deals in "debts", that is the "promises", of nations, and in the "shares" of undertaking whose value depends on certain future dividends . . . These imponderable elements of trade cannot be seen or handled, and the dealing with them trains the mind to a refinement analogous to that of the metaphysician', Walter Bagehot, 'Economic Studies', 1880, in *The Collected Works of Walter Bagehot*, vol. 11, p. 342.
21 Michie, *Guilty Money*, p. vii.
22 Benjamin Scott, *A Statistical Vindication of the City of London*, 1867 (London: Longman, Greens and Co., 1877), p. 57.
23 Ibid., p. 65.
24 Charles C. Turner, 'Living London', 1903, in *The Development of London as a Financial Centre*, vol. 2: 1850–1914, ed. Ranald C. Michie (London: I.B. Tauris), p. 33 and pp. 40–41.

25 Ibid., p. 45.
26 See Reinhart Koselleck, *Futures Past: On the Semantics of Historical Time* (New York: Columbia University Press, 2004), p. 255. As Koselleck further explains, 'experience is present past, whose events have been incorporated and can be remembered. Within experience a rational reworking is included, together with unconscious modes of conduct which do not have to be present in awareness . . . Similarly with expectation: at once person-specific and interpersonal, expectation also takes place in the today; it is the future made present; it directs itself to the not-yet, to the nonexperienced, to that which is to be revealed' (p. 259).
27 Sala, p. 135.
28 Ibid., pp. 138–9.
29 Charles Dickens, *The Uncommercial Traveller*, 1860 (London: Chapman & Hall, 1895), p. 126.
30 Hollingshead, p. 4.
31 Ibid., p. 1.
32 Ibid., p. vi.
33 Ibid., p. 45.
34 Ibid.
35 Ibid., p. 56.
36 Peter Bailey, 'White Collars, Grey Lives? The Lower Middle Class Revisited' *Journal of British Studies* 38, (July 1999), p. 273.
37 Kynaston, p. 141.
38 Hollingshead, p. 263.
39 Ibid., p. 258.
40 Ibid., p. 83.
41 Ibid., p. 86.
42 Walter Begehot, *Lombard Street*, in *The Collected Works*, vol. 9, p. 52.
43 Ibid.
44 Ibid., p. 53.
45 Bailey, p. 288.
46 Ziegler, p. 438.
47 Ibid., p. 449.
48 Amanpal Garcha, *From Sketch to Novel: The Development of Victorian Fiction* (Cambridge: Cambridge University Press, 2009), p. 27.
49 Kornbluh, p. 32.
50 Daniel Novak, *Realism, Photography and Nineteenth-Century Fiction* (Cambridge: Cambridge University Press, 2008), p. 83.
51 Adam Hansen, 'Exhibiting Vagrancy, 1851: Victorian London and the "Vagabond Savage"' in *A Mighty Mass of Brick and Smoke: Victorian and Edwardian Representations of London*, ed. Lawrence Phillips (Amsterdam: Rodopoi, 2007), p. 76.
52 Ziegler, p. 449.
53 Geoffrey Crossick and Heinz-Gerhard Haupt, *The Petit Bourgeoisie in Europe, 1780–1914* (London: Routledge, 1995), p. 13.
54 See Rose, 'The Family Firm', P.L. Payne, *British Entrepreneurship in the Nineteenth Century* (London: Macmillan, 1988) and James Taylor, *Creating Capitalism: Joint-Stock Enterprise in British Politics and Culture, 1800–1870* (Woodbridge: The Boydell Press, 2006).
55 Ziegler, p. 440.
56 Shaw, p. 34.
57 Ibid., p. 94.
58 Kornbluh, p. 32.
59 Scott, p. vi.
60 Ibid.

61 'A Statistical Vindication of the City of London', *The Athenaeum* 2058 (April 1867), p. 445.
62 Scott, pp. 17–18.
63 Ibid., p. 18.
64 Ibid., p. 19.
65 Ibid., pp. 18–19.
66 Ibid., p. 5.
67 Dickens, *Uncommercial*, p. 55.
68 Ibid., p. 52.
69 Ibid., p. 55.
70 Hans J. Rindisbacher, *The Smell of Books: A Cultural-Historical Study of Olfactory Perception in Literature* (Ann Arbor: The University of Michigan Press, 1992), p. 16; on the representations of smells in Victorian novels se also Janice Carlisle, *Common Scents: Comparative Encounters in High-Victorian Fiction* (Oxford: Oxford University Press, 2004).
71 Dickens, *Uncommercial*, p. 127.
72 Ibid., p. 128.
73 Ibid., p. 129.
74 Ibid.
75 Ibid., p. 129 and p. 130.
76 Jasper Schelstraete argues that Dickens's persona, in *The Uncommercial Traveller*, 'cheekily' places himself 'outside of the conventional capitalist economy', see 'Idle Employment and Dickens's Uncommercial Ruse: The narratorial Entity in "The Uncommercial Traveller"', *Victorian Periodicals Review* 47, no. 1 (Spring 2014), p. 53.
77 Charlotte Brontë, *Villette*, 1853, (Oxford: Oxford University Press, 1990), p. 59.
78 David Morier Evans, *The Commercial Crisis, 1847–48: Being Facts and Figures Illustrative of the Events of That Important Period Considered in Relation to the Three Epochs of the Railway Mania, the Food and Money Panic, and the French Revolution* (London: Letts, Sons and Steer, 1849); *The History of the Commercial Crisis, 1857–58, and The Stock Exchange Panic of 1859* (London: Groombridge and Sons, 1859) and *Facts, Failures, and Frauds: Revelations Financial, Mercantile, Criminal* (London: Groombridge and Sons, 1859).
79 Tanya Agathocleous, *Urban Realism and the Cosmopolitan Imagination in the Nineteenth Century: Visible Cities, Invisible World* (Cambridge: Cambridge University Press, 2011), p. 15.
80 Evans, *City Men*, p. 36.
81 Ibid., p. 104–5.
82 Ibid., p. 121.
83 David Morier Evans, *Speculative Notes and Notes on Speculation* (London, Groombridge and Sons, 1864), p. 54 and p. 55.
84 Ibid., p. 107.
85 Poovey, *Genres*, p. 262.
86 Evans, *Speculative Notes*, p. 68.
87 Ibid., p. 66.
88 Ibid., p. 71.
89 See Wayne Parsons, *The Power of the Financial Press: Journalism and Economic Opinion in Britain and America* (Aldershot: Edward Elgar, 1989): 'due to the condition of company or corporate law on both sides of the Atlantic, financial journalism was inherently on shaky ground when it came to being honest to their readers whilst serving the interests of their advertisers. The financial press inhabited a highly unregulated business world . . . even the most responsible of newspapers had to strike a

balance between the need for honest reporting of the more unscrupulous activities of joint stock and the commercial necessity of attracting revenue from company advertising' (p. 39).

90 Evans, *Speculative Notes*, p. 88.
91 Ibid., p. 68.
92 Ibid., p. 89.
93 Ibid., p. 87.
94 Ibid., p. 70.
95 Bauman, p. 6.

Part II

Narrating Capitalism: Charlotte Riddell's Novels of the City

3 Glorious Uncertainty
Too Much Alone

> . . . and indeed, dear reader, in strict confidence between you and me, I doubt whether, as a rule, business-people could keep up heart to weather the adverse winds of trade, but for the glorious uncertainty of what the morrow might bring forth.
>
> Riddell, *Too Much Alone*, 1860

The dictum 'business is business' had several gradations of meaning for Victorian commentators, who denounced commercial immorality just as forcefully as they promoted the benefits of trade. Perhaps the most recurrent connotation concerned the need to keep business 'separated from everything else in its performance', as the author of an article that appeared in the 1865 July issue of *Leisure Hour* peremptorily stated. 'Don't mix it up with pleasure, nor with your household and domestic duties', the writer advised, 'work up to the last stroke of business hours, and then put it by. It gives an additional charm to life when we can divide it and apportion it thoroughly'.[1] Victorian novels, of course, provide salient critical commentary about the charms and harms of a life thus apportioned. Charlotte Riddell's *Too Much Alone* (1860) is a good case in point. The novel revolves around a double axis – 'business' and 'adultery' – and has a dense ideological agenda. A cursory look at the configuration of the story might clarify Riddell's perspective. *Too Much Alone* is a novel of hard facts and uncertain feelings which discusses the commercial uses of the toxic compound cyanogen in the same breath as the subtleties of irregular affections. Maurice Storn, the hero, works as manager and general factotum in a firm located in the City and spends his spare time conducting chemical experiments that will eventually yield substantial financial rewards. He is a champion of social stoicism, a perfect incarnation of the principle that business should not encroach upon home, and therefore makes light of his wife's timid attempts to be more involved in his work, more in contact with the 'trade of [his] affections'.[2] Not only is trade depicted as a field where affections matter, spurring Maurice on to experiment new compounds and market their applications, but domestic serenity itself is shown to be contingent upon the beneficial influence of business. Had Lina Storn been permitted to become familiar with Maurice's business life, had he consented to let the 'shop' enter the parlour, the sanctuary of home would have been protected from the allure of the improper or, more specifically, the temptation of adultery. 'Too much alone', estranged from her husband's business interests, Lina succumbs to adulterous fantasies and desires that gain legitimacy as the narrative accentuates their emotional signifi-cance. The temptation of adultery is invoked to illustrate that business does not, and should not, stop at the threshold of home, that in the modern City, family life is cognate with business life. *Too Much Alone* guides readers to reject the truism 'business is business' and to embrace more malleable forms of integration of home and work, private and public. It does so by mixing genres, grafting the busi-ness novel onto the novel of adultery. The former is self-referentially explained in chapter 4, when the narrator, addressing her preferred constituency of readers, argues for the social and cultural relevance of novels that take business life as their main focus:

> ... business people rarely analyze their feelings, and still more rarely express them in words, and it is perhaps for this very reason that they are the only class in the community who really and truly care to read about themselves. They like to have their feelings, causes of action and modes of thought put into words. A novel about business, about their hopes, anxieties, joys and troubles, throws a new mental light across the page of their life's history; they find everything written there which they have experienced in their own persons, but never dreamt of making a romance about.[3]

The urgent need to mediate between business people and their feelings motivates the production of novels which, by 'turning into poetry the monotonous prose' of bourgeois life, offer a space of self-analysis to those who are least accustomed to the 'anatomical investigation' of their own heart.[4] With this 'daring' gesture of self-authorization, Riddell inaugurates her career as the bard of business.[5] She identifies a niche in the market, a relatively untapped imaginative territory, and lays claim to its significance. Unlike business, adultery is a much more slippery category: the primacy of adulterous desire in *Too Much Alone* does not receive the same degree of validation. The narrator does not step forward to instruct her readers about the function that a novel of adultery might have, but she does pro-vide adultery with an 'emotional style'[6] that differs significantly from contem-porary interpretations of what Barbara Leckie defines as 'the most bourgeois of transgressions'.[7]

Appealing to the pleasures of virtual adultery, Riddell amplifies its emotional resonance at the diegetic level, while keeping transgression within prescribed bounds in the unfurling of the plot. In this chapter, I will focus mainly on the dis-course of the narrator that occupies centre stage throughout the novel, especially as regards the representation of adultery. The voice of the potential adulteress is adopted by the narrator in a sequence of interventions that magnify Lina's 'emotional navigation'[8], test the limits of the im/proper, dwell on extremes of feeling shared nationwide and produce a space of legitimacy where the perils of adulterous desire are held in tension with the affective rewards of cross-gender friendship. What might today appear as the intrusiveness of diegesis in this text – prolonged narratorial musings, often tinged with sentimentality, a surplus of free indirect speech, a profusion of rhetorical questions – was arguably a plausible strategy to negotiate the 'forbidden but not unspoken' topic of adultery.[9] I will also consider how this story of commerce and love configures the interplay of modern affects in the private and public fields. In *Too Much Alone*, the ability to tolerate and manage irregular sentiments comes to identify commercial worth, just as the ability to withstand uncertainty, necessary in business, generates a more clement attitude vis-à-vis the improper. In the world of mixed realities and mixed feelings that Riddell portrays, experiments in affectionate relations do not produce radical results. But they solicit readers to invest in tolerance, to bear ambivalence and to accept the 'glorious uncertainty of what the morrow might bring forth'.[10]

As Nancy Henry states, Charlotte Riddell was 'ahead of her time in seeing the potential of business as material for fiction'.[11] Her novels, especially the early ones, contain explicit pronouncements about the importance of representing business realistically. Riddell's creative investment in the business community and, more specifically, in 'the pathos of the City, the pathos in the lives of struggling men'[12] renders her novels markedly different from other nineteenth-century narrative forays into the world of commerce and finance. John Reed, Norman Russell and, more recently, Tamara Wagner have perceptively discussed how the fascination with financial speculation 'entered the novel genre . . . shaping its development in intricate ways'.[13] Reed argues that 'novels chronicling the rise to business success were commonplace',[14] but Victorian fiction was particularly sensitive to the fraudulent component of financial dealings. Spectacular swindlers, ruthless speculators and financiers of mysterious origins captured the attention and the imagination of literary men and women throughout the century: 'guilty money', as Ranald Michie demonstrates in his book of the same title, was a resilient narrative topic; financial speculation 'worked as a theme, a plot device, and a metonymic representation of an increasingly speculative economy and commercialized society'.[15] Riddell's understanding of what a business novel is (and does) includes the customary denunciation of criminal commercial behaviour but is not entirely defined by this oppositional stance. Rather, her take on business is more attuned to the German 'Poesie des Geshäfts', the poetics of business that Gustav Freytag had immortalised in his 'romance of the counting-house', *Soll und Haben*, translated into English as *Debit and Credit* in 1857.[16] Freytag's novel enjoyed an 'exceptional and long-lasting success'[17] in Germany and was extensively reviewed in the British periodical press, when three different translations appeared within the same year. Like Freytag, and unlike most British novelists, Riddell sought to assign favourable connotations to business activities, encouraging her readers to perceive the buying and bargaining universe with fresh, unprejudiced eyes. A distinctive feature of her poetics of business, as I argue in this chapter, is also the intertwining of private and public issues, the integration of home and work, of the intimate and the commercial that qualifies her understanding of Victorian capitalism.

East and West Intimacy

The opening chapter of *Too Much Alone* introduces the reader to the 'terra incognita' of the City of London: an 'unfashionable locality', situated 'on the wrong side of the Monument',[18] where commerce rather than finance defines the spirit of the place. Unlike Dickens's 'City of the Absent', or Hollingshead's 'City of Unlimited Paper', Riddell's terra incognita is a space of meaningful labour that still holds many promises of social mobility, self-improvement and economic success. An 'over-built and over-populated town', the City is connoted by architectural as well as social hybridity: 'great mansions looking mean and dingy outside' still bear the impress of former grandeur ('wide staircases and massive balustrades and spacious chambers'),[19] poverty and wealth co-exist and the assortment of social types is almost as wide-ranging as the goods traded by City merchants. In this stratified social realm, 'East' and 'West' meet on more equal ground 'over the stream of prejudice which grows so narrow just at that point where the withered banks of pauper gentility and the luxuriant fields of mercantile wealth front and face each other'.[20] With the fading of social distinctions, even 'the estate of beauty' can be allocated more democratically: Maurice Storn (manager) and Gordon Glenaen (manufacturer) are surprisingly 'handsome', their good looks unspoiled by the daily contact with 'filthy drugs and abominably smelling chemicals'.[21] The hybrid character of the City is also reflected in the blending of business and intellectual passion, hard toil and febrile scientific study that turns chemistry into an all-absorbing occupation: for Maurice and Gordon, it was 'the trade of their affections: their warehouses and factories were sun, moon, stars, planets, earth and all to them'.[22]

With these credentials, the City becomes a most appropriate setting for the staging of mixed feelings and amorous attachments that are neither blatantly illicit nor unquestionably proper. The conventional marriage plot is dispensed with by chapter 5, when Maurice Storn, after years of work and prudent investments, reaps his domestic reward: a very young wife, Lina, the only daughter of an elderly gentleman. While the initial joys of their married life are summarily touched upon and declared uninteresting ('Why should I enlarge upon these things, reader?'),[23] the elements of potential discord are paraded, one by one, in a litany of forebodings: 'She knew nothing at all of business, and as little of science. He did not care for music – the books they had read were on topics far as the poles asunder . . . They had no old recollections, no acquaintances in common'.[24] Lina is not allowed into the 'Blue-Beard's chamber' where her husband conducts chemical experiments and is left to her own scanty resources to find a measure of contentment in her proper sphere. Predictably, the rest of the narrative is an extended investigation into domestic unhappiness against a dynamic backdrop of exciting discoveries, sudden reversals of fortunes and enterprising new initiatives that centre on Maurice and his peers.[25] Commercial modernity, the narrative seems to imply, happens outside the domestic sphere: the female denizens of the City who experience this modernity only vicariously are left to wonder what their place in life is:

She . . . was now a cipher in the busy world in which matrimony had placed her. She was given her toys as though she had been a child, and expected to amuse herself for the whole of the livelong day . . . She was to play with these things and never quench the thirst of her active soul with work of any kind – never take part in the labours of those around her . . . never be more than an outsider in the struggle of life – never with the power and the will in her to be of use to attain to a higher position in existence than that of 'suckling fools and chronicling small beer'.[26]

Riddell pictures the 'busy world' of commerce as the fascinating field of action where masculine passions and interests are given free rein, while intimating that the same passions and the same interests dwell in the hearts of middle-class women or wives: the 'power and the will . . . to be of use' is arguably one of the few traits that Lina and Maurice have in common. Modernity does not really stop at the threshold of the home, the inhabitants of the domestic sphere are animated by the same desires as their male counterparts, the same wish to take part in the struggle of life that propels, in Riddell's understanding, the march forward and upward of her bourgeois heroes.

Lina's unhappiness is the prelude to a City story that revolves around adulterous desire. In the late 1850s, adultery was anything but invisible in English print culture, as Barbara Leckie argues:

Between 1857 and 1914, the representation of adultery was neither invisible in the English novel, as Moretti claims, nor invisible in other cultural formations. Instead it was part of a rapidly growing discursive economy in which representations of adultery were both vigorously prohibited by reviewers and readers and actively promoted in the daily journalistic documentation of divorce trials. On the one hand an attempted censorship, on the other hand, an extraordinary proliferation of discursive activity.[27]

Riddell contributes to this 'discursive activity' by assigning adulterous desire a prominent place in her novel, indulging in the representation of both the emotional suffering and the emotional freedom experienced by the parties involved. Like other novels of adultery in the English tradition – Braddon's *The Doctor's Wife* (1864), for instance – *Too Much Alone* expatiates on the 'attraction of impropriety'[28] while eschewing the representation of sexual guilt. When Lina finally decides to elope with Herbert, the news of her husband's commercial demise conveniently intervenes to prevent her own fall. Like Isabel Gilbert and other English heroines, Lina does not faithfully replicate Emma Bovary's trajectory.[29] Interesting, however, is how Riddell adapts adulterous desire for 'home consumption',[30] making it not only visible in the English context, but also plausible as a modern temptation to which many of her female contemporaries surrender. In Riddell's own words: 'God help us – there are such struggles as these going on at many an honest man's fireside in England; a byplay of affections, sentiments, quivering pulses, sleepless nights and wretched days, such as he, snoring in his comfortable easy chair, never dreams of noticing'.[31]

Leckie identifies a number of repeated strategies through which English novelists negotiated the perilous moral territory of extra-marital love. First of all, 'adultery was translated not as a question of passion, but as a question of episte-mology'.[32] Focusing on the perspective of the deceived party, English novelists replaced Flaubert's 'poetry of adultery' with an epistemological quest, the search for clues and signs by which adulterous acts can be detected. Secondly, central to the representation of irregular desires is the figure of the female reader. The addic-tion to reading, which Emma Bovary and Isabel share, is the precondition of their attraction to temptation. As Leckie concludes, in *The Doctor's Wife* 'Braddon conflates adultery and reading and focuses her considerable narrative energies on the indictment of reading. In this context, she does not need to represent adultery because reading carries all the passionate force and moral suspicion of adultery'.[33] Finally, Leckie associates some of the formal innovations introduced by novelists later on in the century with the patterns of divorce court documentation, empha-sising the interconnection between different types of discourses.

Written in the aftermath of the 1857 Matrimonial Causes Act and pre-dating *The Doctor's Wife* by a few years, *Too Much Alone* arguably draws on the same contemporary debates that inspired Braddon and rendered adultery 'sensational, scandalous *and* legitimate'.[34] However, Riddell's narrative strategies differ sub-stantially from the ones Leckie discusses: the addiction to reading has no part to play in her story; the focus is not on the betrayed party, but on the desiring female subject; the search for truth, the epistemology of adultery, is turned inward, as readers learn about Lina's 'emotional navigation', and finally, the narrative places significant value on cross-gender friendship. Riddell's interpretation of adulterous desire is bound up with her unprejudiced view of commercial society, the democracy of business and the potential for change inherent in the modern, urban environment in which her characters dwell. The City setting allows for the exploration of what Riddell calls 'east and west intimacy'[35] in ways that would be more difficult to imagine in a provincial town or a rural area where tradition and continuity set the moral agenda. Lina's dislocation to the City, from her isolated country home, renders her susceptible to new influences: 'She was pleased as a child might have been with the panorama of active life perpetually changing before her eyes'.[36] Like Lucy Snowe in *Villette*, Lina is energised by the encoun-ter with the frenetic activity of the modern City and with the social mixture of people residing or working there. The flexibility of social conventions allows her to come into contact with a variety of new acquaintances including Herbert Clyne (the impoverished heir of an aristocratic family) with whom she is free to spend time, exploring the City's most secluded nooks and crannies, and to con-verse about its venerable history. A shared appreciation of this antiquarian past constitutes the initial basis of their friendship, further strengthened by Herbert's sympathy with the plight of a young woman destined to inaction and dissatisfied with her lot.

Riddell narrates the dawning and development of reciprocal feelings of affec-tion in terms that ensure both the respectful compliance with propriety and the expression of irregular desires. While nothing in Lina and Herbert's social behaviour betrays their intense feelings – 'Herbert never said a word to Lina Storn during these long conferences that all the world might not have listened

to'[37] – the narrator focuses insistently on the inner struggles and emotional turmoil that Lina experiences:

> Can you not feel, as you sit there arguing out that little question of departed
> love, with your own conscience, something at the very bottom of your heart
> reproaching and warning you? Don't you know as well as I do, that it is not
> memory alone, but anticipation, which is sending the blood oftener into your
> face, and making your pulse throb faster, and causing you occasionally to
> tremble and turn cold?[38]

Here the narrator's voice hijacks Lina's, carefully balancing censorship and consensus, (self)reproach and the thrills of anticipation. The ideological pull of the
former is offset by the emotional appeal of the latter. This paragraph is a good
illustration of the rhetoric employed throughout the novel to sustain a sense of
inherent ambivalence, an atmosphere of doubt in which moral judgments are
temporarily suspended. Protracted to the very end, the uncertainty produced by
Lina's hesitancy is magnified in the narrator's discourse, a discourse strewn with
question marks and oscillating between imperative and exhortative modes. The
temptation of adultery does not inspire serpentine twists in the plot or sensational
episodes. Rather, it is constructed as a discursive event to which the narrator's
voice lends authenticity and legitimacy, ensuring that readers perceive its full
emotional impact.[39]

The tension between expression and prohibition was a dominant feature of
public debates about adultery and divorce in the late 1850s.[40] The same tension
informs Riddell's novel: the existence of a 'net of wrong feelings'[41] in which Lina
and many of her contemporaries are caught is openly acknowledged, while, at the
same time, the narrative strives to find sanctioned forms of expression for the kind
of 'emotional refuge'[42] that cross-gender friendship provides:

> And besides, there is not the slightest use denying it, the stolen cup was sweet.
> So felt Herbert Clyne, so felt Lina Storn, as he sate [sic] talking, she listening
> by the winter fire . . . He was confidential – she sympathizing . . . Mr. Clyne
> had nothing to keep from Mrs. Storn. Uncommunicative to the rest of the
> world, he opened his heart to her like a scroll, and read out every feeling and
> anxiety just as it came uppermost . . . He had such a knack of enlisting her
> sympathies in his narrative, such a frank, unreserved way of telling his trou-
> bles, such an easy pleasant flow of small talk about the places he had seen and
> the people he had met, that Lina could not chose but listen.[43]

Many pages in this novel are devoted to similar descriptions that mitigate the
erotic edge of adulterous desire with the less threatening sweetness of the 'stolen
cup' of friendship. The sensuous component of this relationship is not denied,
especially with reference to Lina, whose thoughts hover uncertainly between the
pure and the impure ('she had a vague sense that it was sinful to quiver at the
sound of Mr. Clyne's voice, to shrink and tremble at his touch, to be lonely when

he left her, nervous when he returned').[44] However, Riddell seems also interested in exploring the nebulous region of cross-gender friendship, a region that is perhaps more difficult to chart than adultery itself. There is no conventional 'idiom' by which to name the affective possibilities of friendship between the sexes, a relation that is often perceived only as a prelude to something else, a stage in the progress towards acceptable or illicit forms of love. As Victor Luftig claims, the challenge for mid-Victorian authors was 'to define heterosexual friendship as a *presence* – to declare what it was, rather than to have to admit what it was not', in other words, to write 'a story about "friendship", rather than a story in which friendship cedes ground to something more natural, more visible, more socially sanctioned'.[45]

In *Too Much Alone*, the temptation of adultery and the unnameable rewards of extramarital friendship are held in tension as the reader becomes familiar with both possibilities before the story reaches its 'socially sanctioned' closure. Indeed, considering the prominent position assigned to the friendship between Lina and Herbert and to the emotional ground that they secretly share with the reader, one could argue that adultery is the narrative convention invoked to signify a relationship that would otherwise be difficult to imagine. Riddell locates heterosexual friendship in a grey moral area, where affectionate relations are emotionally legitimate but socially suspicious. Readers are frequently reminded that Lina and Herbert enjoy their 'platonic intimacy' or 'dangerous friendship'[46] in a most innocent way: 'Mrs. Storn was friend and sister, confidante and adviser, all in one. Not a proper relationship for a married lady and a single man, I grant you . . . but still in our case most innocent'.[47] Protestations of innocence such as this reinforce acceptable moral standards, while suggesting that the improper has more than one shade of meaning. The 'by-play of affections, sentiments, quivering pulses'[48] is meticulously scrutinized by a narrator who might be unable or unwilling to 'represent friendship as a *presence*',[49] but is determined to keep its rewards in the foreground. What is improper at one level, feels proper at another.

Revealing in this respect is the impasse in which Lina finds herself when she tries to act honourably and to confide in her husband. The intimacy with Herbert, 'a thing to be felt rather than seen', cannot be put into words, described or confessed because this act of translation would imply a re-naming of friendship in terms of adultery. Riddell understands this impasse as a conflict between emotional freedom and lack of female agency:

> She held a stake in the game of life, and yet still never had a fair chance of taking the cards into her own hands, and playing them out as she would. Without telling her husband all, without confessing that though Mr. Clyne had never offended the dignity of her matronhood by word, or look, or tone, still she cared for him as it did not befit Maurice Storn's wife to care for anyone, there was no help nor protection to be expected from that quarter; and unless she took the initiative with Mr. Clyne, and made a step along the road of love, which is forbidden to all women, married or single, she could scarcely have got rid of him.[50]

Too Much Alone openly enlists the reader's sympathy for Lina and her predicament: she has the 'power and the will in her to be of use' but no legitimate way to act; she has the freedom to be emotionally emancipated but not to articulate her feelings or fears; she is entitled to appreciate the pleasures of friendship as long as they remain unnamed and undisclosed. Her inner turmoil is directly related to the lack of female agency in the social and public sphere. The desire for adultery, as Leckie explains, often indicates that there is not only 'something wanting in the middle-class woman's life in general', but also 'some*one* wanting': this desire is 'the indication of an emerging agency, very much alive and awake, only waiting to be felt and detected like the undercurrent of the body it ignites'.[51] Lina's 'emerging agency' appears towards the end when adverse circumstances – Maurice's bankruptcy – force her to take matters into her own hands. The temptation of adultery is promptly replaced by a more practical aspiration to do and to act that brings satisfaction in the midst of tragedy: 'It was a new thing for Mrs. Storn to have to be up and doing . . . It was new for her to be at once miserable and busy; yet the change proved beneficial'.[52] Thus the narrative naturalises commercial ruin by emphasising its beneficial influence on private morals: Lina's potential fall is averted by introducing a collapse of greater magnitude that restores agency to the female subject. The allure of friendship, on the other hand, however fragmentary and ill-defined, still lingers, informing the final scene and more generally the characterisation of virtuous commercial behaviour. *Too Much Alone* does not advocate innovative forms of intervention for women in the public sphere, nor does it make subversive claims about irregular desires. Rather, it tests the limits of the proper in order to find a plausible use for unregulated sentiments and capricious passions.

Business, Friendship and Tolerance

The mid-Victorian discourse on business was fraught with moral issues. Commanding front-page attention in the periodical press, recurrent financial crises, fraudulent transactions, dubious speculative schemes and plain, old-fashioned stealing were dire reminders that the wealth of the nation was often purchased at the cost of rampant immorality.[53] Even if commerce was regarded as less deplorable than financial speculation, the distinction between honest dealing and rogue trading needed to be reinforced constantly. Riddell's novels provide many examples of downright villainy and as many parables of commercial flexibility and open-mindedness. She finds much to admire in the kind of personality that is better equipped to bear the mixture of good and bad, of vice and virtue, as well as the ups and downs that characterise the life of the market; a personality capable of dwelling in the uncertain without giving way to despondency. In *Too Much Alone*, John Matson embodies this quality in a paradigmatic way: 'I am a tradesman myself though almost on the bottom rung of the trade ladder' – he admits – 'and I know both the virtues and the sins of my class'.[54] In the section of the novel in which his life-script intersects with Lina's, the narrator divides her attention equally between the exposition of commercial and financial technicalities and the

description of Matson's and his wife's powers of endurance. Matson is a chemical sales agent, an intermediary trading goods at a profit, who has to fight a daily
battle with the uncertain:

> . . . there was not the slightest difficulty about getting credit – the real battle
> was to keep it. Somehow, rise as early as he would in the morning – work
> as late as he liked at night – save as much as he could – John Matson never
> felt he was nearing the lee side of fortune by even a solitary point in the
> wind . . . Mr. Matson found himself compelled to use one man's money to
> pay another man's debt . . . and then both husband and wife lay awake at
> night wondering how the dreaded acceptance was to be met. And yet still the
> pair never repented marrying – still they were both happy and cheerful – still
> Mary kept her looks and John his cheerfulness.[55]

The chapter from which this quotation is taken has a seemingly ironic title: 'The
pleasures of trading on nothing'. But there is no mocking of the pretence of trading on nothing. Riddell does not replicate the customary recitation of the dangers
and ills of an overblown credit system that leads investors to ruin. Rather, she
underscores how the couple learns to cope with risk, to accept insecurity and manage anxiety – a steep learning curve, to be sure, but one that will prove profitable
at many levels:

> 'Tomorrow might bring orders,' the wife always in her hopefulness suggested,
> and the husband at her bidding was always ready to believe; and indeed, dear
> reader, in strict confidence between you and me, I doubt whether, as a rule,
> business-people could keep up heart to weather the adverse winds of trade,
> but for the glorious uncertainty of what the morrow might bring forth. The
> wear and tear of struggling forward would be too much for any mind, but for
> the thought that any minute may smooth the onward road. Even when a man
> is trotting at the rate of twelve miles an-hour down the hill, he never knows
> but that something may turn up to turn him . . .
>   It must have been some alternation of feeling of this kind, which preserved
> John Matson from utter wretchedness, as he pursued the tenor of his almost
> uniformly disastrous way.[56]

Faithful to her self-appointed mission, Riddell describes the 'alternation of feeling'[57] that accompanies the exercise of instrumental rationality. The pursuit of
self-interest is not just a question of industriousness, calculation and efficiency,
at least not in Riddell's novels, where capitalism qualifies as a literary topic precisely by virtue of its emotional resonance. An adaptable and elastic mind-set
seems to be required to bear the instability of the market. John Matson emerges
from the experience of trading on nothing with a better understanding of his aspirations and a keener sense of the complexities of modern life. Armed with first-
hand knowledge of what Walter Bagehot famously described as the 'delicacy' of
the credit system,[58] Matson is well equipped to detect Lina's secret uneasiness and

her fondness for Herbert, offering sympathy and understanding in a tactful manner. He is prepared to give her credit:

> Early days those for John Matson to jump to conclusions about the east and west intimacy . . . early days for him to guess so much from so little; but still, after all, it was merely a notion – a thought – a fear which never revealed itself in any way, unless a more earnest desire to help Lina by every means; to give her information about her husband's profession; to aid her studies, and create an interest in her mind for experiments, could be called the revelation of a pity too deep for words; of a knowledge at once of the strength and the weakness of a nature which was fully understood only by one who had no business to have comprehended anything at all about the matter.[59]

Among the various characters paraded in this novel, the most efficient interpreter of Lina's malady is a businessman on the rise. It is the particular position he occupies in the world of work and the knowledge he has gained therefrom that render him suitable to sympathise instinctively with Lina's private troubles, invisible to the rest of the community and only vaguely sensed by Lina herself. It takes a modern subjectivity, the novel implies, trained in the arena of commercial combat and accustomed to deal with uncertainty, to understand intuitively Lina's dilemma and to respond to it in a non-censorious way. This connection between the intimate and the commercial works both ways: adultery is a test not only of Lina's strength of character but also of commercial probity. Those who are blind to her predicament, unable to read the signs of discontent and to imagine her desire, will turn out to be dishonest in their business dealings. Gordon Glenaen has 'a very strict and good notion of what a woman's morals ought to be' and is therefore incapable of even surmising the working of irregular desire. But he is unperturbed by 'laxity in commercial affairs'[60] as his fraudulent behaviour will ultimately confirm. There is no correspondence between commercial dishonesty and domestic treason, they do not feed off each other in the ideological agenda of this novel. More pertinent is the analogy between the experience of uncertainty in the public realm and its equivalent in the private or intimate sphere.

Educating readers about capitalism implies forging the right personality capable of responding to what Riddell sees as endemic in commercial society: not fraud, but insecurity and uncertainty, whether glorious or dreary. *Too Much Alone* offers a lesson in sentimental education addressed to those segments of the middle classes more exposed to precariousness.[61] It does so by placing significance on ambiguous narrative situations that provide a symbolic space for the exploration of conflicting forms of sentiment. As the narrator capitalises on the navigation of feeling, filling up entire chapters with the scrutiny of emotions, readers are called upon to review their own liabilities and expectations:

> Which are the most vulgar? Which the most narrow-minded? Take the merchant's absorption to business; was it worse than [Mr. Clyne's] mother's devotion to society? . . . Was the East-enders love of money to be considered

more ridiculous and snobbish than the country lady's slavish admiration of birth? . . .Was there not just as much intelligence, or more, amongst the traders as amongst the gentry?[62]

Riddell's ideal reader is supposed to refrain from judging new wealth by the standard of old prejudices, learning, instead, how to appreciate the social and cultural hybridity of middle-class workers who are still in the process of adapting gentility to their own needs.[63] Similarly, Victorian readers are expected to gauge Lina's mixed feelings as precisely that, a mixture of pure and impure. Just as in the world of economic transactions virtue does not come unalloyed, so too in the domestic sphere marital virtue is the solid precipitate in a solution that contains 'right' and 'wrong' in equal proportions: 'Right and wrong, she had lost sight of them both', observes the narrator in one of her numerous glosses on Lina's wavering behaviour, 'Floating away down that perilous stream, she neither turned her eyes to the right nor to the left, but listlessly she drifted on'.[64] The sentimental and moral gambling that this novel encourages at the diegetic level, counterbalanced by a more prudent investment in conventional wisdom at the level of plot, performs a significant cultural task. Constantly kept before the reader's eyes, in amplified rhetorical proportions, the representation of the im/proper in the chemistry of adultery provides a kind of training for the conscience of Victorian readers – a schooling in the ability to tolerate ambivalence and to question the postulates of gentility. 'Gambling and reading', writes Gillian Beer, 'are both acts of desire whose longing is to possess and settle the future, but whose pleasure is in active uncertainty'.[65] In *Too Much Alone*, the adultery plot invites readers to make predictions about alternative outcomes, to calculate possibilities and to accept the kind of 'active uncertainty' that is inscribed in Lina's story. However, it is not so much the reader's 'presaging endeavour'[66] but the ability to dwell in the uncertain that this narrative cultivates – an ability shaped and honed through the act of reading itself.

The ending of the novel brings this process to completion. Riddell pushes the limit of plausibility to make room for a 'symmetry that does not often occur in actual life', as Geraldine Jewsbury noticed.[67] Neither of the characters involved in the adulterous plot dies; there is no harsh punishment for Lina, nor indeed for Herbert, even after their passion is made manifest. Instead, the novel offers friendship – different versions of it – as the utopian by-product of socially disruptive behaviour. Herbert Clyne who at the onset of the story is a man without qualities, waiting to inherit the title of baronet, gains a valuable bourgeois prize: a profession of his own. The amorous involvement with Lina and the friendship with men of business whom he learns to respect produce efficient results: he becomes a good doctor, albeit in a distant colony – not the most prestigious of professions at mid-century but one regarded by Riddell with less suspicion than aristocratic titles. Maurice Storn, on the other hand, pursues his career in the world of chemical manufacturing, experiencing all sorts of upheavals that strengthen his capacity for endurance. But never once does he suspect that something riotous is going on at home. His trust is immaculate – or he is too busy to pause and think. The grand finale of this novel is orchestrated so as to show that the threat of adultery is instrumental to the reformation of the man of business *cum* husband. The narrative does not culminate in the scene of reconciliation between husband and wife, when the secret is revealed and forgiveness accorded without reservation. Replete with sentimentality and potentially a fitting closure, this episode is only cursorily glimpsed at: 'What passed between the pair during the interval that followed was never repeated by either'.[68] The narrator makes sure that confession and pardon coincide in one brief sentence and then moves on with the remainder of the story.

The real conclusion imaginatively ties up the loose ends of friendship. Riddell hangs on to the allure of the improper until the last pages, where it is contained within a domestic setting over which a new kind of authority presides. In a gesture of proactive tolerance, Maurice organises a final meeting between Lina and Herbert, making sure that they are left alone to properly settle their own accounts. This scene of reconciliation, unlike the preceding one, is generously detailed: Herbert's eyes are 'dim with the memory of hopes, sinful though they might be – blasted':

> Dim with the agony of a heart that had erred in loving her; but that still, throughout all time, and changes and chances, could never love another . . . Dim for a moment, but he did not show Lina that film; and it was only by an indescribable softening of his voice, by a tone which touched the old chord in Lina's heart that she knew what he was thinking of . . . Going over the old tragedy again . . . pacing over, step by step, the whole of the road that they had trod together, looking fearfully forth into the future which he knew he must travel alone. The whole thing came and passed through Herbert's mind in a moment, and was reflected by the strange sympathy of old in Lina's heart.[69]

Once again the narrator insists on the sense of communion and wordless intimacy that still prevails even if the novel has by now declared it wrong. But the focus of attention has shifted, it is Maurice's enlightened reactions that readers are expected to notice: his benign awareness of Herbert's desire, his newly found perceptiveness and, above all, the offer of friendship to a rival in love welcomed 'as though he had been his son or his brother'.[70] 'It was one of those rare occasions in life on which men speak all that is in their hearts freely and without reserve – when words are uttered and resolutions made which, though they may never be spoken of afterwards, are not forgotten, but influence the life and the conduct thenceforth for ever".[71] The cordial handshake that seals this emotional moment of masculine bonding exculpates Lina completely.[72] Her temptation has proved productive: a reformed husband who feels and acts democratically, a repentant lover who is now prepared to take his part in the struggle of life and a renewed home where family life and business life are no longer at variance. Victorian novels, some of them at least, have a marked problem-solving inclination.

Writing for the *Cornhill Magazine* in 1865, Anne Thackeray Ritchie compared Riddell's modern 'heroines' to their more cheerful 'grandmothers', finding the intense soul-searching of the former rather extreme but not unnatural. 'Does the modern taste demand a certain sensation feeling, sensation sentiment', writes Ritchie, 'only because it is actually experienced?'[73] The answer to this question is unclear: Ritchie seems to consider the 'analysis of emotion'[74] in the novels under review (*Too Much Alone* and *George Geith of Fen Court*) both realistic and slightly exaggerated. But she attributes to this analysis and to Riddell's expressive narrative style the power of creating and sustaining a particular 'bond' with the reader: 'The sympathy between the writer and the reader of a book is a very subtle and strange one, and there is something curious in the necessity for expression on both sides; the writer pouring out the experience and feelings of years, and the reader, relieved and strengthened in certain moods to find that others have experienced and can speak of certain feelings, have passed through phases with which he himself is acquainted'.[75]

Ritchie's review delivers good insights on the relation between the search for consensus and the 'telling' of emotion. In *Too Much Alone*, a great deal of mulling over wayward feelings is necessary to calibrate the internal angle from which both business and adultery are perceived. I have been arguing that this novel constructs adulterous desire not as a stimulus to sensationalistic plot twists, but as a discursive event that demands closer scrutiny for its implications are far-ranging. Riddell's style of narration, with its balancing of expression and prohibition, its propensity to embalm ambiguity in long sentences, carries part of the educational message, guiding readers to accept the uncertain, repackaged as an intense emotional experience. The ideal addressees of this novel, the 'business people' explicitly invoked in chapter 4, are presumed to be immersed in the same world of instability and insecurity in which John Matson and Maurice Storn pursue their nonlinear career paths. In Riddell's view this is the most problematic and contradictory aspect of Victorian capitalism: uncertainty is glorious, inspiring and progressive as well as disheartening and unsettling. Hence the tendency of this novel to value characters who learn to cope with all sorts of unstable situations, including adulterous desire. Matson's tactful intercession and Maurice's open-minded disposition ensure that transgression is adequately contained. The ending is predictable, but the process whereby it is reached is not. This process involves a dynamic integration of private and public, the exploration of affective possibilities and forms of intimacy associated with friendship, and a remapping of the symbolic boundaries of the City of London – a hybrid social realm with great narrative potential, a mixed milieu where the material traces of physical trade have not yet been wiped out by the abstractions of finance. *Too Much Alone*, like the other City novels Riddell went on to write, interrogates a dimension of Victorian capitalism that is ostensibly normal: the everyday running of small firms, the common concerns of business, the life of the market in-between periods of frantic crises. A fair amount of symbolic work and narrative negotiation is necessary to make even such normality acceptable. No matter how pro-business Riddell's novels purport to be, they spell out a whole thesaurus of unease, a lexicon of male and female discomfort that Victorian readers, as Anne Ritchie suggests, might have found rather useful.

Notes

1 'Business', *The Leisure Hour* 705 (1 July 1865), p. 405.
2 *Too Much Alone*, p. 8.
3 Ibid., p. 30.
4 Ibid., pp. 30–31
5 As Decker writes, 'Der erste City-roman der Autorin war sowhol in Bezug auf Tematik als auch auf Struktur ein gewagtes Unterfangen' ('the first City novel was a daring enterprise in terms of both theme and structure'). See Ina Decker, *Mrs J. H. Riddells Londoner Stadtromane, 1860–1881*. (Diss. RWTH Aachen U, 1993. Aachen, Germany 1993), p. 87.
6 'Emotional style', writes Middleton, 'is the normative organization of emotions, their indigenous classification, form of communication, intensities of expression, context of expression, and patterns of linkage with each other and with other domains of culture', see Dewight R. Middleton, 'Emotional Style: The Cultural Ordering of Emotions', *Ethos* 17, no. 2 (1989), p. 188.
7 Barbara Leckie, *Culture and Adultery: The Novel, The Newspaper, and the Law, 1857–1914* (Philadelphia: University of Pennsylvania Press, 1999), p. 1.
8 William Reddy uses the metaphor of 'navigation' to indicate 'the fundamental character of emotional life'; navigation refers to 'a broad range array of emotional changes, including high-level goal shifts', see William Reddy, *The Navigation of Feeling* (Cambridge: Cambridge University Press, 2001), p. 129 and p. 122.
9 Leckie, p. 8.
10 *Too Much Alone*, p. 195.
11 Nancy Henry, 'Rushing', p. 164.
12 Blathwayt, p. 3.
13 Wagner, *Financial Speculation*, p. 6. See also Norma Russell, *The Novelist and Mammon: Literary Responses to the World of Commerce in the Nineteenth Century* (Oxford: Clarendon, 1986) and John Reed, 'A Friend to Mammon: Speculation in Victorian Literature', *Victorian Studies* 27, no. 2 (1984), pp. 179–202.
14 Reed, p. 183.
15 Wagner, *Financial Speculation*, p. 26.
16 Gustav Freytag, *Debit and Credit. A Novel by Gustav Freytag from the Original, with the Sanction of the Author, by Mrs Malcom* (London: Richard Bentley, 1857). *The British Quarterly Review* presented Freytag's novel as 'a sort of apotheosis of that important and rising section of German society. Here we have for the first time, we imagine, a real romance of the counting-house', 'Soll und Haben: Roman in sechs Büchern', *The British Quarterly Review* 27, no. 53 (January 1858), p. 156.
17 See Susanne Stark, 'Dickens in German Guise? Anglo-German Cross-Currents in the Nineteenth-Century Reception of Gustav Freytag's *Soll und Haben*' in *The Novel in Anglo-German Context: Cultural Cross Currents and Affinities: Papers from the Conference Held at the University of Leeds from 15 to 17 September 1997*, ed. Susanne Stark (Amsterdam: Rodopi, 2000), p. 157.
18 *Too Much Alone*, p. 1.
19 Ibid., p. 3.
20 Ibid., p. 73.
21 Ibid., p. 9.
22 Ibid., p. 8.
23 Ibid., p. 45.
24 Ibid., p. 49.
25 Narratives of failed marriages were not unusual at mid-century (see Leckie, chapter 3, and Stern, chapter 4). Less conventional, perhaps, is the amalgam of family and business life that adds a different angle to the topic of conjugal unhappiness.

26 *Too Much Alone*, p. 64.
27 Leckie, p. 13.
28 Ibid., p. 149.
29 Whether narratives which configure adultery as a possibility rather than a textual reality should still be classified as novels of adultery is a moot point. In her reading of *The Doctor's Wife*, Tabitha Sparks suggests that Isabel's rejection of Roland's offer and her refusal to comply with the 'expectation of infidelity' inscribed in the sensational genre produce a re-alignment of the narrative along sentimental lines; half-way through the story, Braddon switches genres, sidestepping the representation of adultery and opting for a conclusion that reaffirms a sentimental lesson: 'wisdom achieved by suffering', see Tabitha Sparks, 'Fiction Becomes Her: Representations of Female Character in Mary Elizabeth Braddon's *The Doctor's Wife*', in *Beyond Sensation: Mary Elizabeth Braddon in Context*, ed. Marlene Tromp, Pamela K. Gilbert, and Aeron Haynie (New York: State University of New York Press, 2000), p. 203 and p. 204. However, according to Leckie, even if *The Doctor's Wife* does not contemplate the consummation of adulterous desire, the novel contributes substantially to redefining the categories of perception through which adultery is rendered visible. In other words, explicit infidelity need not be a *sine qua non* ingredient of the *English* novel of adultery. Only by expanding the historical description of what came to be discussed under the rubric of 'adultery' in English print culture, can one redress the conventional view that 'the representation of adultery was not relevant to the development of the English novel' (Leckie, p. 19). In *Too Much Alone*, adultery remains a central concern throughout the narrative precisely because the possibility of its consummation is left open till the very end, thus allowing for the exploration of wayward sentiments, strong emotions and alternative forms of affectionate relations. It might be useful to compare Riddell's novel to Dickens's *Dombey and Son* (1848). Both texts give prominence (albeit in different ways) to the commercial milieu, but in Dickens's novel the subplot of Edith's adultery functions as further confirmation of the interconnectedness of domestic and financial treason.
30 Leckie, p. 141.
31 *Too Much Alone*, p. 86.
32 Leckie, p. 14.
33 Ibid., p. 141.
34 Ibid., p. 110. It is worth noting that chapter 6 in *The Doctor's Wife* is entitled 'Too Much Alone'. Braddon might have had Riddell's novel in mind as her observations on the lack of communication between City men and their wives, in chapter 10, also suggest. Another parallel could be drawn between Archibald Carlyle, in Mrs Henry Wood's *East Lynne* (1861), and Maurice Storn, both much absorbed in their own professional pursuits and therefore unable to perceive the domestic unhappiness of their respective wives.
35 *Too Much Alone*, p. 154.
36 Ibid., p. 51.
37 Ibid., p. 180.
38 Ibid., p. 172.
39 Although in this paragraph Riddell clearly imagines a female 'you', the assumed reader of her City novels is often masculine and a member of the business community, as she declared in the interview with Blythwait (p. 3). In *Too Much Alone* the appeal to readers of both genders is inscribed in the very structure of the narrative, which revolves around private and public issues that are explicitly seen as deeply interconnected rather than separate.
40 It was also a feature of the Victorian discourse on emotions, see Gesa Stedman, *Stemming the Torrent: Expression and Control in the Victorian Discourses on the Emotions, 1830–1872* (Aldershot: Ashgate, 2002).
41 *Too Much Alone*, p. 116.

42 Here I refer once again to the useful terminology devised by Reddy, who defines 'emotional refuge' as a 'relationship, ritual, or organization (whether informal or formal) that provides safe release from prevailing emotional norms and allows relaxation of emotional effort, with or without an ideological justification, which may shore up or threaten the existing emotional regime' (Reddy, p. 129).

43 *Too Much Alone*, pp. 181–2.

44 Ibid., p. 116.

45 Victor Lufting, S*eeing Together: Friendship Between the Sexes in English Writing, from Mill to Woolf* (Stanford: Stanford University Press, 1993), p. 24.

46 *Too Much Alone*, p. 285.

47 Ibid., p. 289–90.

48 Ibid., p. 86.

49 Luftig, p. 24.

50 *Too Much Alone*, p. 180.

51 Leckie, p. 153.

52 *Too Much Alone*, p. 301.

53 On the deeply disturbing criminal side of Victorian capitalism see Robb, Searle, Stern and Poovey, *Genres*.

54 *Too Much Alone*, p. 83.

55 Ibid., pp. 191–2.

56 Ibid., p. 195–6.

57 Ibid., p. 96.

58 Discussing the system of trade based on borrowed money, Bagehot wrote: 'But in exact proportion to the power of this system is its delicacy – I should hardly say too much if I said its danger. Only our familiarity blinds us to the marvelous nature of the system. There never was so much borrowed money collected in the world as is now collected in London', see Bagehot, *Lombard Street*, p. 20.

59 *Too Much Alone*, pp. 154–5.

60 Ibid., p. 97.

61 Patricia Srebrnik suggests that 'Riddell's novels gained an audience by expressing both the everyday emotional reality and the more fanciful desires of newly emerging socio-economic groups, and especially of women within these groups', see Srebrnik, p. 78.

62 *Too Much Alone*, p. 106.

63 On the relation between gentility and middle-class culture see F.M.L. Thompson, *Gentrification and the Enterprise Culture: Britain 1870–1980* (Oxford: Oxford University Press, 2001).

64 *Too Much Alone*, p. 265.

65 Gillian Beer, *Open Fields: Science in Cultural Encounters* (Oxford: Clarendon, 1996), p. 284.

66 Ibid., p. 279.

67 [Geraldine Jewsbury], 'New Novels' (Rev. of *Too Much Alone*), *The Athenaeum* 1690 (17 March 1860), p. 373. Another reviewer, Anne Thackeray Ritchie, describes the finale in *Too Much Alone* as 'a sad sort of twilight that seems to haunt one as one shuts up the book' see 'Heroines and Their Grandmothers', *The Cornhill Magazine* 11, no. 65 (May 1865), p. 632.

68 *Too Much Alone*, p. 314.

69 Ibid., p. 367–8.

70 Ibid., p. 369.

71 Ibid., pp. 369–70.

72 On the function of homosocial desire and male bonding in literature see Eve Kosofky Sedgwick, *Between Men: English Literature and Male Homosocial Desire* (New York: Columbia University Press, 1985). Sedgwick's revision of the erotic triangles that René Girard analyses in *Deceit, Desire and the Novel* (1965) emphasises the gender

asymmetries in Girard's model, and brings to the fore the role of the female figure within erotic triangles: 'the sexually pitiable or contemptible female figure is a solvent that not only facilitates the relative democratization that grows up with capitalism and cash exchange, but goes a long way – for the men whom she leaves bonded together – towards palliating its gaps and failures' (Sedgwick, p. 160). The type of masculine bonding that Riddell imagines in the conclusion of her novel, however, does not presuppose the woman as victim or as 'pitiable' figure. The friendship between Herbert and Maurice becomes possible only after Lina's agency has been restored in the economic as well as domestic sphere.

73 Ritchie, p. 630.
74 Ibid., p. 637.
75 Ibid., p. 639.

4   Novel Experiments
City and Suburb

> . . . the grand difference between the author and the shop-keeper is but in the power of expression.
>
> C. Riddell, *City and Suburb*, 1861

Although *Too Much Alone* did not attract much attention when it first came out,[1] Riddell insisted on the City theme, advertising it in the very title of her successive novel: *City and Suburb*. Published by Charles Skeet in 1861, this novel has some features in common with *Too Much Alone*. The dual focus on business and domesticity, work and home, is retained and so too is the sense of impermanence and instability associated with commercial modernity. The business hero, Alan Ruthven, like his predecessor, Maurice Storn, aspires to be an inventor and an innovator in his chosen field of action, engineering. Unlike Dickens, who refrains from providing particulars about Doyce's invention in *Little Dorrit*,[2] Riddell takes documentary pleasure in explaining Alan's project and how it could be put to good public use – just as in *Too Much Alone* she had openly discussed the practical applications of cynogen.[3] Finally, the divided affections of the heroine, Ina, bordering on the improper, still play an important role in the narrative's moral economy. Even the choice of proper names – Lina, Ina – signals continuity.

Taken side by side, with their similarities and differences, the first two City novels Riddell produced suggest that she was experimenting with a new pattern, or developing her own formula for the realistic portrayal of local life in the global City. One ingredient in this formula is referential inclusiveness: the text welcomes factual details and salient particulars that point to areas of human experience other authors avoid. Another ingredient is the juxtaposition of office drama, as it were (what goes on in the counting-houses and the sphere of work), and private life (marriages, mostly unhappy, and feelings, mostly irregular), a juxtaposition facilitated by the choice to represent the City not only as functional workspace but also as home to many characters. Just as the City was undergoing a process of drastic de-population, Riddell relocates imaginary people in its streets, houses and shops.

But the most challenging and problematic element in this literary experiment has to do with what Harry Shaw calls the 'procedural' claim of realistic novels: 'By versing and involving us in the workings of historicist metonymy, they promise to involve us in a way of taking in reality which, when we turn from their pages to the world itself, will bring our own distinctively historical mode of being into focus'.[4] Arguing that 'realism doesn't trade in "transparent" representations because it doesn't need to and doesn't want to', Shaw shifts attention to the various procedures whereby the realistic text insistently tries to engage the reader 'not in some sort of illusion of "direct" contact with the world, but in a dialogue in which the stakes are more rhetorical than epistemological'.[5] In the terminology used by narrative theorists, it is in the interaction between 'textual dynamics' and 'readerly dynamics' that the stakes of realism are played out.[6] Realism, writes Ryan, 'is not the art of revealing "how things are", nor the art of imitating real-world speech acts, but the art of getting the reader involved in the narrated events'.[7]

In *Too Much Alone*, the two story lines, grounded respectively on business and adultery, are brought to bear on one another through an effective 'micromanagement of reaction' at the level of narrative discourse.[8] In *City and Suburb*, the earnest endeavor to reach out to a heterogeneous public, to whom the narrator speaks with great frequency and pleasure, is even more pronounced. Direct solicitations to the reader abound in both novels: about 40 in *Too Much Alone* and an increased total of 68 in *City and Suburb*, where 'you' is heavily involved in the mental work of constructing the story world and extracting its significance. The sheer frequency of direct reader addresses and the rhetorical urgency that they convey demand some explanations. As Garrett Stewart argues, 'interpolative passages of reader reference and address'[9] are a key feature of novelistic discourse and a pervasive strategy in the textual rhetoric of Victorian popular fiction. Stewart links the familiarity of address with the kind of 'mainstream confidence'[10] and complacency that Ainsworth's or Bulwer-Lytton's novels radiate: 'For all the occasional simulated heat of its rhetorical urgency, reader address is usually *complacent* in a kind of root sense: at ease *with*'.[11] Later on in the century, the New Woman novel will mainly eschew the 'coziness' of direct reader endearments, so little in keeping with the 'resistant, if tacit rereading of inherited stories'[12] at the heart of the New Woman's ideological agenda. But mid-Victorian novelists, whether popular or elite, willingly employed a variety of reader addresses in the effort to 'reprivatize'[13] the unknown public, the growing constituency of commercial audiences. Drafted by the text as 'silent partners', 'nominated' through apostrophes or 'dramatized' in scenes of reading,[14] the anonymous audiences of nineteenth-century fiction were offered repeated guidelines on how to respond to the stories they were reading.

This 'relentless micromanagement of reaction'[15] has often appeared embarrassing to modern critics. As Robyn Warhol explains, the 'technique of pretending to confide in a "dear reader" is traditionally associated with novels that are, at best, drearily didactic and, at worse, cloyingly sentimental'.[16] It is a technique that always runs the risk of being decoded as a sign of bad writing or as the anti-aesthetic side effect of omniscience. For Warhol, however, the open effort to engage the reader in the world of the story is at one with Victorian women writers' quest for cultural authority; earnest reader address, she argues, was an 'alternative to public speaking "in person"'.[17] Warhol distinguishes between distancing and engaging narrative strategies according to the degree of irony inscribed in the address. She identifies a gendered pattern: engaging strategies tend to occur with greater frequency in female-authored texts, while male-authored novels lean decidedly towards the opposite pole of the spectrum. Such distinctions are not, of course, carved in stone and many permutations are possible. In *City and Suburb*, for instance, Riddell's narrator is rhetorically androgynous; appeals to the response-ability of readers point both ways, towards critical distance as well as emotional proximity – a mixed strategy that has interesting repercussions on what Nicholas Dames calls the novel's 'affective mechanics'.[18] Victorian novel theory, he explains, placed great emphasis on the 'moment-to-moment affects and processes of reading prolonged narrative'.[19] Alert to the dynamics of readerly attention and to the bodily responses elicited by the experience of reading, Victorian critics valued 'the peculiar affective contours of a given writer's procedure, with particular attention to the quasi-emotive, quasi-automatic effects of sequence and speed' (56).[20] What novels *do*, how the experience of reading affects emotions and cognition, is an issue of greater interest to Victorian reviewers and professional critics than the more abstract question of what novels *are*. Dames cites the example of Geraldine Jewsbury, who reviewed for the *Athenaeum* an average of 100 novels a year and adopted the criterion of 'readability' to assess literary form on the basis of the effects it produced on the mind and body of readers. Jewsbury's 'pervasive interest in the physical and cognitive responses of readers', Dames avers, 'is at bottom a physiological informed criterion of judgment'.[21]

This criterion is at work in the review of *City and Suburb* published in the 'New Novels' section of the *Athenaeum* in May 1861. Jewsbury praises the novel as well worth reading ('it will repay perusal with interest'), but detects in the style of telling an 'unpleasant vagueness which baffles and fatigues the attention'. Broken off by 'half-truths and half-revelations' the rhythm of the narrative does not smoothly reproduce the wave-like alternation of excitement and quiescence central in the physiological model of readability: 'if the author would tell a straightforward story', Jewsbury contends, 'it would be much more satisfactory to the reader'.[22] Vagueness, fatigue, bafflement: why does the story Riddell narrates in this novel produce such effects?

Pride and Order

City and Suburb is marked by internal tensions: on the one hand, a strong sense of purpose prevails in the main plot line which centres on Alan Ruthven and his business struggles; on the other hand, an equally pervasive sense of randomness, indeterminacy or 'vagueness' radiates from the representation of urban life in the modern City. At the level of narrative discourse, engaging strategies, which facilitate the reader's immersion in the story world, are offset by distancing strategies which encourage an attitude of criticism and disbelief. Some characters – Alan and his sister Ruby, in particular – are associated with the pre-determined directionality of fate; other characters – Hugh Elyot and Ina – remain surrounded by an aura of indefiniteness. The novel is also divided between the vindication of business as a modern vocation, open to all, and the elitist condemnation of vulgarity and materialism, which Riddell pursues in the scathing accents of social satire. Realism and satire often intermingle in the tradition of nineteenth-century fiction;[23] in *City and Suburb* they are deployed to diversify the symbolic geography of the story world, with the wealthy suburbs, where rich merchants abide, conveniently constrained by the satirical frame, while the cosmopolitan City retains the fuzzy contours of a virtual world rife with possibilities.

The high frequency of direct reader addresses and narrative interventions is related to these internal divisions: the loquacious narrator Riddell imagines is active in the effort to hold the story together and to exert a measure of semantic control on divergent narrative impulses. The process whereby, through the mediation of the narrative voice, readers are 'conscripted' or 'transported' into the simulated reality of the text is worthy of closer scrutiny.[24] Investigating why earnest addresses are so numerous and how and to what effect they are distributed across the textual surface might be more revealing than a simple dismissal of such intrusive occurrences as the embarrassing evidence of an unsophisticated narrative style. If realism, as Ryan claims, 'is the art of getting the reader involved in the narrated events'[25] and if it is through this process that realistic novels 'bring our own distinctively historical mode of being into focus',[26] attending to the rhetoric of narration is as relevant as reading for the plot. Experimenting with a relatively new novelistic subgenre, Riddell lays claim to the significance of urban experience not only by choosing the City of commerce and finance as subject matter (unique though this choice was) but also by elaborating a distinct public rhetoric.

The opening of the novel announces in a straightforward, matter-of-fact way the type of story which is about to unfold, modeled on the familiar paradigm of the quest for money and fortune in the great city: 'Late in the afternoon of a day in August, Alan Ruthven passed under Highgate Archway on his way to London. He was coming to the great city to seek his fortune'.[27] But his approach is slow, interrupted by the narrator's frequent musings and by Alan's indecisions: 'Where should he go? Would anybody stop in his rapid walk to give him the information . . . He wished he had remained for the night in the suburb . . . He wished he had taken a cab . . . Should he take a cab still?'[28] The reader 'you' is summoned several times and solicited to 'break down' prejudices, to 'stand' in a busy thoroughfare in London 'alone, without a friend' and to contemplate from a distance the panoramic view of a 'life different from any life you have ever seen before'.[29] London is presented as a vast agglomerate of hypothetical life stories, branching out in different directions, impossible to predict: 'The woman who shall jilt, the wife who may bless, the friend who will be true, and the man who is to betray – they are all walking about the streets, or sitting in their quiet homes, or busy in their counting-houses, racking not of us, whilst we cannot even picture them'.[30] When Alan turns a corner, and the chapter comes to an abrupt stop, the narrative has successfully hammered home at least one truth about this 'dream-London of every country imagination'[31]: it is a city of strangers and a virtual world rife with unrealised possibilities.

Another pattern is also established in this chapter. Alan, whose movements and thoughts are here the focus of attention, is the subject of a specific type of nar-ratorial intervention – explicit asides that interrupt the natural flow of the story by crossing diegetic levels:

> And yet poets, and philosophers, and savants arrogate thought to themselves, and would make society believe that the fancies and absurdities, truths and falsehoods, wherewith they crowd their pages, are the birthright of genius alone. Break down such a prejudice, reader, if we are to go cordially through this book together. It were as idle to declare that women have deeper feelings than men, because they can tell you all about them, as to affirm that it is only reflective men who think. I tell you, no: the grand difference between the author and the shop-keeper, is but in the power of expression.[32]

On the 'scale of immersivity' – to use Ryan's expression[33] – such shuttling between fictional frontiers, between 'the world in which one tells [and] the world of which one tells',[34] tilts the balance in the direction of self-reflexivity, encouraging dis-tance rather than engagement. A similar effect is obtained, a couple of pages down the line, when the narrator posits 'you, my reader' as incapable of comprehending how hampering pride can be in the race for wealth: 'How very little you, who drive your steeds of ambition, pride, fame and vain-glory successfully into high places, can imagine what different sort of animals these prove when they come to drive you'.[35] Throughout the novel, Alan's thoughts and actions are closely monitored by a vigilant narrator, ready to step in and solicit us to pause, reflect and judge. The 'curse' of Alan's excessive family pride, in particular, never fails to inspire digressions that link his choices to a monocausal explanation. Hence the impression that Alan's story is already set, from the start, in no uncertain terms: he will move forward toward success or failure, but his story will fall into familiar or fairly predictable moral grooves, with pride appropriately chastised in the end and the alleged superiority of rank questioned at every turn.

Nearly each step Alan takes is accompanied by the narrator's vocal interjec-tions. In chapter 4, for instance, when Alan, after some vacillations, settles down as a 'civil engineer' in the City, the narrator adopts a sharply divisive tone: 'At all events he had chosen his trade, and was working hard at it; how hard a self-taught man may guess, and I do not care about anybody else knowing'.[36] Split-ting her audience into two camps, the narrator does not hesitate to alienate the sympathy of readers who happen to have no experience of self-teaching. Such feigned indifference is a rhetorical device that renders the defence of self-help a matter of no contention, but the by-product of this explicit position taking is again distance and estrangement. Of course, there are moments in the novel when Alan's vicissitudes and his heroic business battles inspire a call for sym-pathy, and the narrator's interruptions are designed to beckon the reader into the fictional world. The chapter entitled 'Alan's invention' is a good case in point. The narrative of how he tries to patent his invention is meticulous, rich in factual details, and highly critical of the snares of bureaucracy. The result of this protracted and frustrating encounter with institutional power is a document, 'a sheet of parchment covered with an immense number of useless words, and ridiculous formalities', which Alan finally brings home: 'To the bottom was suspended the great seal, a huge lump of resin, stamped on one side with a seal, meant to represent the Queen's Coronation, and on the other side a design of Her Majesty on horseback. This parchment, and a tin box to hold the resin, was all Alan ever saw for his money – it lies before me now'.[37] The final metalepsis – which turns the fictional document into a 'real' object and the fictional world into an annex of the 'real' world inhabited by the narratee – prompts readers to believe in the reality of the story world, drawing them in by a simple appeal to the narrator's personal memories. On the whole, however, distancing narrative strategies prevail in the account of Alan's progress, piloted into shape by his overmastering pride.

Similarly, a 'certain load of "predestination"'[38] hangs over Ruby's story from the moment she first enters the City stage. Alan's sister, a 'woman without a particle of mind, but with plenty of manner', notable for her 'want of character',[39] is the heroine of a tale that promises few surprises – a conventional marriage plot, in which new money strikes an alliance with impoverished gentility and both parties find the union faulty. Strewn with forebodings and anticipations of unhappiness, Ruby's plot is predicated upon a strict causal logic:

A tiresome, restless, hard-to-manage beauty, whose face had come to her, as his pride to Alan, for a sole inheritance; a snare and a curse; a face that was never looked on by man without admiration . . . can you wonder, oh reader, that Alan's heart was never easy concerning her? Can you not feel where the thorn lay, which the slightest touch drove deeper into his flesh; and even thus early in the story, is it not evident to you that the day must come when the beauty and the pride shall meet and crash together, the weaker thing shivering the greater to pieces.[40]

The emphasis on inherited traits (pride or beauty) and the use of expressions such as 'the day must come' reduce the field of yet unexplored possibilities to a more limited range of options. Though not entirely unsurprising, these options are made to appear pre-ordained, already written in the annals of destiny. Ruby's encounter with a rich merchant, John Perman, in a train carriage, for instance, is soon decoded as the first in a string of similar occurrences that will position this heroine firmly within the jurisdiction of fate. Born into an impecunious family of ancient descent, Ruby, 'poor Beauty', will give in to the desire for wealth, marrying the rich merchant against her brother's will. The predictable result is unhappiness and eventually adultery. The parallelism between Alan's wrestling with his own demon – pride – and Ruby's battle with her inheritance of doomed beauty further strengthen the sense of mono-directionality and convergence that transpires from the double narrative of their descent into commercial modernity from the pinnacles of gentility. And although Ruby's tragic vicissitudes will later on inspire a genuine plea for the reader's tolerance and sympathy, a generalised attitude of critical distance informs the narrator's stance vis-à-vis this character. Soon after Ruby's wedding, this is how the narrative voice liquidates 'Beauty':

> Which mentions of Ruby induces me to remark how exceedingly thankful I feel to be rid of that young person for a while; with what much better spirits I take up the burden of my story when I feel that burden is not about her; how much more willingly I proceed now that Beauty is fairly married, and off, travelling through Scotland with her husband, who is bound by law to pay her future debts, to put up with her caprices, and take all reasonable trouble to keep the wife he has chosen for better, for worse, out of mischief.[41]

Feigning relief and impatience, the narrator is here encouraging readers to consider 'that young person' as a particularly troublesome kind of *fictional* creation. Resembling a host of similar heroines in popular fiction, Ruby can be dropped out of sight, momentarily, without regrets. As far as distancing narrative strategies go, Riddell's rhetoric in this passage is at a par with Thackeray's or Fielding's humorous disavowals of proximity between characters and readers. Emotional involvement is reduced to a minimum when the 'puppeteer' (in Thackeray's metaphor) openly disposes of his fictional characters as best he or she pleases. As Lanser argues, an 'explicit narrative stance provides the readiest mechanism for shaping judgment, but also arrests representation and ruptures the mimetic illusion on which the realist novel depends'.[42] In *City and Suburb*, such ruptures of the mimetic illusion tend to occur more frequently in relation to Alan and Ruby's intertwined stories. The progress of Alan's business struggles, which provides the main plot line, is punctuated by what Lanser calls 'extrarepresentational acts' – 'reflections, judgments, generalizations about the world 'beyond' the fiction, direct addresses to the narratee, comments on the narrative process'.[43] By foregrounding diegesis, these acts interfere with the illusionist aesthetic of mimesis. Similarly, Ruby's plot is contained within a system of explanations that leaves little room for speculations about what she might do or might become. As Dannenberg affirms, 'the ability of texts to create immersive states in the reader is closely bound up with the text's ability to draw the reader into a complex mental engagement with the narrative world by suggesting a variety of possible versions of events'.[44] If the horizon of 'multiple unactualized possibilities'[45] is pre-empted by narratorial warnings, by anticipations and the semblance of order imposed by fate, mental engagement weakens accordingly.

Chance and 'Universal Toleration'

In *City and Suburb*, the creation of immersive states occurs more frequently in relation to the hopes, desires, imaginings and expectations associated with a different set of characters: Hugh Elyot and Ina Trenham, both introduced to the reader as indefinite figures, imperfectly 'sketched'. Hugh's face 'tells no tale about him, he may be anything, or everything or nothing';[46] no demon, no hereditary mark pre-determines his future story. Ina's face is even more puzzling: 'it was a smooth, peculiar, and yet unnational face, which seemed like herself scarcely to belong to any country, or any clime'.[47] This 'unnational' heroine brings into the novel the perspective of detachment associated with cosmopolitanism: 'My father was English, and my mother also; but I, Mr. Elyot, am of no country'.[48] Her voice first appears in the text in the unmediated form of a letter, which a surprisingly silent narrator presents to us verbatim: 'Place is nothing to me, who was born thousands of miles from here; home is nothing to me, who have no home in the wide world; friends are nothing to me, who have none on earth but you; money is nothing to me who have more than enough left to satisfy my wants'.[49] If Ina's non-belonging stands for an idea of detachment that borders on indifference, Hugh is repeatedly associated with an ethos of 'universal toleration' and solidarity – an ethos learnt through years of struggles and observations in the midst of the cosmopolitan City, where 'Irish gentry . . . German counts . . . Scotchmen who came to the south for the sake of its milk . . . foreigners who came vapouring across the Channel with stories of their chateaux and palaces'[50] all stand to win or lose in the race for wealth. The mid-century free trade cosmopolitanism, celebrated in public discourses about the Great Exhibition, is evoked in Riddell's depiction of the City as a multinational aggregation of aspiring individuals.[51] As Tanya Agathocleous argues, a 'vibrant discourse of cosmopolitanism . . . informed the way that Victorian writers thought about their relationship to the rest of the world'.[52] She emphasises the utopianism implicit in such discourse, linking it to Enlightenment dreams of a universal 'brotherhood of men'. In Riddell's novel, cosmopolitanism is primarily an orientation, an attitude of openness towards the 'failings' of others, and a way of making sense of the strange experience of urban modernity:

> I do not think any superficial observer would believe how charitable to the foibles and failings of humanity a long experience makes a thoughtful man in London.
> Seeing constantly fresh beginnings and remembering old ends, renders him tolerant of present arrogance, knowing the pain, and the sin, and the sorrow, he becomes pitiful – reflecting on what the fresh comer must of necessity pass through . . . tends to soften his judgment, and enables him to bear with the impatience of inexperience as he would bear with the restlessness of a child.
> It was thus at all events with Hugh Elyot.[53]

The word 'cosmopolitan' is never used in the text, except for one marginal episode in which it appears in a truncated form, remaining partially unsaid: 'it was only the other day', Ruby says to her sister-in-law, 'she assured me you were not Londoners, and now you assure me you are; I think you must be cosm—what is it, Ina?'[54] Like the interrupted word Ruby does not utter, the cosmopolitan vision, in this novel, is only partially articulated. The fulcrum of this vision is Hugh Elyot, Alan's business partner, a shadowy presence in the text, less prominent than Alan in the progression of the story, but also more insistently associated with what Dannenberg calls 'counterfactuals' or 'what-might-have-been narratives': 'A counterfactual involves a binary pair of events, the *factual* one and the hypothetical other – the *counter*-factual. The counterfactual is thus an alternate world that is viewed, with hindsight, as an ontological subordinate event – something that might have been but was not'.[55] In fictional texts, the suggestion of narrative alternatives or diverging possibilities, whether past or future oriented, may be instigated by the narrator or by the characters' own imaginings. In both cases, suggesting possible worlds is an integral part of plot construction; rather than a 'preexistent given', the progression of the story results from 'the gradual formation of one version from a variety of alternatives'.[56] In *City and Suburb*, counterfactuals occur mainly in relation to Hugh and Ina. It is contact with Ina that stirs in Hugh 'the consciousness of a world outside the little circle in which we live, and move, and have our being – that shadowy glimmering of a might have been and may be, which we have all felt at some period or another'.[57] This 'shadowy glimmering' of alternatives is a refrain in the narrative that stands in stark contrast to the pre-ordained character of Alan's and Ruby's stories in which 'what happens' is almost indistinguishable 'from the more evaluative "it was meant to happen"'.[58]

Several elements contribute to sustaining throughout the novel this sense of productive vagueness or this 'glimmering' of possibilities. Music, for example, creates hidden and sensuous connections between Ina and Hugh, both responsive to its evocative power. Hugh's biographical background remains nebulous and even specific details about the business he runs from his City office ('Analytical Chemist and Assayer') are withheld until chapter 37. His commercial partnership with Alan, of course, is more openly discussed, but an aura of semi-secrecy envelops this character. Where he lives, whether or not he has a family or a wife, where he comes from remain unanswered questions till the very end, thus instigating a series of conjectures about his invisible life beyond the office. When secrecy and business are conjoined in Victorian novels, the character who bears this burden of mystery is usually guilty of fraudulent, underhanded scheming: many financial villains, from Dickens's Merdle to Trollope's Melmotte, are of obscure origins and cultivate a high level of concealment in their daily life. Hugh Elyot does not nurse secret schemes nor does he inspire an attitude of suspicion among those with whom he comes into contact. What he inspires is trust – the same trust he freely offers to a stranger, Alan, accidentally met in a City tavern. This chance encounter sets the story in motion: in the cosmopolitan City, trust among strangers randomly brought together is a valuable asset both in economic and in narrative terms. It provides Alan with his first opportunity of earning a living and of finding an accommodation, and it also provides the true commencement of the business plot: 'And you a total stranger to me and to my people, are doing all this for me out of pure kindness?' asks Alan, 'I am doing a very little for you', replies Hugh 'because I am a man and you are a man – because I have faith in you, and don't care a rush whether you are the son of a beggar, or the son of a duke'.[59]

The cosmopolitan City Riddell represents in this novel is a virtual world, a simulated reality where tolerance, trust, openness towards others and social inclusiveness are not immediately ruled out as implausible ideals; where chance is not synonymous with gambling and the perception of a common vulnerability to the randomness of economic life produces solidarity and cooperation. A utopian vision, difficult to sustain in a realistic novel that purports to chronicle what is and difficult to reconcile with the discourse of selfish greed, vulgar money-grabbing and reckless risk-taking habitually associated with the City of London and explicitly addressed, in this novel, through the medium of satire. It is significant, however, that the story Riddell imagines is not one of utter disillusion. The perspective of cosmopolitan tolerance that pivots on Hugh is not a romantic ideal that will eventually collide with the prosaic reality of capitalist practices and perish in the face of unavoidable circumstances. Rather, this perspective lingers at the periphery of the narrative in the indefinite, counterfactual zone of 'what might have been.'

One episode in which the co-existence of actualised and virtual narrative possibilities is particularly salient occurs towards the end, when the workers Alan and Hugh employ in their factory threaten to go on strike. The partners disagree vehemently on how to respond to the demands of their operatives: Alan opts for a zero tolerance policy, while Hugh is ready to 'concede the point', accepting the request of a pay raise as reasonable. Readers are asked to pause, once again, and to appreciate different positions and orientations:

> What a difference there was between them; between the fierce, dark, handsome face of the one, and the grave, anxious countenance of the other; what a difference between the decision of the stronger will, and the pleading of the truer man . . . between the proud and the lowly, the haughty and the gentle . . . What a wistful, sorrowful gentleness there was in the dark brown eyes; what a tale the expression which lay in them might have told to a dispassionate observer; their expression struck even Alan, and disarmed his anger.[60]

Had Hugh's gentleness prevailed, conflicts and ruin would have been averted, and the frantic last chapters – tracing how Alan loses nearly everything, finds a new employment as 'engine-driver' of express trains, is involved in an accident and in the subsequent inquest – might have taken a different direction. The alternative scenario hinted at in the episode of the strike is an example of what Prince terms 'the disnarrated' – a category which includes 'all events that *do not* happen though they could have and are nonetheless referred to (in a negative or hypothetical mode) by the narrative text'[61]. It is Alan's more ruthless and uncompromising approach that determines the frenzied sequence of incidents in the concluding section of the novel, but this development is held in tension with the 'disnarrated' hypothesis of what could have happened if Hugh's principle of 'universal toleration' had outweighed Alan's pride.

This juggling of the virtual and the actual is also a feature of the love plot, in which the plausible union of equals, Ina and Hugh, which would sanction, under the aegis of romantic sentiment, the cosmopolitan ideals they represent, is affirmed as a possibility and ultimately denied. Ina's love for Hugh is the 'key-note' of the novel, as the narrator specifies in one of her numerous apostrophes: 'And accordingly before three months were over, Ina Trenham loved Alan's friend. Here then is the key-note of my story – listen to the sound!'[62] Ina's feelings are intensely scrutinised by the narrator in a series of interpolations that seek to engage readers by appealing to their own capacity for sympathy and by encouraging an attitude of openness and tolerance vis-à-vis the slight improprieties of Ina's behaviour. Riddell had adopted a similar strategy in her previous novel. But in *City and Suburb*, it is not on the slippery terrain of virtual adultery that the reader's modern conscience is tested. Ina is unmarried, of independent though modest economic means, and in love with a City man whose virtues are unquestionable; she appreciates what he stands for ('From Hugh Elyot she was learning toleration – not the toleration of indifference, which had been a great snare to her previously – but the better toleration of charity') and the democratic sentiments he inspires: 'I think there was a secret longing in her heart to show Mr. Elyot that she, like him, came from the people; that there was no distinction of rank between them, that they twain might clasp hands on the even grounds of social equality'.[63]

Given these premises, and Hugh's interest in Ina, the narrative seems to promise a marriage plot in the making, which, however, is thwarted by small incidents, minor misunderstandings, and more generally by the ungoverned and unspectacular workings of chance. Just as a random encounter in the streets is the unexpected occasion that cements their friendship in chapter 10, an equally accidental occurrence – Ruby's 'excessively tender farewell' to Mr Elyot, observed and misinterpreted by Ina – gives rise to conjectures about Hugh's hypothetical feelings for Ruby that induce Ina to reconsider her amorous investment. Describing Ina's love, the narrator emphasises how 'rash' and 'hazardous' such investment was:

Ina fell in love with him as such women do – quietly, undemonstratively, silently, enthusiastically . . . An exceedingly rash sort of love for a woman to give, doubtless; but still a kind some women will persist in giving till the end of chapter; too transcendental for matrimony not to prove a disappointment, and just simply destructive to happiness should anything occur to render matrimony impossible.

In this description of attachment a woman gives so much of herself away, that, when she finds there is no return to be expected, and reverts to her own resources, she proves to be bankrupt.[64]

In a City novel where gambling and speculation play a decidedly minor role and are evoked only in the end, when the secret of Hugh's father is disclosed, it is amorous attachments that appear caught in the inscrutable game of chance and hurled in unforeseen directions by the randomness of daily life. The crowded, busy metropolis where the story takes place is a most appropriate setting for the staging of causeless accidents that happen unexpectedly. For example, while crossing a busy street, Ina slips and is knocked down by a 'mail-cart', ending up in Bartholomew's hospital with several injuries. A very modern and blameless accident intervenes to deviate the course of her life. There is no attempt to moralise chance, in this episode, or to rationalise the role of indeterminacy and arbitrariness. If there is a lesson to be learnt it is that vulnerability to chance and uncertainty may create a sense of solidarity, as Alan perceives when he sees Ina lying on the hospital bed, looking like a corpse: 'As it was, the spectacle seemed at first to deaden Alan to a sense of his own trouble. He was not one solitary man drowning in the wide ocean of human misery, but one of a ship's crew who were all in jeopardy'.[65]

The accident has repercussions on the development of Ina's story: now conscious of his feelings for her, Alan intervenes to complicate the love plot. Providing much narrative suspense, this love triangle scores high on the 'scale of immersivity', offering the narrator several opportunities to test and encourage the flexibility and open-mindedness of readers. Ina lives in the City with the Ruthvens, Alan and his siblings. When the question of the impropriety of such domestic arrangement is raised, soon after Ruby's marriage, and Ina makes plans (reluctantly) to live elsewhere, irrational chance intervenes. The accident in the street leads Ina to alter her decision; she will remain with the Ruthvens, while the narrator will take this opportunity to cast doubt on accepted codes of propriety: 'I do not attempt to set up Regina Trenham as a model. I am not addressing myself to perfect heroines. I am speaking to imperfect women . . . And I ask you, each and all, under similar circumstances, could you or could you not, have exiled yourself from all you loved, broken the old ties, severed old memories?'.[66] Chance events produce not only a new conscience of collective pain and solidarity, but also slight modifications of the moral order Riddell's readers are assumed to uphold.

The modernity of the City Riddell recreates in this novel is contingent upon the representation of chance and randomness as inwrought in the fabric of life. Retrospectively, of course, all narratives tend to render chance as fate, assimilating random experience into notions of order and design. But Riddell does not capitalise on the play of coincidences that Dickens, for example, introduces in his texts to create a sense of interconnectedness and convergence; nor does she celebrate the magic of coincidental and providential correlations, as Charlotte Brontë does in *Jane Eyre*. The question Dickens poses in the sixteenth chapter of *Bleak House* – 'What connexion can there have been between many people in the innumerable histories of this world, who, from opposite sides of great gulfs, have, nevertheless, been very curiously brought together!'[67] – suggests that random, divergent events follow a logic of causation; they may appear unconnected but are ultimately conjoined. In Riddell's urban realism the 'unexpectedness of occurrences' is appreciated as such:

> It is the mutability of man's life which gives it its interests – the coming on and passing away that varies the narrative of existence, and enables each writer who appears to tell his poor tale, to clothe with fresh vitality the old, old story of life and death, of youth and love, of hopes realized, and disappointed and dead; of struggle and trial, and endurance, and victory, and the instability which lends its prismatic hues to all.
>
> It is this unexpectedness of occurrences, sorrow whence not anticipated; disappointment when least expected; help, when not hoped for; happiness, when despaired of, which makes me, trust, reader, that even this unexciting story of a man's life – a story I am endeavouring to tell just as the events

happened – may still have a human interest for you; not an artistic one – I have no expectations of that – but human.[68]

The most self-reflective narratorial digression in this novel is a comment about the 'unexpectedness of occurrences' and the 'prismatic' effects of chance on human life and the 'narrative of existence'. Linking the story she is telling to this positive understanding of randomness and instability, Riddell, once again, encourages readers to accept mutability and radical uncertainty as an integral component of their own world as well as of the fictional reality of her characters. This attempt to render the disorder of chance, the irruption of the unexpected, simply as a deviation that produces 'prismatic' departures from whatever rational plans individuals are pursuing seems to anticipate late nineteenth-century and modernist conceptions of the role of randomness in life and art. Riddell's insistent focus on metropolitan modernity and her interest in narrating quintessentially urban experiences open up her text to seemingly pre-modernist preoccupations.[69] But the novel remains anchored to mid nineteenth-century realist patterns. Neither the cosmopolitan vision of the City, nor the representation of randomness achieve the kind of textual prominence that Alan's story attains, with its pronounced directionality and overt moral significance. Remarkable, however, is the different attitude of the narrator. If distancing strategies characterise the style in which the main plot is narrated, engaging strategies prevail when the focus is on Hugh, Ina and the possible worlds their wishes and imaginings evoke:

> Have you, my young reader, lost your parents early, and ever turned sick in an instant at the sight of some loving mother welcoming home her son . . . Have you man, lonely and childless, tottering to the grave, felt a pain like a stab when you came unprepared upon a family group, such as may never circle round you? If you have known, or can imagine either of these feelings, then you are able to comprehend the precise blow which the unexpected entrance of these two girls inflicted on Hugh Elyot, for he was a lonely and desolate man.[70]

Appealing to the feelings and imagination of readers, the narrator draws them into the orbit of emotional affinity, counterbalancing Hugh's peripheral role in the development of the story with moments of imagined proximity in which the assonant words 'you' and 'Hugh' are made to mirror each other. The sentimentality of such appeals can hardly be denied. By retracing the well-trodden ways of rhetorical sentimentality, however, Riddell clears a ground for rethinking the novelty of urban experience – a plural experience which includes not only the account of business adventures in the City jungle, but also the exploration of cosmopolitan ideas of tolerance and trust among strangers, of the role of chance in a world ungoverned by providence, and of the shifting borders of morality. To imagine change in the context of commercial modernity, Riddell pursues different paths with different degrees of intensity. The backbone of the novel is constituted by Alan's trajectory and his legacy of pride; a self-made, self-taught man, with ancient blood in his veins, Alan stands for a model of strong economic individuality, capitalist energies and inherited status that Riddell finds particularly compelling. If this structure confers linear coherence to the story, aided by the narrator's rationalising comments, the lateral branches explore alternatives and possibilities that remain partially unrealised. The principle of universal toleration that Hugh represents alludes to ideas of global solidarity that are only glimpsed at in the narrative, enounced rather than enacted, but invested with emotional significance. Similarly, the progression of Ina's story, which, unlike Ruby's, is not pre-constrained by the bonds of fate, introduces in the novel a concern with chance and randomness that Riddell perceives as an integral component of the experience of modernity. The 'unexpectedness of occurrences', however, and the sudden twists and turns that chance produces, are difficult to square with a model of realistic plausibility that values coincidences, causality and semi-hidden interconnections more highly than the simple irruption of the random, unplugged from a matrix of causal explanations. Hence the sense of 'vagueness' that Geraldine Jewsbury detected in this novel, and the 'fatigue' she perceived as a reader. The final resolution of the love plot, with Ina accepting, albeit reluctantly, to marry Alan only to confess, soon after the wedding, that she is still in love with Hugh exemplifies the kind of unnatural situations which Riddell asks her readers to consider plausible. The matrimonial union between Alan and Ina serves primarily an ideological purpose: the more intense is Alan's pride in his ancient family name and his loyalty to an old-fashioned idea of rank, the more requisite will be the lesson in democracy and social inclusivity that marrying the daughter of a yeoman can provide. What militates against the rationality of this compromise is the powerful emotional investment in the alternative union between Hugh and Ina – equals in more than one respect – that the narrative encourages us to see as a possible, and very desirable, outcome. The wish to instruct readers on the democracy of the City and the desire to entertain them with a modern romance tinged with cosmopolitan hues are partially at odds. If *City and Suburb* is deficient in straightforwardness, as Jewsbury claimed, it is also because, in the attempt to render the multiplicity of urban life, the novel follows divergent narrative paths that do not coalesce into a harmonious whole, despite (or perhaps because of) the very visible and vocal supervision of the narrator.

Suburban Wealth and the Business Ideal

The contrast between 'City' and 'suburb' is an explicit line of division in the novel, separating the legitimate ambitions of struggling men of business from the inflated social and political aspirations of rich merchants who have already achieved financial stability. The Permans, with their opulent residences, lavish dinner parties and immoderate hankering after rank, inspire several chapters of biting social satire. Especially when it comes in abundance, wealth is an easy target for scorn. Like Dickens's treatment of the Merdles in *Little Dorrit*, Riddell's represents the Permans as epitomes of the sublime vulgarity of money acquired and spent in the effort to gain acceptance into the restricted circle of the 'upper ten thousand', the highest echelons of society. The house in which Mr Perman lives with his sisters has the exotic-sounding name of 'The Upases' and is described by the house-agent as 'a desirable residence of genteel elevation (perhaps the reader knows what he meant)'.[71] It is a miniature version of a country estate, in line with the 'suburban ideal' popular in the middle decades of the nineteenth century,[72] and explicitly associated with 'the odour of wealth':

> There was an indescribable appearance of opulence about [Mr Perman]; prosperity seemed to encircle him with a halo . . . Money, why it exhaled from him! Money in hand, money in perspective . . . The Upases had the odour of wealth about it. The owner was as good as a bank.
>
> There is no cosmetic like money; there is no autocrat like money; there is no physician like money; there is no self-asserter like money.
>
> I laugh when I hear people say it matters not when we all reach the grave whether we have been rich or poor. They think they have grasped a whole truth when it is only a half one; when we are once in the grave it matters not – but it makes all the difference, oh! my brother, before we get there.[73]

Harping on the familiar motif of money as Mammon – 'let us proclaim money to be in this world Omnipotent'[74] – Riddell attacks the materialist tendencies of her own times with unequivocal vehemence. The ideological ground she is covering is nothing new. The 'vulgar question of money', as Elsie Michie phrases it, is a primary concern in countless Victorian novels. Whether through caricature and comic exaggeration or by imagining marriage plots in which vulgarity is displaced onto the figure of the rich heiress, Victorian fiction actively engages in the complex process of 'thinking through the cultural impact of money'.[75] Riddell's novels are no exception. In *City and Suburb*, the division into two differentiated social and cultural zones circumscribes the potential contagion of repulsive wealth to one specific area: the Permans and the fashionable suburbs embody the negative side of capitalist acquisitiveness so that Alan and Hugh's equally acquisitive desire to make money in the City can be distilled as a legitimate aspiration, untainted by vulgarity. Following a consolidated cultural script, Riddell exposes the ostentatious gentility of the Permans through irony and sarcasm – 'therefore, let us be thankful, readers, that we have done with the city for the present, and can return to The Upases, where we feel as superior and refined as money has power to make us'[76] – endorsing the antimaterialist and moral worldview which readers of Victorian fiction were, to a large extent, primed to expect.[77]

However, in a novel in which all characters are in trade, defining a system of values alternative to rampant materialism is no easy task. For Riddell, this system hinges on business understood as an egalitarian ideal. Being in business is a condition common to all male individuals in the text; the ideological boundaries separating 'city' and 'suburb', therefore, tend to be blurred. To Mr Perman, for instance, is conferred the privilege of speaking, with sincere indignation, in defence of a democratic, egalitarian model of business: 'Do you expect me to forget the insults I have received from you?' Perman asks Alan,

> do you fancy because a man is silent he does not feel – because he is in business that he has no pride? I tell you Mr. Ruthven, it is you and such as you who are the destruction of England; you set class against class – you make the trader hate the gentleman; you make the town detest the country; you put bad blood between one rank and the other.[78]

Riddell's vindication of the dignity of business extends even to those characters that are made to bear the brunt of vulgar acquisitiveness: John Perman, for example, who claims his right to feel, and his uncle, the Alderman, who wears the 'trade skin'[79] with fewer reservations and more sincerity than Alan does. Across the distance that separates new money from old rank, the business ideal emerges as a unifying principle, and the City as a symbol of wholeness. 'For my own part', observes the narrator commenting on the common interests shared by Alan and the Permans,

> I never met the man who was not interested in hearing about City rents, City taxes, City profits, City losses, and all sorts of Herculean City performances . . . Fragmentarily the City is nothing, but collectively it is gigantic; we do not think much of any separate stone in St. Paul's, but we stand and gape at the number of stones that compose the building.[80]

For Riddell, the process whereby individuals pursue their self-interest, the struggles they endure in the effort to achieve economic security and the commercial challenges they encounter are heroic in novelistic terms. Small capitalists, inventors and managers alike are deserving of the prestige of literary representation, even though their immersion in the world of trade verges on the distasteful, according to a criterion of delicacy and refinement that Riddell's novels repeatedly question. But when capitalism is synonymous with wealth amassed and exhibited, when the struggles are over and the enjoyment of money and power comes to the fore, Riddell joins forces with Dickens, Trollope, or Thackeray in satirising the pretensions of those who worship in the 'Temple of Gold'.[81]

Her specific contribution to this discourse, however, consists in defending the dignity of business as a vocation even if its votaries are ultimately swayed by unredeemable materialism. It is a fine ideological line to tread, and one that Riddell will redraw, time and again, in all her City novels. In this text, she uses the ammunition of satire to reinforce divisions and to condemn materialist leanings even though self-interest and money making are declared heroic when associated with Alan or Hugh. She also distinguishes between different types of *homo economicus* by shifting attention to their private behaviours and morals. John Perman turns out to be a violent husband who rejects his wife, Ruby, and bans her from home at the first hint of impropriety, revealing an inflexible and intolerant nature: 'Delicate distinctions, subtle niceties, were not matters with which Mr. Perman had ever troubled his head; a woman was either good or bad; a sinner or virtuous, ergo if she were not good, she must be bad; if she were not without reproach she must be black all over'.[82] The ability to draw delicate distinctions pertains to the liberalism of the City and to Ina's perspective of critical detachment, which also provides the best sanction of the business ideal. She objects to Alan's blind devotion to his 'ancient family' ('Are we not all ancient? Can any of us trace a higher or longer pedigree than the one which conducts us back to Adam?'),[83] she warns Ruby on the inappropriateness of rushing into marriage and admits to liking business exceedingly, imagining herself as a merchant in a hypothetical, alternative life: 'If I had been a man I am sure I would have been a merchant'.[84] More to the point, it is Ina's money that allows Alan and Hugh to set up their own establishment – a judicious investment of her limited resources for which she expects to receive 'large interest'.[85] Ina's pro-business position is also related to a flexible understanding of the rules of propriety; she offers Alan her money, but does not accept his first proposal of marriage, opting instead for a domestic arrangement that in the 'opinion of the world' would be deemed indecorous: 'We emancipate ourselves from the proprieties Ruby and the Misses Perman bow down to and worship', Ina explains, 'and we do the best we can, and try to be as good as an imperfect education will let us'.[86]

The City Riddell portrays is first and foremost a modern world where such experiments with forms of family based neither on marriage nor on blood are possible and social distinctions as well as moral boundaries are questioned. The novel is torn in different directions by the wish to represent the vast potential for change and innovation, in the public and private spheres, that Riddell associates with commercial and financial modernity. On the one hand, as I have argued in this chapter, a sense of pre-destination prevails, on the other, the 'unexpectedness of occurrences' acquires narrative value; likewise, the emphasis on universal tolerance and solidarity is offset by a violent denial of the rights of workers; the idealism of business co-exists with the indictment of the crass materialism of those who have achieved security; and the narrative voice oscillates between critical distance and emotional engagement through a series of earnest reader addresses that render the Olympian vision of omniscience a rather strenuous affair. In *City and Suburb*, Riddell is experimenting with the capaciousness of the novel form, trying out alternatives, carving for herself a position of cultural authority and reaching out to a community of readers whose 'imperfect education', like Ina's, is an asset rather than a liability. If this experiment did not produce a harmonious and well-balanced text, it certainly paved the way for the successive City novel, *George Geith of Fen Court*, which won Riddell widespread acclaim, symbolic recognition and pleasant financial rewards.

Notes

1 *Too Much Alone* was later serialized in *Bow Bells* from January until March 1890.
2 For a discussion of Dickens's reticence and its implications for the novel's symbolic economy see Ruth Yeazell, 'Do It or Dorrit', *NOVEL: a Forum on Fiction* 25, no.1 (Autumn 1991), pp. 33–49.

3 Chapter 33, entitled 'Alan's Invention', contains a detailed description of Alan's meeting with the directors of three railway companies to whom he presents the invention he has designed and patented – an invention which, when properly implemented, would improve the safety features of train carriages. The board's callous hostility towards investing money for the purpose of saving lives is an insurmountable obstacle; Alan fails to sell his idea. In the train accident that occurs in chapter 41, casualties could have been avoided had the railway companies heeded Alan's advice. Both chapters are illustrations of Riddell's realistic take on very topical issues.
4 Shaw, p. xiii.
5 Ibid., p. 39.
6 'Our conception of progression', write Phelan and Rabinowitz, 'arises from a different way of thinking about the larger principle of organization of a narrative, one grounded in the link between the logic of the text's movement from beginning to middle trough ending (what we call textual dynamics) and the audience's temporal experience (readerly dynamics) of that movement. The logic of the text's movement encompass not only the interconnections among events but also the interaction of those story-level dynamics with the discourse-level dynamics arising from the interrelations of implied author, narrator, and audience', see James Phelan and Peter J. Rabinowitz, 'Time, Plot, Progression' in *Narrative Theory: Core Concepts and Critical Debates*, ed. David Herman et al.(Columbus: The Ohio State University Press, 2012), pp. 57–8.
7 Ryan, p. 161.
8 On the management of readers' responses see Garret Stewart, *Dear Reader: The Conscripted Audience in Nineteenth-Century British Fiction* (Baltimore and London: The Johns Hopkins University Press, 1996), p. 21.
9 Stewart, p. 135.
10 Ibid., p. 142.
11 Ibid., p. 154.
12 Ibid.
13 Ibid., p. 9.
14 Ibid., p. 10.
15 Ibid., p. 21.
16 Robyn Warhol, *Gendered Interventions: Narrative Discourse in the Victorian Novel* (New Brunswick: Rutgers University Press, 1989), p. vii.
17 Ibid.
18 Dames, p. 56.
19 Ibid., p. 12.
20 Ibid., p. 56.
21 Ibid., p. 61.
22 [Jeraldine Jewsbury], 'New Novels' (Rev. of *City and Suburb*), *The Athenaeum* 1752 (25 May 1861), p. 692.
23 For an interesting discussion of the blurring of satire and realism in Victorian fiction see Aaron Matz, *Satire in an Age of Realism* (Cambridge: Cambridge University Press, 2010). As Matz argues, 'nineteenth-century realism developed into satire and thereby engendered its own decline. But this is not to say that the fusion of these two modes was a fact of late Victorian literature alone. On the contrary, satire and realism have always existed in close proximity: indeed each has always been embedded in the other' (pp. 2–3).
24 Ryan uses the metaphor of transportation in her discussion of the 'poetics of immersion'(pp. 93–9).
25 Ibid., p. 161.
26 Shaw, p. xiii
27 *City and Suburb*, p. 1.
28 Ibid., p. 9.

29 Ibid., p. 8.
30 Ibid., p. 2
31 Ibid.
32 Ibid., p. 3.
33 Ryan, p. 128
34 See Gerard Genette, *Narrative Discourse: an Essay in Method* (Ithaca: Cornell University Press, 1980), p. 236.
35 *City and Suburb*, p. 5.
36 Ibid., p. 31.
37 Ibid., p. 306.
38 See Genette, p. 67.
39 *City and Suburb*, p. 81 and p. 50.
40 Ibid., pp. 70–71.
41 Ibid., p. 213.
42 Susan Sniader Lanser, *Fictions of Authority: Women Writers and Narrative Voice* (Ithaca and London: Cornell University Press, 1992), p. 85.
43 Lanser, p. 16.
44 Hilary P. Dannenberg, *Coincidences and Counterfactuality: Plotting Time and Space in Narrative Fiction* (Lincoln: University of Nebraska Press, 2008), p. 36.
45 Ibid., p. 39.
46 *City and Suburb*, p. 10.
47 Ibid., p. 54.
48 Ibid., p. 96.
49 Ibid., p. 41.
50 Ibid., p. 23.
51 For a brilliant discussion of the 'Christianized, cosmopolitan brand of political economy around which the Chrystal Palace's globalized fantasy [revolved]' see Paul Young, *Globalization and the Great Exhibition: The Victorian New World Order* (Basingstoke: Palgrave Macmillan, 2009), p. 196.
52 Agathocleous, p. 29.
53 *City and Suburb*, p. 24.
54 Ibid., p. 339.
55 Dannenberg, p. 29 and p. 63.
56 Ibid., p. 64. See also Andrew Miller, 'Lives Unlead in Realist Fiction'. *Representations* 98, no. 1 (Spring 2007), pp. 118–34. Miller speaks of an 'optative, lateral prodigality' which is intrinsic to the realist novel: 'To the extent that realism proposes to give us stories about how things really were, a space naturally opens up within that mode to tell us how things might have been, but were not' (p. 122).
57 *City and Suburb*, p. 77.
58 See Leland Monk, *Standard Deviations: Chance and the Modern British Novel* (Stanford: Stanford University Press, 1993), p. 8.
59 *City and Suburb*, p. 29.
60 Ibid., pp. 389–90.
61 Gerald Prince, *Narrative as Theme: Studies in French Fiction* (Lincoln: University of Nebraska Press, 1992), p. 60. As Prince explains, 'though not essential to narrative, the disnarrated can fulfill many significant functions': it may serve as an instrument to slow down the 'presentation of what does take place'; it can be used as a 'characterization device' and it can help 'to make explicit the logic whereby every narrative progresses . . . by discounting as much as recounting or accounting: the disnarrated, or choices not made, roads not taken, goals not reached'. See Gerald Prince, 'The Disnarrated' in *Routledge Encyclopedia of Narrative Theory*, ed. David Herman, Manfred Jahn and Marie-Laure Ryan (Abingdon: Routledge, 2005), p. 118.
62 *City and Suburb*, p. 94.

63 Ibid., p. 99.
64 Ibid., pp. 272–3.
65 Ibid., p. 239.
66 Ibid., p. 243.
67 Charles Dickens, *Bleak House*, 1852–1853 (Harmondsworth: Penguin, 1994), p. 202.
68 *City and Suburb*, pp. 186–7.
69 Monk argues that 'chance marks and defines a fundamental limit to the telling of any story: *chance is that which cannot be represented in narrative*; but the efforts of British novelists to do just that from the late-Victorian to the modern period resulted in major innovations in narrative form' (p. 9). Riddell's attempt to represent chance and its effects does not produce formal innovations comparable to modernist techniques; but it does produce disruptions in the formal texture of her urban realism.
70 *City and Suburb*, p. 211.
71 Ibid., p. 89.
72 'The ideal suburban home was a kind of country estate in miniature . . . the homes were small, but they included all the elements of larger country estates, including rooms for ladies (drawing rooms and morning rooms), rooms for men (libraries and studies), rooms for children, and even rooms, squeezed under the eaves, for servants', see Lana Baker Whelan, *Class, Culture and Suburban Anxieties in the Victorian Era* (London: Routledge, 2010), pp. 17–18.
73 *City and Suburb*, p. 88.
74 Ibid.
75 Michie, *Vulgar Question*, p. 23.
76 *City and Suburb*, p. 181.
77 On the antimaterialist underpinnings of the notion of individual and 'character' developed in the tradition of British liberalism see Lauren Goodlad, *Victorian Literature and the Victorian State: Character and Governance in a Liberal Society* (Baltimore: The Johns Hopkins University Press, 2003).
78 *City and Suburb*, p. 377.
79 Ibid., p. 139.
80 Ibid., p. 144.
81 Ibid., p. 88.
82 Ibid., p. 360.
83 Ibid., pp. 274–5.
84 Ibid., p. 203.
85 Ibid., p. 222.
86 Ibid., p. 225.

5   Moments of Balance
George Geith of Fen Court

What a thing it is to see the order which prevails throughout his business! . . . What advantages does he derive from the system of book-keeping by double entry! It is among the finest inventions of the human mind.

J.W. Goethe, *Wilhelm Meister's Apprenticeship*, 1795–1796

The publication of *George Geith of Fen Court* marked a turning point in Riddell's career. She stepped out of relative obscurity into the public visibility of media attention. 'While on the subject of books', observed nonchalantly a reviewer in the *Belfast News-Letter*, 'I may tell you that a Belfast woman has made a splendid reputation in the literary world by the production of the novel entitled "George Geith of Fen Court." The lady writes under the *nom de plume* of F.G. Trafford, but the real name is Riddell, and she is married to a gentleman connected with a mercantile house in the City'.[1] Speculations about the identity and gender of F.G. Trafford circulated in the periodical press for a few months soon after the novel came out. The *Saturday Review*, the *Reader* and the *London Review* were quick to conclude, on the basis of 'internal evidence',[2] that the author was a lady, while the *Athenaeum* opted for a gender neutral assessment of the novel's many merits: 'We like this novel better than any of the author's previous ones; the story is more clearly told, and the interest sustained without needlessly teasing the reader', remarked Jewsbury, hinting at the fatiguing 'teasing' she had objected to in *City and Suburb*.[3] Victorian reviewers were by no means unanimous in complimenting the author, yet even the sharpest of critics had to concede that there was something 'intensely interesting' in the story of a clergyman turned accountant in the City.[4] The *Sporting Gazette* had 'no hesitation' in pronouncing *George Geith* 'one of the best novels of the season', strongly recommended for its 'healthy, manly tone . . . which offers a refreshing contrast to the highly-spiced sensation literature to which we have been latterly accustomed, and we welcome the appearance of a novel of this stamp as indicative of the revival, we trust at no distant day, of a healthier and purer type of fiction'.[5] The most enthusiastic review appeared in the *Morning Post*. It is an interesting piece for it attempts to explain what type of popularity the author of *George Geith* could aspire to reach:

It is possible that the author's popularity may be more deep than wide for her style is not adapted to the million; it requires taste, education and discernment;

above all it needs that the reader should not have been vitiated by the sensation school, in order that the beauties and the merits of such novels as 'Too
Much Alone' and 'City and Suburb' should be thoroughly understood and
enjoyed . . . 'George Geith of Fen Court' is the best novel which the author
has written . . . the satisfaction with which it will be read is of that high kind
which arises from the consistency with which an ideal has been carried out, it
is of the kind which the mind derives from symmetry in form, from harmony
in colour, from melody in sound, the penetrating presence of the beautiful.[6]

The newspapers were, on the whole, favourably impressed with the aesthetic
qualities of *George Geith*, commending the well-balanced, measured tone of the
narrative and the sense of harmony and pleasing symmetry conveyed by the story.
Unlike the *Saturday Review* or the *Reader*, the *Morning Post* was also appreciative of Riddell's 'wide and uncommon' range of topics, some of them 'supposed
to be exclusively within the province, if not peculiar to the comprehension, of
men'. It was no small attainment, for a woman writer, to venture into the rough
land of London business and to enrich it with 'such a treasure of association and
ethical meaning'.[7] If the final product would not appeal to the millions, it was sure
to find favour with more discerning, cultivated readers.

Symmetry, harmony, refinement, purity: the ideals evoked by Victorian reviewers to account for the success of *George Geith* suggest that Riddell had hit the
right note, achieving the type of formal and ideological equilibrium that her
contemporaries were likely to find most pleasant. In the following pages, I will
analyse the rhetorical and narrative strategies that contribute to rendering this
novel such a paradigmatic tale of order and harmony. The cautious compromises
and reassuring solutions projected onto the fractured scenario of commercial and
financial modernity are the result of a careful balancing of contrasting elements:
the country and the city, business and leisure, money and prestige, even speculation and morality appear neatly harmonised in the symbolic economy of the narrative. Perhaps it is no coincidence that a novel in which professional accounting
defines the sphere of business should be structured around a principle of balance.
In rational capital accounting 'everything is done in terms of balances', writes
Max Weber, 'at the beginning of the enterprise an initial balance, before every
individual decision a calculation to ascertain its probable profitableness, and at the
end a final balance to ascertain how much profit has been made'.[8] Although such
calculative practices seem antithetical to the modalities of literary signification,
novels too may find the style of bilateral posting quite convenient. *George Geith*
is a good case in point: problematic ideological 'items' are entered twice in the
hypothetical moral ledger of the novel, so that the debit and credit side of the final
balance even each other out.

The Country and the City

A staple of Riddell's urban realism is the topographical imagination typically displayed in the very first chapter of her City novels. In *Too Much Alone*, the 'terra

incognita' where she guides her readers is an 'unfashionable locality' lying 'to the East of Gracechurch Street' and marked on every side by the tangible signs of 'hard-working, bargaining, practical trade'.[9] In *City and Suburb,* the panoramic view of the great metropolis, observed from a distance, amplifies the sense of vastness associated with London and the feeling of isolation of the newcomer. Only in *George Geith* does the City appear in the guise of a peaceful, quiet retreat, caressed by an evening breeze that 'stirs softly and mournfully the leaves above our heads'.[10] Like Mary Russell Mitford, exhorting the 'courteous reader' to 'walk with me through our village',[11] Riddell's narrator kindly invites us to 'sit down for a moment on the churchyard wall' before proceeding to introduce the City that was: 'We are not looking from the present into the past, we are for the moment existing in the years gone by. It is the din of our day which is the dream, and the memories of olden time which are the reality'.[12]

Capturing a beautiful moment of stasis or repose, this sketch is less an echo of Dickens's mournful reflections on the City as necropolis, abandoned by the living, than an adaptation of Mitford's soothing accents – the City is our village.[13] Seasonal changes mark the cyclical passage of time – 'the summer twilight brings silence . . . In the winter it is different. Life hurries along the pavements at a quicker pace' – and the charm of sequestered nooks and inner courts is prevalently rural in spirit: 'There is not a sound to dispel the charm . . . the sparrows have chirped themselves to sleep on their branches overhead'.[14] The collective 'we' reiterated throughout the chapter further contributes to sustaining a vision of the City as 'knowable community' with its natural rhythms and intense local history.[15] Just as the urban and the rural are interwoven in the perception of the self-conscious observer, so too the romance of the City appears rooted in a peculiar amalgam of aristocratic past and bourgeois present: 'no man may ever blot its ancient glory', declares the narrator, 'or its present power and strength, out of the page of history'.[16] Establishing lines of continuity across time and space, using narrative discourse to join distant dots on the cultural map, Riddell opens her novel with a serene evocation of harmony, reflected in a prose that has abandoned or outgrown the syncopated cadences of *City and Suburb*, as well as the frequent urge to apostrophise and conscript the reader directly.

The peculiarity of this City novel, anticipated in the first chapter, is the role played by the countryside and its attendant values in shaping the experience of urban modernity. *George Geith* contains an almost equal number of chapters set in the City, where the accountant lives and works, and in the country, where the Molozanes (his clients) spend the few remaining months of their genteel but impoverished existence, before the last vestige of their once glorious estate is sold. This double structure ensures that the focus on business is counterbalanced by the attention paid to 'unmediated nature' (in Williams's term), to the country as a beautiful landscape from which all traces of productive work have been erased.[17] George's first visit to the Molozanes, in his professional capacity as accountant, occurs early in the novel. Readers have already been entertained with vivid descriptions of the accountant at work in his office, climbing 'Alps and Alps of figures' and restoring order out of 'labyrinths and mazes' of numbers.[18] The narrator also explains that this hard-working, energetic City man, once a clergy-man, willingly gave up a moderately comfortable life in a country parish to pursue freedom and wealth in the City: 'It was just this, he liked business better than preaching or praying, or visiting the fatherless and widows in their affliction'.[19] Callous though it might appear, the preference for profit and independence over a life of Christian compassion is presented as a rational choice that Geith makes not once but twice, with renewed conviction. Initially he works for the 'freedom' that money can buy, the freedom to reinvent his identity and to break with a painful past.[20] But when the secret burden that had pushed him to seek anonymity in the City is lifted, he opts for business once again, rejects the church for the second time and makes money his idol: 'and so for wealth, instead of for freedom, he began to labor, and soon every faculty was stretched in the race he had set himself to run'.[21] All this, without a hint of disapproval from the narrator: the profit motif and the lust for wealth, so forcefully denounced in Victorian novels, do not carry ostensible negative connotations. George Geith is one of the few fictional busi-nessmen who get away with being a slave to Mammon, his reputation untarnished by vulgarity or immorality.

But Riddell is no Ayn Rand. Expressions of pro-capitalist sentiment are inscribed in a structure of feeling that makes ample concessions to pre-capitalist values: the prestige of an ancient family and aristocratic titles (unbeknown even to himself, George is a rightful heir to baronetcy); the refinement of a good upbring-ing; the gentlemanly status acquired by being born into 'one of the oldest and proudest families in Bedfordshire'.[22] In other words, the legitimisation of the profit motif and economic self-interest is held in tension with the respect accorded to traditional ideals of rank and family prestige. Of course, George's unequivocal preference for business and his willingness to step down in the social ladder to prove his individual worth qualify him as a modern, even democratic hero – 'We business men', he explains, 'cannot afford to be other than democrats, and the peer and the peasant stand on equality in a City office, if they bring work in their hands with them'.[23] But the novel steers a mid-course between modernity and tradition, business and status by bringing George frequently into contact with life in the countryside and with the bubble of enduring values surrounding it. Locking focus on the country is an integral part of this novel's strategy to confer symbolic prestige upon business and its votaries.

Riddell does not endorse the 'powerful myth of modern England in which the transition from a rural to an industrial society is seen as a kind of fall, the true cause and origin of . . . social suffering and disorder'.[24] There is hardly any nostalgia in this novel for the alleged simplicity and transparency of rural life. Rather, the countryside is cherished for its recreational value and the physical and spiritual regeneration it provides. It is seen as a temporary antidote to the duress of urban life, not as a viable alternative to it. This 'countryside ideal' was the cultural by-product of urbanisation and industrialisation, as Bunce and Bur-chardt have argued.[25] It was the rise of modern urban civilisation that 'elevated the countryside to a preferential status'.[26] By the mid nineteenth century, 'the countryside of nature, of leisure, of artistic contemplation', in other words the 'countryside as object of consumption rather than as a means of production'[27] was fairly entrenched in the imagination of the urban middle-classes as a dream of affordable leisure. Riddell taps into this popular discourse with the representation of George's commuting back and forth between the City and the country, enjoying the opportunities of both – the profits earned through productive labour and the sensations gained by contemplating a 'summer landscape':

> Dwellers in the country do not know how the sight thereof affects those who dwell in towns. They who have the turf and the fields, and the trees and the flowers always, cannot imagine what sharpened senses gaze every now and then on nature, bask in her loveliness, drink in her perfumes, hearken to her music. To many a citizen, to look on the country in summer is to come fresh on a new creation . . . and how that summer landscape touched George Geith, I could scarcely, my reader, be able to explain.
>
> I only know that all that was noble and good and pure in the man's hard nature was brought out by the sight of the country, and the trees, and the grass; never to speak of the stillness, a stillness which he occasionally stopped to hear, if the paradox may be allowed.[28]

There is a link between the desire to make profits, presented as the legitimate end of business, and the ecological awareness of the perfumes and melodies of a summer landscape: George's ability to appreciate the 'delicious sweetness'[29] of the sensations inspired by the sight of trees and meadows renders his capitalist self less crude and more attuned to all that is 'good and pure and noble' in (human) nature. Ecology – Riddell's version of it – compensates for the stark, matter-of-fact recognition that self-interest is the unapologetic muse of men of business and instrumental rationality their natural driving force. In this respect, the country is truly complementary to the City. George's love of money making for its own sake, the capitalist drive which spurs him on in the race for wealth, becomes acceptable, in ideological terms, because it is embedded in an axiological system predicated on the cohabitation of the ancient and the modern, the rural and the urban, gentry values and bourgeois virtues. There is nothing sordid in George Geith's attachment to business, nor in his desire to become rich as they appear interwoven, in the narrative, with the 'sweetness and light' of his Arnoldian 'best self' reflected in the mirror of an aestheticised conception of nature's loveliness.[30] This mirror also reflects a vision of time in which the past lingers on and is recoverable through the experience of immersion in nature. Mountains, woods, quiet streams and ancient trees, 'these are the places where our lost hours have taken up their abode' observes the narrator:

> Backward and forward they flit softly over the upland, in the depths of the woods they are lying asleep; they climb the sides of the great mountains, and rest under the crags; they look into the darksome pools, lurk in the bluebells, rest among the heather; they are dreaming by the side of the streams, and looking with half-closed eyes out on the calm summer sea. If we want them,

if we would recover the moments and the days, and the years stolen from out our lives, it is in these places we must seek them.[31]

Passages such as this one, moments of heightened aesthetic awareness in which the prose of business makes room for the poetic evocation of a peaceful natural world, would have appealed to the popular taste for the nature idyll or the 'armchair countryside', as Bunce dubs the vision promoted in the literature and arts of the mid-Victorian period – a vision of tamed natural beauty enjoyed or consumed from a distance through the prism of poetry, paintings and natural history.[32] In fact, Riddell's depictions of scenic landscapes and the experience of immersion in a timeless natural realm did take hold of the public imagination, even though it was her 'exquisite delineation of city life'[33] that the periodical press more frequently identified as the hallmark of her novelistic art. The *Penny Illustrated Paper*, for instance, opens an article entitled 'Holiday Scenes' with a long quotation from *George Geith* 'dilating upon the theme' of recreation in the countryside:

> The Easter recess is over; and to many the short spring holiday has already resolved itself into another of those sunny memories prized so dearly because they are so rare. There is a passage in Mrs Riddell's novel of 'George Geith' dilating upon the theme, which will come home to most of our readers: 'While the train by which we travel sweeps through life, quiet country nooks or world-forgotten stations meet our aching eyes, and we feel it would be pleasant to break the journey at some of them and rest a while before proceeding further towards that mighty terminus where the black coach is waiting our arrival'.[34]

The citation comes from chapter 13 ('In the Country'), in which the narrator recounts George's experience of communion with nature while travelling to meet his client. Responding to Riddell's appreciation of the amenity value of the countryside, this article expands on the regenerating potential of holidays spent away from the city, climbing mountains in Wales. In another article, published six years later, *George Geith,* once again, provides the appropriate literary template to entertain readers on the subject of 'Flowers in the City'. The title refers, more specifically, to the annual sermon upon flowers preached on Whit Tuesday evening in the Church of St. Catherine Cree – an ancient usage not mentioned in Riddell's novel but presented by the author of the article as a tradition that Riddell might have limned to great effect.[35] In the popular press, *George Geith* and its 'authoress' are associated with a particular type of charm emanating from the City's rich history of traditional customs and from the pleasant co-habitation of the old and the new, of flowers and finance.

Undoubtedly, there is an element of domestication in this style of reception: the 'authoress' who more boldly than her male colleagues had turned her attention to the modern City and its fierce economic struggles is reframed as the gentle chronicler of 'time-honoured usages', the sensitive limner of pretty urban sketches that have little to do with the more vulgar activity of money making. But it is also undeniable that *George Geith* courts the favour of the public by repeatedly evoking the countryside ideal, appealing to the kind of sensitivity able to appreciate images of natural beauty and repose, especially amidst the clangour and bustle of the City. This compromise, this imaginary union of contraries, is only the first in a series of successful balancing acts performed in the narrative. In *George Geith,* social satire is reduced to a minimum, the tone of narrative interventions (so starkly visible in *City and Suburb*) is tempered down and the distance between materialism and idealism is shortened. Equilibrium prevails, just as it does, in an abstract form, in the practice of accounting.

Furnaces and Ledgers

Why was the story of George Geith, accountant in the City, perceived as more compelling and enjoyable than the story of Maurice Storn, chemical manufacturer, or Alan Ruthven, civil engineer and industrialist? *Too Much Alone, City and Suburb* and *George Geith* are fairly similar as business novels. As I have argued in the previous chapter, in the early 1860s Riddell was developing her own format for the realistic portrayal of City life, a format that she reproduced, with some crucial variations, in *George Geith.* To gauge the difference from her previous novels, it might be useful to compare the representation of the business heroes at work, captured in moments of maximum exertion. For Maurice Storn, in *Too Much Alone,* this moment occurs halfway through the narrative in an episode designed to showcase the strength of his mastery and his exemplary powers of endurance:

> And thus Maurice worked resolutely through the fiery ordeal, while the Bohemian, who had thrown himself on the floor, and lay lounging there with a couple of dogs beside him, watched with intense delight the perspiration pouring from Maurice's temples, and thought, as he listened to every gasp of exhaustion, that his master would give in.
>
> But Mr. Storn did not give in. He would have dropped down dead before failing or fainting in the work he had set himself to do; and thus, as the peel time after time went in empty and came out full, the Bohemian's triumph changed into annoyance; and when, after an hour of pulling, and scorching, and shoving, and perspiring Maurice at last saw his task accomplished, the man got up and stood before him beaten.[36]

Described as a 'valley of desolation by day' and a 'pandemonium by night', the chemical manufactory where Maurice exercises his capitalist energies is a rough environment, stinky, hot, and a place of potential unrest, where German, Irish and 'Bohemian' workers 'resemble ordinary mortals less than spirits in Hades'.[37] Unlike Elizabeth Gaskell, Riddell pays little attention to the plight of workers, concentrating instead on the efforts of manufacturers to keep abreast in a world of tough industrial competition. The 'sweating' of workers and masters, in this scene, may be an accurate realistic rendition of 'life amongst the chemical', as the title of the chapter recites, but it is debatable whether such representation of the sheer physicality of trade would have appealed to the taste of novel readers in the early 1860s. *Too Much Alone* compensates for the roughness of this episode by foregrounding the delicate sensibilities and divided affections of the heroine as well as the inventiveness of the business hero. But the kind of energy unleashed in this scene, paradigmatic of the dynamic, creative thrust of capitalism, appears difficult to contain. After much shoving and perspiring next to the furnace, Maurice falls seriously ill: 'his palms were raw and bleeding . . . he could not stand upright'.[38] The unendurable harshness of industrial work is the problematic flipside of the heroism of business that Riddell seeks to convey.

With the transition from ovens and furnaces to ledgers and journals, in *George Geith*, Riddell redefines the sphere of business: the abstract harmony of double-entry bookkeeping, rather than the tangible scruffiness of trade, connotes the sphere of action where George Geith's mental energies are spent. Office work may be dull and repetitive, but it can be more easily associated with the inodorous realm of professionalism and the service sector, at a safe distance from the controversial materiality of trade. When the accountant is shown at his desk, 'surrounded on all sides by books and balance-sheets, and labyrinths and mazes of figures',[39] a profusion of metaphors is deployed to depict George's mental exertions as acts of bodily valour.

It seems strange that the figures did not dance before his eyes, and chase each other up and down his desk. With many a one the pence would have nodded across to the pounds, and the shillings become confused with their neighbours' columns; but the accountant suffered his puppets to take no such liberties.

In the course of a year he went through miles of addition without a stumble; what he carried never perplexed him; midway up the shillings he never got crazed as common mortals might, but mounted gallantly to the summit as a racer goes straight to the winning-post, without a pause.

The skeins of silk which, in the old fairy tale, the godmother gave to her godchild to disentangle were nothing, compared to the arithmetical confusions out of which George Geith produced order . . . The mass of accounts through which he waded in the space of twelve months was of itself almost incredible. Alps on Alps of figures he climbed with silent patience, and the more Alps he climbed the higher rose great mountains of arithmetic in the background – mountains with gold lying on their summits for him to grasp and possess.[40]

Accounting is hardly a 'subject that quickens the pulse' or a 'glamorous activity', as Carruthers and Espeland admit,[41] but in Riddell's imaginative understanding, totting up profits and losses borders on the marvellous. In this description the accountant is, in rapid succession, a 'puppeteer' fully in control of his dancing 'figures'; a gallant 'racer' determined to win; a fairy-tale prince disentangling his numerical 'skeins of silk' and an indomitable mountaineer climbing 'Alps and Alps of figures' in pursuit of the golden summit. Adventurous and energetic, Riddell's accountant is at liberty to pursue his self-interest untroubled by associations with offensive smells, with the noise and bustle of manufacturing and with the materiality of industrial work. Of course, his profession too can be classed as trade since it involves the exchange of money and services, but it is one that lends itself better to being represented in lofty terms as akin to bracing physical activities of a recreational kind: racing, mountaineering, climbing the Alps, that a gentleman would enjoy as part of the Grand Tour. That George's is a 'lonesome and laborious life', monotonous and demanding, is not denied; on the contrary, the particular quality of his heroism consists in the capacity to endure the routine of work as a racer would bear the physical strain of victory: 'He was fit for the fight he had to wage . . . A man, moreover, who was able to work, not merely fiercely, but patiently; for whom no task was too long, no labour too severe'.[42]

Whereas Maurice Storn and Alan Ruthven, like Samuel Smiles's heroes of self-help, contribute to the march of progress with their industriousness and inventiveness, George Geith's professional task entails the creation of rational order, the harmonising of debits and credits and ultimately the production of statements that prove the balanced nature of economic transactions. He deals in calculations that help organise and make sense of the business world. He sits in his little office all day, yet the representation of his capitalist energies retains the heroic connotations that Smiles and Riddell herself had reserved to inventors and engineers, the more glamorous protagonists of the industrial revolution. Furthermore, as readers are reminded more than once, 'though Mr. Geith was in business, he yet possessed the manners and feelings of a gentleman'.[43] He unites in his persona the best that modernity and tradition have to offer: vigorous instrumental rationality, on the one hand, and the refinement of social and symbolic capital on the other. Small wonder that conservative newspapers, like the *Morning Post*, received the novel in such admiring terms.

Losses and Returns

Riddell's take on the heroism of the accountant was partly at odds with popular sentiment. Beresford Worthington, one of the first historians of the accounting profession, recalls that in the immediate aftermath of the 1862 Company Act and the 1869 Bankruptcy Act accountants were regarded as dubious personages who 'flourished on the ruins of once prosperous undertakings and the wrecks of private fortunes'.[44] Regretting the poor reputation of what to him was a most useful profession, Worthington admits that the word 'Accountant is a most elastic one, and is not infrequently assumed by those mixed up with money lending, bogus company promoting, bookmaking, and other shady occupations'.[45] In the early 1860s, even the *Economist* was cautioning readers about the 'frequent employment of professional accountants' citing as illustrative example 'one of the most disgraceful failures in the crisis of 1857', a failure precipitated by the misconduct of the accountant appointed to examine the company's books who was later found 'guilty of the grossest commercial delinquencies outside the pale of the criminal law'.[46]

A thorough knowledge of double-entry bookkeeping, however, was strongly recommended by the authors of mid-Victorian manuals. Samuel Johnson's advice – 'let no one venture into business while he is ignorant of the method of regulating books' – appears as epigraph in Benjamin Franklin Foster's *Double Entry Elucidated* (1858), a textbook designed for young clerks to make them better acquainted with the 'art' and 'science' of accounting and to convince them of the utmost importance of precision, clarity and order in the keeping of books: 'The first step in the process is to reduce to writing every transaction, in chronological order, and in a language as clear and concise as possible'.[47] For Duncan Macdougal, author of *A Complete System of Bookkeeping* (1862), 'no gentleman is *ably* finished in his education unless he understands book-keeping, because there is no respectable situation in life, either of honour or of trust, that does not require a knowledge of the best methods of keeping accounts',[48] an opinion shared by other practitioners in the field. Double-entry bookkeeping, or the art of arranging accounts so that, as Foster specifies, 'they are at all times in a state of *equilibrium*', was defended as the most efficient formal method to visualise economic transactions and to assess the value of a company at any given moment in time.[49] The rhetorical claims associated with this method are as relevant as the technique itself in ensuring that capitalist practices are perceived as morally legitimate and fully rational, as Carruthers and Espeland have persuasively argued.[50] The conclusion of the balance sheet, James Aho observes, 'is not simply that such and such is the net worth – the capital – of the firm, but that this worth is morally legitimate. This, because it arises from a fundamentally equitable, balanced series of transactions'.[51]

Balance and rationality, equilibrium and legitimacy: accounting provides a powerful way of interpreting the world of economic exchanges as an orderly realm, tidily arranged in symmetrical columns. Its mathematical appeal is indebted to the Renaissance aesthetic of '*divina proportione*' – divine proportion – that Luca Pacioli theorised alongside the double entry method of bookkeeping in the late fifteenth century.[52] In the following centuries, 'accounting became the incarnation of rationality' and the very concept of capitalism came to be viewed as 'indissociable from the representation of economic life shaped by an accounting outlook'.[53] In Werner Sombart's succinct formulation, the relationship between double-entry bookkeeping and capitalism is that of 'form to content'.[54] As a technical and rhetorical device, double-entry bookkeeping contributed significantly to creating and sustaining 'the legitimacy of business ventures', ratifying ideas of justness and fair balance as consubstantial to capitalism.[55]

Riddell's novel does not anticipate Sombart's thesis but it does present the accountant as cultural hero, an iconic figure of capitalist selfhood, unashamed of the profits he makes, and an expert at creating rational order. He is also the fulcrum of a vigorous promotional strategy that aims to grant symbolic legitimacy to business, a modern vocation still lacking the respect of more traditional callings. 'And this is the true fascination of business', observes the narrator at the onset of the story, 'Beyond its weary details, beyond its certainties beyond its endless necessities and countless annoyances, lies the limitless region of possibilities, which is possessed in fancy by thousands who might seem to you, my reader, commonplace men enough'.[56] The transformative power of business is compared to the 'imagination of poets'; it is a visionary faculty that inspires even the most 'silent and undemonstrative'[57] of men to hurry on in pursuit of their dreams. That Riddell's poetics of business should centre on the visions and aspirations of an accountant might also be explained in historical terms: the early 1860s saw an increase in public discussions on the professionalisation of accounting. The first formal organisations of professional accountants appeared in Scotland (Edinburgh and Glasgow) in the late 1850s and in England in the 1870s, although only a decade later, with the foundation in 1880 of the Institute of Chartered Accountants in England and Wales (ICAEW), did accountancy acquire the status of a proper profession. The number of accountants in London, recorded in the *Post Office Directory*, grew rapidly from the 1850s onwards, their services more and more in demand as the legislation changed.[58] Riddell's novel captures (or perhaps anticipates) some aspects of this transition towards increased professionalisation, especially in the representation of George Geith's occupation as anything but a dubious or shady activity – he may have to deal with all sorts and conditions of men, but he remains a most upright translator of foggy facts into transparent figures:

> Bankrupts, men who were good enough, men who were doubtful, and men who were (speaking commercially) bad, had all alike occasion to seek the accountant's advice and assistance. Retailers, who kept clerks for their sold books, but not for their bought; wholesale dealers who did not want to let their clerks see their books at all. Shrewd men of business, who yet could not balance a ledger; ill-educated traders, who, though they could make money, would have been ashamed to show their ill-written and worse spelled journals to a stranger; unhappy wretches shivering on the brink of insolvency; creditors who did not think much of the cooking of some dishonest debtor's accounts – all these came and sat in George Geith's back office, and waited their turn to see him.[59]

This motley crowd of business people, teetering on the brink of insolvency or dishonesty, is a potent reminder of the instability of the market and the ever-recurring suspicion of the immorality of trade. Geith's role is to ensure that mistakes due to ignorance or recklessness are emended and the proper value of properties and commercial concerns is rationally assessed. His centrality in the text promises stability, or at least the semblance of order that derives from the rarefied activity of computation: 'my business lies among certainties', he explains, 'not possibilities'.[60] In the course of the novel, the dealers, traders and 'unhappy wretches' paraded in this passage remain in the background, while the client for whom George mainly works is a country squire, beleaguered by debts and credulous enough to have given in to ill-advised speculations. Geith is employed to ascertain the value of his property in Hertfordshire, and to make sense of the irregularly kept accounts of the Molozane family. It takes him several trips to the country and many sleepless nights of work to come to the foregone conclusion that 'the property must go'.[61] Inefficient management, irrational choices, and random spending patterns: the accumulated failings of generations of Molozanes cannot be put to right. In economic terms, their country assets are valueless.

But not in symbolic terms. While the accountant certifies irreparable economic losses, he also acts as the appraiser of intangible symbolic capital.[62] Living for weeks with the Molozanes, feeling at home in their house, George is in a position to study and appreciate their way of life, which he does in a series of chapters that focus on apparently minor episodes (rambling in the country, going to church, conversing in the evening) and semi-comic domestic vignettes. He falls in love with Beryl, one of the daughters of Mr Molozane. Seen through the eyes of the accountant, Beryl and her sister Louisa are characterised by a charming union of slightly eccentric traits and reliable, old-fashioned goodness. Beryl, whom every reviewer found irresistible, captures the heart of George Geith by virtue of a striking combination of light insolence, comic talent and solid innocence. Beryl mocks her haughty grandmother repeatedly, mimicking her speech and manners to the delight of her relatives; she also takes pleasure in ridiculing the sermons preached in the local church. In other words, Beryl fully enjoys the liberty of being spirited, moderately unconventional and outspoken – a liberty that derives from her social standing and the certainty of belonging to a class that can afford to sidestep strictly bourgeois notions of respectability and proper domestic behaviour. It is fitting that George Geith – 'mentally well balanced'[63] himself – should feel attracted to the combination of opposites that defines Beryl's subjectivity:

> He was commencing to learn wherein this girl's power of attraction lay, viz., in a mental constitution which had the keenest sense of the ridiculous, combined with the deepest sympathy for the suffering; which, while it could see something ludicrous in the most ordinary . . . had yet every cord attuned to echo the slightest breath of trouble, the faintest sigh of woe . . . those people who in themselves combine the two opposites of light-heartedness and sadness, charm us as the Irish melodies charm us.[64]

To the relative poverty and indebtedness of the Molozanes, on the brink of losing even the modest abode where they live, corresponds (on the credit side) the rich and unique individuality of a heroine refreshingly free in her manners, a lover of the country in all its seasons and a modern mind critical of prejudices. 'I like . . . to hear a man stand up for his business, as much as I like to hear people stand up for their country',[65] Beryl admits in a conversation with George that seems designed to stamp the seal of legitimacy and prestige on the word 'business': 'Remember, Mr. Geith, I believe in business, and I only wish I were a man to show what business could do for Molozane Park . . . if trade were not always providing money for the aristocracy, the aristocracy would soon go down to the lowest depths of poverty'.[66] The irony is that no amount of business acumen can actually save the mismanaged property of the Molozanes. But Beryl's words serve a different purpose: the approval of business voiced by a woman accustomed to a leisured country life and to a cultural environment untainted by trade, a character barred by gender from being active in the commercial arena, weighs significantly in the ideological scale of the novel. Beryl's 'I like' is another occasion for the narrative to distil the value of the business ideal, buoyed up by the sanction of a young, upper-class heroine who could have easily turned this ideal into the butt of a joke.

Bilateral Posting

The symbolic capital of the Molozanes – the fund of prestige not yet eroded by lack of money – is expressed not only in Beryl's rich individuality, but also in Louisa's artistic creativity, a talent that inspires mixed responses in the novel. Besides looking at the account books of the family, George is asked to read the yet unpublished pages Louisa writes and to ascertain their value. With characteristic efficiency, the accountant enters the manuscripts twice in his mental ledger, as liabilities and assets, debits and credits. 'I am afraid George anathemised the manuscripts', admits the narrator; the story contained 'nothing original in its treatment . . . there was, certainly, little to interest a man like George Geith, and yet he was interested in the authoress and astonished at her talent'.[67] From this examination, Louisa's literary gift emerges as both an annoyance and a resource, inspiring disillusioned comments on the ordinariness of her imagination – 'Hang the poems!' – as well as dreamy reflections on the power of the creative spirit: 'he could not help marvelling, where, in the name of wonder, the girl had gathered her ideas from . . . How could people whom the breath of passion has never touched, imagine these things? How . . . can they put them into words?'[68] In this case, too, Riddell steers a mid-course between approval and disapproval, neither reproaching the literary aspirations of a young, isolated mind, nor exalting her talent. Luisa will eventually sell her manuscripts for a modicum sum of money, but her career is terminated by a sudden and premature death. The manner in which writing and the idea of literary genius are dealt with in the novel keeps in equilibrium negative and positive judgments. This pattern of assessment – a double entry method of appraisal – orients the treatment of other issues as well, especially those related to the sphere of commerce and finance.

Financial speculation usually receives a bad press in Victorian fiction. Examples abound: form Charles Lever's *Davenport Dunn* (1859) to Trollope's *The Prime Minister* (1876) and Riddell's *Mitre Court* (1885) there is no shortage of accusations levelled against the intemperate greed of the speculator, albeit his daring propensity to risk exerts a strong pull on the imagination of novelists.[69] Riddell introduces the subject of speculation twice in her novel: first when Mr Molozane seeks Geith's advice about the 'shares in those cursed mines' which the country squire has purchased; and then when George himself, much later in the story, no longer resisting the 'allurements of possibilities', takes to speculating 'outside his legitimate business'.[70] In the first case, speculation is synonymous with 'ruin' and George's advice is to get rid of the shares ('I should never invest one sixpence in them').[71] But when the accountant tries the same route, he finds speculation 'safe' and profitable: 'And now the accountant began to do amazingly well . . . He did not speculate in order to sit down idle; he merely did so to accelerate his progress upwards, and to enable him to vary his occupation'.[72] Speculation is regarded as legitimate and ruinous at the same time. Most importantly, it is not overtly linked to immorality, underhand dealings and commercial dishonesty.

This neutral representation of speculative investments is part of a broader picture of the London business world which Riddell keeps within the confines of the rational and the moral. The City men with whom George Geith interacts are all minor characters, since the governing focus of the entire novel is the accountant – an uncharacteristic choice for Riddell who, in her previous and subsequent novels, opts for competing co-protagonists. Here the centrality of Geith goes unquestioned and this ensures that his particular consciousness – his desires, actions, and ethical standards – pervades the representation of the public sphere of business. Minor characters, however, are there to remind us, with the 'strange resonance' of their partial presence,[73] that the world of commerce swings in two opposite directions, towards the grey area of wrongdoing and towards rationality, generosity and cooperation. Mr Bemmidge, the wine merchant, is a loyal friend of Geith's and a fine connoisseur of all the 'tricks' of adulteration commonly employed in his trade.[74] The fraudulent behaviour of Mr Norton, the banker whose failure imperils George's prospects, is counterbalanced by Mr Finch's spirit of cooperation, when he offers George a 'first-rate agency' to help him overcome his difficulties: 'aided by Mr. Finch, and encouraged by Mr. Finch's connections, the business road seemed to the accountant bordered by flowers, carpeted with roses'.[75] If in *City and Suburb* the world of money making was depicted in bold strokes and sharp contrasts, in the attempt to differentiate the materialism of the wealthy from the idealism of struggling characters, in *George Geith* softer hues are employed throughout the narrative to delineate the ethical contours of life in the City. It is a reassuring picture of order and rationality: the deleterious effects of speculation are contained; devious business practices (adulteration) are acknowledged only to be segregated out of view; acts of friendship and generosity among men of business are not infrequent and the City even proves welcoming to the country squire when he relocates to London to work as a clerk in a great shipping-house.[76] Of course, there is a fair amount of dynamism in the City – George reinvents his identity, makes and loses money, speculates – but the rhythm of the narrative, alternating between country scenes and City sketches, and the measured tones of the narration impose a sense of regularity and stability onto this story of modern accounting. The novel rationalises and makes sense of the business world not by disavowing the dark side of the market, but by compartmentalising it as a minor threat – minor in relative terms as it pertains to the 'shadow-space' of marginal characters[77] and is acknowledged only in relation to its opposite. The style of bilateral positing functions as the organising principle of ideologically sensitive issues. Neither condemning nor condoning speculation and regarding commercial misconduct as a momentary lapse in the overall rationality of the market, this novel offers readers a rare picture of fictional equilibrium.

With an eye to the popularity (and marketability) of sensational themes and situations, Riddell spices up her story with a subplot revolving around bigamy. George Geith's secret, the burden he tries to shrug off by moving to the City, becoming an accountant and devoting his life to making money, is a matrimonial union with an unsuitable wife, a mistake of youth which seems quickly repaired in chapter 2 when Geith receives news of the sudden death of a certain person, only much later revealed to be his wife. Marriage too is entered twice in the novel's moral ledger, first as a tragic error and then as an act of love, when George and Beryl are finally united in matrimony. The first wedding is the result of unthinking recklessness and rushed decisions, while the second nuptial concludes a prolonged stage of reflection, in which George accurately weighs his and Beryl's chances of happiness. A principle of balance is at work in the representation of their happiness: 'if their love-making was sadly prosaic, if their wedding was fearfully matter-of-fact . . . they had yet by way of a balance, romance in matrimony, and such happiness, spite of all their anxieties, as do not as a rule go home with those couples, whose marriage has been conducted on the strictest principle of domestic economy'.[78] The romance of love in the City is narrated in a short series of domestic tableaux in which Beryl too is shown 'playing at business': 'she learnt how to arrange his papers, how to keep his bills, his invoices, his receipt-notes, and his letters, so that at any minute she could find him a particular account, or tell him where such and such a proposal was put'.[79] Not an hour is employed 'without a return of some kind', remarks the narrator, 'if she could do nothing to make money, she at least prevented her husband from losing time, which to him was money'.[80] Domestic happiness and profits go hand in hand in Riddell's business-like version of modern love. Beryl's adaptability to the altered circumstances of her life is meant to be commended: gone is her eccentric sense of the ludicrous, while solid bourgeois earnestness takes its place. One of the lessons *George Geith* seems to be teaching is that the *embourgeoisement* of the upper classes brings contentment.

The flipside of such picture of domestic serenity is unconscious bigamy. When 'Mrs George Geith No. 1' (as the narrator calls her) reappears and George gets arrested for 'felonious intermarrying',[81] the novel veers towards sensationalism. The confusion thus irrupting in the story, however, is short lived. In the final section a lengthy courtroom scene is introduced that restores order via a detour into juridical discourse. In this scene, not just George's alleged crime of bigamy but his whole life story appears under examination. In the arguments of the prosecutor, George's guilt extends to his choice of business over the Church: 'Has he been abroad? has he been Christianizing the savages of Africa? . . . has he been existing on some poor stipend in a country parish, or laboring amongst wretched inhabitants of an East of London district? . . . No such thing'.[82] His years of hard work – the story readers have been following so far – are 'spoken of as golden hours of liberty in which he was amassing wealth'.[83] If bigamy is the crime for which he is brought to court, his opting for the City and the chance of making money appears no less suspicious. The counsel for the defence, on the other hand, rehearses the story of how George 'without friends, without capital, without previous business training . . . made his way up'.[84] In his 'unvarnished' tale, the 'days of trial', the 'nights of anxiety', the 'hardships encountered' justify George's economic success. Both perorations are presented verbatim and extensively in a chapter that reads like a final, legal validation of Geith's business life. The verdict of 'Not Guilty' absolves him from all sorts of implicit and explicit accusations.

The conclusion provides one further instance of the double entry model of evaluation that, as I have argued, anchors meanings in this novel: on the one hand, a tragic ending with the death of Beryl occluding private happiness, on the other, a renewed season of commercial prosperity for George, who expands his business to become, on the last page, a 'city magnate'.[85] Sensationalism occupies a relatively marginal position in a novel consistently shaped by the balancing of contrasts. Secrecy, half lies and the suspense created by unconscious bigamy do not contradict the overall vision of rationality and order that the story of George Geith projects. Indeed, most reviewers commended the novel for steering clear of the excesses of sensational fiction. The domestic conflicts introduced in *George Geith* through the topos of bigamy will be more fully explored in Riddell's subsequent novels, *The Race for Wealth* (1866) and *Austin Friars* (1870), where the uneven development of modernity – slow-moving in the domestic sphere and fast-paced in the public realm of commerce and business – becomes the focus of the narrative.

'The True Fascination of Business'

Chapter 4 of *Too Much Alone* begins with a moment of reflection on the usefulness of business novels. Riddell's authorial voice interjects the narrator's to defend the choice of subject matter of the story which is about to unfold. Sealing a pact with a particular constituency of readers, Riddell promises a tale that addresses their specific concerns. A similar moment occurs in *George Geith*, but the context of enunciation is different. George pronounces a passionate defence of his own avocation in Snareham Castle, the property of his aunt, Lady Geith, confuting the prejudicial view of business she entertains and gaining her approval:

> Forgetting the weary drudgery . . . forgetting all the prejudices of society against trade, all old bugbears of gentility, all the ideas in which he had been born and bred up, and only feeling how great and grand a thing it is to have fought the battle of poverty single-handed, to have risen unaided and unpatronized, George Geith grew eloquent, and told the tale of years gone by in words that commended the interest of the listener.[86]

It is significant that the interlocutor singled out as recipient of George's fervent pro-business speech should be a 'Lady' of leisure, representative of a class that this novel wishes to include within the larger group of its implied audiences. Rather than addressing directly the 'business people', who are deemed to be still oblivious of their own peculiar nobility, Riddell turns to 'men of pleasure and men of rank', attempting to persuade them that trade too has its 'glory' – 'I would

I could show to men of leisure and men of rank', exclaims the narrator, 'what trade really is; what an excitement, what a pain, what a struggle, and when honestly and honourably carried out, what a glory too'.[87] Of course the novel does not speak only to the selected few here designated as addressees. But their inclusion is in keeping with the general orientation of a narrative that strives to achieve a credible compromise between competing value systems, praising the economic virtue of self-interest while at the same time imagining strong lines of continuity with the tradition of gentry culture. Awarding the seal of approval to business entails reconnecting the country and the City, closing the gap between the old order and the new, condemning the failings of country squires and families of ancient descent while retaining a fair amount of admiration for their symbolic capital. When the novel was adapted for the stage, by Wybert Reeve in 1877, the story and the setting were rearranged along distinctly gentrified lines: with only one out of four acts taking place in the City, the emphasis on business appears drastically reduced. The play opens in the drawing room of the Molozanes and the curtain falls on a scene of domestic reconciliation, with George and Beryl 'united at last' in the 'home of the baronet'.[88] The heroine does not die and George, reinstated as the owner of Snareham Park, only vaguely resembles the hero Riddell had imagined as a prosperous and dynamic City man in the last chapter of her novel. The stage adaptation brings out the country at the expense of the City, while the novel was predicated on a more balanced approach.[89]

'*Regularity*, not disequilibrium', writes Franco Moretti, 'was the great narrative invention of bourgeois Europe. All that was solid became more so'.[90] Moretti finds this regularity embodied in 'styles more than stories'; it is in the 'laborious prose' of Victorian novels, he claims, that 'the bourgeois' is constructed.[91] *George Geith*, as I have argued, is a novel of equilibrium. The balancing acts performed in the course of the narrative stabilise potential contrasts between competing axiological systems, producing the impression of order and harmony to which Victorian readers responded so approvingly. Riddell's explicit apology of business and economic self-interest acquires credibility by being presented not in opposition to pre-capitalist ideals, although Geith's initial choice to abandon the church is clearly a rupture with the past. This choice, however, occurs early on in a story that soon develops as both a forward movement into commercial modernity (the City, professional accounting, business) and a return to the countryside ideal, redefined according to mid nineteenth-century aesthetic standards. Accounting provides a model of appraisal that proves effective at more than one level, especially as regards the sensitive issue of the morality of the market. Speculation is entered on both sides of the equation, as debit as well as credit, while for every act of commercial dishonesty the novel imagines an equal and opposite deed of good conduct that keeps the final total in equilibrium. I have insisted on the model of bilateral positing not to imply that accounting is intentionally deployed as a master trope, but to tease out the many acts of balance through which the imagined world of this novel is rationalised. That Riddell's contemporaries found her compromises more convincing than the conflicts she had explored in previous novels suggests how deeply felt was the demand for fictional resolutions of the contradictions of modernity. Riddell, however, did not replicate *George Geith*'s successful formula in the City novels she went on to write. Arguably, her imagination was drawn more to the unpolished, rugged aspects of modern disharmonies than it was to the formal balances she proved capable of creating.

Notes

1 'London Correspondence', *The Belfast News-Letter*, 6 January 1865, p. 3. The article also reported 'rumours' that Riddell had received 700 pounds for the sale of the manuscript to the Tinsley brothers, quite a substantial sum of money that confirmed, in the eyes of the reporter, the 'infinitely superior' quality of this novel.
2 'George Geith', *The Reader* 5, no. 108 (21 January 1865), p. 66; 'George Geith', *The Saturday Review* 19, no. 489 (11 March 1865), pp. 290–91; 'New Novels' (Rev. of *George Geith*), *The London Review* 10, no. 241, 11 February, 1865, pp. 181–2.
3 [Geraldine Jewsbury], 'George Geith of Fen Court', *The Athenaeum* 1947 (18 February 1865), p. 233.
4 'George Geith', *The Fortnightly Review* 1 (1 June 1865), p. 254.
5 'Literature' (Rev. of *George Geith*), *The Sporting Gazette, Limited*, 21 January 1865, p. 45.
6 'George Geith', *The Morning Post*, 30 December 1864, p. 2.
7 Ibid.
8 Max Weber, *The Protestant Ethic and the Spirit of Capitalism* (London: Routledge, 2001), p. xxii–xxiii.
9 *Too Much Alone*, pp. 1–3.
10 *George Geith*, p. 7.
11 Mary Russell Mitford, *Our Village*, 1819, (London: Macmillan, 1900), p. 5.
12 *George Geith*, p. 5.
13 On the relevance of the sketch form and Mitford's popular country pictures for the development of the novel see Garcha, pp. 5–24.
14 *George Geith*, p. 6.
15 'Most novels', writes Raymond Williams, 'are in some sense knowable communities. It is part of a traditional method – an underlying stance and approach – that the novelists offer to show people and their relationships in essentially knowable and communicable ways'. In the 'fiction of the city', however, as opposed to the 'fiction of the country', assumptions of a 'knowable community – a whole community, wholly knowable – became harder and harder to sustain', see Raymond Williams, *The Country and the City* (Oxford: Oxford University Press, 1975), p. 165. In the urban-rural sketch with which Riddell commences her novel the pressure of metropolitan experience is temporarily suspended and the local City is reshaped as an object of contemplation, not opaque and threatening, but knowable and enjoyable, albeit for a brief period of time, by the plural 'we'.
16 *George Geith*, p. 2.
17 As Williams argues, idyllic literary representations of rural England frequently hinge on the contrast between what 'seems an unmediated nature – a physical awareness of trees, birds, the moving shapes of land – and a working agriculture, in which much nature is in fact being produced' (*The Country*, p. 3).
18 *George Geith*, p. 12.
19 Ibid., p. 21.
20 The past from which George is trying to escape by moving to London includes an incautious and unhappy marriage. At the beginning of the story, news reaches him of the death of his wife; though free from the burden of the past, George decides to remain in the City and not to go back to his previous life.

21 *George Geith*, p. 24.

22 Ibid., p. 22.

23 Ibid., p. 26.

24 Williams, *The Country*, p. 120.

25 As Bunce observes, the 'countryside ideal' had 'two complementary strands of thought: the one involving a broad critique of urbanization and industrial progress, the other combining romanticism and agrarianism in a general idealization of nature and country life'. See Michael Bunce, *The Countryside Ideal: Anglo-American Images of Landscape* (London: Routledge, 2005), p. 11. In *Paradise Lost: Rural Idyll and Social Change in England since 1800* (London: I.B. Tauris Publishers, 2002), Jeremy Burchardt claims that by the mid-nineteenth century 'Wordsworth's once quite unusual reverence for nature had become part of the cultural atmosphere in which educated English people moved . . . The intensified and elevated awareness of nature popularized by Wordsworth led directly to a privileging of the countryside over the city, in a far more serious way than the pastoral tradition has ever aspired to' (p. 29).

26 Bunce, p. 166.

27 Burchardt, p. 2.

28 *George Geith*, p. 148.

29 Ibid., p. 221.

30 In *Culture and Anarchy* (1869) Arnold famously argued that the word '*Philistine* gives the notion of something particularly stiff-necked and perverse in the resistance to light and its children, and therein it specially suits our middle-class, who not only do not pursue sweetness and light, but who prefer to them that sort of machinery of business, chapels, tea meetings, and addresses from Mr Murphy and the Rev. W. Cattle, which makes up the dismal and illiberal life on which I have so often touched', see Matthew Arnold, p. 75. In each of the three social classes he mentions, however, 'there are born a certain number of natures with a curiosity about their best self, with a bent for seeing things as they are, for disentangling themselves from machinery, for simply concerning themselves with reason and the will of God, and doing their best to make these prevail; – for the pursuit, in a word, of perfection" (Ibid., p. 80). *George Geith* predates Arnold's essays, later collected in *Culture and Anarchy*, by a few years. Yet in the representation of George's 'best self' (albeit mediated by nature rather than culture) a similar emphasis on 'a general humane spirit' (Ibid., p. 81) can be detected.

31 *George Geith*, p. 150.

32 Bunce, p. 30.

33 'Occasional Notes', *The Pall Mall Gazette*, 24 April 1884, p. 2.

34 'Holiday Scenes – No.1', *The Penny Illustrated Paper*, 30 April 1870, p. 285.

35 'There yet linger in the old City whose inner life the authoress of "George Geith" so loves to limn, many ancient customs which we hope will not die out, even in this sordid age of money-making. It is one of these time-honoured usages (in the description of which Mrs. Riddell's pen would revel) that afforded our Artist a subject for the Illustration printed on the present page', see 'Flowers in the City', *The Penny Illustrated Paper*, 10 June 1876, p. 388.

36 *Too Much Alone*, pp. 163–4.

37 Ibid., p. 161.

38 Ibid., p. 164.

39 *George Geith*, p. 9.

40 Ibid., p. 12.

41 Bruce Carruthers and Wendy Nelson Espeland, 'Accounting for Rationality: Double-Entry Bookkeeping and the Rhetoric of Economic Rationality', *The American Journal of Sociology* 97, no. 1 (July 1991), p. 31.

42 *George Geith*, p. 13.

43 Ibid., p. 194.
44 Beresford Worthington, *Professional Accountants: An Historical Sketch* (London: Gee & Co., 1895), p. 4. The 1869 Bankruptcy Act was an extremely controversial piece of legislation (as I explain in greater detail in Chapter 8), which granted professional accountants larger powers; the Company Act of 1862 'offered new fields of lucrative employment for accountants and no doubt did much to attract many ambitious young men to seek their fortunes in the profession', see David Solomons and Stephen A. Zeff, *Accounting Research, 1948–1958: Selected Articles on Accounting History* (New York: Garland, 1996), p. 115.
45 Worthington, p. 1. In England, as Brown claimed in 1905, 'questions of accounting which in Scotland would have been remitted to professional accountants, were dealt with by the Master of Chancery; and estates in bankruptcy or belonging to persons under some legal disability were entrusted to the care of officials of the court. The Scottish system fostered the growth of a body of men relying on their merits for success, the English system maintained a number of court officials and commissioners – many of them ill-qualified to perform accounting work – and left little business for the independent practitioner', see Richard Brown, *A History of Accounting and Accountants, edited and partly written by Richard Brown*, 1905, (London: Frank Cassel & Co., 1968), p. 232. In the English system, in other words, the distinction between professional accountants and 'ill-qualified' practitioners remained blurred till the end of the nineteenth century, when the 'strictest code of professional morality' (Ibid., p. 338) was enforced upon the members of the societies of accountants established throughout the country.
46 These remarks appear in a review of a pamphlet entitled *The Importance of Correct Bookkeeping with Remarks on the General Employment of Professional Accountants, by Simmons and Elles, Accountants* (London 1861), see 'Commercial Literature' The Economist 19, no. 927 (1 June 1861), p. 597.
47 Benjamin Franklin Foster, *Double Entry Elucidated* (London: Bell & Daldy, 1858), p. 31.
48 Duncan Macdougal, *A Complete System of Bookkeeping; or Single and Double Entry Familiarly Explained* (Manchester: Published for the author, Stationers' Hall, 1862), p. 2.
49 'Book-keeping is the art of recording property in such a manner as to show its whole value collectively, and also the value of its component parts . . . In the classification and adjustment of accounts by this system property is regarded as a whole, composed of various parts: the stock accounts exhibits the whole capital, taken collectively; the money, personal and merchandise accounts exhibit the parts of which the capital is composed. Hence there must necessarily and inevitably be a constant equality between the stock account on the one hand and the remaining accounts on the other . . . This equity is the great essential principle of double entry' (Foster, pp. 1–5).
50 In his introduction to *Accounting as Social and Institutional Practice*, Peter Miller makes the point that 'accounting practices are more than the numerical computations of costs, profits, losses and returns. Accounting practices include particular discursive representations and vocabularies'. He calls these representations 'rationales' and argues that 'the economic domain is *constituted and reconstituted* by the changing calculative practices that provide a knowledge of it', see Peter Miller, 'Accounting as Social and Institutional Practice: An Introduction', in Anthony G. Hopwood and Peter Miller, eds. *Accounting as Social and Institutional Practice* (Cambridge: Cambridge University Press, 1994), pp. 3–4.
51 James Aho, *Confession and Bookkeeping: The Religious, Moral and Rhetorical Roots of Accounting* (Albany: State University of New York Press, 2005), p. 72.
52 In Pacioli's book *De Divina Proportione* (1509), 'the geometry of the body is allegorized in terms of its cosmic significance. By contemplating the body's relations and

proportions, says Pacioli, one can indirectly learn about the totality of creation and of its Creator, the divine Geometrician and Architect. Just as the body is a *discordia concurs*, a harmonized diversity, so is the world as a whole . . . Few accounting historians have acknowledged the place of aesthetics in Pacioli's bookkeeping instruction . . . By this omission, they have overlooked still another attraction that DEB must have had to those who adopted it, specifically, its beauty' (Aho, p. 77).

53 Eve Chiapello, 'Accounting and the Birth of Capitalism', *Critical Perspectives on Accounting*, 18 (2007), p. 272 and p. 264.

54 Werner Sombart, *Der Moderne Kapitalismus*, 1916, quoted in Chiapello, p. 266.

55 Carruthers and Espeland, p. 31. The debate on the link between accounting and the rise of capitalism, inaugurated by Sombart's remarks in *Der Moderne Kapitalismus*, is still ongoing. For a brief but accurate review of the current debate see Steven Toms's entry, 'Capitalism', in *The Routledge Companion to Accounting History*, ed. John Richards Edwards and Stephen P. Walker (London: Routledge, 2009), pp. 341–51. Chiapello's article contains a very interesting discussion of Marx's concept of capital which, according to her, 'corresponds to [the representation] given by balance sheets taken from DEB [double entry bookkeeping] accounts of the kind in use in the nineteenth century, at the time Marx was working on the subject' (Chiapello, p. 280). Marx was familiar with the technique of DEB, which he discussed in his letters to Engels: 'Marx found in accounting practices of his time a means to clarify his own concepts' (Ibid., p. 282).

56 *George Geith*, p. 23.

57 Ibid.

58 On the professionalisation of accountancy in both England and Scotland see Chris Pullaos, 'Professionalisation', in *The Routledge Companion to Accounting History*, pp. 247–73. Key events in this process 'involved changes in the insolvency administration'; eventually, as Pullaos claims, 'the Scottish model of bankruptcy was imported into England setting in motion competition between accountants and lawyers and efforts to create shelters *from* the market and to protect professional elites' (p. 251).

59 *George Geith*, p. 24.

60 Ibid., p. 28.

61 Ibid., p. 175.

62 Understood as prestige, consecration or honour, 'symbolic capital' is also defined by Bourdieu as a form of 'credit' which 'under certain conditions, and always in the long run, guarantees "economic" profits', see Pierre Bourdieu, *The Field of Cultural Production* (Cambridge: Polity Press, 1993), p. 75.

63 *George Geith*, p. 98.

64 Ibid., p. 271.

65 Ibid., p. 231.

66 Ibid., p. 232.

67 Ibid., p. 273.

68 Ibid. Riddell had already introduced the character of the female author in *The Rich Husband*, published by Charles Skeet in 1858 and reissued by Tinsley Brothers in 1867; Judith becomes a writer in London after she flees from a violent marriage and a brutal husband. In this novel, authorship is toil undertaken to gain economic independence; there is hardly any room for the more romantic vision of genius that Riddell will later articulate in *A Struggle For Fame* (1883).

69 This is true especially in the 1860s: 'Popular fiction of the "sensational sixties" without doubt most compellingly testified to the growing attraction of speculating villains' (Wagner, *Financial Speculation,* p. 63). Mary Elizabeth Braddon's 'villainous speculators' (Ibid., p. 65) in particular stand out for their excessive exuberance.

70 *George Geith*, 302.

71 Ibid., p. 28.

72 Ibid., pp. 303–4.

73 See Alex Woloch, *The One vs the Many: Minor Characters and the Space of the Protagonist in the Novel* (Princeton: Princeton University Press, 2003), p. 40.

74 In one scene, adulteration is the topic of conversation among men of business: 'The mysteries of the wine-trade were unveiled for the visitors' edification. The adulteration, tricks, the doctoring were all duly discussed over – shall I write it reader? – brandy-and-water' (*George Geith*, p. 53). As part of a convivial scene, this discussion presents dodgy commercial practices as a marginal curiosity within an overall system of sound and safe business transactions. In *George Geith*, indignation about the immorality of trade is almost nonexistent. It will however, resurface in *The Race for Wealth*, a novel that explores the business of adulteration in greater detail.

75 *George Geith*, p. 446.

76 The Molozanes move to London when their house is sold. The country squire finds employment as clerk for a salary of 250 pounds a year – part of this salary is paid out, in secret, by a retired merchant, Mr. Wren, a neighbour of the Molozanes. In this case too, Riddell insists on the representation of acts of generosity and kindness among wealthy men of business. Mr. Molozane takes his job seriously and works hard to 'learn all the ins and outs of the business' (Ibid., p. 363). The novel seeks to convey an image of City life antithetical to habitual representations of the chicanery and deviousness of market players, which Riddell will address in later novels. In *George Geith* the prevailing stance is one of moderation: stock-market villainy and commercial dishonesty, for all their sensational potential, appear far less interesting than the regular running of Geith's own business with its emphasis on clarity and order. The City is also romanticised as the quaint little spot where George and Beryl enjoy their short experience of married love. The extent to which Riddell is willing to go to project a reassuring picture of commercial modernity is, indeed, remarkable.

77 Woloch, p. 40.

78 *George Geith*, p. 452.

79 Ibid., p. 467.

80 Ibid., p. 468.

81 Ibid., p. 518.

82 Ibid., p. 524.

83 Ibid., p. 526.

84 Ibid., p. 530.

85 Ibid., p. 555.

86 Ibid., p. 122.

87 Ibid., p. 123.

88 Wybert Reeve, *George Geith, or Romance of a City Life. A Drama in Four Acts and a Tableau Founded on Mrs. Riddell's Celebrated Novel*, 1877 (London and New York: Samuel French Publisher, 1880), p. 37.

89 According to the magazine *Era*, Reeve's theatrical adaptation of the novel 'proved immensely successful', see 'Theatrical Gossip', *The Era*, 28 October 1877, p. 6. The play was performed in several British locations, including Exeter, Bath, Birmingham, and Derby, and in Australia (Melbourne and Adelaide).

90 Moretti, *The Bourgeois*, p. 15.

91 Ibid., p. 17.

6   Dust and Dirt

The Race for Wealth

Whenever a strict pattern of purity is imposed on our lives it is either highly
uncomfortable or it leads into contradiction.

Mary Douglas, *Purity and Danger*, 1966

The literary reputation gained with the success of *George Geith* resulted in higher
financial rewards for the author. As Riddell's publisher, William Tinsley, recalled
in his memoir: 'We . . . paid her eight hundred pounds for "George Geith", and
close to that sum for several other novels; in fact, I never paid her less than four
hundred pounds for any original novel I had from her'.[1] Arguably, Riddell sought
to capitalise on her moment of fame by producing, in quick succession, three
rather different novels: *Maxwell Drewitt* (1865), set in rural Ireland; *Phemie
Keller* (1866), the story of a failed marriage, serialised in the *Shilling Magazine*;
and *The Race for Wealth* (1866), Riddell's fourth City novel, which tightly interweaves two controversial themes – adulteration and adultery – and was published
in part issues in *Once a Week* from January until September 1866.

Riddell's increased productivity rate was frowned upon by Victorian reviewers, always inclined to question the value of literary merchandise manufactured
in haste: 'novels cannot be produced, like a hundred watch-springs, from a pen-
nyworth of material', observed the *Westminster Review*, 'and certainly two novels
in twelve months are too much for any author'.[2] Similarly, the *Saturday Review*
lamented the negative effects of 'overhaste in production' arguing that the 'inexo-
rable demand for "copy", kept up so steadily and for so long, must tell on the
power of any author, and to this and this alone we trust we are owing the defects
in *The Race for Wealth*, which is far too good a story, too cleverly told, and too
subtle in psychology, to be blemished as it is with certain faults'.[3]

The faults in question were of two kinds: an atmosphere of 'vulgarity', not
in keeping with the 'poetical feeling' of *George Geith*, and an overload of 'long
descriptions instead of dramatic power'.[4] Reviewers responded with a mixture
of disapproval and appreciation to those features that make *The Race for Wealth*
stand out among Riddell's City novels: a distinct focus on the impure messiness
of trade and life in general, and an equally noticeable insistence on what the
Morning Post called 'the rage for the psychological'[5] which frequently interrupts

the unfurling of the plot. Abandoning altogether the countryside theme, with its pleasant harmonies, Riddell locates her new story squarely within the urban environment of Eastern London, marking this return to the City and its immediate surroundings with a renewed emphasis on perceptible materiality: bad odours, urban filth, or in Riddell's own words 'the dust and dirt of our mortality'.[6] In the first chapter, Billingsgate, Lower Thames Street, Fish Street Hill and other localities traced on the map for the benefit of the 'most courteous reader',[7] all emanate distinct smells, mostly offensive for their intensity. In one street, 'the air is literally foul with the smell of foreign fruits'; in another, it is 'salt fish and rotten vegetables, and decomposing head and tails' that combine to create the olfactory spirit of the place; 'open shops' and 'dirty gutters' find themselves in close proximity; and everywhere the traffic in perishable commodities leaves lingering traces that 'make one loathe the sight of food for a month'. With a certain relish Riddell enumerates the many types of fish sold in Billingsgate – 'prawns, shrimps, soles, mackerel, salmon, trout, sturgeon, whelks, winkles' – daring the reader to 'peep up that narrow street' where 'whiffs of a terrible odour are wafted to the senses'.[8]

Strong smells and the repeated evocation of decomposing matter should trigger a plausible reaction of distaste. But the narrator questions such automatic response:

> And yet the men and women who have their homes here . . . love London, and would not go to live in the country at any price . . . There are very strange anomalies to be met with in this region, and it may be that some of the *gamins* in Lower Thames Street . . . may, when they grow into manhood's estate, have as tender memories awakened in their hearts by the odour of a stale mackerel or the sight of a mildewed orange, as are aroused in other breasts by the scent of the jasmine or the gift of a bunch of bluebells.[9]

The memory-triggering potential of odours works at every social latitude: the country and the city may have very different olfactory identities, but for the urban population of eastern London, bad odours are not less evocative than the more delicate perfumes pervading country scenes. Riddell's olfactory imagery, in the first chapter, goes against the grain of the osmology prevailing in high Victorian fiction. Novels of the 1860s, as Janice Carlisle writes, 'reflect a highly refined sensibility to often subtle aromas, turning their imaginative noses away from the disgusting, contaminating stench of the poor to apprehend fainter, though sometimes distinctly distasteful odors'.[10] Flowers and cigars, Carlisle adds, were 'the most frequent odorants' in these novels.[11] The pleasure Riddell takes in detailing the cacophony of smells produced by the trade in food and the insistence with which she defies the delicate sensibility of her imaginary reader are more in keeping with the cultural narrative that David Trotter investigates in *Cooking with Mud*: during the 1860s, 'mess found influential and discriminating patrons among the most prominent English and French writers'.[12] It is in this decade that 'litter began to appear, in increasingly toxic doses, in the works of European writers and painters who thought of themselves as modern'.[13] Ruskin's appreciation of Turner's ability, in his paintings, to 'endure ugliness' and tolerate 'dirt' is a prime example of the new paradigm Trotter analyses in relation to the increasing preoccupation with ideas of 'chanciness' and contingency reflected in mid nineteenth-century literature and art.[14]

The evidence of decay, the stains and stenches of common labour, scattered around in Riddell's initial description of the life of the market, do not carry moral-allegorical meanings; rotting matter is not necessarily synonymous with degeneration. Rather, smells and filth are there to signify primarily this novel's imaginative investment in the impure, in the messy, contingent aspects of commercial modernity, and a concomitant disaffection with static ideals of purity and order. *The Race for Wealth* is, after all, a novel about food adulteration, a most impure and hardly legitimate business activity; as Rebecca Stern claims, it is perhaps the 'only Victorian novel to feature an adulterator as protagonist'.[15] More to the point, the adulterators in this novel, Mr Perkins and Mr Sondes, the senior partners, are not 'bad people' – an interesting ethical twist that Victorian critics did not fail to notice: 'With a praiseworthy superiority to superficial and obvious view of character – remarked the *Daily News* – Mrs Riddell makes both these adulterators anything but bad people . . . they are very honourable and even kind-natured men'.[16] Of course, the novel does not present the business of adulteration as a fully legitimate practice, nor dishonesty as condonable. Rather, *The Race for Wealth* is an extended exploration of ambiguity, of commercial conduct which is not strictly speaking illegal, nor quite right either; it is also a failed-marriage story in which the logic of the plot says one thing and the style of narration another. In short, this novel banks on what Franco Moretti calls 'the *unresolved dissonance of bourgeois life*'.[17] In this respect, it is markedly different from *George Geith*, where conflicts are resolved and equilibrium prevails. *The Race for Wealth* features two competitors, Lawrence and Percy, two heroines, Olivine and Hetta, two social groups within the middle classes; what such doubling achieves, however, is not the clarity of a melodramatic distribution of right and wrong, but the muddling of categorical oppositions and the weakening of ethical codes. Even the reader, drafted into the story through the vocative modality, is dramatised as a gambler at one point and solicited to place a bet on one of the two heroes: 'Which will you bet on, reader? Percy Forbes's horse was entered for the race when his father left him eight thousand pounds. Equal weight, gentlemen riders – which is the favourite? Dark hair or light? The black or the chestnut? You know their points, you may make up your books, for the bell has rung, and the race is beginning'.[18] The figure of the reader as gambler aptly sums up the affective tonality of this novel, which makes the most of the creative potential of messiness and ambiguity.

The Marriage of Chicory and Coffee

In the 1850s and 1860s, food adulteration and gastronomic frauds were a widespread phenomenon that did not go unnoticed. As early as in 1851, the *Lancet* published Arthur Hill Hassall's study, which proved that the food normally consumed by British citizens was extensively adulterated.[19] His findings sparked a public debate that eventually led Parliament to legislate on the matter. Though many commentators found adulteration a most odious evil, others were more lenient towards some adulterating practices, such as the mixing of harmless substances: 'Because we do not like to receive chicory under the name of coffee' – Henry Morley argued in an essay published in *Household Words* in 1852 – 'it by no means follows that we object to receive chicory in its own name, or that we consider it wrong to marry chicory and coffee to each other; the alliance may be advantageous, only let it not be secret'.[20] The public debate on food adulteration was part of a larger set of concerns about the im/morality of the market. The 'frauds upon our stomachs', as the *London Review* put it,[21] were the most horrifying but by no means the only examples of dishonest conduct: 'there is the same adulteration in everything that constitutes the furniture of life', claimed the *Leader* in 1860, 'the Parliament to which you appeal equally share the adulteration . . . commerce itself, as well as the wares transferred in commerce, is adulterated'.[22] Like Adam and Eve tasting the forbidden fruit at their own peril, 'in an unguarded and unlucky moment', British citizens were exposed to 'invisible' hazards lurking in the food they ingested: 'There is a certain ugly little monster of most insidious habits', warned the *Cornhill Magazine*, whose greatest desire is 'to make its way into our stomachs, and, when there, to work all the mischiefs in his power'.[23] The spectre of adulteration hovered over the entire social fabric, threatening to corrupt its texture beyond repair; the *British Quarterly Review* declared Britain 'a nation of knaves' and imagined how disdainful 'natives of other planets would be' if a copy of the report (produced by the Select Committee) were to be dispatched to them: 'They would be ashamed to belong to the same family of worlds. The moon would decline to keep company with such a demoralized orb. Venus would consider us a disgrace to the heavens. Mars would point to us as the most reprobate planet in creation'.[24]

The strong, indignant tones of these and other interventions in the adulteration debate stand in stark contrast with the weak, indecisive institutional attempts, over several years, to suppress (or regulate) the production and circulation of adulterated food, whether poisonous or harmless. A Select Committee was established in 1856 to inquire into the situation. Although the report left little doubt as to the magnitude of the phenomenon and the dangers posed to public health, Parliament and government took a long time to intervene. As Searle writes, 'it was not until 1875 that effective legislation, providing an appropriate mechanism for enforcement, reached the statute book'.[25] The Act for Preventing the Adulteration of Articles of Food and Drink, passed in 1860, was described by most as 'permissive' and therefore inadequate to detect, prevent and punish adulterating practices. Lamenting the many deficiencies of the 1860 Act, the *Westminster Review* denounced the English situation as anomalous within the European context: 'in every continental nation, measures more or less stringent are in force for the suppression of adulteration, and as far as we can learn they are very successful in suppressing it'.[26]

The English anomaly can be ascribed to ideological and political factors, as Searle explains. The economic liberalism of the 1850s and 1860s, hostile to local or central government interfering in commercial matters, played a decisive role in slowing down the implementation of adequate measures to counteract the pervasive circulation of adulterated goods. Appeals to the merits of free trade were also instrumental in casting doubt on the legitimacy of regulatory mechanisms that would, as John Bright claimed, harass the tradesmen and eventually push them to emigrate; and the principle of *caveat emptor* was frequently invoked by opponents of reform and 'ardent free marketeers' for whom even 'modest measures' of control were too restrictive.[27] On the whole, *laissez-faire* positions proved resilient and adulterating practices, even after 1860, went on more or less undisturbed until the late 1870s, making adulteration a most glaring example of *tolerated* commercial misconduct, entrenched institutional ambivalence and unresolved dissonance.[28] Despite much public indignation, the marriage of chicory and coffee, like many other matrimonial unions in the fiction of the 1860s, was not easily dissolved.

Considering the topicality of adulteration at mid-century, Riddell's decision to centre *The Race for Wealth* on such a controversial issue could be viewed as an explicit acknowledgement of how prominent this problem was in the public mind and for the business people to (and of) whom she speaks in her novels. As a contribution to the adulteration debate, however, the novel is oddly non-committal. Alongside a degree of indignation, expressed by characters who object to the alleged honesty of selling non-poisonous adulterated food, the narrative makes ample room for standard *laissez-faire* arguments, namely: the toughness of competition and the increasing demand for cheap versions of exotic goods, which spurs the production of fake articles for mass consumption ('It is the rage for cheapness that induces a trade like ours').[29] Perkins and Sondes, partners in the business of adulteration, and very likeable characters, have almost no qualms about inundating the market with simulacra: 'nutmegs that had never seen a foreign shore; coffee berries that had never grown on a tree; arrow-root extracted from potatoes; rhubarb useless as a medicine; pepper-corns made out of molasses and pea-flour; these were a few of the articles manufactured in Distaff Yard and distributed thence to the length and breadth of England'.[30] Perkins, who runs the Distaff Yard business, enjoys cheating the chemical analysts, feeling 'as proud of inventing any new process likely to delude them, as Watt did of condensing steam-engine, or Arkwright of his spinning-jenny'.[31] If his trade is a 'lie' and 'his business a delusion', still Perkins provides 'little luxuries' for the 'poor' who flock to the cheap shops for a taste of the world.[32] The narrator nonchalantly minimises the illegitimacy of such trade: 'What would have ye, reader? The world is not all honest. There is knavery in the innocent country, as well as due east in London'.[33]

Ironic though these words might sound, Riddell's take on deception seems rather cavalier. She sets the story slightly back in time, before the Act of 1860, so that food frauds can be constructed as unethical or dubious, but not necessarily criminal or illegal.[34] It is the ambivalence of this situation that Riddell exploits and amplifies, implicitly asking her readers to tolerate deception as part of a rather bewildering ethical package. For Arthur Hill Hassall 'it is impossible for a man to be guilty of adulteration and yet be an honest and moral man'.[35] For Riddell, such sharp distinctions are more problematic: in her novel, good, hard-working tradesmen and self-made men of business, respectable, even genteel members or the community, like Mr Sondes, earn money by deceiving the public, but this does not make them particularly detestable, nor guilty according to the law. On the contrary, Perkins is a model of prudence, frugality, contentment and kindness, while Sondes, more upper-class and refined than his partner, dispenses sound business advice to Lawrence, speaking with the authority of experience in tones that echo the very earnest rhetoric of business manuals: 'People go so weary as the years go by, bringing nothing in their wake but failure or moderate success. So many qualities are necessary to ensure even comparative wealth'.[36]

In this highly impure environment, the binary opposition between good and evil simply does not hold. More specifically, what weakens the hold of ethical distinctions is the novel's fascination with borderline situations: goodness of character combined with commercial misconduct; industriousness and regularity in the service of cheating; the infection of right and wrong in everyday business practices, which spills over into the domestic realm, in the second half of the novel. To use Mary Douglas's expression, a 'dirt-affirming philosophy'[37] lies at the heart of this novel as testified by the numerous metaphorical references to 'mud,' 'dirt' and 'stains' which crop up in the narrator's musings. In one description, the personification of Virtue appears as a matron 'walking through the muddy streets, with patched boots, and cotton stocking';[38] in another, the young boy 'sweeping the mud up on the pavement' is said to have the best chance of success;[39] 'experience' means 'getting soiled and stained and sullied' as one goes along 'dangerous roads';[40] if life is compared to a river, the river 'hides in its depth all manner of ghastly corpses';[41] people's 'most holy intentions get soiled with the dust and dirt of our mortality'[42] and even angels are expected to acquire wisdom and knowledge by contact with 'dust, mud, water-carts, and Pickford's vans'.[43]

Dirt exerts a strong pull in the novel at the level of 'scene' and affective investment, even as the plot pushes in a different direction. The 'tension between plot and scene, between the chronological continuum and the eternal affective present', as Frederic Jameson argues in *The Antinomies of Realism*, 'marks out the space in which realism emerges and subsists'.[44] In Riddell's novel, the logic of the plot ultimately reaffirms the value of purity with the death of Lawrence – the adulterous adulterator who has crossed too many lines – and the marriage between Percy, reformed fop, and Olivine, described as a 'lachrymose angel' by the *Saturday Review*, clearly unimpressed by her unsullied goodness.[45] But in what Jameson calls 'the realm of affect' or the 'eternal present' of scene, the dirt-rejecting message of the plot is offset by a persistent emphasis on the impure and the messy in different gradations of meaning, from metaphors of dirt and mud to the literal 'stickiness' of some characters (Ada Perkins in particular); from the elastic ethics of adulterators to the flexible explanations adduced to render adultery plausible. As contemporary reviewers noticed, the twin impulses – narrative and scenic – are off balance in the novel, there is a surplus of 'long descriptions instead of dramatic power', an abundance of 'psychological' analyses accompanying a slender plot.[46] In these non-narrative, pictorial moments, I would argue, ample room is made for the creative exploration of ambivalence.

'Does That Word Shock You?'

The Race for Wealth, like *City and Suburb*, begins with the hero, Lawrence Barbour, slowly making his way towards the City and the chance to prove his worth in the business arena. Unlike Alan Ruthven, Lawrence is not hampered in his progress by family pride, since the impecunious country existence he has endured until then holds very few attractions. London and a future of independence are preferable to inertia in the country, even if that future entails not just going into trade (to which his father objects) but accepting the rough and the smooth of the adulteration business: 'heart and soul he flung himself into the business at Distaff Yard; learning the ins and outs of adulteration thoroughly and rapidly . . . he never loitered in his errands; he never seemed wearied; never grumbled at any work which was put upon him . . . Altogether, Lawrence Barbour's start in London life was a success'.[47]

In this novel, Riddell deploys the same rhetoric, the same earnest tones used in *Too Much Alone*, *City and Suburb* and *George Geith* to celebrate bourgeois virtues and business values. Lawrence's capitalist energies are on a par with Maurice's; his devotion to work proves as unflinching as Alan's and George's absorption in their respective occupations: 'he worked, as Mr. Perkins said, like "a Briton"'.[48] In this respect, engineering, accounting and adulterating are equivalent fields of action where the protagonist's 'economic chivalry' (in Alfred Marshall's expression) is tested and affirmed.[49] Apparently forgetful of the trickery involved in the adulteration business, the narrative proceeds to uphold a system of values – prudence, the nobility of work, habits of regularity – which seems oddly independent of that quintessentially bourgeois virtue – honesty – so glaringly contradicted in the commercial sphere represented in the novel. 'We are adulterators: does that word shock you?'[50] asks Mr Sondes, daring Lawrence (and the reader) to absorb the shock and move on.

It is the murky side of commercial modernity that *The Race for Wealth* confronts with uncharacteristic candour and without much recourse to the abrasive lashes of satire. Sympathy for the adulterator, for example, is boosted in the episode of the accident which occurs quite early in the story. While watching the 'glories of the western hemisphere'[51] parading in Hyde Park, Lawrence launches into an ill-fated attempt to prevent a young lady (Etta Alwyn) from falling off her horse, 'and the next moment he and horse and rider were lying in a confused heap in the middle of the drive'.[52] This unlucky occurrence deprives Lawrence of the most precious form of capital at his disposal, good health and bodily strength, 'turned into weakness from that day forth for ever'.[53] Like other manifestations of the capriciousness of chance, in Riddell's novels, this accident inspires a mood of collective solidarity here anticipated, before the actual event, by a narratorial aside in defence of the 'millions' outside the sphere of 'power' and 'riches': 'How many times has this great show been described, and yet how rarely does any writer seem able to look at it from the plebeian side? . . . Is it that the millions are outside the pale of civilisation, that there is no room for even a thought of them in that heaven where the Upper Ten Thousand dwell?'[54]

The tale of what happens in the park takes up very few pages, while four entire chapters are devoted to the hospital scene (Lawrence in bed at St. George's

Hospital, slowly recovering) and to calibrating the affective coordinates in relation to which this random episode acquires emotional significance. First, the accident generates a plea for global sympathy: 'are we not all one flesh and blood, and is it not hard for one human being to be maimed and lacerated, and probed, and crippled as another?'[55] Then the plea becomes a more specific request of solidarity with the 'worker' who earns barely enough 'to keep himself off the parish': 'the world is not tender to its workers . . . Too many of the rank and file are cut down every day for any strict social account to be kept of their sufferings'.[56] Wounded and enfeebled, lying in a hospital bed, Lawrence acquires a potentially tragic stature as paragraphs accumulate to detail his moods and his silent fight against despondency:

> What should he be, this prematurely old young man? What was to be his lot in life? . . . Did the doctors say he was fit for nothing but vegetating in the country? Then the doctors lied! He, Lawrence Barbour, meant to show to the whole of them, relations, friends, foes, surgeons, what he could yet do in spite of his dislocated ribs and his unsound chest.[57]

Finally, the epic of the hospital: Riddell proffers in these chapters a sincere tribute to the ethic of health care, replete with detailed descriptions of the 'well-ventilated', 'cheerful' ward, where flowers grow 'luxuriantly' in pots, and with grateful acknowledgments of its 'cleanliness' and 'order': 'there was suffering, which skill can oftentimes merely palliate, not cure; but there was charity, there was help, there was constant care'.[58]

This episode and its scenic elaboration ensure that the adulterator is not perceived as a villain. Like many other protagonists in Riddell's novels, he is a struggling young man who will have to fight the race for wealth with the added disadvantage of physical weakness. His serious commitment to adulteration brings him into close contact with dishonest practices, but no reference is made to moral qualms or pangs of conscience. The only indirect acknowledgment that something is not quite right in Lawrence's whole-hearted embrace of such dubious trade is his pronounced distaste not for the 'business taint'[59] but for the Perkins family's way of life, exemplified by the disorder that one minor character, Ada Perkins, introduces to the story. The daughter of Mr Perkins, Ada, is the very embodiment of 'bad form'.[60] Her role is irrelevant to the main storyline, but she comes to the foreground in several scenes in which Lawrence's dislike of her physical presence, strong appetites and general messiness is the main focus. Her 'thick legs' appear almost offensive, her general vivacity always troublesome; the flowers she brings to the hospital are 'wet and sticky' with the sugary residue of the sweets she consumes in large quantities; she has a way of 'flinging herself about', unperturbed by etiquette, that Lawrence (and the narrator) finds disconcerting and fascinating almost in equal measure. Riddell's descriptions perversely linger on Ada's physical attributes:

> Ada's dress was short . . . and her petticoats were many; she had shoes which were a little inclined to wearing down at the heel, as Lawrence could

see, for, as of old, Ada's legs and feet were rather conspicuous than other-wise . . . Her arms were exactly like Castile soap; here white, there blue, there red; generally mottled, and with a development of bone at the elbows which seemed unreasonable, considering the plumpness, not to say the thickness of her figure . . . Go where he would, [Lawrence] still beheld that girl clasping her partner's arm . . . drinking champagne like water, and stuffing tarts down her throat as though she had a design of fattening herself up for market.[61]

Like dirt in Mary Douglas's account, Ada is 'matter out of place',[62] her physical presence evokes lack of restraint – 'dancing, clapping, pirouetting and jumping, to an unlimited extent'[63] – and the disorder of a self indifferent to strict codes of behaviour.[64] Ada, in other words, is meant to bear the brunt of Lawrence's (and the novel's) endorsement of muddled business ethics. Disapproval is displaced onto a female character who, for all her 'minorness', attracts a great deal of attention, since the story often pauses to make room for the carnivalesque element that Ada epitomises. In this case too, the imbalance between plot and scene is revealing: a secondary character, with little to contribute to the story, colonises the narrative at regular intervals; attention to her body brings to the fore not just the primacy of physical appetites, but also the freedom from social restraints that Riddell seems to find particularly inspiring in this novel.

Indeed, Ada has admirers as well as detractors; foremost among the former is Ada's mother, who contrasts her daughter's exuberant vitality with Olivine's static, monumental propriety ('she is looking now like patience on a monu-ment'),[65] voicing a dislike for restrictive ideas of feminine behaviour that chimes with the novel's affective investment in the impure. As Mrs Perkins objects to her husband:

You'd want to pinch your daughter into just such another piece of melan-choly and affectation; but if that's your notion, Josiah, of a nice girl, it's not mine . . . if you have the heart to put a straight-waistcoat on a young creature's high spirits and natural liveliness, I won't stand by and see it done. Who-ever comes and marries our Ada, won't come and marry her for her money, I hope.[66]

The relative freedom Ada enjoys is a question of class, of course, and Riddell does not set her up as an example of positive liberation from the shackles of respect-ability. Lawrence's harsh judgment – 'she is such a forward piece of vulgarity'[67] – is shared to a large extent by the narrator. Ada is the novel's scapegoat, the tar-get of a defensive condemnation of disorder and messiness which appears all the more necessary in a story otherwise open towards the murkiness and ethical impurity of business.

However, alongside this defensive strategy, the novel also questions the sustain-ability of ideals of innocence, purity and good form associated with the domestic sphere. Olivine, Mr Sondes's niece, is indeed a paragon of unpolluted innocence, but the narrator's ambivalence towards this character and what she stands for is hard to miss. Olivine, we soon learn, is the result of an old-fashioned, residual system of education which provides scant emotional resources to face the challenges of modern life: 'This was what the system of education had effected . . . the delicately tuned harp was strung up to its highest pitch, and Olivine could bear no excitement of any kind without the tears starting into her eyes, without her heart being torn and agitated. For an organization like this what was the future likely to hold in store for her?'.[68] With little to do and very few interests to keep her busy, Olivine stands for a model of purity which appears narrow-minded and conservative rather than ideal:

> Furthermore, like some of the sweetest and truest women who have ever breathed, she had no special talent, no great amount of cleverness. Languages were not her forte; for the life of her she could not be made to comprehend why everybody should not speak English, and why people should study the literature of other countries, when there were already, she opined, too many books published in Great Britain.[69]

On the one hand, Olivine is the novel's moral centre, an island of purity and innocence in the midst of much pollution; on the other hand, the narrator takes every opportunity to show that her understanding is limited and her innocence a disadvantage especially when she has to face the complications of an unhappy married life. Put another way, the novel has little use for the absolute standards of Olivine's perspective. When adulteration gives way to adultery, Olivine's predicament as the injured party attracts less narrative attention than Lawrence's motivations, 'involuntary passion'[70] and general restlessness. Adultery is another grey area, another zone of ambiguity, that holds a special interest for Riddell. In *Too Much Alone*, the plot of near adultery hinged on Lina and on the affective rewards of cross-gender friendship. In *The Race for Wealth*, adultery is presented as the plausible outcome of two ill-assorted marital partnerships which, unlike business ventures, cannot be easily dissolved. The conjunction of adulteration and adultery could be viewed, Rebecca Stern suggests, as one further testimony of widespread mid nineteenth-century anxieties about the immorality of commerce invading the domestic realm and adulterating private life. However, in a novel that represents the business of adulteration in non-indignant tones and solicits a great deal of sympathy for the adulterator, a novel that accepts the pervasive influence of the *laissez-faire* philosophy, the treatment of adultery is also, not surprisingly, quite nuanced. Lawrence and Etta's transgression brings to the fore a set of concerns – from the illiberality of marriage laws to the mystifications of class ideologies – which are not entirely dispelled by the redistribution of right and wrong at the novel's close.

'The Die is Cast, the Decision Made Beyond Recall'

The Race for Wealth was originally published in part issues in *Once a Week*. Each weekly instalment, with a few exceptions, commences with a lengthy digression in which the scenic impulse takes over and the plot is momentarily suspended. Quite frequently, Riddell introduces images of impermanence at the beginning of a new episode. She describes a locality about to be altered beyond recognition by sprawling urban developments and then zooms in on one isolated home to emphasise its precarious existence amidst an unstoppable stream of rapid transformations. Chapter 5 (third instalment) is a good case in point. Stepney, the locality where Sondes and Olivine live, has been 'sinking in the social scale' for over a hundred years: 'we connect no tragedy with the spot . . . man finds no interest in loitering here'.[71] The sketch Riddell offers is appropriately fragmented and interrupted; the style of narration underscores the fleeting nature of the present moment: 'Where do these shops find customers? Where? – Alas! This is an age in which if people go hungry they must be clothed – in which –. I must stop at this point and turn back to the Stepney Lawrence Barbour saw when he went to visit Mr Sondes'.[72] Sondes's residence is now 'a common lodging house' where 'any reader' can get a bed 'at a moderate – too moderate charge'.[73] To further emphasise the fast temporality of modernity, Riddell refers her readers back to 'a book written not long ago' and to the house in *City and Suburb* where Alan Ruthven lived:

In all save its name, Marsh Hall was a reality; and now – well, now there is a street through the mansion where those I knew so well lived and suffered; the gable end of Alan Ruthven's factory still remained a few weeks ago, but even that is now, no doubt, level with the ground . . . So the world turns round. How, before these pages are finished, will it be with another house, – with the old-fashioned mansion in which Olivine Sondes had spent all the years of her young existence?[74]

If the suburbs can be described as 'physically transitional spaces'[75] always in the process of being transformed, Riddell's take on urban development typically hinges on the even more unsettling image of houses annihilated to make room for new streets or railway lines. The process of metamorphosis is so quick that readers are left wondering whether the story they are reading will also be derailed, in unforeseen directions, by the invasive rapidity of change. Here one moment, gone the next: this is how Riddell depicts not just Olivine's home, but almost every domestic enclave in the novel; 'we are living now at such a pace', the narrator affirms, 'that actually the things which are here today, are away tomorrow'.[76] Nor is the West End safe from impermanence: 'here, too, all is changed: where there were houses there is now a space of waste ground'.[77] The Alwyns's residence is till standing, but 'changed almost past recognition'; the reader is invited to step in, to look 'at his face in the mirror placed between the windows' and to meditate on how swiftly characters become 'spectres of the past'.[78]

By insisting on transience, these reiterated representations of houses on the brink of disappearance undermine the stability of 'home' itself; the domestic sphere appears shaken even before adultery intervenes to break up the sanctity of marriage. The disappearing house is the objective correlative of an ideal of domesticity that is quickly losing ground as testified by the centrality of the failed-marriage plot. Narratives of marital discontent are not infrequent in the tradition of English fiction, as Kelly Hager argues; the failed-marriage plot, rather than a remarkable exception, is actually 'one of the Victorian novel's favorite stories'.[79] *The Race for Wealth* takes this predilection one step forward, configuring marriage as a point of no return, regardless of its success or failure. On the day of her wedding, Olivine appears to Percy as someone 'who leaves hope behind' and 'accepts the inevitable';[80] floating away 'in a cloud of white' the happy bride seems destined to regret her choice. As for the bridegroom, the shift from satisfaction with 'the great peace of a quiet domestic existence' to restlessness and longing for 'the busy life' is immediate.[81] It takes Lawrence a very brief honeymoon to realise that 'he was much more interested in hearing of orders, than in listening to Olivine's ecstasies'.[82] The tale of this instant failure of matrimonial promises is narrated from Lawrence's point of view, in a nocturnal scene which expatiates on his feelings of entrapment in sharp contrast with the dynamism and freedom of the public sphere of work. A few weeks after his honeymoon, while lingering in the crowded City streets, reluctant to go home, Lawrence clearly realises how hopeless his situation has become. 'There is nothing perhaps so terrible to a man', confirms the narrator, 'as the feeling that he has matrimonially made a mistake':

> Everything else in life can be remedied – save this. The years are before him, and may be full of gold, rank, fame; the mines of existence are still untouched for him to dig what he will, out of it; there is wealth for the winning, fame for the striving, land for the buying, distinction for the working . . . If he makes a mistake in one thing, he can rectify it by doing right about another; if one mine be unproductive, or one field barren, he can try for gold in some fresh direction . . . but to find one has chosen wrongly in marriage, is as when a man discovers, just as his sun is close upon setting, that he has erred through life; there is no retracing either road; there is no getting rid either of the spent existence, or of the lawful wife; the day is gone, the die is cast, the decision made, beyond recall.[83]

Remarkable in the narrator's commentary is the view of marriage as a tragic deadend, a final verdict with no possibility of appeal. Set against the unlimited opportunities that commercial modernity has to offer, even to those who make mistakes, the strictures of the laws and conventions regulating matrimonial unions appear unbearable. Errors cannot be remedied, nor bad decisions undone. If business transactions are never 'beyond recall', love contracts seem hopelessly final. The only option is breaking or bending the rules, in other words adultery. And just as the adulterator was deserving of the reader's sympathy in the hospital scene, so too the husband in love with another woman, and conscious of his errors, ought not to be summarily condemned. Riddell compares Lawrence's nocturnal, melancholic brooding on the subject of marriage to his heroic fights against the bonds of fate soon after the accident in Hyde Park: 'He felt then as he had felt in St. George's, when he lay there bruised and maimed, and battered, viz., that any fight would have been preferable to endurance. Pity him, friends, striding over the pavements'.[84] Lawrence's impure desire for Etta inspires several pages of intense scrutiny: his feelings, thoughts and inner struggles are dissected by a narrator determined to frame adultery as the plausible result of both 'involuntary passion' and a voluntary quest for freedom, the freedom to rectify one's mistakes, to dissolve matrimonial partnerships and ultimately to modernise the private sphere.

Published nine years after the passing of the 1857 Matrimonial Causes Act, which legalised divorce in England, *The Race for Wealth* suggests scepticism about the actual social and cultural impact of this piece of legislation.[85] Divorce is mentioned in the novel when Percy hints that Olivine ought to offer Lawrence 'the chance of marrying Mrs Gainswoode, and retrieving his position'.[86] Etta Gainswoode, however, disdains the prospect of a marriage which would entail losing control of her wealth ('every shilling I have in the world goes from me if I take to myself a second husband').[87] Divorce is clearly not a realistic option; the significance of wedlock as a permanent bond, and an unfair one for women in possession of a fortune, is still firmly in place in this novel.[88] This insistence on the permanence of marriage serves as a prop to sustain the imaginative investment in ambiguous situations: the adulterous husband, for example, whose predicament is presented as a struggle between bondage and freedom; or the adulteress, Etta, who comes to the fore, in the second part of the novel, as a sharp critical voice, debunking upper-class myths of social harmony and genteel prejudices as well as exposing the unfairness of marriage laws.

Like Olivine, whose standards of purity are simultaneously affirmed and called into question, Etta is the seductress, the manipulative enchantress of melodrama who, however, defends liberal values and unmasks the bad faith of adulterators turned arbiters of morality. Etta Alwyn accepts to marry the wealthy Mr Gainswoode in the attempt to salvage her father's declining fortunes, but she finds the burden unbearable: ' "Better bread and water and freedom", she decided; "better hips and haws in the woods than sugar and biscuit inside gilded wires" '.[89] Etta's dissatisfaction with her lot is the occasion for the narrative to launch into a semi-satirical expose of the society of the 'Upper Ten Thousand' with 'their frigid propriety, their dignified exclusiveness' and utter lack of 'independent opinions'.[90] Etta's passionate dislike for the conventionality of genteel life in the country and for the 'sublime indifference to everything' vaunted by the selected few who passively enjoy their wealth qualifies her as the novel's female champion of individuality, a staunch defender of the right to oppose what John Stuart Mill called the 'tyranny of the prevailing opinion and feeling'.[91] Her stance is a mixture of liberalism and capriciousness; but the narrator takes her side when it comes to criticise patrician notions of distinction:

> Those individuals who, tracing their descent back to some illiterate baron, or rough-and-ready chieftain of the good old times of misery, when might was right, but right of itself never was might, firmly believe that God made the earth and all that therein is for them and theirs, have an agreeable way of making other people think that by getting on in the world they are running counter to Heaven's high decree.[92]

This tirade against the prejudices of blood occurs, appropriately, at Malingsford End, the former country residence of the Barbours, purchased by Mr Alwyn, colonial broker, and later sold to Etta's husband, Mr Gainswoode. In this scene, Etta sets the record straight, unmasking the pretensions of Mr Barbour senior and reminding Mr Sondes that defending commercial morality (as he does by questioning the legitimacy of Alwyn's business ventures) is incongruous for a professional adulterator: 'I suppose there is no strict honesty to be looked for in any business', remarks Etta, 'not even in that of an adulterator'.[93] Etta's role as the critical voice deflating high-sounding ideals of social status and moral rectitude is not meant to be exemplary. But her impatience with conventions clearly resonates, later in the story, in a long passage in which the narrator, just before concluding the adultery plot with a new, hopeful marriage, turns to sarcasm, depreciating Olivine's angelic propriety – 'the very citadel of her purity' – and her indignant response to Percy's confession of love:

> Supposing (which is one of the unlikeliest suppositions possible) an angel were to descend from Heaven, and take a walk down Cheapside on a muddy day, there can be little doubt that the angelic pedestrian would find its equanimity discomposed when at nightfall it came to enquire into the conditions of its wings.
>
> In the better land, neither taint nor soil could ever touch its snowy plumage; and, as it is with the angel's wings, so it is with many a woman's purity.
>
> She cannot endure that aught so gross as the dust of earth should sully the whiteness of her garments . . . it is simply that the woman does not know what the world is, nor of what materials the men and the women who make up the world are composed.
>
> To some people it is a great shock to find, not merely that their neighbours are only mortal, but also that they themselves are capable of receiving splashes as they travel along the common highway of existence.[94]

The splashes of mud tainting the 'snowy plumage' of domestic innocence are there to remind readers that even as the plot reinstates moral order at home, the value of impurity is not gainsaid. In an ambivalent rhetorical gesture, Riddell undermines the affirmation of moral righteousness with which the novel ends, insisting once again on the strange honesty of dirt, on its metaphorical alliance with knowledge or experience and its power to undo illusions. In this respect, Riddell's style of narration is itself impure or adulterated, a mixture of dirt-affirming rhetoric and dirt-rejecting narrative logic, quite appropriate, one could argue, in a novel that represents moral pollution as intrinsically more interesting than moral indignation. In one final, ironic twist of the business plot, Olivine's money is reinvested in the Distaff Yard enterprise, enabling Mr Perkins 'to carry it on so successfully that doubtless . . . he will be able to portion the daughters liberally and start his sons in good businesses on their own account'.[95] Before the novel ends, Olivine becomes the capitalist who finances adulteration – purity and its opposite finally converge in this wry annotation on the limits of sharp distinctions.

Gambling and Speculation

On 10 May 1866, the long established bill-broking house, Overend, Gurney, and Co. (Limited), stopped payment causing immediate 'panic' in the City and the subsequent failure of other important banking establishments. Astonished commentators agreed that the magnitude of this crisis was unprecedented and extremely distressing: 'The panic which exists in the City' – noted the *Saturday Review* – 'is described as beyond anything which was witnessed even in 1847 and 1857'.[96] About two weeks later, on 26 May, readers of *Once a Week* were offered the chronicle of a similar collapse, albeit on a smaller scale, in the opening paragraph of the 21st weekly instalment of *The Race for Wealth:* 'Great was the astonishment expressed in mercantile circles when the failure of Alwyn and Allison, Colonial Brokers, was announced; but this astonishment proved nothing in comparison to the dismay felt when it came to be understood the house had not merely stopped payment, but was rotten and bankrupt to the core'.[97] Whether this matching of facts and fiction is a coincidence or a deliberate nod to contemporary events, the timely collapse of Alwyn's business contains a distinct echo of the notorious panic that was very much alive in the public mind. Joining a chorus of critical voices, Riddell includes in her novel an impassioned denunciation of 'the devil of speculation' and the 'mania for companies' licensed by the Limited Liability Act of 1855: 'The cholera and Limited Liability reached a point at about the same period' she writes, equating the spread of the epidemic with the 'deluge' of company promotions.[98]

Like adulteration and adultery, however, speculation too generates some ambivalence in the text. First of all, the distinction between legitimate and illegitimate business practices is bound to appear problematic in a novel that concentrates so much attention on the normality of the illicit trade in adulterated food. When the narrator presents Lawrence's speculations as an 'illegitimate' form of business in opposition to 'his regular trade',[99] the ethical boundaries thus established are rather dubious. Secondly, both Lawrence's allegedly regular trade and his speculative activities are constructed as battlefields for the productive release of his capitalist energies; speculation gains prominence as trade proves increasingly constrained by the overmastering authority of senior partners. In other words, speculation intervenes when innovation and progress are hampered by conservative tendencies. Finally, not speculation but its next of kin, gambling, is encouraged by Riddell in a rhetorical move meant to increase the reader's absorption in the textual game: 'Which will you bet on, reader?' asks the narrator. Betting on characters, Lawrence or Percy, raises the excitement of participating in the play of predictions, speculations and hypothesis that the act of reading entails: 'Gambling and reading' writes Gillian Beer 'are both acts of desire whose longing is to possess and settle the future, but whose pleasure is in active uncertainty'.[100] The reader-gambler ignores 'parsimony' enjoying the power 'to amplify the text with multiple alternative outcomes, to weigh chances, to foresee and determine, to experience loss and gain, to *hope*, particularly against the odds'.[101] In the speculative game of reading that Riddell imagines, contradictory signals are disseminated in the text. As Percy slowly emerges as an alternative hero and possibly the safest bet for the reader – he wants nothing to do with adulteration or speculation and admires the purity of Olivine – Lawrence's risk-taking propensities attract increasing emotional attention and forcefully drive the plot forward into the overlapping terrains of adultery and speculation. Lawrence may not win the race for wealth, but his dashing style of racing keeps the thrills coming till the very end.

In the account of Lawrence's speculations much emphasis falls on his desire to find new outlets for the release of his productive energies, constrained by what he considers unfair partnership arrangements: 'I will never hereafter be at the beck and call of Mr. Sondes . . . There is not a thing I do pleases him. I never knew the meaning of the word slavery till I became a partner'.[102] Like his adulterous desires, these energies chafe against restrictions and the 'slavery' of dependent work. More to the point, Lawrence stands for progress and innovation in business against the conservative tendencies of his senior partner: 'unfortunately the character of our trade is changing . . . the other sugar houses are shooting past us like express trains' he complains to Percy, 'imagine the door being shut on every new process; fancy that I dare not try an experiment at my own expenses'.[103] The spirit of capitalism, which Lawrence embodies since his first appearance in the City, retains positive connotations in this as in many other novels by Riddell, even though *The Race for Wealth* focuses on shady and dubious enterprises. The chapters Riddell introduces in the second part of the novel, detailing how Lawrence and Percy join forces to try and keep the sugar refinery from collapsing under the pressure of competition, are a paean to that spirit. When Sondes undermines the chances of success by withdrawing twenty thousand pounds to purchase a property in the country, Lawrence embarks upon a speculative frenzy which appears as the natural development of his indomitable capitalist spirit, in an excess of passion not condoned in the story, but hard to distinguish from the energies he has so far devoted to bettering the prospects of both Distaff Yard and the refinery: 'and as a spirited horse released from control gallops madly on over every obstacle, so in those days Lawrence ran a course of speculation through which nothing but his own clear intellect, his indomitable perseverance, and his amazing good fortune could have carried him safely'.[104]

The celebration of individual force and freedom in the characterisation of Lawrence blurs the distinction between good and bad passions. If the 'cholera' of Limited Liability is a collective disease with negative social implications, Lawrence's speculative tendencies are the expression of a vital force intrinsic to the model of *homo economicus* Riddell endorses in this novel. In the 'kaleidoscope of finance' as Alex Preda defines the 'public positive discourse on markets and speculation' that developed after the 1850s, speculation is both a 'civilizing factor' and an 'untamed natural force':

> While the civilizing side is characterized by hard work, attention, observation – all qualities intrinsic to speculation as a privileged form of knowledge – the wild, adventurous side means taking risks, developing emotions, being caught in the ardour of the game as a means of escaping the boredom and dullness of ordinary life.[105]

Being caught in the ardour of the game: Riddell's novel captures quite well this cultural connotation of the speculative game. The creativity of the inventor or innovator, which ensures the forward progress of his 'regular trade', exists on the same symbolic continuum as the spirit of adventure of the speculator or the gambler. 'The fact is', wrote Edwin Freedly in 1852, 'there is a certain quantum of the spirit of wild, and eager, and hazardous adventure ever in the community, and it *will* seek exercise and gratification in some form or another'.[106] Riddell's novel configures financial speculation as the natural outcome of Lawrence's restlessness, hopes for upward mobility and sheer force of will – his disregard for moderation (in business as in love) is what keeps the race going.

A similar disregard, a tendency towards excess, is inscribed in the very style of Riddell's prose: amplified semi-philosophical interpolations at the beginning of nearly each instalment; prolonged dialogues that occupy entire chapters; frequent self-referential observations that yank the reader away from the comforts of mimesis; descriptions and scenes that develop elaborate bubbles of metaphors, like the metaphor of the muslin dress 'with the starch out' employed (over several paragraphs and in association with other metaphors) to convey the feeling of depletion experienced the morning after a large party; a linguistic exuberance in the use of different verbal registers, from Mrs Perkins's rambling sentences to Percy's upper-class mannerisms. In other words, the centrifugal tendency of the novel form is gladly seconded in *The Race for Wealth*, as the impulse towards scene takes over, time and again, complicating or adulterating the straight chronological and moral trajectory of the story.

In this chapter I have deliberately focused attention on these lateral excesses, as it were, to clarify how and to what extent Riddell invests imaginatively in the impure, showing a willingness to push the limits of conventional moral standards even as the story works to confirm them. This is not a novel that strikes the indignant note, although adulteration and adultery were both topical issues in the 1860s which inspired much public outcry. Riddell's reworking of these issues in her fiction is further evidence of the singularity of her vision. The novel takes unresolved ambivalence as its starting point, redefining the sphere of business as intrinsically flawed or inconsistent, framed on the one hand by dishonest but not illegal practices and on the other by a sincere commitment to the virtue of hard work and individual exertion, reconfirmed as the motor of upward mobility. The tolerated contamination of right and wrong prevailing in the market does not inspire a didactic tale of reform or repentance hinging on the ideal purity of the domestic sphere. In the story of ambition that Riddell narrates domesticity is not safe from contagion. However, her reading of both commercial and domestic frauds is less anxious than inquisitive. Probing moral limits: this is what the novel does. This probing is achieved in the realm of affect rather than plot; it is a question of how things are described, as opposed to what narrative destiny prescribes. The attraction of the impure, detectable in the style of telling as well as in the choice of subject matter, works against the certainties of melodramatic binaries, producing a different sort of realism from the one tested in *George Geith* to much public acclaim. Risking the displeasure of her readers, Riddell turns away from the nature idyll, from the balancing of contrasts and from the image of market life as a triumph of rationality. *The Race for Wealth* is not a more honest rendering of the realities of capitalist competition; but it is a more intrepid and speculative rewriting of the narrative of modernity.

Notes

1   William Tinsley, *Random Recollections of an Old Publisher* (London: Simpkin, Marshall, Hamilton, Kent & Co., 1900) vol. 1, p. 98.
2   'Belles Lettres', *The Westminster Review* 30, no. 2 (October 1866), p. 526.
3   'The Race for Wealth', *The Saturday Review* 22, no. 567 (8 September 1866), p. 307.
4   The *Saturday Review* observed: 'there are scenes and characters in this book which are neither playful nor humorous, though aiming at being both, but which are simply and nakedly vulgar' (Ibid., p. 307), while the *Westminster* questioned the excessive reliance on 'long descriptions' and the lack of the 'poetical feeling', found in generous doses in *George Geith*, which had made Riddell 'stand out from the herd of novelists' ('Belles Lettres', p. 526). In both cases, the noticeable differences between this novel and *George Geith* baffled the reviewers who were still inclined to give Riddell credit (comparing her to George Eliot, for instance) but were also disconcerted by what appeared as a radical departure from a narrative style that had proved so successful.
5   'The Race for Wealth', *The Morning Post*, 14 September 1866, p. 3.
6   Charlotte Riddell, *The Race for Wealth* (Leipzig: Bernard Tauchnitz, 1866) vol. 1, p. 107.
7   Ibid., p. 7.
8   Ibid., pp. 9–10.
9   Ibid., p. 11.
10   Carlisle, p. 17.
11   Ibid., p. 14.
12   David Trotter, *Cooking with Mud: The Idea of Mess in Nineteenth-Century Art and Fiction* (Oxford: Oxford University Press, 2000), p. 115.
13   Ibid., p. 79.
14   In the fifth volume of *Modern Painters* (1860), Ruskin expatiates on Turner's 'tolerations and affections' for images of 'dinginess, smoke, soot, dust': 'to the very close of life, Turner could endure ugliness which no one else, of the same sensibility, would have borne with for an instant. Dead Brick walls, blank square windows, old clothes, market-womanly types of humanity – anything fishy and muddy, like Billingsgate or Hungerford Market, had great attraction for him . . . you will find these tolerations and affections guiding or sustaining him to the last hour of his life; the notablest of such being that of dirt. No Venetian ever draws anything foul; but Turner devoted picture after picture to the illustrations of effects of dinginess, smoke, soot, dust, and dusty texture', see John Ruskin, *Modern Painters*, 1860, (London: Smith, Elders and Co.: 1873), vol. 5, p. 293. Ruskin's willingness to find aesthetic and affective value in Turner's visions of dirt signals, according to Trotter, a paradigmatic shift in the way modern writers 'think *with* mess as well as *about* it' (Trotter, p. 8). In *The Race for Wealth*, thinking with mess is an integral part of Riddell's realist take on both adulteration and adultery.
15   Stern, p. 107.
16   'The Race for Wealth', *The Daily News*, 14 November 1866.
17   Moretti discusses unresolved dissonance with reference to Ibsen's works. Ibsen 'can look at bourgeois ambiguity without having to resolve it . . . What draws Ibsen to the grey area', Moretti adds, is that 'it reveals with absolute clarity the *unresolved dissonance of bourgeois life*. Dissonance, not conflict. Strident, unsettling . . . precisely because there are no alternatives', see Moretti, *The Bourgeois*, p. 178. Nor is Riddell's

novel centred on the conflict between the honest and the fraudulent bourgeois, but on a more ambiguous mix of deception and legality, which remains 'grey' throughout the story.

18 *Race for Wealth*, vol. 1, p. 240.
19 Hassall also wrote two books in which he exposed the pervasiveness of adulterating practices and provided instructions to help consumers detect gastronomic frauds, see Arthur Hill Hassall, *Food and Its Adulterations* (London: Longman, Brown, Green, Longmans, and Roberts, 1855) and *Adulterations Detected; or, Plain Instructions for the Discovery of Frauds in Food and Medicine*, 1857 (London: Longman, Brown, Green, Longmans, and Roberts, 1861).
20 [Henry Morley], 'Justice to Chicory', *Household Words* 6 (13 November 1852), p. 208.
21 'The Adulteration of Food', *The London Review* 13, no. 326 (29 September 1866), p. 342.
22 'Adulteration of Credit', *The Leader* 6, no. 287 (22 September 1855), p. 742.
23 'Adulteration, and its Remedy', *The Cornhill Magazine* 2, no. 7 (July 1867), p. 87.
24 'Adulteration of Food, Drinks, and Drugs', *British Quarterly Review* 23, no. 45 (January 1856), p. 288.
25 Searle, p. 91.
26 'Adulteration of Food and Drugs', *The Westminster Review* 35, no. 1 (January 1869), pp. 201–2.
27 See Searle, pp. 92–3.
28 According to the *Westminster Review*, the three years that elapsed between the publication of the report and the passing of the 1860 Act saw an actual increase in food frauds: 'the evidence collected by the Committee . . . proved in the interval quite a mine of useful information to adulterators, whose fraudulent resources had hitherto been unequal to their wishes', see 'Adulteration', *Westminster Review*, p. 193.
29 *Race for Wealth*, vol. 1, p. 58.
30 Ibid., pp. 27–8.
31 Ibid., p. 29.
32 Ibid., p. 28.
33 Ibid.
34 It is unclear when exactly the story is set, but internal evidence suggests that it takes place in the 1850s. There is an explicit mention of the Limited Liability Act of 1855 in the second volume, which allows speculators such as Lawrence to reap hefty but unstable profits. In the third chapter of the first volume, the narrator ironically states that 'Doubtless there is no such thing as adulteration now . . . but in the days when Mr. Perkins did business due east, matters were differently managed' (p. 28), thus suggesting that the events recounted are set before the 1860 Act. As Rebecca Stern writes, 'The principle of sampling and self-protection . . . accurately describes the only recourse most consumers had. There were no effective laws to regulate, discipline, or discourage food adulteration, and the attempts of the Parliamentary Select Committee to pass legislation indicate the larger legal climate' (pp. 101–2).
35 Hassall, *Adulteration Detected*, p. 22.
36 *Race for Wealth*, vol. 1, p. 57.
37 Mary Douglas, *Purity and Danger: An Analysis of Concepts of Pollution and Taboo*, 1966 (London: Routledge, 2001), p. 165.
38 *Race for Wealth*, vol. 1, p. 234.
39 *Race for Wealth*, vol.1, 122
40 Ibid., p. 242–43.
41 *Race for Wealth*, vol. 2, p. 12.
42 *Race for Wealth*, vol.1, p. 107.
43 *Race for Wealth*, vol. 2, p. 298.
44 Fredric Jameson, *The Antinomies of Realism* (London: Verso, 2013), p. 83. Jameson's reading of realism is genuinely dialectical. The storytelling function of novels forms

part of an opposition and 'must be defined against something else' which he terms 'the realm of affect' (p. 8): 'the regime of the past-present-future and of personal identities and destinies is at its outer limit the realm of the récit; while the impersonal conscious-ness of an eternal or existential present would at its outer limit govern pure scene, a showing that was altogether divorced and separated from telling and purified of it' (p. 25). Whereas récit presides over the emergence of realism, affect or the eternal present of scene gains visibility the more realism approaches its point of dissolution.

45   'The Race for Wealth', *Saturday*, p. 308.
46   'The Race for Wealth', *The Morning Post*, 14 September 1866; the article mentions the 'rage for the psychological' as a feature many novelists, not just Riddell, seemed to appreciate (p. 3).
47   *Race for Wealth*, vol. 1, p. 87.
48   Ibid., p. 187.
49   See Alfred Marshall, 'The Social Possibilities of Economic Chivalry', *The Economic Journal* 17, (March 1907), pp. 7–29. Marshall refers nostalgically to 'the bracing fresh air which a strong man, with a chivalrous yearning for leadership draws into his lungs when he sets out on a business experiment at his own risk' (p. 17). Writing at a time when corporate capitalism was on the rise, Marshall looks back at a strong model of economic individuality trying to revive its symbolic potency by associating it with the ideal of chivalry.
50   *Race for Wealth*, vol. 1, p. 58.
51   Ibid., p. 85.
52   Ibid., p. 90.
53   Ibid.
54   Ibid., p. 86.
55   Ibid., p. 92.
56   Ibid., p. 93.
57   Ibid., p. 112.
58   Ibid., p. 106.
59   Ibid., p. 134.
60   As Kent Puckett remarks in *Bad Form: Social Mistakes and the Nineteenth-Century Novel* (Oxford: Oxford University Press, 2008), the representation of 'bad form' and social mistakes is inextricably linked with formal literary features: '"Bad form" will thus both name a particular kind of mistake and refer to the fact that that mistake's appearance tends to coincide with moments where the social authority and the formal coherence of the nineteenth-century novel (thought of in relation to characters, plot, and narration) are paradoxically and sometimes elaborately secured' (p. 16). Bad form is an index of the character's distance from rules of etiquette; however, as Puckett argues, 'the vulgarity of the thing appears as legible not when it stands simply opposed to style or elegance. Rather, it is the messy, sumptuous mix of the two that makes bad form speak' (p. 17).
61   *Race for Wealth*, vol. 1, pp. 337–8
62   Douglas, p. 41.
63   *Race for Wealth*, vol. 1, p. 158
64   As Mary Douglas states, dirt 'is never a unique, isolated event. Where there is dirt there is system. Dirt is the by-product of a systematic ordering and classification of matter, in so far as ordering involves rejecting inappropriate elements' (p. 36). In *The Race for Wealth*, Ada's inappropriateness always emerges in relation to Lawrence's ideas of order, style and elegance. Her messiness seems to reinforce the desirability of order.
65   *Race for Wealth*, vol. 1, p. 335.
66   *Race for Wealth*, vol. 2, p. 48.
67   *Race for Wealth*, vol. 1, p. 331.
68   Ibid., p. 64.

69   Ibid., p. 296.
70   Ibid., p. 168.
71   Ibid., p. 48.
72   Ibid.
73   Ibid., p. 49.
74   Ibid., pp. 50–51.
75   Whelan, p. 7.
76   *Race for Wealth*, vol. 1, p. 105.
77   Ibid., p. 129.
78   Ibid., pp. 130–31.
79   Kelly Hager, *Dickens and the Rise of Divorce: The Failed-Marriage Plot and the Novel Tradition* (Farnham: Ashgate, 2010), p. 23.
80   *Race for Wealth*, vol. 2, p. 43.
81   Ibid., p. 42 and p. 54.
82   Ibid., p. 54.
83   Ibid., pp. 74–5.
84   Ibid., p. 76.
85   As Poovey explains, the 'Matrimonial Causes Act that Parliament adopted in 1857 did not disturb either women's relation to property or the sexual double standard'; the Act 'made significant contributions to legal reform . . . Nevertheless it did not actually remedy the anomalies it set out to address', see Mary Poovey, *Uneven Developments: the Ideological Work of Gender in Mid-Victorian England* (Chicago: The University of Chicago Press, 1988), p. 84 and p. 85.
86   *Race for Wealth*, vol. 2, p. 294.
87   Ibid., p. 306.
88   It is uncertain whether this section of the story is set after the passage of the 1857 Divorce Act, as the text provides no clear indication on this score. Unlike the Limited Liability Act, the Matrimonial Causes Act is not explicitly mentioned. Riddell's emphasis on the indissolubility of marital bonds suggests that in the story-world divorce does not appear as a solution.
89   Ibid., p. 88.
90   Ibid., p. 83 and p. 85.
91   John Stuart Mill, 'On Liberty', 1859, in *On Liberty and other Writings* (Cambridge: Cambridge University Press, 1989), p. 8.
92   *Race for Wealth*, vol. 2, p. 127.
93   Ibid., p. 123.
94   Ibid., p. 298–9.
95   Ibid., p. 319.
96   'Panic in the City', *The Saturday Review*, 12 May 1866, p. 547. For an interesting discussion of popular responses to the commercial crisis of 1866, see James Taylor's books, *Creating Capitalism: Joint-Stock Enterprise in British Politic and Culture, 1800–1870* (Woodbridge: The Boydell Press, 2006), pp. 176–209 and *Boardroom Scandals: The Criminalisation of Company Fraud in Nineteenth-Century England* (Oxford: Oxford University Press, 2013), pp. 140–51. In 1865 Overend, Gurney, and Co. had been converted into a limited company 'but its heavy liabilities had been deliberately concealed from the investing public by the company's new directors'; as a result of its collapse and the subsequent crisis, 'the workings of the corporate economy were subjected to intense public scrutiny, (Taylor, *Creating*, p. 177). See also Kynaston for a detailed historical account of the crash of the 'corner house' (pp. 235–47), and Poovey, *Genres*, pp. 248–54.
97   *Race for Wealth*, vol. 2, p. 55.
98   Ibid., p. 176.
99   Ibid., p. 173.

100 Beer, p. 284.
101 Beer, p. 279.
102 *Race for Wealth*, vol. 2, p. 93.
103 Ibid., p. 208.
104 Ibid., p. 277.
105 Alex Preda, *Framing Finance: The Boundaries of Markets and Modern Capitalism* (Chicago: The University of Chicago press, 2009), p. 179.
106 Freedly, p. 153.

7   A Liberal Education
Austin Friars

It really is of importance not only what men do, but what manner of men they are that do it.

John Stuart Mill, *On Liberty*, 1859

She had sense enough to know it is impossible for any one to be man and woman too.

Charlotte Riddell, *Austin Friars*, 1870

In December 1867, Charlotte Riddell succeeded Anna Maria Hall as editor of the *St. James's Magazine* – a literary monthly launched in 1861 with the intention of promoting 'the Interests of the Home, the Refinements of Life, and the Amusement and Information of all Classes', as Maria Hall announced in the first issue.[1] A rival of the *Cornhill*, the magazine featured articles on a variety of topics (from 'Artificial Illumination' to 'Historical Misrepresentations') as well as serial fiction, travel writing and poetry.[2] When Riddell undertook its editorship, the *St. James* had 'gradually declined below the average of its numerous competitors' or so the *Sporting Gazette* claimed: to resuscitate this publication from its 'moribund condition' was Riddell's specific task. Reviewing the first two issues of the new series in 1868, the *Sporting Gazette* congratulated the editor on the successful performance of her 'duties of resuscitation', which had restored the magazine to 'a place of honour among its contemporaries'.[3] In a more analytical piece published in the *Morning Post*, Riddell's style of editorship was praised for its 'agreeable blending of the entertaining and the instructive'. In particular, the new focus on politics – with articles discussing the value of local self-government, county politics and Disraeli's premiership – was appreciated as a welcome innovation, likely to 'tempt a pleasant list of new subscribers'.[4] In a brief note, even *Punch* offered its 'courteous salutation' to the new editor, 'a lady who has just stepped into the editorial arena, gracefully and without *fanfaron*, as might be expected from the author of *George Geith*'; wishing her good luck, the writer did not fail to notice (with characteristic irony) the political tenor of the publication: 'We further compliment Mrs. Riddell on going in, as becomes a woman, for good old Toryism'.[5]

Judging from these contemporary responses, the new interest in politics played a significant role in Riddell's successful revamping of the *St. James*. The magazine continued to publish fiction, poetry, travel writing and entertaining articles on a variety of themes, but the political questions of the time received an increased share of attention. Under her editorship two new series were introduced – 'Cabinet Photographs' (1869–1870) and 'Political Summary of the Month' (1869) – arguably intended to satisfy the demand for discussion of pressing political issues.[6] It is worth recalling that Riddell's seven-year editorship coincided with Gladstone's ministry of 1868–1874, a particularly exuberant phase in the political life of the nation in which the pace of legislation accelerated considerably and a number of historically significant Acts were passed that affected the domains of education, the civil service, the army and trade unions, amongst others.[7] Even if politics, unlike economics, did not capture the imagination of the City novelist, in her capacity as editor Riddell quite shrewdly secured the contribution of writers who could address controversial political matters. In addition to the two new series mentioned above, the *St. James* featured articles on such topical issues as 'The Irish Land Bill' (October 1869), the reformed House of Commons ('The Birthday of a New Era', October 1868); the 'University Reform' (April 1868); the question of education ('The Educational Question in Bengal', October 1871); Scottish liberalism ('A "Liberal Nation"', October 1868); and 'Womanhood Suffrage' (April 1868). Mainly conservative in outlook, these and other contributions responded to the liberalising political climate of the time providing readers with timely discussions of parliamentary life and political debates.

Liberalism, as a political and cultural project, was an intensely interesting object of critical scrutiny for some of the collaborators Riddell employed. To what extent she personally shared this interest is difficult to say, but the novel she published soon after starting her term as editor, *Austin Friars* (1869–1870), bears witness to the pervasive influence of the 'multiform and sometimes contradictory web of ideas labelled "liberalism"'.[8] While all Riddell's novels resonate with concepts and beliefs associated with classical economic liberalism (the centrality of *homo economicus*, the emphasis on individual energy and industry, the philosophy of self-reliance), *Austin Friars* more specifically engages with the procedures of liberalisation and the pedagogy of self-cultivation: 'There are some people of whom it has been said', observes the narrator, 'that to know them is a liberal education'.[9] Proffering her own version of what a 'liberal education' does and how it is fostered, Riddell writes a story of commerce that revolves around three 'embodiments' of liberalism: the liberal fallen woman, the liberalised male subject, and the liberal intersubjectivity of the commercial sphere. I do not use the word 'embodiment' to refer to specific material practices in tension with liberalism's many abstractions, as Elaine Hadley does in her account of Victorian political liberalism and the forms of 'abstract embodiments' through which it was 'lived'.[10] I use it in a less specific sense to signify the fictional instantiations of liberal ideas or their incorporation, at various levels, within the story world. In the 'golden age of liberal reform',[11] Riddell turned her attention to the political scene, in her role as editor, and to the rhetoric of cultivation, the 'techniques of liberal individuation',[12] in the fiction she wrote. As I argue in this chapter, *Austin Friars* is a reformed City novel: it extends the textual franchise to the representation of female liberal agency (though not in triumphant terms); it focuses on the process of self-development that produces the ideal citizen, the City man in this case, endowed with a capaciousness of vision, and it describes in meticulous detail how in the commercial sphere transcending self-interest might yield efficient results.

In Riddell's 1860s novels, women are not directly involved in the running of business ventures; only in the 1870s – with *Austin Friars, Mortomley's Estate* (1874) and the unusually humorous *Frank Sinclair's Wife* (1874) – is the hyper-masculine City imagined as a terrain where women attempt to claim their right to trade. Though their endeavours are limited in time and scope, motivated by extreme circumstances, and in one case lampooned, the presence of women in business is nonetheless a noteworthy innovation in Riddell's canon, particularly poignant in *Mortomley's Estate*, a bankruptcy novel in which the author reworks the traumatic experience of the liquidation of her husband's business. What aligns *Austin Friars* with the narrative of mid-Victorian liberalism is the primacy of liberal education as a 'regulative' ideal. David Thomas distinguishes between a 'substantive' and a 'regulative conception of liberal agency': in the latter the 'promise of reflective agency much more than its realization and static maintenance' is emphasised.[13] In *Austin Friars*, this promise is apparent in Luke Ross, the City man who learns how to think along liberal lines: his inner self-development is more significant than the process of wealth accumulation he pursues. But there is a particular twist added to this scenario: Luke's liberal education is sparked and facilitated by his encounter with (and love for) 'a woman who has sinned',[14] an adulteress, who also assumes a business identity. The novel explores the consequences of her choices and the beneficial effects of Luke's increased self-reflectivity on both affective and commercial matters, projecting a liberal vision of the small business community represented in the text.

Some elements in Riddell's fictional reworking of liberal ideals jarred against the aesthetic and moral values habitually held by Victorian reviewers. The *Saturday Review* declared *Austin Friars* 'an immoral book' berating its 'curious confusion of moral principles and almost total absence of moral impulses'.[15] In a similar vein, the *Athenaeum* questioned the 'moral' of the story 'if it may so be called' – a moral hinging 'on the mistaken notion that there is too much decency in the world at present, or at least that being strait-laced is the crying evil of the age'.[16] Even for the critic of the *Graphic*, a periodical usually benevolent towards Riddell's publications, *Austin Friars* played a tad too loosely with the 'ethics of fiction'.[17] The novel appeared misaligned with expectations regarding the boundaries of realism – for its overload of technical financial knowledge – and too liberal in the representation of exceptional individuals rising above ordinariness and mediocrity, especially when the individual in question was, as the *Saturday Review* put it, 'an ambiguous woman dressed in sad-coloured garments and living in the office' or a City man who 'will run the risk of ruining himself to accommodate a lying, shifty scoundrel'.[18]

In this chapter, I analyse the text bearing in mind that, as Amanda Anderson, Elaine Hadley, David Wayne Thomas and other scholars have recently argued, 'any attempt to reappraise the Victorians requires a serious look at the liberal project'.[19] Economic liberalism is the discourse and ideology most openly reimagined in Riddell's business novels. With *Austin Friars*, self-education and cultivation become more prominent, alongside a new focus on women's liberal agency as expressed in the business world. Almost inevitably, one could argue, Riddell faces the contradictions of the liberal project – 'it is impossible for anyone to be man and woman too' she writes – while also sustaining the belief in a 'liberal vision of many-sidedness'[20] or, in her own phraseology, in a 'more extended and comprehensive view of life'.[21] There is nothing particularly exceptional in this embracing of critical distance; it is fairly typical of the Victorian novel, Hadley contends, to produce 'a form of social disinterestedness that sanctions many opinions, and thus many characters'.[22] What perhaps deserves attention is how Riddell's investment in the idea of liberal cultivation ends up producing an 'immoral' tale, a story deemed out of the ordinary by Victorian critics but for all the wrong reasons.

Yorke's Business Plan

That modernity wears a feminine garb in *Austin Friars* is apparent in the novel's incipit. To describe the rapid pace of change in the locality selected for this story (Scott's yard), Riddell reverts to the image of trains sweeping in and out of the new Canon Street Terminus:

> Behold the locality! Where the great City station and the great City hotel now are, there stood formerly a City bank and a City insurance company. Peace be to their memories! Over their remains the trains sweep grandly in and out as a great lady of the olden time swept, in her magnificent selfishness, over all inferior feelings, loves, passions, regrets.[23]

If trains are an unoriginal signifier of progress, their association with the 'magnificent selfishness' of a 'great lady' signals a vision of modernity very much alert to female self-interest. The novelty of the present is condensed in the figure of a woman who stands aloof, wrapped up in her own glorious individualism. The story that unfolds from this imaginative premise appropriately features a heroine with an androgynous name, Yorke, who asserts her right to the 'liberty of tastes and pursuits' which, in Mill's formulation, coincides with the liberty 'of framing the plan of our life to suit our own character'.[24]

When the novel opens, Yorke has already chosen to alter the conventional social destiny in store for her by abandoning her husband and a marriage she does not want. She moves to the City, like George Geith, Alan Ruthven and other business heroes before her, and works alongside her lover, Austin Friars, in the unspecified business venture they have launched, a venture supported by the money (1,000 pounds) Yorke has inherited from her former employer. This narrative 'situation', as the reviewer of the *Graphic* stated, 'is strong, even for a novel of the period'.[25]

What makes it even more startling is the calculated untruth the narrator tells in the first chapter, leading readers to assume that Yorke and Austin are happily married – 'they had never grown indifferent, never fallen into the state of conjugal rudeness which makes a woman less courteous to her husband than she would be to a guest'[26] – only to uncover, a few pages later, the *more uxorio* reality behind the façade of demure domesticity. Riddell arranges the disclosure of details about Yorke's past to maximise the surprise effect: readers discover Yorke's 'fall into sin' when Austin declares his intention of marrying Mary Monteith, the daughter of a rich merchant who has agreed to take on Austin as a partner. To this revelation, which throws Yorke into the uncomfortable position of the jilted woman, corresponds an immediate reaction that reverses the passivity of desertion. Yorke may be a sinful woman and the victim of circumstances, but she is determined to frame the plan of her life: 'She was a lonely woman thrown upon her resources at a moment's notice, and not an instant, she felt, must be lost in forming her future plans'.[27]

As Amanda Anderson has argued, the 'rhetoric of fallenness' in mid-Victorian culture was predicated on two recurring features: the 'attenuated autonomy and fractured identity of the fallen figure'.[28] The idea of fallenness was primarily defined in opposition not only to feminine purity but also to normative masculinity or more specifically 'to a masculine ideal of rational control and purposive action'.[29] Riddell's interpretation of the fallen woman initially acknowledges the lack of self-control and self-consistency that was habitually associated with the atrophied selfhood of 'lost' female characters, ensnared by their own uncontrollable impulses and desires. Yorke's life, the narrator explains, 'was now but a tangled, twisted skein the threads of which might never more be separated and made smooth – a knotted confused mass of contradictory feelings, impulses, sins, sorrows, virtues – strands of different colours mingling and intermingling – memories, regrets, fears, mixed up together, beyond the possibility of extrication'.[30] But the equation between fallenness and lack of coherence is short-lived; it is instantly contradicted by Yorke's decided deviation in the direction of rational planning, self-control and economic agency:

Pride, indignation, wounded affection, and a perfect horror of dependence, all stimulated her desire to strike out some course which she might at once follow. Project after project she looked at and rejected; and it was only when the first grey of morning appeared in the sky that a sudden idea occurred to her, which grew into shape, and formed itself into a more practicable plan the longer she looked at it.[31]

What Yorke devises is more specifically a business plan: with Austin gone, she intends to carry on the business herself, with the help of Luke Ross, 'book-keeper in a third-rate City house'.[32] The scene in which she communicates her intentions to Luke reads like a full-blown liberal fantasy in which the fallen figure is metamorphosed into a 'character', a liberal subject defined by her rationality, self-interest and self-sufficient moral consciousness.[33] This metamorphosis entails a degree of gender crossing or the transition to a form of selfhood conventionally understood as masculine. As Yorke explains to her bewildered interlocutor:

> Do you think me a perfect idiot? Do you not know that the sort of education I have had for years has made me feel like a man, judge like a man? Do you imagine I am going to be either dependent upon the Monteiths for my daily bread, or satisfied with the thirty-five or forty pounds a year I should get from my thousand pounds if I invested it safely?[34]

That Yorke's desire for self-assertion and independence should take a commercial shape is not surprising considering Riddell's preference for business. What need remarking, however, are the liberal underpinnings of this configuration. For John Stuart Mill, 'great energies guided by vigorous reason' are mostly channelled in the arena of business: 'There is now scarcely any outlet for energy in this country except business', he writes, 'The energy expended in this may still be regarded as considerable'.[35] Yorke's entrepreneurial energies appear even more pronounced and daring because they stand in sharp contrast with Luke's timid and excessively prudent hesitations: 'vexed at his male stupidity, which failed . . . to grasp the full brilliancy of her plan',[36] Yorke appeals to his latent desire to rise, offering him a better job than the one he holds and the prospect of higher returns. It is worth quoting the passage at some length, as it provides one rare instance, in the annals of Victorian fiction, of a fallen woman redeemed not by sympathy or compassion for her victimhood, but by a vigorous assumption of liberal subjectivity and economic rationality:

> She proceeded to remark that although the certain income the business could at first afford might be small, yet that it would be larger than the salary he, Mr.Ross, was receiving from Messrs Hurward & Gaskarth. She proposed, she went on to explain, that a portion of the £1000 should be mentally devoted to salaries, rent and so forth. She enlarged upon the fact that, no matter how long he remained with Messrs Hurward & Gaskarth, or how hard he worked for them, he could only hope to better his position a little; whereas if this venture proved successful, he might ultimately make a large fortune. She grew eloquent in advocacy of her plan, for she had set her heart on carrying out the scheme.[37]

In this scene, Yorke embodies the spirit of entrepreneurial, risk-taking capitalism more convincingly than the prudent City man to whom she lays out her plan. She also proves capable of mastering the rigorous logic of argumentative rhetoric; 'the power of expressing her ideas forcibly and persuasively'[38] is conveyed through the anaphoric structure of this paragraph in which the grammatical subject stands out at the beginning of each sentence: she proceeded, she proposed, she grew eloquent, overwhelming her interlocutor with the force of her arguments – 'Yet still he remained silent'.[39] Wielding such power of speech, Riddell's liberal fallen woman is anything but a fractured self and her agency, rather than attenuated, appears linked directly to both the assertion of economic self-interest and the affirmation of rationality. It is a liberal utopia, an optimistic take on the possibilities of character redemption or reform open not just to women, but to those among them who have been in the thrall of uncontrollable feelings, impulses, regrets, fears and sins 'beyond the possibility of extrication'.[40] As Amanda Anderson argues, 'Victorian fallenness served as a charged cultural site for some of the most acute anxieties about agency, character and reform in mid-century Britain'.[41] In Dickens's novels, for instance, fallenness typically emblematises a form of determinism, of subjection to larger social and cultural forces that lacks any transformative capacity. The women writers Anderson considers, Elizabeth Gaskell and Elizabeth Barrett Browning, revise the rhetoric of fallenness in less deterministic terms: Aurora Leigh, unlike David Copperfield, identifies herself with not against the fallen woman. In Riddell's revision, the fallen figure becomes the agent of her own reform, which is configured as a movement towards increased autonomy (financial and moral), accentuated purpose and self-development: Yorke has quickly learned the art of performing masculine roles and appropriating the liberal notion of 'character' in opposition to which the otherness of the fallen was conceptualised. So successful is this appropriation that Yorke's 'character' can be detected, as the narrator points out, 'even in the sweeping sound of her dress'.[42] Furthermore, her business plan proves effective, at least for a while: 'Yorke had been right', Luke has to concede, 'there was a business, and a good one, to be made after the manner in which she suggested'.[43]

In the first ten chapters of *Austin Friars*, the basic narrative outline of Riddell's City novels appears altered or reformed. First of all, the aspirational discourse of business and self-reliance is transposed onto a female character who rejects dependence and passivity to pursue what Luke defines as her 'mad desire for self-assertion';[44] secondly, the eponymous hero, Austin, choses marriage as a shortcut to wealth accumulation, contravening the fundamental belief in the virtue of hard work and industriousness that had characterised his predecessors' *Weltanshaaung*; finally, the competing co-protagonist, Luke Ross, 'a prosaic commonplace creature',[45] hardly qualifies for the role of proud business hero, forward-looking, inventive and ambitious, celebrated in Riddell's previous novels. The City is still a land of opportunities, but male characters seem now poorly equipped to take advantage of them. As regards the private sphere, adultery is still on the agenda and in a more prominent position; the portrait of the relationship between Austin and Yorke, as Nancy Henry remarks, 'is daring for its sexual frankness'.[46] Alternative domestic arrangements have become a fact of modern life and they are presented as such by a narrator who is little inclined to question their irregularity. The adulteress is also the initiator of the business plot, which hinges on her decision to claim the right to trade: 'what is to prevent the business being carried on by Y. Friars, as well as it was by A. Friars?'.[47] In the short space of a few chapters, Riddell condenses the crossing of many boundaries, creating a type of narrative disorder that calls for some resolution, some symbolic readjustment of formal borders.

Self-Cultivation in the City

Austin Friars begins as a relatively progressive narrative in which both 'home' and 'business,' the two interlocked spheres of action in Riddell's novels, have acquired more malleable contours and female economic individualism has been pushed to the fore, while the masculine contingent shows unequivocal signs of exhaustion. Austin's decision to marry a rich merchant's daughter is rightly decoded by Yorke as one such sign ('I now understand you were waiting for some one to bring you the fortune you ought to have made yourself');[48] Luke Ross, on the other hand, though hard-working and honest, is hampered by an excess of lower-middle-class 'mediocrity' and respectability which Riddell presents as the outcome of an 'orthodox' life devoid of cultivation and higher refinement:

> For a home less calculated to develop the higher part of a man's nature, more likely to dwarf and cramp his mind, it would be difficult to conceive. The terribly monotonous, orthodox existence; the day filled with small interests; the evening spent in listening to paltry gossip and petty talk; the life, into the consciousness of which there entered the conception of nothing great or grand, of nothing tragic or inexpressibly pitiful; which bounded the horizon of existence with the view obtainable from its own poor windows; which had no cognisance of great oceans, of the desert plains, of the lofty mountain peaks, of the soft green valleys; which understood nothing, not even the vastness of its own mediocrity – what could all this do for a man save render him a Pharisee, save make him pin his faith to accurate figures, and punctual attendance at office six days in the week, and to best clothes and morning and evening service on the Sabbath?[49]

In this description, there is a reverberation of Mill's social diagnosis: 'the general tendency of things throughout the world', he states, 'is to render mediocrity the ascendant power among mankind'.[50] Luke Ross is one of those 'individuals lost in the crowd' who quietly succumb to what Mill calls the 'despotism of custom'.[51] Small interests, petty talks, restricted vistas and a general atmosphere of oppressive domesticity render Luke Ross quite atypical in the pantheon of Riddell's City heroes. Like George Geith, Luke is an accountant or book-keeper by profession, but his conformity to the limited horizons of 'self-satisfied commonness'[52] casts a long shadow even on the bourgeois values (prudence, punctuality, regularity, industriousness) that Riddell had glamorised in her portrait of George's capitalist energies. Whereas his style of bookkeeping was compared to intrepid mountaineering, Luke's dealing with 'accurate figures' is the symptom of a conformity to routine and 'collective mediocrity'[53] that fails to pass the test of liberal heroism. It is Yorke's eccentric, unorthodox existence and 'wild' schemes, not Luke's prudence, that best represent the 'progressive principle' or the 'spirit of liberty' invoked by Mill as 'antagonistic to the sway of Custom'.[54]

The stumbling block in this symbolic reallocation of individuality, this gendering of liberty that Riddell so openly advances in the first chapters of her novel is, of course, gender itself: how plausible would it have been, in the early 1870s, to narrate the story of a woman and an adulteress who enters the business arena, 'goes down where men wage fierce war together',[55] and carves her way to position and fortune, sustained by her originality and genius? If the novel welcomes the ideology of liberalism, it also stumbles upon its abstractions, which, as Hadley writes, 'blithely erase particular physical and socialized bodies – women, the poor, the disabled'.[56] No sooner does Yorke try to implement her business plan, than she realises that 'it is impossible for any one to be man and woman too'.[57] The way out of this impasse consists in redirecting the narrative of liberalism: *Austin Friars* turns out to be a novel about the 'liberal education' not of women but of men and of men of business in particular. After the initial chapters, Yorke becomes gradually more disengaged from business interests and economic life, while what she stands for – the spirit of liberty, the ethos of tolerant judgment, self-cultivation – survive in the abstract form of inspirational principles that guide Luke's liberal self-development. 'There are some people', the narrator observes, 'of whom it has been said that to know them is a liberal education'.[58] Yorke is one of those people: the encounter with this unconventional woman transforms Luke into a proper 'character', endowed with a wider capacity for self-reflective agency and a finer appreciation of 'the blessedness of a life in which mind takes precedence of mere matter'.[59] Riddell insists more than once on this ideal of a liberal education transmitted through love and facilitated by contact with a woman repeatedly connoted as 'free':[60] 'Already Luke Ross was scarcely the same man he had been . . . already standing by the river's edge, that liberal education, previously mentioned, had begun – begun in a different sense than that of making him merely discontented – it had commenced to enlarge his mind, to extend his sympathies, to teach him a wider charity, a more tolerant religion'.[61] The story of Yorke as businesswoman, the potential tale of her professional or vocational trajectory, remains untold in the novel; in this respect she is rendered peripheral. But it is noteworthy that the story Riddell narrates instead focuses on the shaping of a liberal subjectivity (Luke's and arguably the reader's) that flourishes by being in close proximity with the strangeness and otherness of a woman 'who has sinned' and remains proudly independent. It is her example that inspires in Luke the attitude of cultivated detachment so dear to liberal thinking:

It is not from any mental valley, from any sequestered nook, however safe, that a human being can take an extended and comprehensive view of life; rather he must, if he would behold eternal truth, mount where he can see not merely the poor personal world which has hitherto confined his view, but the lives lived, the sorrows endured, the temptations resisted by other men and women – brothers and sisters of his own, in the eye of God, though he has never hitherto acknowledged the relationship. That it should have come to this! With an amazed surprise, Luke Ross felt, as he walked home to Homerton, that the old landmarks of his faith had been swept away, and that strange waters were rushing in over the arid land formerly his sole possession, to nourish, to beautify, and clothe with gladness and with verdure.[62]

The 'expanded and comprehensive view of life' recommended in this passage, predicated on distance from the partiality of one's own position ('the poor personal world'), is to a certain extent the philosophy of this novel. Luke's progress from narrow-minded conformism to a broader appreciation of 'many-sidedness' provides the central pedagogical trajectory of the narrative.[63] Significantly, however, his advancement towards increased liberal agency and cultivation corresponds to Yorke's inverse movement towards decreased autonomy: as the story unfolds, Yorke is gradually removed from the City scene and returned to her husband, while the restitution of the thousand pounds which Austin owes her catalyses the attention of the small commercial community represented in the text. By shifting attention from Yorke's liberal claims to Luke's inner self-development, Riddell anchors the narrative to a more stable set of meanings: the progress of Luke, both in the private sphere (his relationship with Yorke) and in the public world of commerce, is undoubtedly more conceivable than Yorke's potential ventures as a trader into the rough land of London business. Furthermore, Yorke's regress to a position of marginality is accompanied by the insisted representation of 'tortured moments of self-reading',[64] moments in which her initial bold determination is re-read as the infelicitous result of impulsive action: 'Bitterly enough now memory reminded her that first and last she had acted on impulse, and that her impulses had caused the unhappiness of everyone with whom she came into contact'.[65] In the novel, we get a glimpse of the alternative stories that commercial modernity could potentially license, but Riddell's assessment of the promises of liberalism is quite sober: as the intertwined but opposite trajectories of Luke and Yorke reveal, liberal agency remains the prerogative of the male subject though forcefully claimed, at the commencement of the novel, as a possible option for the female denizens of the City who, like Riddell herself, command a fairly good knowledge of business practices.

'Those Little Bills'

If Yorke does not quite develop into the business heroine she could have become, her money plays no minor role in cementing intersubjective relationships among City men. As Ranald Michie writes in *Guilty Money*, with *Austin Friars* 'Riddell produced what was almost a eulogy to the commercial City';[66] the activities of merchants not only take centre stage, they are also portrayed as fundamentally sound and less dubious or guilty than the activities connected with finance.[67] The twists and turns of the commercial plot have to do with the fluctuating value of 'those little bills'[68] which represent Yorke's capital. The thousand pounds Austin borrows from her (and is asked to repay when Yorke and Luke set up their own business)[69] are returned to her only after a long and meticulously detailed process which involves the circulation of bills – acceptances and accommodation bills – discounted, renewed and at one point dishonoured. All the merchants and City men featured in the novel are involved in this process at various levels: Austin as the borrower and speculator who overextends himself; Luke as the antagonist who, nevertheless, accepts renewed bills so as not to compromise his and Austin's credit; Monteith, Collis and Turner as traders willy-nilly stepping in to defend their interrelated commercial interests. Initially, Luke finds no difficulty in discounting the bills at either private banks or joint stock companies 'once it was clearly understood that the A. Friars who signed them was the A. Friars of Monteith, Friars & Co., Leadenhall Street'.[70] The quality of these bills is contingent on the quality of the signatures they contain, in other words, on the creditworthiness of the individuals whose names appear on the bills and on the probability that they would be willing to pay the bills' face value.[71] But even good bills, renewed one time too many, decrease in value and eventually fail to get discounted; as Luke anxiously observes: 'they had been renewed and renewed and renewed till the bills stank in the nostrils of discounters and bankers'.[72] Austin is impatient with slow progress ('he hated drudgery, he detested monotony')[73] and is well acquainted with 'every expedient by which just payment could be deferred, or avoided altogether';[74] he borrows in order to speculate 'on his own account' thus impairing the credit of his and Monteith's name. Each stage in the progress of 'those little bills' is accurately detailed, as if Riddell's intention in this novel were to provide readers with rudiments of financial education, alerting them to the complex interconnectedness of the credit system which ensures the negotiability of paper promises. Most reviewers considered these particulars as 'almost too technically related' or 'unintelligible to the ordinary reader', while simultaneously admiring Riddell's commercial expertise. Even the *Saturday Review* had to admit that 'the facility with which she handles commercial slang is remarkable in a lady'.[75]

Among Riddell's City novels *Austin Friars* is indeed the one most saturated with technical facts and information about negotiable instruments. As the *Times* observed, *Austin Friars* is 'as full of the tricks and turns of City brokerage and speculation as though its plot had been hatched within the quiet and respectable precincts from which it took its name'.[76] The focus on bills of exchange and on the mechanisms whereby credit is transferred confers upon this novel an abstract quality that the focus on chemical manufacturing (*Too Much Alone*), engineering (*City and Suburb*) and even accounting (*George Geith*) did not have. Little is known of the specific businesses of the various merchants (what they trade in remains undefined), while a fair share of attention is devoted to the formal agreements, the binding contracts they stipulate – the bills – which create an interconnected network of debtors and creditors hinging on consensus. No bill can be renewed without the mutual consensus of the interested parties: the segment of the business world portrayed in *Austin Friars* is, to a certain extent, reminiscent of the bourgeois public sphere; reaching agreement, achieving consensus and cooperating are described as necessary for the survival of the system as a whole.[77]

There is an analogy in the text between the defence of Yorke's honour and the quality of the bills issued by Austin: just as the value of this 'ambiguous woman' is championed by all the City men with whom she comes into contact, so too the value of the bills representing her wealth is never allowed to fall below a certain level, despite Austin's commercial negligence, speculative proclivities and downright dishonesty. Riddell's main concern seems to be the delicate equilibrium of the credit system and, related to that, the need for cooperation rather than

competition among businessmen. Translated into commercial terms, the quality
of tolerant judgment, which characterises the liberal education Luke derives from
Yorke's example, becomes instrumental to the correct functioning of the credit
system, even though tolerance involves pardoning (at least partially) Austin's
many mistakes. As is typical of Riddell's narrative art, private and public issues
are interwoven in a series of scenes focusing alternately on commercial and affective concerns. Yorke's honour is the object of discussion among City men, just
as much as the uncertain value of 'those little bills'. Collis, an honest, upright
merchant of the old generation, objects to Yorke's scandalous presence in the
City once he discovers that she has fled from her husband ('you must get her
away from Scott's Yard' he intimates to Luke);[78] Luke, trained in the art of liberal
understanding, finds Yorke's transgression heroic 'spite of the distance she has
wandered, notwithstanding the sorrow and the sin her eyes have seen'.[79] Likewise,
when it comes to renewing Austin's bills during 'a period of tightness in the City'
when 'pecuniary depletion is felt by every class in the community',[80] Collis takes
a conservative position, pressing Luke to expose Austin's insolvency, while Luke
is inclined to be more lenient, to explore other options and be guided by principles
that clash with Collis's stern commercial ethics. The narrator takes this opportunity to emphasise how Luke's understanding of commercial matters is affected by
his liberal education:

> This man, you will observe, had one of God's elements of success about
> him – Charity. For my part, I never yet knew one who climbed the world's
> ladder of competence, happiness, and social consideration who lacked this
> divine gift.
>   Yet there was a day when Charity and he were almost strangers, only *she*
> had taught him – she who never but once took up an antagonistic attitude in
> the hour of her extremity . . . We help, we refuse, we believe, we deny credit –
> and behold in the one case we help a man over the stile of starvation, or leave
> him to turn a corner, or we put up the shutters and assist at a commercial
> funeral. In a City of millions, where God (seemingly) leaves the units to
> us, our responsibility is great; and so Luke Ross felt it walking back to his
> office.[81]

Since Austin is from the outset the business villain of the novel, the extent to
which the community of merchants is willing to go to prevent, on more than one
occasion, the collapse of his credit is remarkable. Riddell's plea for commercial
charity in a City where God has 'seemingly' disappeared and the 'millions' rise
or fall, are pushed over the brink or survive more or less randomly, is an appeal
to cooperation and flexibility that complicates the notion of instrumental rationality. True to the philosophy that inspires Luke, Riddell defends the expediency of
disinterestedness, the opportunity of transcending one's interest in order to sustain
the interconnected network of commercial credit. Cooperation, in other words, is
portrayed as more efficient than competition at certain critical junctures. Much as
he resents Austin's lies and financial recklessness, Monteith, his senior partner,

intervenes more than once to repay Austin's dishonoured bills; similarly, Luke goes out of his way to accept bills that are worth little more than the paper they are written on; and even when Austin commits a felony, forging the signature of his father-in-law, the small community of merchants devises a plan that allows the forger to escape and his debts to be repaid. The dishonest element is eventually expunged from the system, but to achieve this result a fair share of toleration towards Austin's recklessness has to be mustered. More to the point, none of the City men can afford to be over-fastidious or too scrupulous when it comes to commercial morals: insolvency, so tightly interconnected with its opposite, cannot simply be denounced and unmasked without compromising the delicacy of the system of credit upon which the reputation of each individual depends – hence the novel's focus on the process whereby agreement is created among competing economic actors. The quality or the honour of the bills is an elaborately constructed fiction sustained by the concerted efforts of merchants who temporarily forego their self-interest in view of future, collective gains; to do this, they bear with dishonesty, cover up Austin's felony and finally help him flee to the continent. Luke's perspective in particular is defended as morally unconventional:

> It is said that the state of mind which pities a sinner instead of condemning him is morally low . . . Let it be as it may, however, Luke . . . determined that if any stone he might turn could save Austin, the man should not be taken up before Alderman Turtle, and duly committed for trial, and tried at the assizes, and found guilty, and sentenced . . . Afterwards Austin Friars said his friend's kindness on that eventful evening prevented his committing suicide.[82]

Riddell's reflections on business morality and commercial honour, in this novel, contain a repeated demand for leniency and flexibility, in tandem with the open request for tolerant judgment and respect elicited by Yorke's story. The reference to suicide, in this passage, is particularly meaningful, as the tragic ending was the one favoured by other Victorian novelists – Dickens, Trollope, Gissing – who tended to wind up the career of rascality of their fictional financiers in cathartic moments of self-destruction. Nancy Henry has argued that the 'trope of suicide . . . was part of an attempt to find the right language and images with which to represent the financial sector that had long been considered unsuited and inappropriate for fiction because of genteel and literary society's distaste for trade, business, and finance'.[83] Riddell opts for a different ending, eschewing the melodrama of suicide in favour of a more prosaic (and potentially more confusing) resolution and writing self-consciously against literary conventions:

> There are people in these days who, gathering their ideas of commercial morality from the columns of some favourite daily paper, think the 'honest and honourable British merchant' either an altogether mythical individual, or a thing of the long ago past, like the dodo or the mastodon; but against this delusion I would earnestly raise my voice . . . if fair dealing, honest trading, honourable feeling were not more common than the reverse, commerce

would soon come to a standstill – a point I hope more fully to demonstrate in some future work, seeing that the majority of writers who have undertaken to portray business know nothing on earth about it, and know, if that be possible, a trifle less about the men who work hard to keep wife and children above want while they live.[84]

For today's apologists of capitalism, the argument expounded in this passage is common knowledge: as Deirdre McCloskey writes, 'modern capitalism does not need to be offset to be good. Capitalism on the contrary can be virtuous';[85] when stealing rather than dealing prevails, the system as a whole does not work, 'By doing evil we do badly. And we do well by doing good'.[86] For Riddell, writing within a well-established tradition of 'literary irritability about bourgeois life'[87] as well as against a backdrop of commercial and financial scandals, the point is not so much to show that honesty works and is more efficient that stealing, but to problematise how fiction represents the distinction between honesty and dishonesty. As the novel suggests, the credit of both women and merchants in dire straits is best supported when sharp distinctions are set aside. More than once the narrator solicits readers to appreciate the 'many-sidedness' of existence: 'There is a reverse to all pictures', she writes, 'the back of the canvass of sorrow and sin might occasionally show something, reader, capable of ennobling our poor humanity'.[88] The liberal vision of many-sidedness that came to prominence in the mid-Victorian period found many equivalents in novels.[89] Riddell's specific interpretation, however, is peculiar in that it leans towards that type of relaxed moral stance which Victorian critics were primed to reject. If the moral of the story appeared dubious, it is arguably because the narrative leaves commercial felony unpunished (though not uncondemned) and rewards Yorke with solid wealth, a new husband (Luke) and a good life, albeit only after a period of tortured repentance. 'It is rare that a lady novelist has the courage to give her heroine to three men in the course of her three volumes', noted the *Saturday Review*, 'but this is the day for female courage, and the authoress of *Austin Friars* has not been behind the rest of her sex'.[90]

Whether courageous or not, Riddell's liberal imagination seemed too elastic, even for a female author who had already established her credentials as insider to the business world. The 'ambiguous woman' idealised in the text, 'devoted, unselfish' and yet 'guilty' of 'sharp practice', could not be quite deciphered as either a sensationalistic figure or a realistic (plausible) character, just as Luke's liberal heroics could not be squared with conventional views of the selfishness induced by money making.[91] The ubiquity of 'those little bills' negotiated in a series of meticulously detailed verbal exchanges was also bound to appear abnormal even for the capacious standards of fictional realism. By opening up the text to the technicalities of commercial life, which actually drive the plot, Riddell pushed realism in the direction of abstraction: too much knowledge produced, or was said to produce, not clarity but unintelligibility. It is difficult to say whether her contemporaries, the real historic readers of her novels, found the vicissitudes of the bills hard to grasp; some of them (the business people to whom Riddell addresses herself) might have had much greater familiarity with negotiable instruments and the kind of situations described in the novel than critics cared to admit. But in terms of fictional forms and literary conventions, structuring a plot around the exchange of bills, or the transfer of credit, as reviewers observed, fell short of meeting the aesthetic criteria of good novel writing. Yet, the sense of urgency with which Riddell plots and narrates insolvency – real or potential, honest or otherwise – suggests that she considered this issue of great relevance for the constituency of readers she had in mind. To them she recounts not only what little dramas the renewal of a bill entails, but also what mental attitudes, what moral dispositions are better adopted to ensure that the fall of one individual does not compromise the entire system. The emphasis is on how to behave, how to conduct oneself, in the commercial sphere, when the quality of credit deteriorates. With respect to this, the novel's moral is not confusing: appeals to charity (broadly understood), to cooperation beyond the clash of competing interests and to tolerant judgment are scattered throughout the novel; offering instead of withholding help is described as an economically rational decision. Liberal education and financial education overlap. That they do so in a novel so painstakingly committed to redeeming the *faux pas* of a woman whose commercial as well as erotic knowledge is well above average, further testify to the liberalising tenor of this tale of commerce and love.

Something else might also have inspired this intensification of interest in the porous boundaries between solvency and insolvency, credit and discredit. Riddell's husband declared bankruptcy in 1871: the events that precipitated the crisis are partly clouded in mystery, but one can surmise that for the author of *Austin Friars* pressing financial difficulties, the anxieties attendant upon bills coming due and the spectre of insolvency were household matters of some urgency in the months leading up to the collapse of Joseph Hadley Riddell's small business venture. The novel is hopeful and optimistic (almost utopian) in the way it imagines the management and resolution of the crisis determined by the discovery of Austin's forgery: money is generously advanced to avoid collective losses, debts are repaid, Turner obtains what he wants, Yorke comes back to the City to ensure the smooth functioning of the rescue plan, credit is safe – fiction confirms its problem-solving vocation. Things worked out differently, in real life, for Riddell's husband. The bankruptcy novel she wrote after his fall, *Mortomley's Estate*, teems with vehement passions (anger, in particular) and a widespread sense of perceived injustice – it is also the only business novel which revolves entirely around the actions, decisions and responsibilities of a woman, a 'small' individual, waging battle against 'big' financial organisations and what she perceives as abuses of legal power. When Riddell zooms in on 'Economic Woman', she turns combative *against* the City, in an interesting reversal of her previous position.

Notes

1 See Laurel Brake and Marysa Demoor, eds *Dictionary of Nineteenth-Century Journalism in Great Britain and Ireland* (Gent and London: Academia Press, 2009), pp. 551–2.
2 Before becoming editor of *Belgravia* in 1866, Mary Elizabeth Braddon published *Only a Clod* and *The Lady's Mile* in *St. James's Magazine*.

3 See 'Literature', *The Sporting Gazette, Limited,* 13 May 1868, pp. 402–3.
4 See 'The St. James's Magazine', *The Morning Post,* 9 April 1868, p. 6.
5 See 'Santiago!', *Punch, or the London Charivari,* 11 April 1868, p. 157.
6 In an article entitled 'Non-Thinkers', published in the issue of October 1870, the writer laments the fact that 'the vast majority of people never condescend to think, or when they do so condescend, are utterly incapable of thinking to any good or useful purpose. . . And this is particularly the case in reference to politics. Can we not, each of us, reckon on our fingers . . . those of our acquaintance who ever venture to have an independent opinion upon any political question?' see 'Non-Thinkers', *St. James's Magazine* 6 (October 1870), p. 406. The need to encourage political debates and to foster the formation of 'independent opinions', especially among the so-called non-thinkers, had evidently become a priority for the *St. James's Magazine.* I am not contending that Riddell's editorship radically altered the general orientation of the journal, but attention to political matters intensified during her service, while other features remained unchanged. The series 'Cabinet Portraits' was commissioned to Wemyss Reid, see Stuart Reid ed., *Memoirs of Sir Wemyss Reid* (London: Cassell & Co 1905), p. 142.
7 As Parry states 'there was much more legislation after 1868 than before' (Parry, p. 224); for a detailed analysis of the new political order see, in particular, chapter 10, 'Liberalism exuberant, 1868–85' (pp. 227–46). According to Hoppen, however, a 'combination of energetic surface disturbance and submarine stability applied – at least in the short and medium terms – to many of the changes introduced by the ministry of 1868–74', see Theodore Hoppen, *The Mid-Victorian Generation, 1840–1886* (Oxford: Oxford University Press, 1998), p. 601. On liberalism as a mass movement and on Gladstone's charismatic style of leadership see Eugenio F. Biagini, *Liberty, Retrenchment and Reform: Popular Liberalism in the Age of Gladstone, 1860–1880* (Cambridge: Cambridge University Press, 1992), pp. 369–95.
8 Peter Cain, 'Radicalism, Gladstone and the Liberal Critique of Disraelian Imperialism', in *Victorian Visions of Global Order: Empire and Relations in Nineteenth-Century Political Thought,* ed. Duncan Bell (Cambridge: Cambridge University Press, 2007), p. 215. As Goodlad observes: 'Nineteenth-century British liberalism was not a monolithic discourse or political rationality but a cacophony of diverse, though mainly optimistic, viewpoints on culture and society. Broadly construed, liberalism included, but was not limited to, the high-minded cooperation sought by John Stuart Mill; Thomas Chalmer's Christian and civic community; Harriet Martineau's vision of a society fueled by individual self-improvement; Walter Bagehot's staid confidence in the dynamism of civil society; Samuel Smiles's populist assertion of individual will; Matthew Arnold's conviction in the enlightening potential of a cultured elite, and Bernard Bosanquet's fin-de-siecle citizen ethic. What united these and still other identifiably liberal positions was their common adherence, though typically pressured and often contradictory, to an antimaterialist and moral worldview' (Goodlad, pp. 21–2). Similarly, Hadley claims that 'Liberalism in mid-Victorian Britain encompassed such a diversity of opinion and personality that it has always frustrated efforts at definition, reducing many descriptions to seemingly banal references to progress and reform, themselves dating back to Victorian formulations', see Elaine Hadley, *Living Liberalism: Practical Citizenship in Mid-Victorian Britain* (Chicago: The University of Chicago Press, 2010), p. 60.
9 Charlotte Riddell, *Austin Friars,* 1869–1870, (London: Hutchinson, n.d.), p. 40.
10 Hadley defines 'abstract embodiment' as a 'purposefully paradoxical neologism that seeks to encompass liberalism's desire for a political subject who is abstract (and capable of abstract thought) but also individual, abstract and yet concretely materialized, "free", though in its place' (Hadley, p. 28). Taking issue with the notion of 'a universalized liberal subject awash in abstractions (p. 32), Hadley concentrates on the 'lived practices of liberalism': 'many of the abstractions that define this period, especially the human being, become complexly encoded in the forms of embodiment that liberalism supplies' (p. 34). The forms of abstract embodiment discussed in her book are: the

liberal individual, the 'signed opinion piece' (in the *Fortnightly Review*), the liberal citizen in the ballot box, the liberal politician, and Gladstone's embodiment of liberalism in the Midlothian campaign.

11 Parry, p. 224.
12 See James Vernon, 'What Was Liberalism and Who Was Its Subject?; Or, Will the Real Liberal Subject Please Stand Up?', *Victorian Studies* 53, no. 2 (2011), p. 305.
13 See David Wayne Thomas, *Cultivating Victorians: Liberal Culture and the Aesthetic* (Philadelphia: University of Pennsylvania Press, 2004), p. 7 and p. 12. Thomas's book, like Hadley's, rethinks liberal subjectivity challenging current critical assumptions about liberal culture and the scepticism that has prevailed in academic discourse towards modern as well as Victorian notions of liberal agency. His analyses intend to 'carve out some space for a relatively affirmative reading of liberal agency, and on terms other than those of a conventionally neoconservative nostalgia for the humanist subject' (p. 5). The difference between substantive and regulative liberalism is formulated in analogy with the Kantian distinction between '*regulative* ideas', hinging on how we think, and '*constitutive* knowledge' which turns on what we think (p. 15). With reference to *Middlemarch*, Thomas writes: 'if it is clear that readers of all sorts are invited to identify not with Farebrother but with Dorothea, that is because Farebrother's substantive liberal agency is less persuasive finally than the regulative ideal of liberal conduct apparent in Dorothea' (p. 12).
14 *Austin Friars*, p. 224.
15 'Austin Friars', *The Saturday Review* 29, no. 762 (4 June 1879), p. 748.
16 [Robert Collyer], 'Novels of the Week' (Rev. of *Austin Friars*), *The Athenaeum* 2222 (28 May 1870), p. 707.
17 'All the circumstances disclosed are required to soften the situation, which is strong, even for a novel of the period . . . It is questionable how far the ethics of fiction justify the fact – but the guilt of the woman seems light compared with the heartless selfishness of the man', see 'Austin Friars', *The Graphic* 27 (4 June 1870), p. 635.
18 'Austin Friars', *Saturday*, p. 748.
19 See Rohan MacWilliam, 'Liberalism lite?', *Victorian Studies* 48, no. 1 (Autumn 2005), p. 104 and Hadley: 'To move beyond [the] current analytical impasse between the liberated citizen of liberal idealism and the disciplinary subject of post-structuralism, mid-Victorian liberalism must come back into sharper focus' (p. 34).
20 This is Thomas's definition, see p. x.
21 *Austin Friars*, p. 51,
22 Hadley, p. 93.
23 *Austin Friars*, p. 2.
24 Mill, p. 16.
25 'Austin Friars', *Graphic*, p. 635.
26 *Austin Friars*, p. 6.
27 Ibid., p. 27.
28 Amanda Anderson, *Tainted Souls and Painted Faces: The Rhetoric of Fallenness in Victorian Culture* (Ithaca, N.Y.: Cornell University Press, 1993), p. 2.
29 Ibid., p. 36. Anderson argues that the concept of fallenness reveals multiple anxieties 'about what constitutes human agency and selfhood . . . Through depictions of fallenness, the many perceived threats to the self – to its coherence, freedom, and distinct recognizability – could be both exaggerated and displaced, and also eventually diminished and dismissed, ushered off the scene, as were so many fallen figures in Victorian literature'; Anderson concentrates on the figure of the prostitute often perceived, 'distortedly as the mere effect of systemic forces – environmental, economic, sexual, and aesthetic' (p. 198). Although Yorke is an adulteress not a prostitute, the consciousness of her sexual 'fall' is no less prominent in the text.
30 *Austin Friars*, p. 26.
31 Ibid., p. 27.
32 Ibid., p. 7.

33 As John Stuart Mill famously put it, 'A person whose desires and impulses are his own . . . is said to have a character' (p. 60). Yorke comes closer to embodying this abstract notion when she assumes a business identity. On the centrality of the idea of character in 'Britain's liberal path to modern governance' see Goodlad, p. 24. She argues that to 'invoke character in the nineteenth century was, typically, to regard the individual's spiritual condition as inseparable from collective purpose of some kind. Throughout the century this moral worldview vied with its materialist antithesis, a competing foundation for modern truth claims in which character lost its transcendent and intersubjective possibilities and was reduced to the product of external determinants, bourgeois competition and representation' (p. 189).
34 *Austin Friars*, p. 45.
35 Mill, p. 69.
36 *Austin Friars*, p. 47.
37 Ibid., p. 45.
38 Ibid., p. 46.
39 Ibid.
40 Ibid., p. 26.
41 Anderson, *Tainted*, p. 65.
42 *Austin Friars*, p. 48.
43 Ibid., p. 117.
44 Ibid., p. 33.
45 Ibid., p. 29.
46 Henry, 'Charlotte Riddell', p. 201.
47 *Austin Friars*, p. 44.
48 Ibid., p. 13.
49 Ibid., pp. 29–30
50 Mill, p. 66.
51 Ibid., p. 70.
52 *Austin Friars*, p. 33.
53 See Mill, p. 66.
54 Ibid., p. 70.
55 *Austin Friars*, p. 52.
56 Hadley, p. 23.
57 *Austin Friars*, p. 52.
58 Ibid., p. 41.
59 Ibid., p. 120.
60 This is how the narrator glosses Austin's desertion of Yorke: 'Deserted! Ah, friends! Should we not rather, remembering what he was, write it 'free' – free to begin a new life afresh, with eyes from which the cloud that had lain between them and honour, between them and truth, was brushed away for ever' (Ibid., p. 177).
61 Ibid., p. 57.
62 Ibid.
63 As David Thomas remarks, ' "many-sidedness", understood as a personal disposition to consider alternative vantage points in private and public issues . . . is one facet of the period's discourse of *character*' (p. 26), although, he adds, 'in neither Mill's nor Arnold's case does many-sidedness emerge as a specially coherent or predictable stance'; Thomas sees it mostly as a 'regulative aspiration' (pp. 39–40).
64 See Anderson, *Tainted*, p. 89.
65 *Austin Friars*, p. 256.
66 Michie, *Guilty Money*, p. 71.
67 Michie argues that the 'place of the City in British culture that emerged [in the middle years of the nineteenth century] was a rather mixed one. To some it remained a commercial City to be lauded as the greatest of its kind in the world, as with Charlotte Riddell. To others it was where financial fraud took place' (Ibid., p. 76).

68 *Austin Friars*, p. 202.
69 'Of course you are aware', Yorke tells Austin, 'I cannot live on air, healthy as the City is reported to be; and though I do not desire to trouble you about money matters, still I may just mention that I want you to repay me that legacy of Mrs. Clissod's'; this request is presented as necessary to ensure Yorke's financial independence: 'I would rather provide for myself', she objects, 'and with that money I believe I can do so. At all events, I mean to try' (Ibid., p. 92).
70 Ibid., p. 118.
71 For a concise but very clear account of how the system of exchange by bills came into being in the mid-sixteenth century see Felix Martin, *Money: The Unauthorized Biography* (New York: Alfred A. Knops, 2013), pp. 105–8. As Barbara Weiss explains in *The Hell of the English: Bankruptcy and the Victorian Novel* (Lewisburg: Bucknell University Press, 1986), the commercial bill was 'a promise of future payment based usually upon dock-warrants or warehouse receipts. It could be passed on from one creditor to another, each one endorsing it, and thus by the forties the bill of exchange had become a sort of substitute currency among ordinary business men . . . An even less secure form of credit was the accommodation bill. Unlike the bill of exchange, which at least had its origin in a commercial transaction, with an accommodation bill the acceptor received no collateral at all for what was basically a promissory note' (p. 26). Poovey's *Genres of the Credit Economy* contains an excellent discussion of the multitude of factors that affected the value of a given bill: 'The complications in form, due date, and value help explain why every bill purchased by a bank (discounted) was immediately submitted to the bank's accountant for verification and evaluation . . . The complications also help explain why the use of bills was restricted to merchants for most of the nineteenth century . . . and why a flourishing bill-broking industry developed in London after 1825' (Poovey, *Genres*, pp. 40–41).
72 *Austin Friars*, p. 151.
73 Ibid., p. 146.
74 Ibid., p. 150.
75 See 'Austin Friars', *Saturday*, p. 758.
76 'A Life's Assize', *The Times*, 14 January 1871, p. 4.
77 In Habermas's theory, the bourgeois public sphere emerged in the eighteenth century as a realm where private individuals came together as a public and used rational discussion to analyse and critique the power of despotic States, see Jürgen Habermas, *The Structural Transformation of the Public Sphere. An Inquiry into a Category of Bourgeois Society*, 1962, (Cambridge, Mass: The MIT Press, 1989).
78 *Austin Friars*, p. 190. It is interesting to note that Riddell deploys the sensational stratagem of the painting to uncover Yorke's secret; like George in Braddon's *Lady Audley's Secret* (1862), Collis is able to connect the dots after he looks at the painting of Mr Ford's long lost wife, recognising in it Yorke's semblance. This sensational trick, however, is soon put to good realistic uses when the narrator invites readers to consider the 'back of the canvass' and to reflect upon the 'transcending of . . . purity' it reveals (p. 177).
79 Ibid., p. 185.
80 Ibid., p. 204.
81 Ibid., pp. 208–9.
82 Ibid., p. 350.
83 Henry, 'Rushing', p. 163.
84 *Austin Friars*, p. 235.
85 Deirdre McCloskey, *The Bourgeois Virtues: Ethics for an Age of Commerce* (Chicago: The University of Chicago Press, 2006), p. 1.
86 Ibid., p. 4.
87 Ibid., p. 10.
88 *Austin Friars*, p. 178.

89 As Hadley argues: 'Novels seek not surprisingly to educe the liberal individual through their formal operations, such as third-person narration, when, for instance other sites of contestation – the newspaper, the hustings – do not' (p. 3).

90 'Austin Friars', *Saturday*, p. 748.

91 Again, it is the *Saturday Review* that insists on the ambiguity of Yorke and the implausibility of Luke's generosity: 'As for Luke, such an innocent as he would find the City but a dangerous airing ground, all things considered; and with his generosity and weakness, unselfishness and romantic honour, would find money-making about as hard a piece of business as the transmutation of metals', see 'Austin Friars', *Saturday*, p. 748. Both the *Saturday Review* and the *Graphic* take note of the sensational elements in the tale, but conclude that *Austin Friars* could not be classified as a sensational novel – which for the former is a further sign of failure (even sensationalism fails to work its usual magic) and for the latter, on the contrary, a confirmation of quality.

8   Rewriting the Crisis
Mortomley's Estate

Thus the bankrupt becomes a clear man again; and, by the assistance of his allowance and his own industry, may become a useful member of the commonwealth.
Blackstone, 'Of Title by Bankruptcy', *Commentaries on the Laws of England*, 1811

Joseph Hadley Riddell's financial collapse did not fail to capture the attention of late nineteenth- and early twentieth-century critics who wrote journalistic accounts of his wife's literary career in which much emphasis is placed on her domestic existence – on the houses where she lived, the gardens she tended, the countryside she admired and even the cats keeping her company. Invariably, the tranquillity of the modest existence that the novelist presumably led in the late years of her life appears as the calm after the storm. Of the financial storm itself not much is revealed, but the presence of this traumatic event is nonetheless crucial to the structuring of Charlotte Riddell's life story. In *Notable Women Authors of the Day* (1893), Helen Black reports Riddell's words verbatim when it comes to breaching the subject of her husband's crash:

> Mrs. Riddell regarded her husband as one who was very early in life overborne by a weight of business cares too heavy for his nervous nature to sustain: 'Courageous and hopeful, gifted with indomitable energy, endowed with marvellous persistence and perseverance; modestly conscious of talents which ought to have made their mark he, when a mere lad, began his long quest after fortune, one single favour from whom he was never destined to receive'; and in her story, Mortomley's Estate (1874), she added, she 'but told the simple story of what, when in ill-health and broken in spirit, he had to encounter before ruin, total and complete, overtook him'.[1]

Described by his wife as a distressing event, 'total and complete', Joseph Riddell's descent into irreparable insolvency marked a turning point in their life: he was never able to resume trading, while Charlotte, urged by economic necessity, intensified her productivity and also turned towards popular genres – the ghost story, supernatural fiction – much in demand in the 1870s and 1880s.[2] The stigma of bankruptcy, of which Riddell writes eloquently in her novel, must have been difficult to shake off. The artist and illustrator Henry Furniss, writing in 1923 and reminiscing about the mid 1870s, when he encountered the Riddells, throws in an unsubstantiated piece of gossip about their unhappy marriage and Joseph's alleged imprisonment for debt: 'Mrs. Riddell had made a great reputation with her "prize novel", *George Geith*', he writes, 'but she was unhappily married, at least, I believe her husband through some queer way in business was resting somewhere at his country's expense'.[3] Over 10 years later, in 1934, Stewart M. Ellis dismisses Furniss's 'mischievous suggestion' as 'entirely indefensible': 'It is true that at this date Mr. Riddell was involved in grave financial difficulties, with which, by temperament, he was quite unfit to cope. But that he committed any malfeasance leading to imprisonment seems highly improbable'.[4]

However, even for a sympathetic commentator such as Ellis, the association with a bankrupt name is detrimental to the reputation of the writer; he is perplexed about the writer's choice to continue signing her novels as 'Mrs. J.H. Riddell' 'despite the clouds that overwhelmed Mr. Riddell in his closing years, when his name could be of no possible service, but entirely the reverse, at the launching of a book'.[5] The disgrace of bankruptcy evidently lingered on in the perception of posterity. In Ellis's account, in particular, references to the 'storm' are also used to sustain his conjectures about the underlying melancholia of Riddell's outlook on life: 'I think she read in the gentle yet melancholy beauty of the Middlesex landscape', he claims, 'some wistful presentiment of the changes and sorrow and financial ruin that, storm cloud-like, were already massing on the horizon of her life'.[6] Casting a long shadow, financial ruin is construed by later readers as a life-defining moment, a dramatic occurrence that alters the course of one's existence. Furniss, Ellis and to a lesser extent Black still operate within a value system that sees failure as suspicious, and bankruptcy as an infection of sort, spreading its viral contagion over a long expanse of time – a view that Riddell had criticised, in no uncertain terms, in *Mortomley's Estate* (1874).

The only account in which Joseph Riddell himself appears in the picture (and even speaks a few words) is the one contained in the *Memoirs of Sir Wemyss Reid* (1905) – it is hardly a flattering sketch of this man of business, the husband of the famous writer, who seems lost amidst a vociferous crowd of urban 'bohemians'. Reid relates how he met the novelist in a 'cellar beneath a shop in Cheapside' where 'this gifted woman' was 'acting as her husband's clerk, and engaged in making out invoices'.[7] Of her business habits as editor of the *St. James's Magazine*, however, he has a very low opinion, claiming that the magazine was never ' "out" on the proper day'[8] and that she lost one of his manuscripts. Of her abilities as host, likewise, he speaks with condescension, recalling the Riddells's 'rambling old house', the 'choice specimen of Mr Riddell's wares' on display in the rooms, and George Augustus Sala's 'jocosely brutal' remarks on one particular occasion:

> The literary men who frequented Mrs. Riddell's house were not, I am sorry to say, so respectful to her husband as they might have been . . . again and again the attempts of Mr. Riddell to contribute to our entertainment by some

long-winded narration had been vigorously and successfully repulsed. At last the unhappy host found an opening, and had got so far as 'What you were saying reminds me of an interesting anecdote I once heard', when Sala, striking his fist upon the table, thundered a stentorian 'Stop, sir!' Mr. Riddell looked at him, half frightened, half indignant. 'If the story you propose to tell us', continued Sala, 'is an improper one, I wish to tell you that we have heard it already; and if it is not improper, we don't want to hear it at all'. Yes, clearly one had wandered into Bohemia in those days.[9]

Whether apocryphal or not, Reid's anecdote is in keeping with the cultural model of disdain towards trade that Riddell's novels, especially the early ones, sought to redress. For all their appreciation of the City theme that had made Riddell famous, later commentators seem rather keen to keep her reputation untarnished by excessive intimacy with the reality of trade, rhapsodising on the tame domestic charms of her isolated life and glossing over the tale of ruin, though registering its enduring emotional impact.

The history of Joseph's bankruptcy is an incomplete puzzle: we get some glimpses of the disruption it caused in the accounts I have quoted above; we can infer how critical the situation was from the legal documents kept in the British National Archives and we have the fictional re-enactment of the crisis in the novel Riddell published in 1874 – a text that bears some relation to the actual event, as the author declared to Helen Black, though not necessarily a mimetic one, as I argue in this chapter. *Mortomley's Estate* is a highly uncharacteristic tale of ruin, atypical with respect to other Victorian novels of bankruptcy.[10] Its singularity, uniqueness even, may be rooted in painful autobiographical memories of the bankruptcy and its aftermaths, but the relation that works of fiction entertain with memories, especially traumatic ones, is rarely direct or literal.[11]

We can get a sense of the disruptive effects of Joseph's financial collapse by looking at the court records of the litigations in which the couple were involved. In 1871, after Joseph Riddell declared bankruptcy or, more specifically, went into liquidation, Charlotte sued both her husband and one of his creditors in the attempt to prevent her own earnings from being confiscated. The Bill of Complaint she filed and the answer of the defendant, James Smith, stove manufacturer in Glasgow, contain references to several negotiations conducted by the plaintiff, Charlotte, on behalf of her husband who was indebted to Smith for the sum of 2,000 pounds. Smith describes the plaintiff as 'an experienced woman of business' who 'has had for many years extensive business transactions with me in reference to her husband's trade of stove manufacturer and has had extensive correspondence with me by letter'.[12] Charlotte went to Glasgow several times, before the bankruptcy, to meet with the creditor and his lawyer and to discuss the settlement of the debt. Eventually, she offered as security the copyrights to some of her novels – *The Rich Husband* (1858), *Maxwell Drewitt* (1865), *Phemie Keller* (1866), *The Race for Wealth* (1866), *Far Above Rubies* (1867), *My First Love* (1869), *My Last Love* (1869), and *Austin Friars* (1870) – as well as to the *St. James's Magazine*, of which she and her husband were proprietors. The Bill of Complaint was filed after the passage of the Married Women Property Act in 1870 in the attempt to defend Charlotte's future earnings; the 'prayer' of the plaintiff states that the indenture previously signed 'ought not to bind any other separate estate of the plaintiff than the books and magazine thereby specifically assigned' and requires that the indenture be 'reformed accordingly'.[13] Interestingly, the document also reports that 'the plaintiff had expressly told the defendant that she was determined upon one thing, which was, that she would never work for any creditor again, and that, if he imagined she was going to work any more to pay her husband's debts, he was quite mistaken'.[14] The defiant tone of this assertion is quite striking; empowered by the provisions of the Married Women's Property Act, Riddell sought to keep her estate separate from her husband's liabilities, and to distinguish her identity as 'authoress' from her role as 'experienced woman of business', a role that the defendant claimed she had performed repeatedly. As Nancy Henry writes, 'To Riddell, major legislation of the mid-Victorian period, including the Bankruptcy Act of 1860 and the Married Women's Property Act of 1870 . . . were not abstractions. Rather, these Acts affected her material wellbeing almost immediately upon becoming law'.[15] She was fighting to protect her professional earnings, possibly the only source of income on which the family could count after the bankruptcy.

How the litigation went on and was eventually resolved is unclear, since half the case is missing. We know, however, that this was not the only legal case involving Riddell's works. In April 1873, Charlotte, her husband and the publisher Routledge & Son were sued by another publisher, Hurst and Blackett. The latter invoked the Married Women's Property Act in the attempt to recover the money owed by the Riddells; Hurst and Blackett also tried to prevent Routledge from publishing Charlotte's Christmas Book, *Fairy Waters*.[16] It is not necessary to report the tortuous twists and turns of this complicated case. Suffice it to say that, over a period of several years, the Riddells's financial troubles were many and pressing, creditors were quick to seize upon every asset and especially upon the only valuable property – Charlotte's literary works – that still promised future yields. How 'inglorious' the resulting uncertainty must have been is not difficult to surmise. In *Mortomley's Estate*, Riddell reconfigures the crisis, using the form-giving power of fiction to reset the whole scenario of legal, economic, personal and impersonal matters. She favours a hyper-technical reading of ruin, focusing on the new liquidation clauses contained in the 1869 Bankruptcy Act and going against the grain of well-established literary conventions presiding over the fictional representations of scenes of bankruptcy. The 'archetypal pattern of prosperity followed by catastrophe' which, as Barbara Weiss has argued, structures the narrative of failure in many Victorian novels (*The Newcomes, Little Dorrit, The Way We Live Now*, for instance)[17] is replaced by an almost exclusive concentration on the downward slope, the moment when Fortune's wheel takes a turn for the worse and things fall apart. What precedes this moment – prosperity, domestic serenity, ambition even – lies outside the story's perimeter. Moreover, the figure of the bankrupt is notable for his textual invisibility: ill, enfeebled and confused Archibald Mortomley disappears behind the scenes at 'the first mutterings of the storm',[18] while his wife, Dolly, takes upon herself the task of managing the crisis, dealing to the best of her abilities with powerful creditors, absent lawyers, sleazy accountants and a little crowd of zealous bailiffs.

As I argue in this chapter, the novel's disturbed linearity, its fixation on technical legal knowledge, the animosity displayed against accountants and City men, the distortions of this story of ruin are cracks in the representational system Riddell had devised and tested in her previous business novels. In other words, when the crash becomes fictional, fictional models crash. What emerges is a City novel that turns against the City and a narrative of failure that strays off the literary tracks delineated in the tradition of Victorian fiction. I shall analyse the text as the re-enactment of the painful experience of ruin, the effects of which, however, can only be communicated, as Hartman suggests, through 'distortions' and 'displacements'.[19] What kind of testimony is Riddell offering in *Mortomley's Estate*, if it is a testimony at all? What can be inferred about the emotional impact of bankruptcy from the way in which the story is (dis)organised and from the fantasy of compensation it projects? What understanding of ruin is conveyed through the deviations from patterns of symbolisation recurrent in other Victorian novels of bankruptcy?

'What On Earth Is Liquidation?'

In the *London Gazette* of 3 October 1871, the following announcement appeared:

> The Bankruptcy Act, 1869
>> In the London Bankruptcy Court
> In the matter of Proceedings for Liquidation by Arrangement or Composition with Creditors, instituted by Joseph Hadley Riddell, of No. 155, Cheapside, and No. 3, Liverpool-street, both in the city of London, trading and carrying on business on both such places as an Engineer.
>> NOTICE is hereby given, that a First General Meeting of the creditors of the above-named person has been summoned to be held at the Guildhall Tavern, Gresham-street, in the city of London, on the 24th day of October, 1871, at twelve o-clock at noon precisely – Dated this 26th day of September, 1871
>> BENJN. HARDWICK, Attorney for the said Joseph Hadley Riddell[20]

As can be evinced from this notice, Charlotte Riddell's husband was one of the many traders in dire straits who, after the passage of the Bankruptcy Act of 1869, opted for what was then considered a less hostile form of arbitration of a debtor's liabilities, namely 'liquidation by arrangement'.[21] The Act had introduced, for the first time, a distinction between bankruptcy and liquidation by arrangement or composition with creditors. The main difference consisted in the fact that whereas in bankruptcy the debtor was subject to public examination and judicial supervision extended over the administration of the bankrupt estate, liquidation by arrangement was viewed as a more amicable form of settlement, unsupervised by officials of the court; the administration of the estate was placed in the hands of a trustee and of an administrative body 'left to work as it likes, free from any special control of the Court of any kind'.[22] Furthermore, as Lester explains, liquidations were 'exempted from the provisions of the Act of 1869 requiring the audit of the trustees' accounts and judicial approval for the discharge of the debtor'.[23] In other words, the liquidation clauses were the most direct expression of the philosophy behind the new reform, which aimed at minimising the role of the State or the court, abandoning the system known as 'officialism' while giving creditors increased powers in the administration of the estate.

Introduced by Lord Brougham's Bankruptcy Act in 1831, 'officialism' entailed 'direct official involvement in the day-to-day management of bankrupts' estates';[24] court-appointed official assignees were the nominated administrators of bankruptcy cases, thus replacing the figure of the assignee selected by the creditors.[25] This system remained in place until 1869, 'when the pendulum swung in the other direction and creditors again took control'.[26] Lester claims that the reform was instigated by 'a vocal section of the business community' represented by new organisations such as the National Association for the Promotion of Social Science and the Associated Chamber of Commerce of the United Kingdom which effectively pressured Parliament, denouncing the high cost of bankruptcy administration and clamouring for the introduction of a scheme that would enable creditors 'to dispose of what was substantially their own property in their own way'.[27] The creditor-managed system of administration lasted only 14 years, until 1883 when officialism was again introduced. By the early 1870s, Lester writes, 'disenchantment with the new Bankruptcy Act had become widespread'.[28] As the *Saturday Review* stated in 1879, 'the present system is so bad that a legislator must be singularly unfortunate if he suggested any change that was not for the better'.[29] Among the many drawbacks of the 1869 Act, the 'gigantic evil' of 'liquidation by arrangement' was frequently singled out for special notice: for the *Saturday Review* it was a nasty system 'fostering a tribe of harpies who fatten on bankruptcies';[30] for the *Examiner*, likewise, the uncontrolled power of trustees in liquidations was 'liable to the grossest possible abuses';[31] the rapid increase of liquidations by arrangement was decoded by most as symptomatic of a fallacy in the system that encouraged improper forms of collusion between debtors and trustees.

In Riddell's novel, liquidation is a much-debated topic and the target of fierce criticism; the question 'What on earth is liquidation?'[32] is posed repeatedly, leading characters (and the narrator) to engage directly with the specific clauses of the new Act. The novel, in other words, falls right into the midst of contemporary diatribes about the functioning of the system of administration licensed in 1869, and it does so in ways that are distinctly polemical and fastidiously specific. Below is one example of Riddell's style of intervention:

Whether the gentlemen, commercial and legal no doubt, who concocted the Bankruptcy Act of 1869, and the other gentlemen of the Upper and Lower Houses who made it law, ever contemplated that an utterly irresponsible person should be placed in a responsible position it is not for me to say, but

I cannot think that any body of men out of Hanwell could have proposed to themselves that the whole future of a bankrupt's life should be made dependent on the choice of a trustee, since it is simple nonsense to suppose a committee selected virtually by him and the petitioning creditor have the slightest voice in the matter.

And if any man in business whose affairs are going at all wrong should happen to read these lines . . . let him remember liquidation means no appeal, no chance of ever having justice done him, nor even remote contingency . . . of setting himself right with the business world.

He who goes into liquidation without first being sure of his trustee, his lawyer and his committee passes into an earthly hell over the portals of which are engraved the same words as those surmounting Dante's 'Inferno'.[33]

For Carlyle, the universal 'terror of "Not succeeding", of not making money, fame, or some other figure in the world' represents the 'somewhat singular Hell' of which the 'modern English soul' is most in dread.[34] For Riddell, liquidation is a decidedly more technical kind of Inferno, hopeless for those who cross its threshold and fall into the legal traps strewn along their path. As Victorian reviewers lamented, this novel presupposed a familiarity with the ins and outs of recently passed legislation that neither the average reader of fiction nor the critic could be expected to possess: 'It is scarcely fair to the ordinary reviewer of novels' – complained the *Saturday Review* – 'to publish such a book as *Mortomley's Estate*. Familiar though he is with all the regular crimes, and hand in glove though he has been kept through a long course of reading with the worst criminals, he still does not profess to have any exact knowledge of the working of the Bankruptcy Act of 1869'.[35] Accusations of excessive technicism had already been levelled at Riddell after the publication of *Austin Friars*. But the extent of legal knowledge exhibited in *Mortomley's Estate* is considered even less appropriate for it gets in the way of the linear development of the story. As *The Spectator* noticed, it takes some time before the 'complicated business relations to each other of the people in the book' become less obscure and some clarity is reached over what this 'strangely realistic and most touching narrative' is all about.[36] It is not immediately apparent, in other words, whose story is to grab the reader's attention.

Indeed, the straight chronological order that typically structures Riddell's City novels (the beginning of the narrative coincides with the arrival of the hero in London and the start of his career) is disrupted in this novel. The first two chapters plunge the reader into the midst of 'complicated business relations', alluding to events that are fully related only later on. The scene is set in one of the new, big offices that have sprung up in the City, and the dialogues reported revolve around business and legal matters connected in a yet unspecified way with Mortomley's bankruptcy. Characters of different nationalities are paraded – accountants, managers, men of business – who speak in brisk sentences of 'petitioning creditors', 'pressing creditors', 'private settlements', 'trustees' and 'liquidation', reporting conversations (informal negotiations) they have had with Mrs Mortomley which will be described in full only half-way through the narrative. One character, the accountant Mr Asherill, receives the benefit of a fuller characterisation, but his presence in the story will turn out to be more marginal than the initial scene seems to suggest. The significance of the episode and of the dialogues reported in the initial chapters becomes apparent only *a posteriori*; in particular, one detail, the choice of the solicitor who is to act on behalf of the debtor, mentioned *en passant* amidst other business matters, will prove of crucial importance in the subsequent reconstruction of what went wrong. The opening scene, in other words, seems deliberately arranged to mystify the reader, overexposing one minor character, Asherill, underexposing relevant details, and alluding to negotiations between accountants and creditors that presuppose some knowledge of the new clauses of the Bankruptcy Act to be fully deciphered.

What this beginning achieves, at the cost of straining the conventions of realist representation and confusing the reader, is to perform an act of symbolic dispossession: the story of Mortomley's estate is not really *his* story, it is hijacked by the professional figures emboldened by the new Act who take centre stage at the commencement of the narrative and remain in charge throughout; their authority will be questioned in quixotic ways only by the bankrupt's wife, Dolly, a 'little madam with the big temper' (as she is described by a German creditor, Kleinwort), sublimely ignorant of all matters legal and financial. The truth about liquidation is not just the one the narrator spells out in the passage quoted above – no possibility of appeal, no chance of justice, no redemption. It is also the emotional truth obliquely conveyed through the dispossession enacted in the first three chapters and the sense of displacement that the disturbed chronology indirectly expresses. To be in the hands of creditors, trustees and accountants is in a deeper sense the origin of the story here narrated, hence the repositioning of this scene before the events that lead to it have been reconstructed. This is not a major disruption of narrative linearity, to be sure, but it stands out as a significant deviation from both Riddell's habitual preference for straight chronology and the typical trajectory from prosperity to ruin which novels of bankruptcy tend to follow.

Big versus Small

Another effect of this bewildering beginning is to redefine the City of London as the kingdom of 'Limited Companies' and 'liquidators': the 'new class of buildings' in which they operate 'are tenanted by a more wonderful race of men than Captain Cook discovered in the South Sea Islands'.[37] The City where Alan Ruthven, George Geith, and Lawrence Barbour strove single-handedly to mould their destiny is now quite clearly the centre of corporate power, of joint-stock companies located in edifices remarkable for their lack of character: 'they all resemble each other more or less – more indeed rather than less'.[38] In this City, 'big thing[s]' are always being 'floated' and money is coined 'out of the blood drawn from men's hearts, the anguished tears of women, the broken hopes of youth, and the disgrace heaped upon old age'.[39] The days of small partnerships and 'economic chivalry' seem long past; the heroic individuality of entrepreneurs, engineers, chemical manufacturers and even food adulterators that Riddell had so vividly represented in her previous novels has been replaced by a formidable 'race' of City men indistinguishable from one another.[40] Inimical to the expression of individual business talent, the corporate identity and mentality of the City is presented as hegemonic: in the thrall of 'big' interests, 'small' subjects seem destined to exhaust their energies without achieving much, or so Riddell implies in this novel.

The tension between 'big' and 'small,' between corporate and individual enterprise, is one of the polarities that give shape to this narrative of failure. Framed as a combat between powerful creditors (the 'General Limited Chemical Company') and self-interested public accountants on the one hand, and a one-man firm ('one small thing', the White Lead and Colour Works of Archibald Mortomley)[41] on the other, the tale of bankruptcy Riddell narrates is marked by a starkly defined reallocation of right and wrong. Mortomley has accumulated liabilities through a mixture of mismanagement, excessive generosity and bad luck. How his affairs got so entangled as to render ruin inevitable is not really explained. What captures the attention, rather, are the manipulations of Forde (manager of the limited company), Swanland, accountant *cum* trustee, and Kleinwort, a German creditor and speculator with a suspiciously unctuous mien. It is a paranoid reading of ruin that shifts responsibility onto the creditors and their representatives, while portraying the debtor as fundamentally the victim of a system of power too consolidated to be challenged by one single individual. Of course, this configuration has the added advantage of eliciting immediate sympathy for the insolvent debtor, trapped in a complicated legal and financial web not of his own weaving. The 'ropes which bound Mortomley to the wheels of the General Chemical Company's chariot' cannot be easily severed, enmeshed as the former is in commercial relations that are anything but transparent:

> Goods were charged for which never entered the gates of Mortomley's factory; when a bill was renewed, the old bill reappeared at some unexpected juncture, and was treated as a separate transaction; when drugs so inferior that nothing could be done with them were returned, no credit was given on the transaction. Receipt notes, when the carmen could obtain such documents, were treated as waste paper or as referring to some other affair from that under consideration. In fact, let who else be wrong, Mr. Forde and the General Chemical Company must be right. That was the manager's solemnly expressed conviction. According to his bewildering creed, if an entry were wrong in the first book, supposing such an impossibility possible, it was made right by being repeated through twenty other books, and finally audited by two incompetent gentlemen, who would thankfully have declared black to be white for a couple of guineas a day.[42]

What Riddell is describing here is crony capitalism at its worst: the collusion between auditors and managers; the falsifying of accounts; the cheating of smaller clients by the concerted efforts of unscrupulous managers and accountants working for their own profit; the smug pretension of correctness. Even before failure intervenes, the Company is running the show, artificially swelling Mortomley's account and eventually pushing him over the brink of ruin. This configuration – based on a well-defined opposition between corporate capitalism and individual entrepreneurship – is not mimetic with respect to Riddell's personal experience of bankruptcy. In the light of available evidence, one can reasonably argue that Joseph Riddell was not the victim of unethical machinations concocted by a large joint-stock company; his main creditor was a trader like himself, not a corporate power. If there is documentary mimesis in the text, it is continuous with the broader economic and legal history of the second half of the nineteenth century, rather than with the author's personal experience. The two are interrelated, of course, but it is significant that in turning biographical material into fiction, Riddell rewrites the outline of the personal (or referential) story so as to identify a clear set of enemies (predatory managers and accountants), a series of objective circumstances (the rise to power of limited companies and private liquidators), and a backdrop of capitalist malpractice against which bankruptcy seems indeed a minor type of shame. Appealing to popular sentiment, hostile towards the very principle of general limited liability and distrustful of corporate enterprise,[43] Riddell finds a cultural and affective mould within which to tie the loose ends of experience and to shape the personal in ways that resonate with collective significance. *Mortomley's Estate* is arguably not a 'truthful' account replicating the story of her husband's 'total and complete' ruin, but it is a testimony to the feelings of entrapment, alienation, impotence and even anger that are likely to have complicated her perception of failure. These feelings are amplified in the fictional configuration that pits 'big' powers versus 'small' subjects, the canny ability to manipulate others versus the innocent incompetence of the debtor and his wife. Some blame falls on them too (they make mistakes), but the rationale of the novel is largely exculpatory.

The distressing implications of Joseph's bankruptcy can be perceived indirectly in the textual traces they have left, dispersed over the surface of the novel; they can be detected in the disturbed linearity or chronology, as I have argued, which tells a tale of dispossession, or in the sharp distinction between the wrongdoing of corporate entities and the relative innocence of their victims, which brings to the fore a diffuse sense of impotence but also the fictional clarity of neat classifications. Both the disruption of linearity and the stark differentiation between right and wrong, heroes and villains, are fairly uncharacteristic of Riddell's representational strategies, alert as they often are to the rich narrative potential of ambiguity. To picture the City in very negative terms is also quite unprecedented for this author. The *Saturday Review* declared Riddell 'too severe on the men of business of the present as she is upon the Bankruptcy Act . . . We place little credit in the charges that are made against all classes of men'.[44] For a novelist who had gained a reputation of partiality towards men of business and the unsuspected charms of the City, turning against her own ideal was not a creditable move. Yet, in the wake of the crisis, Riddell's urban realism changes valence and the City appears almost exclusively as a dystopian domain in the hands of large interest groups, foreign speculators and untrustworthy accountants. There are, of course, exceptions. Mr Gibbons, for instance, is a kind creditor and good man of business: 'to men of this sort', observes the narrator, 'who are willing to sow in the spring and patient enough to wait for the ripening in the autumn, England owes most of her prosperity'.[45] But the healthy, honest component that 'men of this sort' represent is portrayed as powerless or residual, just as powerless and enfeebled Mortomley appears to be until, towards the close of the novel, he comes out of his stupor and starts trading again. It is not within the masculine contingent of the business community, however, that rescue is to be found. The novel's utopian streak centres on women, Dolly and her friend Leonora, and on their problem-solving lateral activities. The contrast between Dolly and the law is another polarity that gives shape to the novel and to the fantasy of redress it projects. But before analysing the role she plays, it is important to explain how the law – the Bankruptcy Act itself – functions as a structuring principle of the plot.

Reckoning with Failure

As the narrator points out, there is something about failing in business that defies simple comprehension: 'It may not require any great amount of brains for a man to know his affairs are becoming involved; but it does require a certain order of intellect, at all events, to state the precise causes of his want of success. In trade, when once one thing begins to go wrong, so many others immediately follow, that it is difficult to lay a finger on the real seat of disease'.[46] The genealogy of failure, in other words, unlike the forward-looking trajectory of success, is difficult to reconstruct; the downwards path is strewn with misread signs, false hopes, negligence, good intentions, bad luck and unforeseen circumstances out of which no linear narrative can conceivably be fabricated to explain with precision when and how things begin to fall apart. In Mortomley's case, the narrator offers some generic retrospective explanations, interspersed with a very brief account of his moderate and short-lived accomplishments. Archibald Mortomley has inherited his father's once prosperous business; though highly inventive, he lacks the business acumen of his progenitor, is too generous towards his niece and nephew and does not pay enough attention to simple commercial matters (the writs he receives, for example) that will eventually do him in. 'There is an inevitable decay in some great business houses as there is in some great families'[47] the narrator states, invoking the abstract concept of 'inevitable decay' to fit this story into some sort of pattern. The ancestor who first set up the colour business, Hildebrand Mortomley, might have been the protagonist of a typical upward mobility tale: 'A story of a successful man's life might have been written about this first Mortomley, who, forsaking the paths hitherto trodden by his progenitors, struck out one for himself which led to fortune and domestic happiness'.[48] The epigone, Archibald, coming at the end of the line, becomes the invisible protagonist, the absent centre, of a tale of ruin that speaks of the crisis not only of a family business but of the forms of representation through which business and failure were habitually narrated.

A startlingly prevalent phenomenon, bankruptcy had already acquired by the early 1870s its own artistic and literary profile: 'Victorian art is filled with paintings, dramas, fictions that exhibit a fear of economic disaster amounting almost to paranoia', claims Barbara Weiss, 'and yet with rare exceptions manage to avoid lingering upon the unpleasant details of the experience of bankruptcy'.[49] Victorian novels offer nuanced interpretations of bankruptcy and several variations on what Weiss identifies as an 'archetypal pattern . . . of economic prosperity, loss, debt, and then final catastrophe'.[50] The pivotal moment in this cycle is the profoundly disturbing household clearance scene, a scene that typically describes the dreaded violation of the hearth when personal possessions are turned into mere commodities or even into inert matter, as Trotter remarks.[51] In the texts Weiss considers, bankruptcy is frequently construed as a kind of fortunate fall 'in which all the old falsehood, false values, mistaken goals are swept away and a new and purer beginning is possible',[52] as *Dombey and Son* and *The Newcomes* testify.

Riddell's novel does not follow the same narrative arc. The story zooms in on the actual fall and its aftermaths, painstakingly detailing the process of going into liquidation (including the informal negotiations with creditors before the decision is made); Dolly's mistakes and her consulting with lawyers; the first official meeting of creditors, as required by the law, and the administration of a the estate by a trustee, Mr. Swanland, who understands very little about the manufacturing of colours. In other words, what structures the plot is the letter of the law, the step-by-step procedure itemised in the 1869 Bankruptcy Act. If this Act is the ultimate villain, it is also what gives order to an otherwise episodic narrative.[53] The plot closely follows the progression sanctioned by the liquidation clauses contained in the new Act, conveying a sense of inescapable development, a kind of pre-determined rolling down, interrupted here and there by Dolly's interventions. An impression of didacticism, of course, emerges from this arrangement of episodes, as the reviewers noticed, lamenting the fact that 'the hero of this story is the Bankruptcy Act of 1869, and the heroine, winding up an estate by liquidation'.[54] Just as the genealogy of failure is ultimately explained or rationalised by intensifying the opposition between 'big' and 'small' and exacerbating the contrast of right and wrong, what the crisis entails, the actual downward slope of ruin and loss, is structured along impersonal lines according to the sequence that the 1869 Act had devised. The 'services of an attorney' rather than of a 'literary critic', the *Saturday Review* objected, are required to properly 'review the case'.[55]

There is some truth in this allegation. An entire chapter, for instance, is devoted to chronicling the first meeting of creditors. With a good deal of sarcasm, Riddell describes the alleged impartiality of the trustee, Swanland, who 'posed himself as Justice, and held the scale, I am bound to say, with strict impartiality between debtor and creditor'.[56] The chapter reports in detail discussions among creditors; selected specimens of Swanland's oratory ('he went in for the Turneresque effects'); the objections voiced by small creditors such as Gibbons; the different positions taken by those who represent the Company's interests and the resolutions adopted, all the while registering how legal power is wielded to indulge the wishes of Forde and his Company. All happens according to what legislation prescribes, down to the specific particulars of how the certificate of discharge is to be obtained. It is a sarcastic excursus into legal procedures, at once validating and undermining them. The law provides a framework within which to arrange the narrative of liquidation, fiction offers salient critical commentary through the narrator's voice intended to indict the supposed impartiality of the professional figures emboldened by the Act. In this case, Riddell's strategy is openly confrontational.

Less belligerent is her reworking of the house auction. The slow process of liquidating private assets is expanded over so many chapters that it becomes almost unrecognisable – unrecognisable, that is, according to the literary models repeatedly honed by Riddell's fellow novelists. So frequent are scenes of seizure and auction, in Victorian fiction, that they can be considered 'set-pieces'; as Trotter writes, they are second only to death-bed scenes in terms of the profoundly disturbing effects they have.[57] Descriptions usually dwell 'lingeringly upon familiar objects imbued with great emotional significance that are roughly removed by strangers: Amelia Sedly's "little" piano, Paul Dombey's "little" bedstead, Colonel Newome's silver cocoa nut tree, Mrs. Tulliver's china and linen, Maggie Tulliver's books'[58] Objects predominate in these scenes; the 'pretty' things embellishing middle-class drawing rooms derive significance from their relation with subjects and the melancholy of loss.[59] The poignancy of such descriptions is contingent upon the rapid transition from 'singularization' to 'commoditization' (to use Kopytoff's terminology), or from the sentimental aura of domestic possessions, to their reduced status of inert things indifferent to subjects.[60]

Riddell takes a different approach. The invasion of the domestic enclave by 'men in possession' is not resolved in one scene, rather it is a prolonged and extenuating process involving a large set of individuals (clerks from Asherill's office, bailiffs, auctioneers, the omnipresent trustee), a series of preliminary assessments, the inventory of things, the negotiations over what property is indivisible among creditors and finally the selling up of the house and factory. The first mention of 'wolves . . . howling round the doomed estate'[61] occurs in chapter 9, accompanied by Dolly's mournful appreciation of 'the room, the flowers, the soft evening light'[62] soon to be appropriated by strangers. It is only in chapter 21 that Dolly and her husband finally leave Homewood – once their property. In the intervening chapters, of course, much happens that does not have to do with the auctioning of domestic possessions, but this prolonging of the loss over many pages is strikingly inconsistent with literary conventions, allowing for a more detailed account of the stages of the process and, related to that, for a different understanding of the feelings involved, especially Dolly's.

What drives the slow unfolding of the clearance process is the focus on Dolly's slow realisation of what liquidating means. Even when the bailiffs are solidly installed at Homewood, 'Dolly could not yet realise the fact that her husband was bankrupt, that a trustee ruled at Homewood, that the last man in possession was his lord-lieutenant, that the men were no longer Mortomley's men, but belonged to Mr. Swanlad, as did the works and everything else, themselves scarcely excepted, about the place'.[63] We see her dealing with Swanland, when he first supervises the colour manufactory; with a series of bailiffs and auctioneers, who come and go from Homewood, inventorying its contents; with servants who try to hide things away, but never is she pictured contemplating one particular 'pretty' thing (except perhaps for the garden), one object of great sentimental value in which the sense of bereavement at the impending loss is condensed. When the final day arrives and her loyal maid asks: 'What will become of all the things?' Dolly's reply is notable for its curtness: 'I do not care what becomes of them'.[64] Furthermore, the objects that are actually mentioned as part of the repossession are a motley group of inanimate things and animate creatures, devoid of any particular aesthetic or sentimental aura: 'The horses in the stables, the chemicals and colours in the works, the bed the sick man lay upon, the flowers in the garden, the exotics in the greenhouse, the cat curled up before the hall fire, the dogs raving at the length of the chain at the intruder'.[65] Nostalgia for the ideal of middle-class domestic happiness reflected in the singularised object – the piano, the silver tea-pot, the little things gracing bourgeois drawing rooms – is less relevant for Riddell than the painful process of tracing with precision how a home is dismantled and how difficult it is to realise what is going on and to face the inevitable, which Dolly is inclined to deny ('I do not care what becomes of them') until avoidance becomes impossible. Her denial is what the protracted household clearance scene repro-duces, its tempo slowed down by her false hopes – 'sometimes Dolly felt angry and sometimes sad, but she never felt hopeless'[66] – and by the vague belief that the inevitable might be averted.

Reckoning with failure means, in a rather literal way, slowly absorbing the shock, getting used to the irruption of the abnormal into the ordinary dimension of existence. Even a cursory look at the swelling lists of bankrupts in the *London Gazette* or *The Times* is sufficient to get a sense of the normality, the ordinariness even, of bankruptcy in mid-Victorian England. Statistics, though not always accu-rate, reveal to what extent failing in business was a widespread phenomenon.[67] Yet, for those directly involved the experience of bankruptcy, despite its normal-ity, was a moment of extreme distress, as Victorian novels in many ways testify. Bankruptcy is both normal and abnormal; no matter how plural it is, it remains singular in the extreme. Riddell's representational strategy captures something of this singularity: the household clearance remains a pivotal moment, but its prolonged duration registers the stupor, incredulity and denial of those directly affected, further emphasised by the contrast with what the law-based plot, the nar-rator, the professional liquidators and the readers know to be unavoidable. A pre-determined outcome – the house auction – is represented not as a rapid transition into dispossession, but as a series of incomplete scenes, interspersed with other episodes, that revolve around Dolly's unprocessed experience of what is happen-ing, her simultaneous knowing and not knowing what liquidation actually means. In this case, the novel's realism veers towards the 'traumatic'[68] registering the distance between experiencing and understanding in the protracted act of selling up and in the sense of incredulity accompanying it.

Dolly's Battles

In the preceding sections, I have paid attention to those features of the text that sig-nal indirectly what Rothberg calls the 'nonintegrated presence' of the 'extreme'[69] manifesting itself in the distortions of representation – distortions that can be gauged in relation to both individual and collective representational models. Riddell's fictional template, the form she tested and honed in her City novels, cracks under the pressure of extreme contingency: the disturbed chronology, the melodramatic conflict between 'big' and 'small,' right and wrong, the negative affect imbuing descriptions of the City, the reliance of the plot on the letter of the law are the resulting effects. The literary conventions that other novelists found congenial when treating the subject of bankruptcy appear strangely skewed in *Mortomley's Estate*, causing reviewers to attack Riddell's 'foolish language' and her surrender to legal rhetoric. However, her veering away from tradition – in the representation of the house auction, for example – could also be seen as a way of reckoning with the emotional impact of failure, or of registering its long-term effects through a form of traumatic or disrupted realism that evokes distress in the suspension of, or deviation from, consolidated models of representation.

But *Mortomley's Estate* is also a story of resilience in which the spirit, rather than the letter, of the law is reaffirmed. As Blackstone stated in his *Commentaries on the Laws of England,*

> At present the laws of bankruptcy are considered as laws calculated for the benefit of trade, and founded on the principle of humanity as well as justice; and to that end they confer some privileges, not only on the creditors, but also on the bankrupt or debtor himself. On the creditors, by compelling the bankrupt to give up all his effects to their use, without any fraudulent concealment; on the debtor, by exempting him from the rigor of the general law.[70]

One of the social aims of bankruptcy legislation, which provides *ex post* relief mechanisms, is to allow the debtor to stand on his feet and to become 'a clear man again' – 'a useful member of the commonwealth'.[71] With the introduction of the liquidation clauses, the 1869 Act promoted a potentially less severe attitude towards the debtor, who could avoid the public shame of going through the bankruptcy court and could continue trading if the business was deemed valuable – under some form of supervision. Rehabilitation of debtors is in the spirit of the law, as befits a commercial society interested in the smooth running of its operations.

In Riddell's novel, the process of becoming 'a clear man again' is contingent upon female agency, heightened in a situation of crisis.[72] It is perhaps no coincidence that *Mortomley's Estate* features what is arguably Riddell's most interesting and unclassifiable heroine (and City wife), Dolly. She is ostensibly different from the serious-minded, pro-business, non-frivolous female figures – Mary Watson, Ina Trenham, Beryl Molozane, Yorke Forde – who populate her novels as apt companions of earnest men of business. Indifferent to financial matters, Dolly is portrayed as a 'little heathen' and a 'lazy little sinner',[73] with a 'biting tongue', a marked 'tendency to flame up',[74] a penchant for complicated hairdos and fashionable clothes, but 'possessed of a wonderful temper – of a marvellous elasticity' and unflinchingly loyal to her husband (no adultery in this case).[75] She hardly fits the bill of what the sensible wife of a City man should be, as the narrator likes to point out. Indeed, so unorthodox is the mixture of traits that combine to create this character that she projects a negative aura of foreignness, which instigates xenophobic sentiments in the City circles she frequents: 'the ladies who called upon her . . . disliked her as nation dislikes nation, as class dislikes class, as sect dislikes sect, as diverging politicians dislike each other'.[76] Dolly, in other words, is an outsider, treated with condescension by City notables and their spouses, compelled to become insider by the sheer pressure of circumstances.[77]

Her ignorance of both business and the law causes her to make mistakes: she accepts Forde's proposal to employ the Company's lawyer, Mr. Benning, as Mortomley's legal representative. This minor glitch is invested with huge significance; it is the straw that breaks the camel's back, leaving Mortomley entirely at the mercy of his creditors: 'when Dolly consented that Mr. Benning should step into the shoes of their own solicitor, they virtually threw up their cards and gave the game to their adversaries'.[78] Anticipated in the initial scene, this detail functions as a monocausal, *a posteriori* explanation of disaster: much seems to hang upon the uninformed decision Dolly makes. The senselessness of failure is thus contained: to be able to point at a probable cause, a slip that precipitates events, is preferable than to dwell indefinitely in the inexplicable. Dolly's misgivings – 'she did not feel satisfied on that point . . . Dolly vaguely comprehended there were dangers and difficulties ahead'[79] – are also the trigger that sets her off on a mission, a 'campaign' of redemption, fought with the legendary bravery of a knight in armour. 'Mortomley himself out of the battle, his wife took up the sword on his behalf',[80] declares the narrator: 'She was in the middle of the battle, and the Gerace nature knew no faltering when the trumpet sounded, and every man (or in default of man, woman) was called to do his best'.[81] Metaphors of war are sometime deployed by Riddell to convey the fierceness of the race for wealth, but in this case it is an appeal to ancient, archaic notions of bravery and honour that qualifies the heroism of a female character sporting the incongruous name of Dollabella Gerace. Her role in the story is configured according to a simple pattern: the battle of a solo adventurer against organised systems of power. And just as in the adventurous romances of old brandishing a sword is not enough to win, in this novel too some clever trick must be deployed: Dolly's trick is to gain some leverage on Asherill and then to trade the information she has on him (which he does not want to divulge) for the certificate of discharge her husband needs to resume his activity.[82] She also arranges secret meetings with Lang, the former manager of the Colour Works: with his help, and the timely arrival of a pecuniary gift (a hundred pounds) from her friend Leonora, Dolly establishes a new business venture, where her husband's secret formulas – the only intangible property that was not taken away from him – are again put to good use in the production of his famous 'blue' and 'yellow'.[83]

Over many chapters, Dolly is the focal point of the narrative, as she quickly learns precious life lessons, also intended for the benefit of the reader, becoming a paragon of resilience. She takes 'the business bull by the horns',[84] proving a tough negotiator in her dealings with Lang: 'Who would have supposed that a lady who twelve months before could not have told ochre from umber should all at once develop such an amount of business capacity as to understand precisely which way Lang's desires led, and at once put a padlock in the gate by which he hoped to reach his goal?'[85] She does not hesitate to vent her anger against relatives ('rats leaving the sinking ship') and friends, who shun the bankrupt fearing his contagion, or to storm into the offices of accountants and attorneys, fully attired in colourful clothes, 'speaking her thoughts out loud'.[86]

A fantasy of compensation is inscribed in Dolly's chivalric adventures; not only is she successful in procuring her husband's discharge (the sacred grail of bankrupts), she also fends off possible competitors, writes to old customers inducing them to come back, and supervises the activities of the new colour manufactory, set in a remote corner of Hertfordshire, until Mortomley recovers from his illness. The strong wish to rectify things, to paint the hopeful picture of a new possible beginning after the fall, is antithetical to the main dystopian strain of the narrative. A partial synthesis between these two opposing tendencies is achieved by dint of direct narrative interventions: anxious anticipations of a happiness to come are scattered here and there in *ad hoc* asides that hurriedly create a sense of closure in the midst of the crisis. For example, when Dolly is summoned to Swanland's office to be told that even the money she assumed was hers (an inheritance of 8,000 pounds) will be distributed among creditors, the blow she thus receives is counteracted by the narrator's swift reassurance that 'sunshine' will soon come: 'my dear . . . all unconscious your feet were already treading a path leading into the sunshine – through dreary wastes it is true – along places stony and thorny; across wilds hard to traverse, but still a path conducting to the sunshine, out of the blind, maddening, perplexing darkness, into light'.[87] It is rare for Riddell to address a character as 'my dear' and even more unusual to state halfway through the story that the happy ending is a certainty. The same strategy is repeated at the close of the house auction scene: Dolly has a heated verbal exchange with the auctioneer, Mr Meadows, regarding 'the modest bonnet box and portamenteau' she is entitled to keep. This confrontation is recorded by the narrator as a moment of 'victory' and a turning point in the story of failure:

> . . . but it is only after a battle any one engaged can tell when the tide of war began to turn. It turned for the Mortomley's then.
>
> It turned when Mrs Mortomley's lifted up her voice and defied Mr. Swanland's bailiff. In that moment, she ensured ultimate success for her husband – at a price.
>
> The years are before him still – the years of his life full of promise, full of hope – the past of bankruptcy, recent though it may be, is, nevertheless, an old story, and the name of Mortomley is a power once more.[88]

It is unclear how the verbal skirmish between Dolly and the bailiff can carry so much tactical weight, affecting in one single move the direction of Mortomley's future at the moment when that future seems most overdetermined by forces beyond his control. Rehabilitation and the promise of happiness do not emerge as natural outcomes of Dolly's victorious battles. Rather, they are forcefully willed by a narrator determined to offer the kind of 'justice' and 'humanity' that the law avows to protect, but does not seem automatically to guarantee. In this case too the representation is strained; the narrator's words abruptly produce the happy denouement ahead of the events leading to it. If the initial disruption of linearity amplifies a sense of dispossession (Mortomley's story, like his house, belongs to his creditors), this forestalling of closure is indicative of how much Dolly's brave romance is a fantasy of literary justice, a sort of fictional reparation covering up with a layer of hopefulness 'the places stony and thorny' where both heroine and author have dwelt. There is also another puzzling element: after all the anticipations of serenity and success, Riddell opts for the death of the heroine in the last chapter, as if Mortomley's return to normality and prosperity could only come at a further cost. Sacrificing Dolly, killing off her bravest and most resourceful heroine, can be seen as one final distortion of Riddell's habitual plotting: even adulteresses are rewarded in her fiction, but Dolly has to pay with her life, though no specific sin justifies the tragic end. She becomes the ultimate victim of bankruptcy – a choice that perhaps suggests the intensity of the sacrifices Riddell herself had to make.

Literary Aftermaths

Published in the same year as *Mortomley's Estate*, the one-volume novel *Frank Sinclair's Wife* takes up the theme of bankruptcy once again. The tone of this story is unusually light: Riddell uses the City setting to conduct a humorous experiment in gender inversion. The wife, Bella, unable to find any satisfaction in her dreary domestic routines, is invited by a disgruntled and neglected husband to step into his shoes and take his place as head of the firm, while he remains at home to look after the children, manage the servants and pour endless cups of tea. 'Bella and I have changed sexes' – writes Frank in his diary – 'she is now a man and I a woman; and . . . we have changed natures as well, since she is now amiability itself, and I – well, the less I say about my own feelings and temper the better'.[89] Bella accepts this challenge willingly and enjoys her new identity – for a while. Free from office cares and business anxieties, Frank takes pleasure in writing a journal and even courts the idea of turning to literature as a profession.

Bella and her female mentor sympathise with 'women's rights': 'For my own part', the narrator adds, 'if women choose to go out and work with and like men, it seems to me that it is simple folly to raise any objections'.[90] Yet, objections are raised in the novel, as Bella's limited understanding of how the credit system works, how business activities are managed not on the principle of 'cash only', delivers her husband into the hands of angry creditors. Bankruptcy inevitably ensues, but this time it is viewed more conventionally as a fortunate fall, a meaningful accident that resets the social and familial order disrupted by women who clamour for their rights and underestimate the complexities of business. In the process, Bella becomes 'humble and docile',[91] while Frank serves some time in prison before returning to the City and to a fresh season of prosperity. A new home in the country seals the final ideological victory of tradition over innovation. Designed to puncture inflated expectations, comedy seems to deliver a univocal lesson in this novel: home and work are best kept separate, under the supervision respectively of women and men; crossing symbolic borders leads to ruin. Yet, As Eileen Gillooly reminds us in *Smiles of Discontent*, 'feminine humour functions as a sustained, if diffusive, undercover assault upon the authority of the social order itself'.[92] Riddell's comic take on ruin expands into a gentle mockery of the literary patterns according to which the fall from material grace is usually narrated and rationalised: if Bella's feminist pretensions are laughed at, so too are the moral lessons one is supposed to derive from exemplary stories of bankruptcy. 'I am at a loss to decide', concludes Bella, 'whether it is well or ill for people thoroughly to understand such misery . . . Give me neither complete non-understanding nor complete understanding . . . give me just enough knowledge to sympathise with these people's troubles, but spare me the knowledge of how their troubles came to be deserved'.[93] Comedy does not stop short of ridiculing the godly morality of the fortunate fall this novel reproduces and lampoons.

Spurred by the need to increase her earnings, Riddell went on writing with renewed energy in the years successive to the bankruptcy. The ghost stories and supernatural tales for which she is still famous today – *Fairy Waters* (1873), *The Uninhabited House* (1875), *The Haunted River* (1877), to name just a few – began to appear in the mid seventies.[94] The spectral homes, the restless ghosts, the recurring dreams, the persistence of the past in the present, in short, the scenario of indefinite fears that the genre of the ghost story codifies may have proved congenial to Riddell in the aftermath of the crisis. Here was a form designed to evoke and assuage fears, to thrill readers with uncanny returns of the past and to reassure them that justice would ultimately be done – a form well-suited to capture the structure of the crisis, the breach of ordinary reality that the intervention of the supernatural, like the irruption of the extreme in the everyday, produces. If the bankruptcy, with its heavy legacy of uncertainties and worries, was a haunting presence in Riddell's household, the phantoms she summons in her ghost stories often haunt the present as a result of economic torts or to reveal unavenged murders motivated by greed (*Old Mrs. Jones; Nut Bush Farm; The Old House in Vauxhall Walk*).[95] As Bleiler notes, the 'ideas in Mrs. Riddell's ghost stories were not novel; they were shared by most of her contemporaries who wrote such fiction'.[96] She invented nothing new but became a proficient practitioner of the genre, returning in numerous stories to that perturbing moment when a breach in the normal texture of reality 'suddenly bursts open . . . and changes lives'.[97] Like most of her contemporaries, Riddell assigns to phantoms specific motivations: her ghosts hover between life and death in a spectral quest for justice. These providential apparitions, like Dolly Mortomley before them, are problem-solvers: they unveil the last piece of the puzzle, ensure that justice descends on earth and then vanish. Hauntings serve a purpose in the practical world of Riddell's imagination.

And a very practical purpose was also served by the publication of ghost stories – much in demand in those years and therefore, arguably, a reliable source of extra income for the author. Whether material or symbolic motivations (or both) are behind Riddell's frequent incursions into the Victorian gothic, these incursions suggest that the ghost of bankruptcy did not evaporate in a sudden puff. From the serious realism of *Mortomley's Estate*, to the comic vein of *Frank Sinclair's Wife* and the haunted atmospheres of the ghost stories, bankruptcy persists displaced in various literary forms – not exactly an 'unclaimed' experience, but certainly one that could not simply be left behind.

Notes

1 Black, pp. 19–20.
2 On the popularity and marketability of the ghost story see the introduction to Michael Cox & R.A. Gilbert, eds. *Victorian Ghost Stories: An Oxford Anthology* (Oxford: Oxford University Press, 2003). Cox and Gilbert suggest that women writers 'took to the ghost story so successfully' due to the 'practical – often pressing – need of a certain type of educated woman to earn a living . . . As ghost stories were consistently in demand it was natural that women, who provided so much fiction for the magazines, should provide these too' (p. xiv). Riddell produced ghost stories 'to make up the financial deficiencies of her husband' (p. xiv). The final section of this chapter briefly considers her contributions to this genre.
3 Henry Furniss, *Same Victorian Women – Good, Bad, and Indifferent* (London: John Lane, 1923), p. 6.
4 Stuart M. Ellis, *Wilkie Collins, Le Fanu, and Others*. 1934 (London: Constable 1951), p. 287.
5 Ibid., p. 282.
6 Ibid., p. 285.
7 Reid, p. 141.
8 Ibid., p. 142.
9 Ibid., p. 145.
10 Barbara Weiss considers 'novels of bankruptcy' those texts such as Dickens's *Dombey and Son*, Thackeray's *The Newcomes*, George Eliot's *The Mill on the Floss*, Trollope's *The Way We Live Now*, among others, in which scenes of bankruptcy, charged with emotional significance, are crucial turning points in the narrative.
11 In this chapter, I rely on some of the conceptual tools provided by trauma studies. Cathy Caruth, for instance, writes eloquently on trauma as an 'unclaimed experience': 'trauma is not locatable in the simple violent or original event in the individual's past, but rather in the way that its very unassimilated nature – the way it was precisely *not known* in the first instance – returns to haunt the survivor later on'. In other words, 'it is only in and through its inherent forgetting that [trauma] is first experienced at all', see Cathy Caruth, *Unclaimed Experience: Trauma, Narrative and History* (Baltimore, The Johns Hopkins University Press, 1996), p. 4 and p. 17. Hartman explains that 'the knowledge of trauma, or the knowledge which comes from that source, is composed of two contradictory elements. One is the traumatic event, registered rather than experienced. It seems to have bypassed perception and consciousness, and falls directly into the psyche. The other is a kind of memory of the event, in the form of a perpetual troping of it by the bypassed or severely split (dissociated) psyche. On the level of poetics, literal and figurative may correspond to these two types of cognition', see Geoffrey Hartman, 'On Traumatic Knowledge and Literary Studies', *New Literary History* 26, no. 3 (Summer 1995), p. 537. Although the experience of bankruptcy may not be traumatic in the technical, psychoanalytic meaning of the word (a violent event that 'falls' into the psyche), I would contend that some of the peculiarities of Riddell's fictional writing of disaster can best be explained as expressions of a traumatic kind of

knowledge. For a reading of financial crises as traumatic events see Paul Crosthwaite, 'Is Financial Crisis a Trauma?', *Cultural Critique* 82 (Fall 2013), pp. 34–67.

12 See Riddell v. Riddell and Smith. R133 (1871). British National Archives C16/747.
13 Ibid.
14 Ibid.
15 Nancy Henry, 'Economic Exhaustion and Literary Energy: Charlotte Riddell', Paper presented at the annual conference of the Interdisciplinary Nineteenth-Century Studies (INCS), Houston, Texas, 27–30 March 2014.
16 See Collinson v. Riddell, Riddell, Routledge Brothers, and Whiffin. C92 (1873). British National Archives C16/852 C92 C588778.
17 Weiss, *The Hell*, p. 17.
18 Charlotte Riddell, *Mortomley's Estate*, 1874, (London: Hutchinson, n.d.), p. 75.
19 Hartman, p. 537.
20 *The London Gazette* 23781 (3 October 1871), p. 4148.
21 'The popularity of liquidations by arrangements and compositions' writes Lester 'can be readily seen in the records of their use. In 1872 just under 7,000 liquidation by arrangement petitions were filed. The number of these petitions had increased by 1879 to 14,574. While some of this increase can be attributed to economic problems, none of those debating the issue acknowledged economic factors and only saw the dramatic increase in filing as a sign of improper evasion of the bankruptcy system', see Markham V. Lester, *Victorian Insolvency: Bankruptcy, Imprisonment for Debt, and Company Winding-Up in Nineteenth-Century England* (Oxford University Press, Oxford: 1995), p. 180.
22 See 'The New Bankruptcy Act', *The Economist* 27, no. 1372 (11 December 1869), p. 1458.
23 Lester, p. 178.
24 Ibid., p. 40.
25 The official assignees were paid out of the proceeds of the estate, though they were considered officers of the court: 'the officials that served the bankruptcy system tended to remain in their position over a considerable period of time. As a result, the system was run by almost the same group of public servants throughout its thirty-year existence' (Ibid., p. 83).
26 Ibid., p. 41.
27 Ibid., p. 123 and p. 157.
28 Ibid., p. 171.
29 'Bankruptcy', *The Saturday Review* 27, no. 712 (19 July 1879), p. 69.
30 Ibid.
31 'Our Bankruptcy Law', *The Examiner* 3687 (28 September 1878), p. 1227.
32 *Mortomley's Estate*, p. 84.
33 Ibid., p. 210.
34 Thomas Carlyle, *Past and Present*, 1843, in *Carlyle's Complete Works. The Sterling Edition* (Boston: Estes and Lauriat, 1885), vol. 12, p. 142.
35 'Mortomley Estate', *The Saturday Review* 38, no. 989 (10 October 1874), p. 481.
36 'The Mortomley's Estate', *The Spectator* 2422 (17 October 1874), p. 23. Whereas the *Saturday* was quite dismissive, the *Spectator* praised the novel in no uncertain terms.
37 *Mortomley's Estate*, p. 1.
38 Ibid., p. 1.
39 Ibid., p. 2 and p. 3.
40 On the slow 'transition from "family capitalism" to a more modern, corporate form of enterprise' within the City see Kynaston, pp. 301–14. In the historical examples he considers, the decision to go public is often fraught with doubts; in the textile sector of the City, for example, 'by 1873 a series of firms . . . had decided to incorporate, thus giving up traditional family control' (p. 303), but incorporation was only grudgingly

accepted by long-established family firms. The development of corporate capitalism in the second half of the nineteenth century, as Taylor argues 'did not dominate the economy in the way that it was to in the twentieth century; it has been estimated that even by 1885, at least 90 percent of "important business organistions", excluding one-man firms and public utilities, were partnerships. Nevertheless the multiplication of new joint-stock companies dazzled contemporaries, for it was unlike anything that had been witnessed before', see Taylor, *Creating*, p. 6.

41 *Mortomley's Estate*, p. 12.
42 Ibid., pp. 113–14.
43 There is countless evidence, in popular culture, of the social antipathy towards joint-stock companies and speculation that emerged in response to changes in the legislative framework, as Taylor's books, *Creating Capitalism* and *Boardroom Scandals*, persuasively document.
44 'Mortomley's Estate', *Saturday*, p. 481.
45 *Mortomley's Estate*, p. 286.
46 Ibid., p. 114.
47 Ibid., p. 29.
48 Ibid., p. 31.
49 Weiss, *The Hell*, p. 66.
50 Ibid., p. 82.
51 David Trotter, 'Household Clearances in Victorian Fiction', *19: Interdisciplinary Studies in the Long Nineteenth Century*, 6 (2008), p. 9, http://www.19.bbk.ac.uk (accessed 2 May 2015).
52 Weiss, *The Hell*, p. 110.
53 As Dolin argues: 'Legal procedure provides such an influential model of reality-construction in the modern West that fictional critiques of the law are often unable to escape its forms and its rhetoric' see Kieran Dolin, *Fiction and the Law: Legal Discourse in Victorian and Modernist Literature* (Cambridge: Cambridge University Press, 1999), p. 19.
54 'Mortomley's Estate', *Saturday*, p. 481.
55 Ibid.
56 *Mortomley's Estate*, p. 278.
57 Trotter, 'Household', p. 1.
58 Weiss, *The Hell*, p. 105.
59 In *Framley Parsonage* (1861), Trollope adopts a tone of gentle teasing when describing Mrs. Robarts's feelings for the beautiful objects contaminated by the touch of the 'philistines' in the house: 'O ladies, who have drawing-rooms in which the things are pretty, good and dear to you, think of what it would be to have two bailiffs rummaging among them with pen and ink-horn, making a catalogue preparatory to a sheriff's auction; and all without fault or extravagance of your own', see Anthony Trollope, *Framley Parsonage*, 1861, (Oxford: Oxford University Press, 1980), p. 527.
60 In his essay 'The cultural biography of things', the anthropologist Igor Kopytoff analyses the cultural strategies whereby objects move out of the commodity state: 'the singular and the commodity' tend to be seen as opposites, but in many empirical cases, he writes, 'the forces of commoditization and singularization are intertwined in ways far more subtle than our ideal model can show', see Igor Kopytoff, 'The cultural biography of things: commoditization as a process', in *The social life of things: Commodities in cultural perspective*, ed. Arjun Appadurai (Cambridge: Cambridge University Press, 1986), pp. 87–8.
61 *Mortomley's Estate*, p. 82.
62 Ibid., p. 84.
63 Ibid., pp. 223–4.
64 Ibid., p. 242.

65 Ibid., p. 209.
66 Ibid., p. 239.
67 For a thorough discussion of how insolvency statistics were compiled and how 'susceptible to misrepresentation' they are see Lester, pp. 241–86. Weiss claims that there was a 'sharp increase in bankruptcy from the middle of the eighteenth century to the later Victorian period'; by the mid nineteenth century, 'bankruptcy had become a necessary refuge for those marginal entrepreneurs who were unable to survive the vicissitudes of a capitalist economy' (Weiss, *The Hell*, p. 24 and p. 40).
68 See Rothberg on the definition of traumatic realism: 'I would suggest that traumatic realism is an attempt to produce the traumatic event as an object of knowledge and to program and thus transform its readers so that they are forced to acknowledge their relationship to posttraumatic culture. Because it seeks both to construct access to a previously unknowable object and to instruct an audience in how to approach that object, the stakes of traumatic realism are both epistemological and pedagogical', see Michael Rothberg, *Traumatic Realism*, (Minneapolis: University of Minnesota Press, 2000), p. 103.
69 Ibid., p. 137.
70 William Blackstone, *Commentaries on the Laws of England, A New Edition with the Last Corrections of the Author* (London: William Reed, 1811), vol. 2, chapter 31, p. 471.
71 Ibid., p. 488.
72 Hunter has analysed the role of daughters in bankruptcy scenes, arguing that 'While Victorian novels rarely represent financial ruin as an outright benefit to daughters, they frequently suggest that daughters are positively transformed or liberated by such misfortunes', see Leeann Hunter, 'Communities Built from Ruins: Social Economics in Victorian Novels of Bankruptcy', *Women's Studies Quarterly* 39, 3 & 4 (Fall/Winter 2011), p. 137.
73 *Mortomley's Estate*, p. 38 and p. 42.
74 Ibid., p. 44 and p. 38.
75 Ibid., p. 42. Dolly shares some traits with other heroines in Riddell's previous novels (Ada Perkins, for instance, or Ruby in *City and Suburb*) who are notable for their misalignment with respectable standards of behaviour and for their association with disorderly conduct, bad form, or 'vulgarity': they flaunt a certain disregard for moderation that, in Dolly's case, is turned into an asset rather than a liability. Remarkable are the descriptions of Dolly's clothes, mostly shocking for their elaborateness and strong colours especially in relation to the enforced modesty and humbleness imposed by the bankruptcy context. Dolly's dresses are the objective correlative of both her singularity and her non-acceptance of the reality of disaster.
76 Ibid., p. 61.
77 To explain the unexplainable antipathy towards Dolly and her daughter, Riddell quotes Charles Lamb. In 'Imperfect Sympathies', Lamb ascribes to imponderable matters of 'taste' all sorts of ugly feelings projected onto the 'other', see Charles Lamb, 'Imperfect Sympathies', 1821, in *The Essays of Elia* (London: The Walter Scott Press, n.d), pp. 91–9. Dolly's otherness or foreignness might also contain an echo of Riddell's personal history; as an immigrant moving to London in the mid 1850s she might have encountered prejudices similar to the ones Dolly has to contend with in the City.
78 *Mortomley's Estate*, p. 148.
79 Ibid., p. 147.
80 Ibid., p. 119.
81 Ibid., p. 137.
82 Ibid., p. 422.
83 In her study of 'giving women' in Victorian culture, Jill Rappoport examines the 'peer alliances women established with one another through gift-giving' recovering, as she

argues, 'a complex history of bourgeois women's strategies for achieving economic agency during a period when most lacked property rights and professional opportunities. Through gifts that ranged from small tokens to their own bodies, women entered into volatile and profitable economic negotiations of power and created diverse forms of community' (p. 5). The monetary gift Dolly receives from Leonora is clearly connoted as feminine: i.e. the money is Leonora's own, not her husband's and as such can be accepted by Dolly without any qualm. The money is then used as start-up capital to establish the new colour manufactory outside of London, in an idyllic natural enclave, a community of sorts, where Leonora too will find refuge after her husband's financial collapse and subsequent suicide.

84 *Mortomley's Estate*, p. 364.

85 Ibid., p. 311.

86 Ibid., p. 234. Dolly's bouts of anger typically take the form of curt letters she fires off in moments of intense distress. In one of these missives, like an improvised Caliban, she curses. Upon realising that Henry, Leonora's husband, considers the Mortomleys contaminated by the stigma of bankruptcy and therefore unfit to be seen in his house, Dolly writes to her friend: 'I would wish that the man you have had the misfortune to marry might be beggared and ruined tomorrow – beggared, more completely ruined, more utterly even than we have been' (p. 261). And sure enough, the man in question quickly succumbs to a disastrous financial calamity. Affect theory reminds us that anger 'lies at the root of an intuitive and manageable sense of daily justice and is not to be confined to such primitive forms of justice . . . as the revenge or honour system which we pride ourselves on having replaced by our idea of a civilized life under an objective system of explicit laws and impersonal justice', see Philip Fisher, *The Vehement Passions* (Princeton: Princeton University Press, 2002), pp. 172–3. In the novel, Dolly's capacity for 'correct' anger is an integral part of her desire to restore some sense of justice.

87 *Mortomley's Estate*, p. 225.

88 Ibid., p. 248.

89 Charlotte Riddell, *Frank Sinclair's Wife and Forewarned, Forearmed*, 1874, (London: Hutchinson, n.d.), p. 183.

90 Ibid., p. 73

91 Ibid., p. 256.

92 Eileen Gillooly, *Smiles of Discontent: Humor, Gender, and Nineteenth-Century British Fiction* (Chicago: The University of Chicago Press, 1999), p. 24.

93 *Frank Sinclair's Wife*, p. 265.

94 'Riddell is notable amongst Victorian writers for her longer supernatural novels and for producing one of the first collections of ghost stories, which were only beginning to appear in collected form by the 1870s and the 1880s', see Emma Liggins, 'Introduction' in *Weird Stories by Charlotte Riddell* (London: Victorian Secrets, 2009), p. i.

95 In her analysis of Riddell's and Oliphant's 'uncomfortable houses', Edmundson observes that 'Women writers of the supernatural frequently used the motif of the haunted house to comment on property, class and economic issues. In many of their stories, these "uncomfortable houses", as they were popularly called at the time, are troubled because of some injustice or social inequality that left the past inhabitants seeking for help from the current owners of properties', see Melissa Edmundson, 'The "Uncomfortable Houses" of Charlotte Riddell and Margaret Oliphant', *Gothic Studies* 12, no. 1 (2010), p. 51.

96 Bleiler, p. xvii.

97 Ibid.

9   Past and Present
The Senior Partner and
Mitre Court

> We have made for ourselves strange gods, and we live in a stage of transition to a
> yet unknown order . . .We hold enlarged conceptions of our place in the scale of
> the peoples of the earth, but what England's mission really is we have not quite
> decided.
>
> T.H.S. Escott, *England: Its People, Polity and Pursuits*, 1879

At the end of a troubled decade, in 1879, the journalist and social historian
Thomas Hey Sweet Escott (1844–1924) described the condition of England as
one of relative stasis or 'partial stagnation': 'we have come to occupy a position
in which we are no longer progressing', he states, 'but rather appear to be standing still, if we are not even falling back. And at this precise time it is that we find
other nations able to compete with us to an extent as we have never before experienced . . . Things are in a critical way with us.'[1] Overviewing the specific situation of 'commercial and financial England', Escott speculates about its imminent
future, wondering whether his country will ever 'resume the sceptre of an autocrat
in trade' or whether the signs of decline he diagnoses announce the permanent loss
of what once was a position of unquestioned power. His conclusion is hopeful:
'prosperous times may again be looked for', he reassures his readers, but they will
not come 'unless our traders abandon the ways of trickery and deceit, and learn
the virtues which distinguished their forefathers in the proud days in which English mercantile honour was unstained, and when the name of English goods was
synonymous for excellence'.[2] The proud days of mercantile glories serve as a prop
to sustain a vision of the future in which decline or degeneration is averted by a
vigorous revival of the 'spring and elasticity' of English trade on a global scale.
   Perceptions of economic decline were widespread in the 1880s. As Theodore Hoppen remarks: 'the coincidence of increasing industrial maturity, rapid
advances by rivals abroad and spasmodic bad time in the years after 1873 induced
repeated contemporary assertions that the late Victorian economy was somehow
in decline'.[3] Economic historians have demonstrated that Britain's decline in the
last quarter of the nineteenth century was not as severe or extensive as previous
analyses believed it to be.[4] But for late Victorian observers, who experienced or
witnessed slow internal growth, loss of competitiveness in international markets

and the downward drift of prices and interest rates, the spectre of permanent deterioration loomed large. 'A strange darkness appears to have fallen upon the earth', declared *Tinsley's Magazine* in January 1879, 'Progress halts in her onward march. Civilisation pauses'.[5] In some cases, gloomy predictions of prolonged stagnation came escorted by unflattering comparisons between England and its closest competitors, Germany and America, which laid bare the 'shortcomings of the British merchant':

> For a long time past consular reports and travellers' books have been telling the public the same universal story of the German pushing himself into every branch of business in every part of the world, and the British merchant either letting him occupy unopposed the new market, or allowing himself to be more or less thrust upon it.[6]

Where once the British merchant or trader dominated entire regions 'with an authority unquestioned' – so the narrative goes – now German as well as French and Italian trading adventurers are reaping the rewards of vigorous entrepreneurship. A nostalgic vision of the British merchant, 'the pioneer of commerce', transpires behind impassioned denunciations of the nation's failings: 'There was a time when what the German trader is now everywhere doing was being done by ourselves . . . Wherever the explorer discovered a new highway the trader followed, and obstacles a hundred times more difficult than the merchant has to face to-day were treated as trifles by the pioneers of commerce'.[7] In the pages of the periodical press, the mercantile heroism of 'olden times' received a fair deal of attention. In 1879–1880, *London Society* ran a series of article entitled 'Fortunes Made in Business'; though not specifically focused on English merchants, these illustrations of successful entrepreneurship in the not too distant past cast commercial vitality and individual ingenuity as national virtues that ought to be properly celebrated or protected from extinction.[8] The author of 'Romance in Business', published in the *Blackwood's Edinburgh Magazine* in 1882, evokes the 'stirring romance of the olden time' not to reminisce about warlike adventures, but to extol the fascination of 'the story of trading' up to the present time.[9] Commentators inclined to defend the dignity of business and commerce in the face of declining returns frequently used the rich heritage of the past to project a hopeful vision of the present and the future: 'The merchants of Venice were statesmen and princes', writes the author of 'Noblemen in Business', but 'our London merchants, in their honest broadcloth, [are not] inferior to those who once wore the Tyran dye or the Venetian velvet'.[10] In a different spirit, but with an analogous inclination to romanticise the archetypal figure of the merchant, the writer James Payne recalls his youthful desire to become a merchant in 'The Literary Calling and its Future', which appeared in the December 1878 issue of *Nineteenth-Century*:

> I do remember (when between seven and eight) having a passionate longing to become a merchant. I had no notion, however, of the preliminary stages; the high stool in the close street; luncheon at the counter, standing . . . and

imprisonment at the office on the eves of mail night till the large hours of pm . . . The sort of merchant I wanted to be was never found in *Post Office Directory*, but in the *Arabian Nights*, trading to Bussorah, chiefly in pearls and diamonds.[11]

In the cultural narrative of national economic decline, the figure of the once heroic merchant crops up in various shapes and sizes, his daring often contrasted with contemporary weaknesses, the romance of his adventures with the prosaic reality of stagnation or dull office work. The most magniloquent defence of the value of commerce and business and of the exemplarity of the 'Man of Business Absolute' appeared in the pages of the *New Monthly Magazine* in a series of long articles signed 'Launcelot Cross,' running from June 1879 to January 1880. Immortalised in Cross's orotund rhetoric, is an abstract conception of business as the essence of history: 'the essence of all History is the History of Business', he claims.[12] Piling up references to the classics, from Homer to Plutarch, Cross indulges in high-sounding declarations: 'In dark moments, [Business] has a divine potentiality. When prophets fail, and present substance seems to melt beneath the feet . . . it will then catch at every jutting, frieze, buttress to sustain itself by: find the music of hope in any chance syllable: accept any call or summons to new endeavours, or to substantiate the old'.[13] The lavish show of erudition; the emphatic attempt to distil timeless truths; the vertiginous accumulation of historical *exempla* all betray the urge to reconnect past and present and to revive a sense of nobility, strength and valour against the fears of exhaustion haunting late Victorian culture. The 'Hero' of business, Cross concludes, 'may appear as Prime Minister . . . or he may be a merchant or shopkeeper, but wherever he is he has an equal purpose, and is inspired in equal manner'. Most importantly, 'He is never without success'.[14]

The City novels Charlotte Riddell wrote in the 1880s register late nineteenth-century anxieties about economic decline. In *Mitre Court* (1885), England is described as a 'foolish nation impelled along the rails of life by the force of its own weight';[15] while the story narrated in *The Senior Partner* (1881) rules out any vision of progress. The worthy British merchant and his nemesis, the pushy German trader – frequently evoked in tandem by Victorian commentators – occupy centre stage in *The Senior Partner* and *Mitre Court* respectively. The symbolic valence of these iconic figures, whether positive or negative, is confirmed in Riddell's fictions of decline. In both novels, the prevailing mood is one of disillusionment. The modern orientation towards autonomy that in her business stories used to drive the biographical trajectories of youthful protagonists, who sought and found in the City a space of self-determination, still animates the aspirations of a new generation of market players. But their struggles recede into the background, while domineering Victorian fathers come to the fore, their monumental presence obfuscating the narrative destinies of their progeny. Overshadowed by imposing middle-aged fathers, younger sons find little to rejoice in their condition of posteriority. For them modernity is not synonymous with progress, individual development and social mobility. Relative stasis, rather than restless dynamism, characterises their present. In narrative terms, their textual existence is well-nigh plotless: youth no longer serves as the master trope of modernity.[16]

What takes its place is a reified opposition between mature adulthood and restless, discontented youth, between overbearing fathers and frustrated sons locked in a combat that has no real development. As the notion of progress or modernisation is subject to intense critical scrutiny, the plot of development hinging on the youthful individual coming to terms with the demands of socialisation appears stunted, inhibited and interrupted rather than brought to completion. Narratives of 'stunted youth', as Jed Esty observes, abound in the late Victorian era. 'In later iterations of the novel of youth', Esty writes, 'the ideological fantasy of bounded growth – of restive youth bent to the asymptote of stable adulthood – becomes more conspicuous as a problem and thus becomes subject to dramatic estrangement and startling revisions'.[17] The manner in which Riddell problematises or revises the allegories of self-making she had repeatedly articulated in her previous novels entails a decided veering away from 'narration' towards 'observation', observation of character, in particular, with a marked preference for obsolete literary figures. The miser clad in threadbare clothes (*Mitre Court*) and the extremely parsimonious merchant dealing only in cash (*The Senior Partner*) bring with them the memory of a much earlier stage in the development of capitalism when primary accumulation and monopolistic advantages sustained the mercantile fortunes of the nation. These heritage characters, celebrated and berated in literary texts over the centuries,[18] compete for the reader's attention with a more modern breed of businessmen, a small cohort of cosmopolitan traders, brokers and promoters who are declared representative men of the present.[19] Nothing speaks more clearly of a demoralised, non-progressive temporality, in these novels, than Riddell's intense focus on characterisation as a state not a process, connected to the progression of the story by dint of minimal intersections. Young or old, honest or dishonest, these characters are going nowhere.

Indeed, in a very literal sense they are stuck in the City, now promoted to the status of an isolated setting, unrelated to suburban or rural spaces and only tenuously connected to the domestic sphere. This narrowing down of the novel's geography re-invents the City as a rather claustrophobic locale precisely at a time when the actual City was consolidating and expanding its strategic role as the hub of international trade and finance.[20] The more global becomes its reach, the more problematic it is, for Riddell, to imagine the City as a space of opportunities. The freedom to reinvent oneself, which Alan Ruthven, George Geith, Lawrence Barbour and other business heroes had enjoyed with varied degrees of success, is exposed as a myth, a fable that does not really deliver what it promises.

In addition to confirming late nineteenth-century fears of decline and the disenchantment with narratives of progress that Riddell shares with other novelists in this transitional period, *The Senior Partner* and *Mitre Court* still retain a residual realist agenda and a serious commitment to investigating the changing dynamics of commercial modernity. In *The Senior Partner*, it is the tradition of British personal or family capitalism that comes under the spotlight, as the emergence of 'big business' threatens the survival of small firms or one-man partnerships;

while *Mitre Court* resonates with late Victorian concerns about cultural heritage and the urgent need to protect architectural testimonies of the past threatened by decay and by what William Morris called the 'forgery' of restoration.[21] A central presence in this novel is the beautiful and decrepit house in Botolph Lane where Sir Christopher Wren used to live, a real building that Riddell translates into a fictional place with the explicit intention of redeeming it from oblivion. Preserving the past from the destructive impetus of modernisation, as I argue in this chapter, is the realist *enjeu* of Riddell's semi-naturalist fiction. Her preservationist stance is most noticeable in the attempt to protect both historical landmarks and old forms of economic subjectivity, psychological as well as material architectures whose heritage value is memorialised in her writing. This caring attitude towards the past, however, is in tension with the critical, even corrosive perspective of the disenchanted late nineteenth-century narrator, resulting in a somewhat uneasy cohabitation of the residual, empathic affectivity of realism and the more deterministic streak of incipient naturalism. Both novels evoke the past as heritage, but only to suggest that there is no going back.

Family Capitalism in *The Senior Partner*

Business historians agree that the family firm tradition, in the British context, was remarkably resilient, its influence over business organisation extending well into the twentieth century.[22] More contentious is whether this tradition fostered managerial inefficiency and conservatism, thus contributing to determining the substantial loss of market share that Britain experienced in the late Victorian era. Alfred D. Chandler has argued that the 'continuing commitment to personal management and therefore personal capitalism' is directly related to the failure of British entrepreneurs 'to make the essential three-pronged investment in manufacturing, marketing and management in a number of capital-intensive industries in the Second Industrial Revolution'.[23] Objecting to Chandler's hypothesis, Mary Rose claims that 'the causal relationship between family run firms and economic decay can be overdrawn': the family firm, Rose explains, is not necessarily 'a harbinger of conservatism and stagnation', just as large-scale firms 'cannot be seen as a universally appropriate business strategy'.[24] By the last decades of the nineteenth century, increased foreign competition (due to the industrialisation of Germany and the United States) altered the international economic environment; as more players entered the game, 'Britain's share of the world's manufacturing output declined from nearly 20 per cent in 1860 to 14 per cent on the Eve of the First World War'.[25] But the national preference for family firms and personal management should not be cast as the villain in the narrative of macroeconomic decline.

In addition to contesting Chandler's thesis of the negative influence exerted by a moribund family-firm model, Rose identifies in the question of leadership transition and intergenerational succession a problematic element in the history of nineteenth-century British firms: 'there is considerable evidence to suggest that the majority of family firms did not enjoy longevity, and that at least part of the problem lies in the failure of business leaders to plan for their own succession'.[26] Other factors are more commonly adduced to explain the deteriorating performance of family firms; foremost among them is the so-called 'Buddenbrooks syndrome': 'families become wealthier, later generations become gentrified, neglecting their business or withdrawing altogether'.[27] The Buddenbrooks syndrome, however, Rose contends, is an unsatisfactory explanation of the problems encountered by maturing family firms in the late nineteenth and early twentieth centuries. The slow survival rate of the majority of these firms was heavily affected by the 'failure to provide for a smooth and effective succession'.[28] It was not uncommon for successful nineteenth-century businessmen to cling to their position of power for too long, delaying retirement and failing to make formal provision for the transmission of leadership from one generation to another: 'It is ironic', Rose concludes, 'in looking at nineteenth-century entrepreneurs, to find that the very character traits which made them successful in the first place, could lead them into entrepreneurial failure in later life'.[29]

With characteristic perspicacity, Riddell zooms in on the question of intergenerational succession in *The Senior Partner*.[30] The story is set in the late 1850s and early 1860s, but the focus on the problem of continuity and interpersonal relationships within family firms alludes to a set of historical concerns that were being thrown into relief by the emergence of big business – 'large scale, vertically-integrated and hierarchically organized firms'[31] – on the national and international scene in the last decades of the nineteenth century. It is not uncommon for Riddell to tackle in her novels topical issues related to the changing dynamics of the business world: the rise of the professional accountant in *George Geith*, the much debated question of food and drink adulteration in *The Race for Wealth* and the controversial bankruptcy legislation in *Mortomley's Estate* are good cases in point. *The Senior Partner* captures a moment of transition in the history of British business when the traditional family-firm model came under pressure as new forms of business organisation materialised; in the words of Thomas Escott: 'everywhere small establishments have been swallowed up in large, the private firm is absorbed in the limited company; the private bank in the joint-stock'.[32]

The senior partner of the novel's title, Mr. Pousnett, willing to experiment with new methods of doing business, turns his firm into a limited company at the earliest opportunity: ' "Pousnetts" was about the first house with a great reputation to take the initiative of "allowing the general public to participate in its profits", and the general public proved itself grateful for the chance afforded'.[33] In stark contrast to Pousnett's pro-modern orientation, the novel features the anti-modern tenacity of Robert McCullagh (Old Rob), Scottish merchant and wholesale dealer in confectionary, who leads his successful one-man partnership like an autocrat, with little consideration for the development of any strategy that might involve the delegation of responsibility to his potential successors: 'It's strange', he reflects at one point, 'that out o' four sons there's not one o' the lot I'd care to see carrying on this business after me'.[34] Squeezed between the generous character space allotted to these senior personages (and the business alternatives they embody), is a generation of disoriented sons and cousins, some of them used as commercial pawns by Old Rob, others more inclined to strive for autonomy and to take considerable risks in the hope of attaining their share of prosperity and independence. Unlike his brothers, marginal to the story, Robert McCullagh junior is a co-protagonist in a plot that pits his attempts to gain independence against the machinations of Pousnett and the pertinacious refusals of his father. Seduced by the prospect of a partnership in the House of Pousnett, Robert borrows money at an exorbitant rate of interest to secure his appointment, and spends the remainder of the story partially regretting his choice and smarting under the yoke of his debt. The senior partner bequeaths to his own son and to Robert a tainted legacy of fraudulent management, falsified accounts and liabilities that the junior partners are unable not only to administer but to rectify. Decline follows rapidly for Pousnett & Co. and when the company founders the blame falls on Robert. His father, on the other hand, manages to stay afloat in a volatile economic environment (the crash of Pousnett & Co. is soon replicated by the fall of the Corner House which disseminates panic in the City), though his profits follow a decreasing curve. Father and son are reconciled in the end through the auspicious mediation of Robert's wife, Janey, who nurses the ailing progenitor while Robert attempts, without success, to make his fortune in America. Back in England, he accepts the very modest job that his father offers.

This is the bare outline of the novel's plot. The vicissitudes of family firms drive the story forward with only minimal concessions to lateral sub-plots: romance, falling in love and the unfolding of reciprocal affections occur off stage; while adultery and irregular feelings are simply ruled out. The connection of the intimate and the commercial is severed in this City novel which is almost entirely devoted to observing an older generation of businessmen bent on retaining their position of power and a motley group of epigones who are trapped in a condition of suspended 'middleness', neither success nor utter failure awaiting them at the end of the line. Unsavoury though this type of story may sound, some Victorian reviewers found much to praise in Riddell's novel. The *London Standard* proclaimed *The Senior Partner* Riddell's 'best production': 'We think we may go further and pronounce her present work to be her masterpiece'. What makes this novel an accomplishment, according to the anonymous reviewer, is the refinement of characterisation, extolled via a comparison between Riddell's Old Rob and Dickens's Scrooge that casts the former as a superior creation:

> There is all the difference between a Rembrandt and a Rowlandson, between the character painting of a great artist and the burlesque distortion of a clever caricaturist. It is true that, like Scrooge, the Scotch confectioner softens in the end, but the process which leads to his conversion is no machinery of ghosts and shadows . . . And here it is that Mrs. Riddell shows herself the true artist we have called her.[35]

The *Pall Mall Gazette* pronounced *The Senior Partner* 'as unsentimental as a novel well can be' and applauded the author for the audacity shown in choosing Plutus rather than Cupid as her muse: 'it is money and not love which makes the world go round. Nevertheless, some courage is required of an author to desert the traditions of the school, and to invoke Plutus, instead of Cupid, as the inspiring genius of a novel in three volumes'.[36] The main interest of the novel, the reviewer claims, lies in its 'illustrations of character' with respect to which plot is deemed secondary.

Unsentimental, mainly descriptive and with a slender plot: Riddell's novel eschews sensational elements (adultery) and thrilling incidents, elaborate twists in the plot and the pleasure of suspense, in favour of a more static kind of chronicle, marked by undramatic beginnings and endings, and by a decisive investment in the power of narrative middles to sustain the reader's attention. Nineteenth-century novelists 'were absorbed in the experience of middleness *per se*'; they spent 'hundreds of pages in *medias res*, absorbed in complex processes of *Bildung* and characterization, carefully deploying suspenseful cliffhangers and ironic interruptions, managing mistakes and crises, interludes, digressions, and transitions'.[37] The slow middle of sprawling nineteenth-century novels, Levine and Ortiz-Robles maintain, was likely to have been appreciated by Victorian readers who 'enjoyed a leisurely, dilatory, plotless middle much more than we have ever recognized'.[38]

In *The Senior Partner*, no process of *Bildung*, complex or otherwise, and no suspenseful cliffhanger, disturb the dominion of the 'characterological middle'[39] monopolised by the rather obsolete figure of Old Rob, 'the architect and builder of his own fortune'.[40] His adherence to an absolute ideal of self-help, attachment to traditional business values and refusal to use credit instruments of any denomination ('bills are the Satan of trade')[41] mark him as an eccentric emissary from the past. Like the old, once grandiose house he inhabits, which 'appeals mutely against the purposes to which it has been turned',[42] 'plain old Rab' is firmly resisting the modern ways of commerce, preaching to his sons the long-term benefits of extreme prudence and self-denial, while openly distrusting their ability to replicate his success. When Pousnett offers Robert the partnership, his father's surprise ('*why they would take you!*') is thus decoded by the narrator: 'There was nothing remarkable in his words, but the tone in which Mr. McCullagh spoke italicised every one of them. It implied, "Here is a poor, weak, vain, useless creature; what can a big firm like that want with a brainless idiot I would not give a pound a week to for entering goods in the day-book?"'.[43] Abrupt and domineering, jealously defending his business from the potential encroachment of young talent ('what I have, I have made myself; what I own I'll keep for myself'),[44] Old Rob is nonetheless the quintessence of 'the worthy merchant'[45] whose commercial integrity is elevated to the status of a precious relic in a world dominated by unscrupulous business practices.

There is something wholesome in the patently anti-modern attire of the Scottish merchant; 'a scent of Windsor soap, and a perfume of fragrant linen and broadcloth laid aside with lavender-bags between'[46] emanate from his well-tailored Sunday clothes as well as from his well-structured, simplified architecture of beliefs. For the critic of the *London Standard*, this 'hard, avaricious, vindictive, close-fisted' merchant is endowed with a 'rugged tenderness' that is almost 'poetical': 'in the range of modern English literature we rarely remember a character more original, more complex, and yet more consistent with itself'.[47] Victorian professional

readers responded appreciatively to what they saw as the charming unpleasant-
ness of a character so out of tune with modern life and so evocative of old times
that even his unashamed self-interest could appear endearing rather than greedy.
It is the residual status, the heritage value of Old Rob and what he represents that
Riddell immortalises in her fiction. His struggles to build singlehandedly the fortunes he now jealously guards; the heroic phase of capitalist accumulation briefly
summed up in the account of the merchant's rise from rags to riches ('Little by
little, month by month, year by year, the business grew and flourished')[48] and
the enduring faith he has in self-denial, parsimony and cash allude to an earlier
commercial era in which the myth of the energetic individual attaining prosperity through self-help, thriftiness and unflinching honesty was the most significant
cultural narrative of capitalist modernity.

In *The Senior Partner*, this myth becomes the object of a backward-looking
curiosity; the perspective from which the novel observes its survival in the present
is divided between nostalgia and ironic distance, between an undeniable sympathy
for the timeworn character of the worthy merchant and a diffuse scepticism about
the values he embodies. Riddell grants him the lion's share in the novel's character system and includes a few scenes that seem designed with the sole purpose of
enlisting the reader's sympathy for this character and the past he represents. For
instance, at one of the lavish dinner parties organised by the Pussnetts, the merchant shines with charming quaintness and supreme self-confidence: 'Amongst
all that grandeur he sat unmoved as the Sphinx in the desert . . . Mr. McCullagh
might have been sitting at great men's feasts all his life far aught any one could
from his manner have told to the contrary'.[49] His vigorous singing, conversational
skills, impressive knowledge of the art of knitting and above all his 'irresistible'[50]
originality single him out from the more anonymous aggregate of City guests.
Unperturbed by the spectacle of prosperity, the merchant devotes himself 'to
doing the agreeable'[51] betraying no sign of embarrassment. Like the Sphinx, he
enjoys the dignity of antiquity.

While the novel certainly encourages a protective attitude vis-à-vis this character and his oddities, it also casts doubt on the authenticity of his narrative of
self-making, demystified as a construction, a retrospective fiction. Already in the
second chapter, the narrator explains that 'Accident had a larger share in compassing Mr. McCullagh's worldly prosperity than that gentleman would have cared to
acknowledge'.[52] More specifically, as the story unfolds, it becomes clear that Old
Rob's steady profits derive from the monopolistic advantage he has enjoyed for a
very long time:

> Few persons in business had ever experienced less harass in his trade than
> the merchant who had risen so fast and done so well. Hitherto he had been
> in the enviable position of having the market all to himself; and like every-
> one whom Fortune has favoured, he believed he owed his prosperity less to
> her kindness than to some extraordinary merit and capacity on his own part.
> Actually, he had felt so sure of himself, so satisfied that the Scotch trade
> in provisions meant Robert McCullagh and none other, that even the very

notion of competition never entered his mind until Mr. Pousnett's slight reference to such a possibility came like a jarring discord across the harmony of
nearly thirty years' success.[53]

Objective circumstances – the absence of competitors in the market – rather
than subjective virtues – honesty – have ensured the continuous flow of profits
and the position of dominance of the one-man partnership run by the merchant.
The heroic striving and the capitalist ethos of the founder of this small firm
are simultaneously memorialised, arranged on a most prominent plinth, and
declared a bit of a sham by a disenchanted narrator whose perspective oscillates
between conserving and dissecting the cultural narratives of capitalism. On the
one hand, the novel displays self-help in its purest form, encased in the figure
of the stubbornly autonomous merchant; on the other hand, Riddell insinuates
doubts about the veracity of Old Rob's proud tale of self-making, exposing it as
delusionary.

In the remainder of the story, the act of preservation that the novel performs
becomes increasingly difficult to sustain as the focus on the very topical question
of intergenerational disputes within the family firm brings to the fore the tyranny
of the past over the present. The novel's understanding of historical continuity is
deeply divided: if the discourse of preservation promotes a caring attitude towards
the past, the thematic focus on the unresolved conflicts between fathers and sons
showcases in all its negative splendour the despotic rule of the past. As the story
progresses, Old Rob's fierce independence and obstinate refusal to plan for his
succession, to devise a strategy for the future of the firm, appear distinctly self-
serving. It is true that he manages to defend his profits even when competition
appears on the scene, but he does so by blatantly exploiting his sons, David and
Archie, as commercial pawns: David is hurriedly called back from Scotland when
his father needs him to manage lateral branches of his firm;[54] then, when David
and Archie's requests for innovation become too insistent, Old Rob pays them off
('the new ways ye're so fond of aren't mine')[55] and calls in his old bookkeeper,
Mr Roy, only to liquidate him soon afterwards, jealous of the power Mr Roy has
acquired in the warehouse. In other words, a series of sudden, despotic decisions
rather than strategic, rational planning is the merchant's response to altered economic circumstances. In the light of Mary B. Rose's hypothesis that the failure of
British entrepreneurs to provide for succession determined the lack of longevity
of the majority of family firms, *The Senior Partner* can be considered a fictional
interpretation of the drawbacks and contradictions of personal capitalism. When
faced with rising competition, the merchant falls back on an autocratic model
of management, disposing of his sons as best he pleases and undermining any
prospect of innovation; his short-term earnings are maximised at the expense of
long-term income generation.

In the novel, innovation is synonymous with limited liability and fraudulent
schemes, as the quick rise and rapid demise of the global enterprise of Pousnett &
Co. testifies. There are, in other words, no real alternatives for the younger generation of participants in the race for wealth; they do not find either in the past or

in the present of family capitalism any space for self-realisation. The struggles of Robert junior and his cousin, Alf Mostin, are narrated through the lens of incipient naturalism: there is a marked emphasis on heredity as an almost absolute determinant of one's character; the sagacious use of free will is the prerogative of fathers, while deterministic constraints limit the choices of their sons and sabotage their chances of ever achieving the financial independence they seek.[56] Fathers – Old Rob and Pousnett – live in a liberal world where individual freedom still has meaning; for their progeny, the world of capitalist competition is an incubus of determinism. Alf has successfully internalised a fatalist outlook on life, seeing himself as an 'unlucky devil' doomed to perpetuate the same mistakes; 'Has a man power to alter his nature?' he reflects:

I don't believe a word of it. Did 'plain auld Rab' endow himself with that bump of caution which has proved of such service? Can his son help being a conceited prig, or Snow a liar, or Pousnett a rogue, or I a fool? Absurd! We are born to limp through life, or squint at life, or make a good thing or a bad thing out of it. We are unable to escape our fate.[57]

Having inherited all the failings of the Mostin family, foremost among which is 'inveterate laziness', Alf manages 'to rub along somehow';[58] the companies he establishes, halfway through the narrative, begin life and collapse in the short space of a page, leaving him without a 'sixpence to go on with'[59] and with a commercial reputation damaged beyond repair. Alf's failures match the philosophy of fatalism he has assimilated.

The novel does not present his 'case' according to standards of impersonality or objectivity; the narrator is still a recognisably realist voice that has not abdicated her ideological function and the urge to communicate approval or disapproval of a character's motives and actions. There is a residual sense of exasperation at Alf's inability to effect change in the narrator's glosses on his failures: 'and yet, as he walked discontentedly along the path leading to Temple Mills, he had again, could he only have believed the fact, a fresh chance given to him – the ball of life at his foot once more!'.[60] The realist belief in the possibility of change and progress, however, does not drive the commercial plot; no matter how many new chances come his way, Alf is destined to take the wrong turn. A victim of nature and circumstance, this character nonetheless is able to seize the first opportunity to perform chivalrous acts of altruism that win the sympathy of the narrator: 'Poor Alf Mostin, who was ever ready to lie with so glib a tongue, whose commercial morals were of the very worst, and yet whose heart was of the truest gold, who, looking down at the tear-stained face of that "little girl", as he mentally called her, was filled with the wildest indignation to think any woman should so be made to suffer!'[61] It is in the private sphere not in the marketplace that his actions deliver positive results: through his intercession, Janey and her mother are saved from utter destitution – and the novel recuperates a brand of sentimental realism that sits uneasily with the mood of disillusionment enveloping the narrative destinies of youthful protagonists.

In other words, in *The Senior Partner* Riddell continues to explore the possibilities left in Victorian realism while testing the potentialities of new narrative modes. The contrast between fathers and sons upon which the novel hinges is also a contrast between realism and its later distillation into naturalism. Loyal to the former and drawn to the latter, Riddell writes a City novel which, unlike its predecessors, has almost no lesson to teach, no axe to grind, no firm ground from which to view the business world she had encouraged her readers to reconsider with fresh, unprejudiced eyes in earlier novels. *The Senior Partner* shows undoubtedly a memorialist orientation, a will to preserve stories, cultural narratives, characters that are out of sync with late nineteenth-century sensibilities; but it also exhibits a corrosive desire to undermine their validity and a naturalist penchant for the observation of failure and the logic of inevitability that comes with it. These contradictory impulses produce a punitive type of plot, one that is propelled forward by a regressive logic. The business plot begins with the merchant's firm refusal to go into partnership with his son and ends on the same note: 'I always said I'd never take a partner, and I never will',[62] declares Old Rob on the last but one page. The very modest job he offers Robert comes with one chillingly castigatory requirement – unconditional obedience: 'I want somebody that'll do what I want as I want'.[63] Beaten down by a series of ill-fated attempts to prove his worth, Robert is only too 'thankful' to comply. Family capitalism has become a mechanism for enforcing submission, or so the novel suggests. The worthy merchant succeeds in weeding out ambitions and desires that clash with his immediate self-interest, defending the firm at all costs from the threatened injection of new talent.

This illiberal conclusion provides a wry commentary on the ideological uses of the past in times of crisis: reviving old national glories, or revamping traditional myths and narratives in the attempt to imagine a future beyond decline produces a story of failed progress and paralysis. Riddell's take on the British merchant, the pioneer of commerce, the heroic adventurer nostalgically evoked in the periodical press in the early 1880s, is at the same time appreciative and sceptical; the symbolic valence of this archetypal figure of capitalism triumphant is affirmed by granting him substantial character space and it is eroded over the course of the novel by casting the merchant as a tyrannical father – an 'autocrat in trade' like England was said to be in Escott's account. Ultimately, *The Senior Partner* is a novel about an unlikable present – limited companies and their frauds, incompetent and ill-starred newcomers – and the contested legacy of the past. Between these two extremes, there is hardly any room to imagine the 'realizability of modernity as a historical project'.[64]

Preserving the Past: *Mitre Court*

Reviewing *Mitre Court* for the *Academy*, James Ashcroft Noble dismissed the novel as 'more aggressively cityish' than Riddell's previous productions. In lieu of a well-delineated plot, with the right amount of suspense, he argues, this 'tale of the great City' offers the dubious pleasure of 'enthusiastic antiquarianism': 'she has very little story to tell; and, if it had not been for antiquarianism, the orthodox three volumes could not possibly have been filled. Indeed, one has to get nearly to the end of the first volume before one perceives that there is any story at all'.[65] Noble also questions the accuracy of Riddell's 'fearful and wonderful knowledge of matters financial' contesting the plausibility of the financial plot that hinges on the villainous figure of the German trader, Mr Katzen, ('whose purse is empty, and reputation shady'), who manages somehow to raise 300,000 pounds and to accomplish a 'piece of scoundrelism' that remains 'entirely out of the reach of the law'.[66] Implausible villainy and an excessive concentration on antiquity make for a 'poor' tale, according to Noble. For the *Saturday Review* the lack of a proper plot – 'the one thing needful in such books as Riddell's' – is a major defect: 'in *Mitre Court* we have not a novel, but descriptions of many households with very little connecting link between them'.[67] Only the *Atheneum* considered *Mitre Court* 'a very good specimen of Mrs. Riddell's work', regretting however the story's exclusive concentration on the City: 'the story never takes the reader out into the open country which she can draw so well, and which she has at times – and notably, of course, in *George Geith* – used so effectively as a contrast to her pictures of City courts and alleys'.[68]

As Victorian reviewers noticed, the novel interweaves two narrative strands that do not integrate harmoniously: on the one hand, a fascination for historical remains (the old house in Botolph Lane) and their symbolic potential, which finds expression in an abundance of descriptions loosely related to the plot; on the other hand, an 'aggressively Cityish' type of story that parades unpunished 'scoundrelism' to illustrate, in a rather cynical manner, the ways of modern business. The relation between these two narrative strands appears strained: there is an imbalance between narration and description that suggests, in George Lukács's terms, the loss of 'epic significance': as he explains in 'Narrate or Describe', 'description becomes the dominant mode in composition in a period in which, for social reasons, the sense of what is primary in epic construction has been lost. Description is the writer's substitute for the epic significance that has been lost'.[69] Lukács relates the predominance of description in naturalism to the 'continuous dehumanization of social life, the general debasement of humanity', in other words to 'the objective facts of the development of capitalism'.[70] His charge is specific: the descriptive mode is a mode of 'passive capitulation' to 'capitalist inhumanity'.[71] Of course, one does not have to embrace wholeheartedly Lukács's critique of naturalism to appreciate his insights about the social and historical determinants of literary styles. Riddell's style, in *Mitre Court,* is a hybrid mixture of realism, satire and quasi-naturalist sensibility as befits an age in 'transition to a yet unknown order'.[72] However, the dominance of the descriptive mode does not bring with it the ideological capitulation of which Lukács speaks, quite the opposite, in fact. The descriptive 'antiquarianism' of *Mitre Court*, attuned as it is to contemporaneous discourses about the preservation of cultural heritage, is arguably the only residue of 'humanist revolt' (Lukács's words)[73] that this novel imagines, while a disillusioned, even cynical vision transpires in the way the financial plot is narrated. To the global City of international finance, where the likes of Katzen hold sway, Riddell responds with a pronounced imaginative investment in the national and local past of the City that was. The formal inconclusiveness of the novel (which Victorian reviewers criticised) is the result of a divided vision, torn between nostalgic 'revolt' and cynical 'capitulation'.

What Noble liquidates as the antiquarianism of Riddell's perspective can best be apprehended in the context of the late nineteenth-century debate about cultural heritage and the 'preservation' rather than 'restoration' of ancient buildings – a debate sparked and kept alive in the public mind by the interventions of John Ruskin, William Morris, Henry Brewer, Thomas Hardy and other members of the Society for the Protection of Ancient Buildings (SPAB), founded in 1877.[74] As Morris declared in the SPAB's manifesto: 'We of this Society at least know the beauty of the weathered and time-worn surface of ancient buildings, and have all of us felt the grief of seeing this surface disappear under the hands of the 'restorer' . . . the untouched surface of ancient architecture bears witness to the development of man's ideas, to the continuity of history'.[75] Like Ruskin before him, Morris was critical of the practice of 'restoration' pursued by Victorian architects. In its extreme form, such practice entailed the drastic alteration or destruction of many good quality structures that failed to match the Gothic Revival style. As Andrea Donovan explains, restoration was 'a form of destruction falsely packaged as the reconstruction or representation of an original form. It was the practice of claiming to restore the appearance of the original building without regard for its original function or the kind of community and person that built it'.[76] Aiming to recover some ideal moment of perfection, Victorian restorers re-created facsimiles of the past passed off as original historical entities, as Cowell observes.[77] For preservationists such as Morris, Ruskin and Hardy, on the other hand, taking proper care of monuments and ancient buildings meant conserving the integrity of historical structures that changed and evolved over time. Their goal was 'to preserve buildings in the state they had naturally arrived at over time by keeping them as untouched as possible',[78] allowing only minimal interventions in order to protect historic sites from the damages of time or negligence: 'Take good care of your monuments' Ruskin admonishes in *The Seven Lamps of Architecture,*

> and you will not need to restore them; watch an old building with anxious care; count its stones as you would the jewels of a crown; bind it together with iron where it loosens, stay it with timber where it declines. Do not care about the unsightliness of the aid; better a crutch than a lost limb; and do this tenderly, reverently, continually, and many a generation will still be born to pass beneath its shadow.[79]

Among the historic landmarks in need of the kind of tender care that Ruskin and Morris promoted, City churches, especially those designed by Christopher Wren, were often singled out for special attention.[80] In the 1860s, writes John Earl, 'it was possible to dismiss Wren's churches as impediments to free traffic movement',[81] but the threatened demolition of these small, unobtrusive buildings did not go unquestioned. Even before joining the SPAB, Henry Brewer was campaigning in the pages of periodicals against the demolition of City churches, some of which feature in *Mitre Court,* flanked by imposing warehouses and lofty modern edifices, in a state of precariousness.[82] In 'The Proper Use of City Churches', published in *Nineteenth Century* in 1880, Paul C. Kegan adopted a militant tone to raise awareness of the menace incumbent upon ancient monuments in the City: 'The reckless spirit of destruction' – he warned – 'sweeps away every old monument because its use is not at the moment apparent';[83] since the 'little-out-of-way churches' seemed to serve no special function, they were most likely to be pulled down and effaced from memory, though their churchyards still provided to the busy City man 'the same rest, in kind, though not of course in degree, that the Alps bring to the tired worker on his yearly holiday'.[84] Kegan values old buildings in the City for their 'sentimental' function; in a place that 'does not suffer from an excess of that quality' they are all the more precious.[85] In its early years, the SPAB conducted a successful campaign to save the historic church of St. Mary-at-Hill in the City of London.[86] This church, alongside Wren's old habitation in Botolph Lane, ranks high in the preservationist platform of *Mitre Court.*

There are distinct echoes of the heritage debate and the larger set of concerns it addressed in the third chapter of Riddell's novel, where the author, speaking directly as 'the writer of this book',[87] mixes memories and desires in an impassioned plea to salvage historic landmarks (churches and houses about to be swept away by the march of improvement) and the intangible cultural heritage (rituals, traditions, stories) associated with them. A conservationist aesthetic orients the descriptions of the house in Botolph Lane, redeemed from decrepitude by the story we are reading, protected in literature, though not in real life. At the time of writing, the house had already been turned into a school, reclaimed by the 'Philistine utilitarianism'[88] of speculative builders. The novel reverses this process by repopulating Wren's house with imaginary inhabitants who instinctively appreciate its value. First, Riddell mourns the loss of many 'old landmarks' in the City and many ancient customs and traditions 'fallen into desuetude'.[89] Then, she turns her attention to a secluded spot, comprising Botolph Lane, Love Lane and the church of St. Mary-at-Hill, reclaiming its heritage value in words that recall a preservationist understanding of history: the streets are 'rich in ancient architecture, streaked with those tones of colour it needs the passage of centuries to paint to perfection'.[90] The 'wonderful old mansion' in Botolph Lane, which 'stands apart and quiet, as a gentlewoman of the olden time',[91] is observed with the clinical eye of a conservationist who takes due notice of the marks left on the building by time and negligence. Riddell introduces the house to her readers in a descriptive passage that traces the building's state of disrepair:

By the steam given off from those and other nuts, the boards have been prized from their nails, and lifted from an inch to half an inch. Strange, is it not? And yet, perhaps, no stranger than that the panels painted by one Robinson (whoever he might be), in the year of grace 1670, as all who choose to go and see can read, are strained and cracked by a similar action on the part of oranges'.[92]

The chapter in which this description appears is entitled 'A Plaint' and contains the author's open protestation against the indifference of administrators and public bodies towards the rich cultural heritage of the City:

> Methinks were I, the writer of this book, . . . in any capacity free of the City of London – say liveryman, common councillor, deputy-sheriff, sheriff, alderman, Lord Mayor – I would make the City – which after all cannot be accounted very big, though undoubtedly it is very great – my study: I would know every court, lane, alley, house, exhaustively; and were there still left an old mansion, hallowed by fact or tradition, I should try to save it; and if I could not I would enter my protest . . . against the Philistine utilitarianism of an age which, desecrating the word 'progress', sweeps away, for the sake of accursed Mammon, every ancient landmark.[93]

Adding her voice to the chorus of critical interventions in the heritage debate, Riddell adopts in this novel a preservationist methodology: the plaint articulated in the third chapter is an open denunciation of the destructive impetus of modernisation; the story she then narrates seeks to repair the damaged past and to ensure the survival of the house and its fictive inhabitants in an imaginary reversal of the negative progress deplored in the passage quoted above. Against the extremes of 'Philistine utilitarianism', *Mitre Court* promotes an aesthetic appreciation of historical remains, including in this category not only old houses but also characters and stories that seem to hold a special attraction though they are no longer fruitful in narrative terms. Riddell resumes character types – the miser (Brisco), the foundling (Abigail) – and narrative devices – the agnition (in the last volume Frank is revealed to be Brisco's long lost son), the unexpected inheritance – that confer upon the story a slightly antiquated look, in stark contrast with the modern focus on the business of global finance. Brisco, the current occupant of the house in Botolph Lane, and Katzen, the German speculator who sets up office in Mitre Court, embody the 'Spirits of the Past and the Present' respectively:[94] the former looks as much out of place in Katzen's office 'as a dingy "old master", its frame tarnished and broken, would seem in the drawing-room of a *nouveau riche*'.[95] Whereas the plot revolves around the new City man and his dubious enterprises, Brisco's appearances in the text have little to add to the story. Often he is the object of visual descriptions that place him inside the house, restively pacing its rooms, a ghost-like presence haunted by memories: 'There seemed a certain fitness', the narrator points out, 'in seeing a wasted figure wandering like a ghost through the building, flitting from room to room in the twilight when business was over and the offices closed . . . It was then – clad in an old grey dressing-gown, and wearing a pair of list slippers that made no sound – he roamed through the solemn stillness, making no echo'.[96] Riddell imagines the occupants of the house in Botolph Lane, Brisco and Abigail, as sensitive to the beauty of the place, able to appreciate its features.[97] Abigail may be 'a waif'[98] of uncertain origin, but she has a keen instinctive sense of the pleasure to be derived from contemplating architectural art: 'The old house – with its leads, its long passages, its steep back-stairs, its brewhouse, its inlaid circles on the drawing-room chimney-piece, its panelling – was to her a kingdom, the resources of which seemed inexhaustible'.[99] There are several moments in which the story is arrested to allow for the contemplation of this 'strange abode' and to register the effects that its beauty and ancient dignity have on the mind of the beholder – on Frank, for instance, who imagines the house as a living organism: 'Somehow, as he stood, the fancy struck Frank that in its stately separation from the surrounding meanness and turmoil it was like some great soul on the earth, but not of the earth; associating with things vile, yet remaining unstained by them'.[100] Guided by aesthetic considerations, Riddell's preservationism turns the house into a character itself, serving no other function than that of being a material remain, a trace of the past in the present to be treasured as such. Like the mansion he looks after, Brisco, an unsociable misanthrope ('as morose as Diogenes')[101] and a miser who has 'dropped behind the world',[102] has almost no impact on the story, except towards the end when he objects to the marriage between Abigail and his long-lost son Frank. Yet his presence is summoned up frequently by a narrator who clearly counts among her duties the task of remembering.

This task also extends to fictional forms: in *Mitre Court*, Riddell replicates narrative conventions that have lost their explicatory power and survive in the novel as hollowed out forms unmoored from their ethical substratum. This is noticeable, for instance, in the way the domestic sub-plot, centred on the relationship between Brisco and Abigail, is played out. The traditional framework is still in place: Abigail possesses all the virtues that would make her the perfect heroine in a story of redemption or reformation in which the cold-hearted, guilt-ridden miser, softened by the moral influence of his sentimental putative daughter, finds a way to come to terms with his past.[103] While the novel certainly vents this possibility, Brisco remains immune to the transformative power of Abigail's exemplary devotion. The discourse of domesticity rings hollow, though Riddell seems reluctant to sidestep it altogether. A similar attachment to narrative paradigms that have lost their momentum can be detected in the story of Frank, the only character in the novel who closely resembles Riddell's typical business hero. Hard-working and honest, striving to prove his worth in the City – 'He was an assiduous worker, always ready, always willing, always punctual, always well'[104] – Frank is a reformed gambler who has willingly overgrown his bad habits. For him, however, there is virtually no plot worthy of the name: he is instrumental in uncovering the secret machinations of an unscrupulous manager; consequently, he obtains a better job – end of story. To provide some kind of closure, Riddell interrupts the prosaic tale of Frank's very slow advancement in the business world to bring him back into the fold of his original family as Brisco's prodigal son; after the death of his father, Frank will marry Abigail in a modest ceremony performed in the church of St. Mary-at-Hill.

The late nineteenth-century crisis of realism is reflected in the half-hearted loyalty shown to narrative paradigms that carry little symbolic power but are not entirely discarded. They serve as counterweights to the satirical mode prevailing in the narrative of Katzen's rapid progress towards success. The foreign adventurer, who speaks five languages and has sharpened his speculative skills in Germany and America, becomes 'Consul for New Andalusia' early on in the story. The novel follows his financial exploits, and his creepy attempts to woo Abigail, in a crescendo of absolute disillusion. Katzen is cast as a villain, but in a City where rascality is hegemonic, his ingenuity shines. Of his ability to float companies, raise money, and manipulate savvy City men, a disheartened Riddell writes:

> He managed to keep just within the law, though how, sailing so near the wind, he contrived to do this he alone could have told. For indeed he did things quite beyond the law. He established different houses in various parts of the world, and drew upon those fictitious firms with a cool disregard of possible consequences . . . Yet somehow it all came right'.[105]

Relinquishing any hope of correction, Riddell narrates with great gusto how Katzen's grandest scheme, the New Andalusia Loan, takes wings, how he dupes even sagacious City men into entrusting their money to him and how he emerges unscathed from the collapse of his project: 'neither guilty nor not guilty' (III, 277) is the final verdict.[106] Undoubtedly, the negative energies Katzen expresses are more productive, in narrative terms, than the feeble, residual desires mobilised in the sub-plot centred on Frank, Abigail, and Brisco. What the narrative condemns through ruthless satire is more inspiring than the pale fictions deployed to counteract the hegemonic hold of deception and unfettered rascality.

The novel attempts to draw a distinction between past and present, between the City where old houses, old stories and old characters linger on as valuable traces of a different, less contemptible reality, and the City where grand fraudulent schemes and their perpetrators have become the sole interpreters of progress and dynamism on a global scale. But it is an attempt in which Riddell seems to have little faith, as the tired re-proposition of exhausted narrative conventions suggests. Furthermore, the text registers, at a subliminal level, a deep line of continuity linking the aesthetic beauty of the past to the moral ugliness of the present. Two scenes, in particular, bring this to the fore: they are both ekphrases, moments in which the story pauses to make room for descriptions of works of art – minor pieces in this case, but carrying a particular message from the past. The house in 5 Botolph Lane was a real house, with its own history, which Riddell transposes into a fictional place. Its main artistic attraction was the Painted Room, decorated by Robert Robinson (1635–1706) in 1696 with exotic scenes, partly Chinese, partly Peruvian, featuring a 'composition of pagodas, pavilions, palm trees, princesses and other oriental exotica'.[107] Commissioned by a rich merchant of the East India Company who was, at the time, the owner of the house, the paintings are, according to Pratt, good examples of an allegorical style of decoration with colonialist underpinnings.[108] Europe is typically placed 'as the fount of civilization, of arts and letters' while the other continents 'tend to occupy the extreme edges of the design . . . On the level of the formal arrangement, then, these figures were symbolic of the global reach of European powers into the corners of the world'.[109]

In *Mitre Court*, the Painted Room is an object of curiosity for visitors who invariably find the geography, the objects and the creatures represented in the panels quite bewildering. The first visitor who attempts to extract some sense out of these baffling visual images is Katzen: 'There are two funny fellows riding on rhinoceros, and there are others gathering tobacco-leaves, and there are chariots drawn by some deer, and something like a church, and white people, and sea and mountains'.[110] Out of this list of mismatched exotic items, Katzen cannot piece a story together: 'The series of paintings constitutes, I suppose, a whole story; but what that story might be no one can tell'. On second thought, however, he does find a prophetic meaning in the paintings, an anticipation of his future mission as promoter of the New Andalusia Loan: 'it has just occurred to me that I could have said the tale the panels told me was the colonisation and civilisation and Christianising of New Andalusia'.[111] The second ekphrasis is even more fragmented: Mrs Jeffley (who runs the boarding-house where Katzen and Frank lodge) wanders 'hopelessly from scene to scene' noticing disparate details: 'something like a church', a cat in a boat, a lady among 'savages', 'a particularly jolly-looking savage riding with a companion on a rhinoceros'.[112] But she is unable to decipher the whole picture: 'And what is the meaning of all these things?' she asks Abigail, 'We should all be so glad if anyone could tell us that' is the curt reply.

Allegorised in the original paintings, refracted in Katzen and Mrs Jeffley's fragmented descriptions, the history of colonialism survives in the Painted Room as a tale whose significance has been lost or forgotten. The novel alludes to it, the cynical Katzen even reads in the panels a self-serving prophecy, but this historical referent remains unrecoverable, impermeable to interpretation within the fictive world Riddell reconstructs around the house. It is significant that the City landmark memorialised in this fiction, caringly preserved through the work of writing, should contain the splintered representation of the pre-history of global finance capitalism, whose later developments Riddell criticises in *Mitre Court*. It is also significant that the line of continuity thus established should be so tenuous, barely visible, no sooner remembered than forgotten. The act of aesthetic preservation is enabled, at least in part, by an act of forgetting. The late Victorian City that Riddell describes as a 'mere aggregation of offices and warehouses, swollen with wealth, insolent with prosperity'[113] casts a long retrospective shadow on the City she had 'loved' in better times, 'the London of my dream and of my memory'[114] celebrated in her fiction. To keep that dream alive, or to preserve the cultural value of her imaginative investment in the City, the present must appear discontinuous with the past, the City of speculators and insolent wealth must be disentangled from the City where George Geith, Hugh Eliot and York Forde 'lived and played out their little tragedies'[115] though the differences may be hard to grasp. Hence the act of forgetting (which leaves its textual traces in the ekphrases) and the aesthetic appreciation of material, historical remains which replaces, in this novel, the pro-business, pro-capitalist ideology of Riddell's more militant fictions. In *Mitre Court*, the author casts a retrospective look not only on the real and fictional

City of her memory, but also on her career as the novelist of the City, drawing a final balance that tilts towards the negative:

> O City! Once interesting beyond all power of speech . . . With an exceeding love have I, an alien, loved you. In your better time I knew you, and there was scarce a stone in your pavement, or house in your streets, but had a fascination for one who deliberately elected to strive and interweave the touching romance of daily life and eternal struggle with the dry details of commerce . . . Scarce a man or woman in your midst but whose face held to my fancy a story and a pathos no one, perhaps, would have felt more astounded to see into print than its owner; with toil and travail I learned the ins and outs of your commerce; of the best God vouchsafed me, I gave you all, and for myself the result has been well-nigh *nil*. I piped to you and ye did not dance, I mourned and ye did not weep; yet this I could have borne, for in authorship, as in all art, there is a reward the world wots not of. What I cannot bear, however, is your changed and desecrated face.[116]

In this bleak self-assessment, the novelist's professional life is couched in the same narrative of disillusion that moulds the destinies of her characters in *The Senior Partner* and *Mitre Court*: Riddell's intense and prolonged affective investment has yielded but a paltry result. It is difficult to say how the result is measured, whether in financial or symbolic terms. But it is certainly made to appear as a sign of partial failure, as if her writing had failed to protect the City from desecration or to have any impact on its recent developments. Implicitly, Riddell's self-assessment attributes to fiction an enormous power, the power to effect changes, to act in the societal domain, to steer the course of history one way or the other. Of course, it is only when this power falters against the stubborn resistance of reality that its ideal force is thrown into sharp relief. The discontent of the novelist, in this case, is contingent upon the belief she still holds in the promises and ideals of Victorian social realism: interweaving the 'romance of daily life' with the realities of commerce, putting into print the 'pathos' of the City, addressing her readers directly, while taking stock of their unresponsiveness ('I piped to you but ye did not dance'). 'In the future' – Riddell concludes – 'who will be found possessed of sufficient courage to write a novel about your present?'[117] This question emphasises the courage she herself had mustered to produce the City stories mentioned in the long, slightly valetudinarian speech delivered in the third chapter of *Mitre Court*. A sense of failure and a certain pride are intermingled in the rhetoric that Riddell adopts, though it is the glumness of her vision that prevails.

As I have argued in this chapter, the perspective from which Riddell narrates the City in *The Senior Partner* and *Mitre Court* points in two directions: nostalgia and scepticism, realism and satire, an aesthetic of preservation and a corrosive counter-impulse to distrust the messages from the past cohabit uneasily in the texts. The formal inconclusiveness of *Mitre Court* bears testimony to Riddell's divided ideological alliances. Opting for a backward-looking perspective, but attuned to emerging modes of representation, Riddell restricts her field of vision to one isolated segment of that social reality which, in her earlier novels, included the City *and* the suburbs, urban spaces *and* the countryside, the sphere of work *and* the equally troubled domestic sphere where the irregular desires of the female denizens of the City matched the modern restlessness of their male counterparts. Veering towards specialism, Riddell re-imagines the City as an exclusively masculine place of work, cut off from private life, amorous attachments and the complications attendant upon them – an 'aggressively Cityish' locale, perhaps, certainly an impenetrable world for the few, marginal heroines skirting along the borders of the narrative. Their shadowy presence is, arguably, the most drastic negation of the idea of progress to be found in Riddell's novels. Janey and Abigail belong to the past in more than one way –modernisation has passed them by. But the heroine Riddell imagines, in the same years, at the very centre of her *Künstlerroman*, *A Struggle for Fame* (1883), is the protagonist of an altogether different story, one in which failed or denied progress is not the dominant script.

Notes

1 Thomas H.S. Escott, *England: Its People, Polity and Pursuits*, 1879, (London: Cassell, 1881), p. 114.
2 Ibid., p. 116.
3 Hoppen, p. 305.
4 See James Foreman-Peck ed., *New perspectives on the late Victorian economy: Essays in quantitative economic history, 1860–1914* (Cambridge: Cambridge University Press: 1991) and David McCloskey, 'Did Victorian Britain fail?' in *Trade and Enterprise in Victorian Britain: Essays in Historical Economics* (London: Allen and Unwin, 1981).
5 Joseph Hatton, 'England's Commercial decline', *The Tinsley's Magazine* 24 (March 1879), p. 256.
6 Charles Marvin, 'English Merchants and German Traders', *Time* 16 (February 1887), p. 136.
7 Ibid., p. 137.
8 The articles were later collected in a volume, *Fortunes Made in Business* (1884), which I have discussed in Chapter 1. For the *Athenaeum*, this volume was a much-needed reminder of a time when trade was buoyant: 'the recital of such tales as are here told', observed the reviewer, 'might fairly be expected to have a consolatory and stimulating effect'. See 'Fortunes made in Business', *Athenaeum*, p. 401.
9 'Romance in Business', *The Blackwood's Edinburgh Magazine* 131, no. 796 (February 1882), p. 221.
10 'Noblemen in Business', *London Society* 33, no. 195 (March 1878), p. 214.
11 James Payn, 'The Literary Calling and its Future', *Nineteenth-Century* 6, no. 34 (December 1879), p. 986.
12 Cross, 'Leaves from Life. No. IV, Business', p. 641.
13 Ibid., p. 642.
14 Cross, 'The Man of Business—Absolute', p. 613.
15 Charlotte Riddell, *Mitre Court: A Tale of the Great City* (London: Richard Bentley and Son, 1885), vol. 1, p. 290.
16 The obvious reference here is to Franco Moretti's work on the *Bildungsroman*, see Moretti, *The Way of the World*.
17 Jed Esty, *Unseasonable Youth: Modernism, Colonialism, and the Fiction of Development* (Oxford: Oxford University Press, 2012), p. 41.

18 See John McVeagh, *Tradefull Merchants: The Portrayal of the Capitalist in Literature* (Routledge: London, 1981).

19 The expression 'heritage character' is meant to sum up the following traits: 1) a fairly stereotypical type of character – the miser; the parsimonious merchant – whom readers might easily recognise from his frequent appearances in literature, whether in novels, plays or poems; 2) the non-modern connotations of this character whose attitudes and fixations evoke a time prior to that of the story; 3) his re-evaluation as a trace of the past surviving in the present of the narrative, a precious relic that the text cherishes as such.

20 As David Kynaston succinctly puts it: 'The world was the City's oyster'; for a detailed analysis of the increasing internationalisation of City's businesses see Part IV of his *The City of London*, pp. 250–422.

21 William Morris, *Manifesto* (London: SPAB archive, June 1877) quoted by Andrea Elisabeth Donovan, *William Morris and the Society for the Protection of Ancient Buildings* (London: Routledge, 2008), p. 106.

22 See Rose, 'The family firm in British business', pp. 61–87. On the evolution of family businesses in a historical and comparative perspective, see Colli.

23 Chandler, p. 235.

24 Rose, 'The family firm in British business', pp. 61–2.

25 Ibid., p. 70.

26 Mary B. Rose, 'Beyond Buddenbrooks: the family firm and the management of succession in nineteenth-century Britain' in *Entrepreneurship, Networks, and Modern Business*, ed. Jonathan Brown and Mary B. Rose (Manchester: Manchester University Press, 1993), p. 128. Rose includes in the category of family firms both partnerships and limited companies 'where a family or families were overwhelmingly represented amongst partners or boards of directors. They should as a result be involved in the strategic planning of the firm' (p. 130).

27 Ibid., p. 131.

28 Ibid., p. 133.

29 Ibid., pp. 135–6.

30 The novel was serialised in *London Society* from January to June 1881.

31 Rose, 'The family firm in British business', p. 61.

32 Escott, p. 4.

33 Charlotte Riddell, *The Senior Partner* (London: Richard Bentley, 1881), vol. 3, p. 106.

34 Ibid., p. 109.

35 'New Novels' (Rev. of *The Senior Partner*), *The London Standard*, 27 February 1882, p. 1.

36 'Mrs. Riddell's New Novel' (Rev. of *The Senior Partner*), *The Pall Mall Gazette*, 11 January 1882, p. 5. *The Graphic* also praised the novel as one further example of Riddell's specific art – 'the art of finding romance in price lists, and both comedy and tragedy in the multiplication table'. Regarding the 'harsh-grained, close-fisted Scotch tradesman' Riddell portrays, the reviewer concludes: 'For once, the words 'painful and unpleasant' must be used as terms of praise', see 'New Novels' (Rev. of *The Senior Partner*), *The Graphic*, 11 March 1882, p. 254.

37 Caroline Levine and Mario Ortiz-Robles, 'Introduction' in *Narrative Middles: Navigating the Nineteenth-Century British Novel*, ed. Caroline Levine and Mario Ortiz-Robles (Columbus: Ohio State University Press 2011), p. 7.

38 Ibid., p. 18

39 The characterological middle is defined in relation to the 'person or persons . . . at the center of the novel's consciousness' (Ibid.).

40 *The Senior Partner*, vol. 1, p. 121.

41 Ibid., p. 67.

42 Ibid., p. 2.

43 Ibid., p. 59.
44 Ibid., p. 60.
45 Ibid., p. 9.
46 Ibid., p. 113.
47 'New Novels', *London Standard*, p. 1.
48 *The Senior Partner*, vol. 1, p. 39.
49 Ibid., p. 121.
50 Ibid., p. 126.
51 Ibid., p. 122.
52 Ibid., p. 20.
53 *The Senior Partner*, vol. 2, p. 129.
54 'With this laudable purpose he wrote in hot haste to his third son David, whom he had sent . . . to a place very far north in Scotland . . . All of a sudden, however, his father decided David's energies would be better employed in London. Like many other lesser and greater persons, Mr. McCullagh did not care to invest those belonging to him with independent power' (Ibid., p. 131).
55 *The Senior Partner*, vol. 3, p. 99.
56 See the entry 'Naturalism' in Raymond Williams's *Keywords: A Vocabulary of Culture and Society*, 1976, (Oxford: Oxford University Press, 1983). Referring to both the French school of 'naturalisme' (whose major exponent is Zola) and the English tradition, Williams mentions the 'study of heredity in the story of a family' as well as the 'new and properly naturalist sense of the determining or decisive or influential effect of an environment on a life' as defining features of literary naturalism (p. 217); the emphasis on description 'based on *ad hoc* observation' is also a trait associated with the naturalistic method, see Georg Lukàcs, 'Narrate or Describe?', 1970, in *Writer and Critic and other essays* (Lincoln, NE: Authors Guild Backinprint, 2005), p. 139.
57 *The Senior Partner*, vol. 2, p. 249.
58 *The Senior Partner*, vol. 1, p. 160 and p. 161.
59 *The Senior Partner*, vol. 2, p. 235.
60 Ibid., p. 250.
61 Ibid., p. 73.
62 *The Senior Partner*, vol. 3, p. 288.
63 Ibid.
64 From the middle of the nineteenth century, Peter Wagner explains, the project of modernity was subject to a series of critical inquires that identified basic problems in its practices: 'In the historical development of modernity as a "liberal" society, the self-produced emergence of overarching structures, such as capitalism and the market, organization and bureaucracy, modern philosophy and science, and the division of labour, is identified. These structures work on the individual subjects and their possibilities for self-realization – up to the threat of self-cancellation of modernity. The more generalized modern practices become, the more they themselves may undermine the realizability of modernity as a historical project' see Wagner, *Modernity*, pp. 19–20.
65 [John Ashcroft Noble], 'New Novels', *The Academy* 709 (5 December 1885), pp. 371–2
66 Ibid., p. 371.
67 'Three Novels' (Rev. of *Mitre Court*), *The Saturday Review* 61, no.1577 (16 January 1886), p. 96.
68 'Novels of the Week' (Rev. of *Mitre Court*), *The Athenaeum* 3033 (12 December 1885), p. 765. For the *Graphic*, on the other hand, with *Mitre Court* 'Mrs Riddell fully equals, if not surpasses, her early triumphs in 'George Geith' and its immediate successors, and in their more mature rival, 'The Senior Partner' . . . The story, though slight, is a finished piece of construction – without a stroke too much, and it is perfectly adequate to its purpose – that of the complete development of character, without the aid of direct

analysis or reflection', see 'New Novels' (Rev. of *Mitre Court*), *The Graphic*, 19 December 1885, p. 26.
69 Lukàcs, p. 127.
70 Ibid., p. 127.
71 Ibid., p. 146.
72 Escott, p. 2.
73 Lukàcs, p. 147.
74 On the history of what today is called heritage see Ben Cowell, *The Heritage Obsession: The Battle for England's Past* (Chalford: Tempus, 2008); chapter 6, in particular, contains a brief overview of the restoration *vs* protection debate. In Cowell's definition 'heritage' is 'an ongoing concern for the tangible and intangible remains of the past, for the benefit of present and future generations' (p. 10). See also Michael Hunter, ed. *Preserving the Past: The Rise of Heritage in Modern Britain*, (Stroud: Alan Sutton, 1996) and Donovan, *William Morris*.
75 Seventh Annual Report: SPAB (London: SPAB, 1884), quoted by Donovan, p. 8.
76 Ibid., pp. 8–9.
77 Cowell, p. 73.
78 Donovan, p. 8.
79 John Ruskin, *The Seven Lamps of Architecture*, 1849, (Leipzig: Bernhard Tauchnitz, 1907), p. 261.
80 As the population of residents in the City dwindled, City churches began to be demolished to make room for 'commercial palaces': 'By 1871 there were 75,000 residents in the City and 200,000 daytime workers, by 1881 the respective figures were 51,000 and 261,000. Many City churches were demolished' (Kynaston, p. 287).
81 John Earl, 'London government: a record of custodianship' in Hunter, *Preserving*, p. 59.
82 See Henry Brewer, 'The Demolition of City Churches', *The Academy* 100 (4 April 1874), pp. 371–2.
83 Paul C. Kegan, 'The Proper Use of City Churches', *Nineteenth Century* 7, no. 37 (March 1880), p. 487. Several articles appeared in the *Nineteenth Century* throughout the 1880s and 1890s that address the question of material remains and the urgent need to protect them, see Virginia Zimmerman, ' "The Weird Message from the Past": Material Epistemologies of Past, Present, and Future in the *Nineteenth Century*', *Victorian Periodicals Review* 42, no. 2 (Summer 2009), pp. 114–35.
84 Kegan, p. 490.
85 Ibid.
86 See Cowell, p. 76.
87 *Mitre Court*, vol. 1, p. 66.
88 Ibid.
89 Ibid., p. 55.
90 Ibid., pp. 62–3.
91 Ibid., p. 63.
92 Ibid., p. 66.
93 Ibid., pp. 66–7.
94 Ibid., p. 273.
95 Ibid., p. 272.
96 Ibid., p. 81.
97 Abigail is an orphan whom Brisco 'adopts' after finding her hiding in his house. She performs domestic duties for her putative father and tries to win his love.
98 *Mitre Court*, vol. 1, 115.
99 Ibid., p. 176.
100 *Mitre Court*, vol. 3, p. 91.
101 *Mitre Court*, vol. 1, p. 115.

102 Ibid., p. 74.
103 Abigail promises to be a slightly different version of Florence in *Dombey and Sons* or of Amy in *Little Dorrit*. Like Dickens's heroines, Abigail makes the most of the circumstances that restrict her field of action, finding a *raison d'être* in her devotion to a stern father figure and in the spotless performance of domestic duties.
104 *Mitre Court*, vol. 2, p. 9.
105 *Mitre Court*, vol. 1, p. 260.
106 *Mitre Court*, vol. 3, p. 277. On the craze for foreign loans that seized the City in the 1870s see Kynaston, pp. 260–70. He mentions Honduras, the Republic of Santo Domingo, Costa Rica and Paraguay: 'the loans for all four states were characterized by the creation of artificial premiums and the unloading of stock on the public just before the price fell like a stone' (p. 270). Riddell's New Andalusia Loan might have been inspired by these historical precedents.
107 See Peter Earle, *The Making of the English Middle Class: Business, Society and Family Life in London, 1660–1730* (Berkeley: University of California Press, 1989), p. 74. 'By 1700, the aristocratic taste for paintings had filtered down to those of the middle station, many of whom owned scores of pictures and some of whom rivaled their betters in the commissioning of decorative art in their homes such as the East India merchant who in 1696 got Robert Robinson to paint his paneled room in Botolph Lane' (Ibid.).
108 See Stephanie Pratt, *American Indians in British Art, 1700–1840* (Norman: The University of Oklahoma Press, 2005), p. 19.
109 'The figure of America seen in combination with the other three continents can be found in a number of ambitious decorative schemes of this period, among them. . .the painted panels of 1696 by Robert Robinson that originally decorated a house at 5 Botolph Lane in Aldgate' (Ibid., p. 19).
110 *Mitre Court*, vol. 1, p. 41.
111 Ibid.
112 *Mitre Court*, vol. 1, pp. 126–7.
113 Ibid., p. 67.
114 Ibid., p. 68.
115 Ibid., p. 71.
116 Ibid., p. 68.
117 Ibid., p. 72.

Epilogue: *A Struggle for Fame*

Charlotte Riddell produced over 40 novels. Some of them – *Maxwell Drewitt* (1865), *The Earl's Promise* (1873), *Berna Boyle* (1884) and *The Nun's Curse* (1887) – are Irish-themed novels, dealing with the fraught relationship between landlords and tenants and with the disrupted history of Ireland.[1] Others can be classified as domestic fiction, although the middle-class domesticity they narrate sometimes spins in unusual directions. In *Miss Gascoigne* (1887), for instance, the love plot traces the growing intimacy between a young man and a woman over 10 years his senior; *Home, Sweet Home* (1873) and *Her Mother's Darling* (1877), despite the overt demureness of the titles, recount the rough adventures of female singers and musicians; while *Mysteries in Palace Gardens* (1880) delves into the brooding psychology of an upright City man attracted and repulsed, in equal degrees, by the *femme fatale* he has married. In the late 1880s, Riddell also ventured into co-creation: *The Government Official* (1887), a novel about civil servants, is the result of an anonymous collaboration with Arthur Hamilton Norway, who lodged with her for a few years. On the whole, in a career that spanned four decades, Riddell experimented with several novelistic subgenres, returning to the City novel at regular intervals.

This book has charted the progression of her imaginative commitment to the City of London, from the early 1860s when the brave new world of capitalist enterprise appeared to her promising and dynamic up until the mid 1880s when disenchantment became prevalent. This trajectory is aligned with broader historical developments in the conceptualisation of modernity: 'After the dust of the great revolutions had settled', writes Peter Wagner, 'a series of major critical inquiries into the dynamics of modernity was elaborated successively from the middle of the nineteenth century up until the middle of the twentieth century'.[2] In Riddell's case, the transition from enchantment to disenchantment may have been aggravated by personal circumstances (the bankruptcy) that darkened her vision. Noticeable, however, is that disillusion and the narrowing of possibilities did not cause her to turn away from the City and the broken promises of progress. Rather, her later novels focus even more intensely on a restricted City setting, dominated by different generations of male characters, with only minor concessions made to the lateral presence of female figures. As the horizon of expectations shrinks, the space of experience appears increasingly unbalanced in terms of gender. In this

Epilogue, I shall concentrate on a text that is not, strictly speaking, a City novel, but shares with Riddell's fiction of the 1860s a firm belief in the narrative of self-determination, re-purposed this time to fit the desires and aspirations of a female subject. Read in relation to the template of her City novels, *A Struggle for Fame* suggests that Riddell was not indifferent to the demands for change that women were articulating in increasingly pressing ways on the political, cultural and social scene of the time.

There is no scarcity of men of business in Riddell's City novels, but women of business are rare. Yorke Forde in *Austin Friars* and Dolly in *Mortomley's Estate* are the only female characters who get to savour the mixed blessings of a business life. Yorke assumes the mantle of the liberal individual who claims her right to trade albeit for a short period of time; while Dolly experiences a radical transition from innocence to shrewdness, becoming the fulcrum of a business epic that sees her battling like a knight in armour against commercial and legal dragons of various denominations. However, no sooner is this vision articulated than it is forcefully denied: first, in the one-volume novel *Frank Sinclair's Wife*, where Riddell liquidates the question of women's rights as humorous if not ludicrous and, later on, in *The Senior Partner* and *Mitre Court* where female characters are relegated to such peripheral roles as to become ineffectual and almost invisible in the story world. Plotting modernity via allegories of self-making centred on 'new women' is not a path that Riddell seemed willing to follow, despite the increasing cultural prominence, in fiction and society, of female-centred plots of emancipation and self-development. The story of the successful or unsuccessful woman of business remains untold, as if this development of late nineteenth-century modernity – women reclaiming their share of progress – were non-narratable.

There are some glimpses of unrealised female economic aspirations in both *Mitre Court* and *The Senior Partner*. In the former, Mrs Jeffley, who runs a boarding-house, dreams of taking advantage of the 'custom of the City' which, she claims, enabled a wife to 'trade independent of her husband, sue and be sued, rent a house, carry on a business, "keep what she made for herself", exactly as if she had never seen John Jeffley'.[3] The text registers these aspirations when she makes her first appearance in the story: but this energetic, loquacious lady will remain trapped within the confines of her Cockney identity, her ambitions belittled by the moderately sardonic and conservative tone of narratorial interventions. In *The Senior Partner*, another lower-middle-class character, Effie, tired of being dependent on her relative (Old Rob), manages to find a job; but soon afterwards a villainous clerk robs Effie of her savings and her hopes for a better future. If the aspirations of these minor characters have no future, upper-class women fare no better. Indeed, they do not even become desiring subjects: Janey, in *The Senior Partner*, and Abigail, in *Mitre Court*, are notable for their bland acquiescence with their lot. The arrival of Janey on the novel's stage is described ironically through the rapturous words of Robert, instantly hit by Cupid's arrows when he first sets eyes on her: 'How pretty she was! How pleasantly she laughed! How modestly she blushed! . . . What an exquisite rose-pink tinted her cheeks! What threads of gold flecked her brown sunny hair'.[4] Janey is a formulaic 'vision of loveliness' and will perform her silent domestic duties to perfection, hardly intervening in the novel, except towards the end when the need to find some type of closure for the open-ended strife between Robert and his father pushes her nursing skills to the fore. Abigail has a larger share in the novel's character system, as she plays the traditional part of the sentimental daughter taking good care of Brisco and asking almost nothing in return. However, even her minimal desire to humanise the old miser is frustrated: upon the return of the prodigal son, Brisco's affections shift away from her towards Frank. Left on her own resources, Abigail earns a modest living by becoming a seamstress, until a providential distant relative appears and takes her on a European tour that hurriedly prepares the foundling to be reinstated in the social class she rightly belongs to. The fictional life of this character is a pale rendition of stories already told and partly worn out.

One could argue that the very marginality of female characters in Riddell's later novels and the determination with which they are pushed to the edges of the narrative or enlisted in cultural scripts which have lost momentum are symptomatic of the pressure of contingent historical forces on the construction of the stories of decline Riddell narrates. There is a sense of denied modernisation in the way these novels refuse to plot female progress, to imagine scripts that acknowledge the direction in which the history of modernity was going especially after the 1860s, when the issues of education, work, married women's property, divorce, the suffrage, and sexual morality were extensively debated, and traditional beliefs fervently challenged. By making women lateral, Riddell closes off the possibility of introducing into the narrative of decline a counterpoise not grounded in the past but in the future. This choice might very well have been determined by lack of sympathy with late Victorian feminism (as *Frank Sinclair's Wife* clearly suggests), but also by the very specific thematic focus on the City of London, on the world of commerce and finance which was not yet opening its doors, in any obvious way, to female traders or businesswomen. How plausible would it have been, even in the mid 1880s, to narrate the story of a woman who embarks upon a business career in the City? It would take about a hundred years for such a figure to appear in the firmament of fictional heroines, and when she does her story falls into the grooves of popular genres – the financial thriller, the City memoir – not into the less formulaic moulds of what today goes under the name of literary fiction.[5] That Riddell did not pursue this path is understandable from an historical point of view.

If the female trader in the City was an implausible chimera in the 1880s, the woman struggling in London to achieve literary fame was less so. Riddell's semi-autobiographical *Künstleroman*, *A Struggle for Fame*, traces the parallel careers of Bernard Kelly and Glenarva Westley, both of Irish origin, trying their luck in the London literary marketplace. With the story of Glenarva, Riddell rehearses the progressive plot of development that had structured her City novels up until the early 1870s, adapting it to the altered circumstances of a woman author's life. *A Struggle for Fame* is not a City novel, but it retains the narrative skeleton of *George Geith* or *The Race for Wealth* with one substantial revision – the representative subject is a woman, not a man; hers is the story of progress and self-affirmation that *The Senior Partner* and *Mitre Court* had rewritten as failure. Like Alan Ruthven, George Geith, and Lawrence Barbour, Glen descends from an impoverished upper-class family; the move to London opens up opportunities for self-realisation unthinkable in the isolated, rural setting of Ireland. Like her male predecessors, Glen is endowed with determination, 'tireless energy', 'dogged industry'[6] and a generous dose of self-reliance; like them, she experiences the alternation of gains and pains which, in Riddell's understanding of the philosophy of self-help, always complicates the representation of characters making their own fortune. To a certain extent, *A Struggle for Fame* reproduces this pattern in its purest form, by imagining a dual trajectory which differentiates between chance and freedom along gender lines: Bernard Kelly will attain success aided by fortune, while Glen's adventures in the marketplace are the prototypical expression of undiluted self-help.

This novel, unlike most of Riddell's texts, has captured the attention of critics in recent years. Linda Peterson, in particular, reads *A Struggle for Fame* in relation to the myths of authorship formulated by Elizabeth Gaskell in her biography of Charlotte Brontë: 'In *A Struggle for Fame* Riddell invokes – indeed, reproduces and interrogates – this seminal narrative as it influenced a generation of mid-century women writers, popularized a "parallel currents" model of authorship, and then came into conflict with the professional realities of the later nineteenth-century professional field'.[7] As Peterson observes, Romantic and Brontëan myths of authorship – myths of genius, inspiration, literary talent, solitude and tragedy – are aligned in the novel with Glenarva's vocation, while Barney Kelly's professional life is associated with a 'market-driven, Bohemian approach'.[8] Riddell 'reverses usual gender alignments by affiliating Glen with genius and Kelly with the cog in the capitalist wheel', thus accruing 'cultural capital for the woman author'.[9]

It is certainly true that Glen is depicted in the novel as a later incarnation of Romantic subjectivity and that 'the gold of genius'[10] is not Kelly's prerogative. However I would contend that Riddell's own myth of strong economic individuality provides the deeper structure, the internal scaffolding of Glen's progression from Irish immigrant to celebrated author. Narrative attention is equally divided, in this novel, between the linear destiny of Bernard Kelly – writer, journalist and Darwinian survivor (like Jasper Milvain will be in Gissing's 1891 novel *New Grub Street*) – and the vocational trajectory of Glen Westley, modelled on Riddell's memories of her own experience in the mid nineteenth-century market for fiction. Whereas Bernard's progress is propelled by fortuitous circumstances, by a propitious mix of chance and adaptability, Glen's progression is presented more heroically as the result of unadulterated self-help, virtuous individual striving and an open confrontation with market forces in which chance or fate play a decidedly minor role. Chance encounters and odd coincidences aid Bernard's advancement from the time of his arrival in London. Riddell pushes the limits of plausibility to insert in the story apparently accidental episodes that turn out to be 'merciful interpositions'[11] of providence. A good case in point is the humorous sketch 'How is Maria?' related in the second chapter: Bernard unwittingly and gratuitously offends his uncle (whom he does not recognise in the 'contemporary Brummel' sitting opposite him on the omnibus) thus curtailing the possibility of ever benefitting from his patronage. This episode sets in motion a play of coincidences that leads to Bernard's first publication (a short story), facilitated by the intercession of his Bohemian friends, the Dawtons. As Kelly is quick to admit: ' "How's Maria?" had indeed done something for him . . . he accounted the loss of his uncle's patronage a gain'.[12] Barney finds himself on several occasions in the position of beneficiary of other people's altruism. For instance, when money is most needed, his mother sends him five pounds alongside a sermon on his incompetence: 'It is a burning shame for an able-bodied man to be writing home for money like a helpless child';[13] and when literary skills fail him, the Dawtons compensate for his deficiencies by revising his short stories extensively, making them 'airy, sparking, vivacious'[14] and therefore fit for publication. Later on in the story, 'Barney's luck'[15] manifests itself in the shape of a wealthy widow, a woman he had wooed in his youth, who opportunely reappears in his life when his profession necessitates a boost, which she provides by introducing him into her upper-class circle of powerful acquaintances. The narrator ironically emphasises how fit Bernard is to emerge victorious from the struggle for fame – 'this young man had every element in his nature for compassing success: a cool head, a cold heart, a selfishness which was instinctive as his love of ease and money'[16] – but euphoric chance clearly determines the felicitous outcome of the race he runs. Bernard Kelly adapts well to circumstances, churns out the kind of literature the market wants – entertaining urban sketches – and nurtures the ambition to write a novel though he has no genius for that; he may be a cog in the capitalist wheel, but he is not a victim of the kind of gloomy determinism at work in *The Senior Partner*. His struggles in the literary marketplace benefit from the assistance of Tyche as a positive force; each random twist is a gain. The point is not that Bernard is portrayed as a lucky fellow; rather, Riddell constructs the narrative of his professional progress as a series of accidental occurrences, minimising the role of his agency and free will.

Conversely, Glen's parallel story follows a narrative trajectory that reads like a pure distillation of self-reliance and heroic individual striving. Glen embodies the modern orientation towards autonomy and self-determination which in *The Senior Partner* and *Mitre Court* appears either reified as paternal despotism or denied to younger participants in the race for wealth by the predominance of a fatalistic outlook on life. Of course, the gift of genius and inspiration helps Glen to stand out among the bevy of competitors, male or female, who vie for a place in the history of literature. But the narrative of her slow rise to success is constructed so as to accentuate self-help and individual entrepreneurship against a backdrop of cultural prejudices and adverse circumstances that sharpen Glen's ability to become the maker, the architect of her own fortune. The novel offers a bleak portrait of author-publisher relations, insisting on the sense of frustration experienced by newcomers (like Glen) and on the affective, emotional price paid by writers whose brains, as Trollope famously put it, remain 'unbought'.[17] After several failed attempts to place her manuscripts, Glen begins to doubt her own talent: 'She did not now believe in herself or her fitness to become an author'.[18]

Not only the publishers' negative responses, but also her father's and her future husband's mistrust in her 'fitness' to achieve literary fame provide a front of opposition in relation to which Glen's heroic isolation stands out: 'The girl did not look as if the making of a writer was in her – no fire of genius burnt in her eyes . . . It was hard upon Glen that no human being believed she was the right person in the right place'.[19] Not even when she strides into fame, do her friends or relations 'realise that it was really Glenarva who had won success, and not some quite independent power associated with her in an unaccountable and uncanny sort of alliance'.[20] Riddell insists repeatedly on the cultural hostility surrounding Glen's attempts to live by the pen: 'There never yet lived a wise man who wished women to turn artists, actresses, or authors',[21] the narrator states; Glen's fiancé, Mr Lacere, values her needle-work more highly than her manuscripts, which he does not even bother to read: 'he took the fragile scrap of work in his hand almost as tenderly as he spoke, and looked at it as he was never likely at any manuscript which she might present to him'.[22] Remarkable is the narrator's unwillingness to contest preconceptions openly or to question Lacere's condescending attitude; rather, they are presented objectively as the expression of a common structure of feeling, a shared understanding of what the role of women in society should be, which the narrator has no wish to dispute directly. The more hostile the environment, the more Glen's achievements can be made to appear as a victory against all odds, unassisted by fortune or by the help of relatives, in an extreme celebration of autonomy and will power.

If in Barney's narrative the fortunate play of coincidences tests the limits of the plausible, in Glen's parallel story incidents that appear contrived, or slightly out of sync with verisimilitude, serve the ideological purpose of highlighting Glen's exercise of free will. The story of how she manages to obtain her first, substantial financial gain is illustrative. When Mr Lacere offers his assistance and immediately finds a publisher willing to print her novel, Glen decides not to go ahead with the publication. Riddell describes her lack of joy upon hearing the good news that a publisher has finally been found – 'why is it that I do not feel more elated at my success? Why do I not dance and sing with delight?'[23] and concocts a rather elaborate explanation to justify Glen's resolve to retrieve her manuscript (the content of the novel would have been distasteful to Irish friends and relatives). Later on, with two novels already in print, one purchased 'before the ink was dry',[24] Glen has no qualms when it comes to the decision of selling the 'manuscript she formerly besought Mr. Lacere to take out of the firm that had bought it'.[25] This time, relying solely on her exertions and bargaining skills, Glen obtains what Riddell presents enthusiastically as a memorable victory and a moment of sheer capitalist joy:

> The fact being that Glen by sheer force of audacity had got fifty pounds for a novel that would have been dear at five. She wanted money so badly and she was so determined to have it, that she extracted an acceptance of the work and cheque in payment from a publisher who otherwise might have coquetted with the matter for a long time, and then 'declined the story with thanks'.

Till the last day of her life Glenarva will always remember two cheques she
received; and that fifty pounds was one of them.[26]

Striking a hard bargain (bordering on dishonesty), making a hefty profit, imposing her own terms to the counterpart are all valued, in this scene, as the rightfully
earned proceeds of a strenuous battle, fought in splendid isolation by a self-made
woman. That she possesses literary genius is beyond doubt, since the novel casts
Glen as the inheritor of Romantic subjectivity from the very beginning; that she
also possesses the power to impose her will in the marketplace is, on the other
hand, something which Riddell takes pain to demonstrate, ensuring that Glen's
steps, all along the way, are hindered by hostile prejudices, indifference, and
self-doubt that serve to highlight her heroine's double achievement: as creator of
literary value (novels that encounter the favour of discerning readers) and as successful producer of merchandise commanding fairly high prices in the market. In
this respect, *A Struggle for Fame* is more akin to Trollope's *Autobiography* (1883)
than it is to Gaskell's *Life of Charlotte Brontë*. Trollope's materialism, which took
his contemporaries by surprise, is certainly more pronounced and his business-
like approach to novel writing more radical. Riddell retains the idealism of myths
of authorship which, as Peterson argues, allowed her to differentiate, along gender
lines, between prestige or cultural capital and market-driven productivity. But she
grafts these myths onto the narrative of self-help, the great plot of *male* bourgeois
life, conferring upon the vocational trajectory of her heroine an aura of economic
romanticism. Though not a business novel, *A Struggle for Fame* still reproduces
fictional templates dear to the novelist of the City. In Glen's plot of development,
progress rather than decline is still a possibility, relocating to London opens up
fresh opportunities for the exploration of alternative lives and, as in Riddell's
earlier City novels, the emphasis falls on the struggle itself, the capitalist contention between the self and the market, often beset by private tragedies. Like
her male predecessors, Glen finds the balance between professional success and
private happiness rather unstable: for instance, to her advancements as an author
correspond private losses, first the death of her father, then her husband's commercial troubles and eventually his death. This uneven distribution of success and
happiness could of course be interpreted as a sign of ambivalence, on the part of
Riddell, vis-à-vis the possibility of imagining the harmonious integration of public and private commitments, of genius and domesticity, in the life of a woman
writer. However, Riddell's City heroes are often apportioned the same share of
private pains in relation to business gains as Glen is in this novel: the formulaic
equation between 'fame' and 'death' (embarrassing to modern readers, as Peterson observes) is a new version of the equally predictable correspondence between
economic success and affective losses which we find in the story of George Geith,
for instance, or Lawrence Barbour. When the subject of modernity changes gender, no longer a man of business but a woman author, the tensions inherent in
the way Riddell plots individualism and economic agency are reconfirmed. Like
George Geith, Glen attains the future she wished for minus the affections that
would make it more stable. These characters are both illustrations of Riddell's

philosophy of individualism – a philosophy which places a premium on the struggle qua struggle, factoring in tragedies and private losses, in the careers of men as well as women, to reflect the ineradicable precariousness of life under capitalism.

More interesting is the way in which the novel downplays domestic femininity. A doting daughter, Glen nonetheless systematically ignores the telling signs of her father's illness until it is too late. Mostly depicted when she is not at home but roaming the London streets in pursuit of her own career, or when she sits at her desk forgetful of the world around her, Glen has few domestic virtues to speak of. In her married life, she distinguishes herself on two fairly non-domestic fronts: an open hostility towards her husband's relatives – 'a provoking sort of antagonism'[27] exacerbated by Glen's sarcastic style of repartee – and a knack for business that more or less sum up her contribution to domestic serenity: 'Glen was never happier than in those days when doing her poor best to help a sadly overweighted man . . . she could write his letters, she could get through a mass of correspondence that might well have appalled a man'.[28] And to further emphasise the distance between this character and conventional ideals of domesticity, Riddell lists among her (few) domestic accomplishments the writing of a commercial 'pamphlet' which 'given away by thousands, caused such a division in families as pamphlets probably never did before . . . When Glen wrote it, which she did more out of despair and annoyance than from actual hope of effecting any good, she had not the slightest idea of creating such a glamour. Never one of her books was read, criticised, praised, and pooh-poohed like the three-page bill'.[29] The novel seems impatient when it comes to reassure readers that female authorship need not clash with domestic duties: Riddell shows little interest in exploring the happy convergence of the two or, alternatively, their disharmonic divergence. She keeps the focus of the narrative steadily on Glen's profession and vocation, which provide more material for reflection and narratorial interventions than do domesticity, romantic love and private affections. Glen is at her most 'disagreeable' when performing the part of the wife entertaining relatives and inflicting on them 'lacerating wounds';[30] there is no particular reason why such scenes should be included. They add nothing to the progression of the story, but they certainly suggest disaffection towards a vision of tamed femininity that hardly chimes with the model of strong subjectivity Riddell favours in relation to Glen.

This model is rooted in two cultural traditions: Romantic genius and *homo economicus* as paradigms of self-assertion. It is noticeable that Glen's creativity or genius is associated with the ability to exert a degree of control on market forces. For example, only after the prodigious triumph that Glen obtains with the sale of a novel worth five pounds and commanding 10 times as much, is her genius fully activated, resulting in the writing of a book which will finally make her reputation, a novel about 'the trials, the sorrows, the self-denials, the successes of trade',[31] reminiscent of Riddell's City narratives. Later on in the story, Glen becomes 'common property'[32] in the hands of 'speculative publishers' who dictate the terms of her contract, offering hefty sums of money but requiring servitude in return: '[Mr. Felton] had exactly the same feelings about his authors that some mistresses have about their servants'.[33] Subjected to a heavy round of marketing activities, Glen experiences a long period of sterility: 'words slipped away from memory; ideas, if not instantly written down, were difficult to reproduce; unless she took her mind firmly in hand and shook it, she failed to arouse the faculty of attention'.[34] The decision to leave the big firm of Laplash and Felton, with their speculative style of publishing, produces a renewed bout of creativity: 'So she wrote on steadily with a vigour, a determination, and a happy spirit of cheerfulness that it may be her labours had hitherto lacked'.[35] In other words, the power of Romantic genius is not immune to the pressures of the market: Glen's creative juices flow more steadily when she retains some control on her freedom to trade.

A Struggle for Fame is a retrospective fictionalised account of Riddell's professional life. Some episodes are loosely based on facts, or memories, of the author's experiences in London: the character of Vassett may be a thinly disguised version of Charles Skeet, Riddell's publisher in the early stage of her career; Laplash and Felton could stand for Tinsley Brothers; Barney Kelly, in Linda Peterson's interpretation, recalls George Augustus Sala or even Thackeray and Dickens; Mr Lacere, like Riddell's husband, is a man of business who does not shun the help of his wife when it comes to composing commercial letters; and Glen achieves success with a novel about business, Riddell's own specialty. In this respect, like *The Senior Partner* and *Mitre Court*, the novel looks back at the past – the personal past of the author, reworked into a narrative which provides a pattern, an overall significance to the struggles of both author and heroine.

The main difference, however, is that the female-centred novel not only contradicts the vision of decline projected in the male-centred novels of the 1880s but also suggests a way forward, in line with emerging cultural and political discourses that placed women and their liberal agency at the forefront of modernity. The image with which *A Struggle for Fame* takes leave of its readers is emblematic in this respect: a man, Ned, looks at the figure of a woman, Glen, and describes her through a series of negatives: 'not a girl in her first youth', 'not a daughter seated beside a cultured gentleman', 'not a struggling woman', 'not a wife'; while Glen simply watches his retreating figure, 'feeling almost as though she were looking on one dead'.[36] Glen and Ned are united by bonds of affection rooted in childhood's memories. In this parting scene, they are physically separated by an unnamed river. The scene is reminiscent of *The Mill on the Floss*'s closing moments – but there is no death by water for Ned and Glen, and only one clear survivor.

In the early stages of her career, Riddell had already published a novel – *The Rich Husband* (1858) – in which nearly all female characters nurture literary ambitions and some of them succeed in becoming authors. Conceived before Riddell opted for the City and business, *A Rich Husband* contains extended reflections on authorship as a vocation and a trade. The main plot revolves around the story of a failed marriage – a marriage that fails before the nuptials are celebrated, since it is presented as a crude economic transaction, a cold, rational deal stipulated between Judith, who needs money to take care of her ailing sister, and the rich husband of the title, Mr. Mazingford, a tyrannical and violent despot who has no intention of fulfilling his side of the contract. Authorship is a desperate remedy that Judith adopts seeking to redress the many torts life has in store for her. The metaphors deployed to describe the profession of writing are contradictory: it is alternately a 'fever' coming upon the writer with 'virulence and hopelessness',[37] a 'parasitical convolvulus'[38] demanding attention, or a powerful 'medicine' acting as 'anti-depressant';[39] while authors are likened to sailors desperately pumping water during a shipwreck or to engineers and other traders simply doing their job. Mostly, however, authorship is the result of chance, an unexpected deviation that alters the course of one's life: 'Life chances turn on the merest atom of a pivot – and so, we doubt not, there are scores now earning their bread by the labours of their pen, who would never have tried their hand at authorship but for some strange chance or domestic misfortune'.[40] *The Rich Husband* is a recursive and sprawling text, with several intersecting story lines, some of them barely developed. One common thread connects these disparate stories: the pressing urgency, especially for women, to find some degree of economic independence from abusive husbands or relatives. Authorship appears as the only plausible field in which they can 'accidentally' wander and earn some money. Before embarking upon her career as the bard of business, Riddell had imagined embattled stories of female economic agency mostly ending in tragedy: in *The Rich Husband*, Judith dies after a series of melodramatic vicissitudes that include the forging of her husband's signature on a cheque. Savvy enough to know what do with the cheque, Judith pockets the money and soon afterwards changes 'the large notes into small ones, the small into large'[41] so that they cannot be traced. The financial expertise this character demonstrates is remarkable, but the felony committed does not go unpunished.

The Rich Husband was published two years before *Too Much Alone*: the melodramatic contrasts of the former are tempered down in the latter, and the representation of female economic agency (tormented and extreme) gives way to the more linear, less convulsive depiction of businessmen on the rise. The formal confusion of *The Rich Husband* may reflect the difficulty of imagining and plotting the economic subjectivity of female characters in a world in which the hegemonic narratives of economic individuality were gendered male, as the texts considered in Chapters 1 and 2 clearly indicate. The focus on the City of London and businessmen arguably allowed Riddell to recalibrate the formal structure of her novels by anchoring it to a recognisable cultural pattern. When she revisited the subject of female authorship in *A Struggle for Fame*, the same philosophy of self-help that she had contributed to honing in story after story was reedited to tie up the threads of events hinging on Glenarva's progression from obscurity to fame.

The paradigmatic tale of the self-made man (more narratable than the atypical story of the self-made woman) is not reproduced or appropriated, in Riddell's fiction, without emendations, additions and re-interpretations that place it more squarely in relation to the domestic sphere (with its internal fractures), the private realm of affections (often irregular, verging on the improper) and the changing dynamics of Victorian personal capitalism. For Riddell, narrating capitalism entailed testing the limits of what novels can or cannot do, according to the aesthetic standards of her time. Though frequently criticised for flaunting an excess of financial and legal knowledge, Riddell continued to interrogate the impact of capitalist modernity on the lives of 'sober plodders', instructing her readers on how best to cope with an unstable and only partially regulated economic sphere. That she was not deterred by negative criticism is to her credit. That she consistently tried to understand and to explain, in a profusion of specific particulars, how mid-Victorian capitalism worked, what challenges it posed, what demands it placed on the lives of middle-class men and women, is what sets her writing apart (for better or for worse) from the tradition of Victorian fiction. Riddell used the novel form primarily to give structure and meaning to the experience of *capitalist* modernity. Her vision is not all-inclusive; the conflict between capital and labour, for instance, is only summarily touched upon in *Too Much Alone* and *City and Suburb*. She writes about capitalists (mainly small), not the working classes. Her sympathies are with the plights of individuals, not collectives. Nonetheless, Riddell's City novels address concerns and preoccupations which, it is plausible to assume, were widely shared by the unknown public of potential readers; foremost among these preoccupations is the ever recurring spectre of insolvency, which haunts the pages of her novels though her protagonists are not battling with penury on a daily basis. The reverse of this picture is Riddell's pro-business orientation, her belief in the power of individuals to shape their destiny through work, ingenuity and determination – a quintessentially Victorian myth which her novels refashion in various permutations, including pejorative ones.

'Capitalism must be explained, not assumed': these words appear in the 2014 Manifesto of capitalism studies, an interdisciplinary field of research that has gained momentum in the aftermath of the 2008 crisis.[42] One premise upon which this manifesto is built is that economics is insufficient to explain capitalism as a social process and to account for the political, social and cultural embeddedness of markets. Thomas Pikkety's study, *Capital in the Twentieth-First Century* (2014), relies on historical data and economic theory to bring to light the patterns of inequality associated with the development of capitalism, while also looking at nineteenth-century fiction for literary evidence of social immobility. Whether his take on fiction is accurate or not, it exemplifies a renewed interest in cross-disciplinary approaches to the study of capitalism. While my book cannot claim to be a literary study of nineteenth-century capitalism, Riddell's business novels come close to that description: they certainly illustrate how deeply felt was the desire to explain, rather than assume, the relatively new reality of capitalism with which her fiction repeatedly engages. Her novels have suffered from neglect partly because her embracing of the City and business was expressed and communicated through formal and thematic patterns that bear a scant relation with the tradition of high Victorian fiction. Much of what was written in the nineteenth century still remains dormant in the obscure storehouses of passive cultural memory. As John Sutherland claimed in 1989, 'Over the last 88 years, our map of nineteenth-century fiction has shrunk to Lilliputian dimensions. The tiny working areas of the "canon", the "syllabus" and the paperbacked "classics" are poor reflections of what the Victorian novel actually meant to the Victorians'.[43] With the massive enterprise of digitization, however, the 'lost continent'[44] of nineteenth-century fiction is gaining a new lease of life. Not so long ago, Riddell's novels were available only in a few select libraries; now most of them can be downloaded from the Internet Archives website and the Europeana online library. The transition from print to digital has the undeniable advantage of rendering more texts potentially available to a greater number of readers. But digitization does not automatically entail new visibility. For the recovery of what was lost to proceed beyond the scanning process, further steps are needed. Starting from the assumption that the mechanisms presiding over the selection and transmission of literary heritage have often penalised women's contributions, the central aim of this book has been to provide a critical platform for the recirculation of Riddell's forgotten words. My readings have sought to highlight, on the one hand, the interaction between her novels and the broader discursive framework of Victorian business culture, and on the other, the narrative strategies, the formal solutions through which her fiction reconfigured pressing topical issues, from food adulteration to bankruptcy, from the instability of credit to the precariousness of ancient buildings, from adultery to commercial morality. Harriet Martineau's *Illustrations of Political Economy* (1832–1834) had set the tone of the early nineteenth-century conversation between economic ideas and literature, attributing to fiction a crucial mediating and educational function. Riddell's City novels dispense with tackling theories to concentrate on the practical side of business. But both authors consider the new economy of their time a worthy subject of literary experiments. The hybridity of Martineau's *Illustrations*, as Deborah Logan has observed, 'accounts both for its immediate success and for its lack of staying power or long-term relevance, the standard traditionally employed to measure literary worth'.[45] Likewise, the hybrid mixture of financial and literary writing that characterises Riddell's novels captured the attention of her contemporaries and arguably affected her rapid fall from grace. In both cases, the reputation diagram is a bell-shaped curve. Martineau's works have recently enjoyed an upsurge of interest among publishers, literary and cultural critics. Will Riddell's novels follow suit?

Notes

1 James H. Murphy briefly discusses Riddell's Irish novels in *Irish Novelists & the Victorian Age* (Oxford: Oxford University Press, 2011). 'In all of these novels', he concludes, 'there is an apparent diffidence about Irish identity but it is a diffidence that appears to be masking feelings which at times amount to revulsion. Riddell, far from being indifferent to Irish identity, is in fact quite passionate about it' (p. 8).

2 Wagner, *Modernity*, p. 17.

3 *Mitre Court*, vol. 1, p. 6. The 'custom' Mrs Jeffley mentions here refers to the long established tradition of conferring the Freedom of the City of London to both men and women; upon marriage, however, women would have their right suspended. 'The Freedom of the City is not confined to the male sex. Freewomen are called free sisters, but cannot transmit their freedom, which is, moreover, suspended during coverture' see William Ferneley Allen, *The Corporation of London: Its Rights and Privileges*, 1858, http://www.gutenberg.org/cache/epub/5609/pg5609.html, last accessed 22 April 2015. It would appear that Riddell's interpretation of this ancient custom is more progressive and liberal than the custom itself.

244 *Epilogue*

4 *The Senior Partner*, vol. 1, p. 156.
5 See, for instance, Suzana S. *Confessions of a City Girl* (2009) and Venetia Thompson, *Gross Misconduct* (2010).
6 Charlotte Riddell, *A Struggle for Fame*, 1883, (Dublin: Tramp Press, 2014), p. 198.
7 Peterson, p. 151.
8 Ibid., 160.
9 Ibid., 160.
10 *A Struggle*, p. 199.
11 Ibid., p. 61.
12 Ibid., p. 137.
13 Ibid., p. 59.
14 Ibid., p. 206.
15 Ibid., p. 297.
16 Ibid., p. 66.
17 'Brains that are unbought', Trollope declares, 'will never serve the public much', see Anthony Trollope, *An Autobiography*, 1883 (Oxford: Oxford University Press, 1987), p. 107.
18 *A Struggle*, p. 184.
19 Ibid., p. 185.
20 Ibid., p. 185.
21 Ibid., p. 189.
22 Ibid., p. 188.
23 Ibid., p. 229.
24 Ibid., p. 285.
25 Ibid.
26 Ibid., p. 286.
27 Ibid., p. 325.
28 Ibid., p. 327.
29 Ibid., p. 331.
30 Ibid., p. 326.
31 Ibid., p. 290.
32 Ibid., p. 346.
33 Ibid.
34 Ibid., p. 378.
35 Ibid., p. 400.
36 Ibid., p. 407.
37 Charlotte Riddell, *The Rich Husband*, 1857, (London: Tinsley Brothers, 1867), p. 226.
38 Ibid., p. 226.
39 Ibid., p. 193.
40 Ibid., pp. 116–7.
41 Ibid., p. 247.
42 Julia Ott and William Milberg, 'Capitalism Studies: A Manifesto' *Public Seminar Review* 1, no. 2 (Summer 2014) http://www.publicseminar.org/2014/04/capitalism-studies-a-manifesto/#.VVRp0dqqqkp last accessed 5 May 2015.
43 John Sutherland, ed. *The Stanford Companion to Victorian Fiction* (Stanford: Stanford University Press, 1989), p. 1.
44 Ibid.
45 Deborah Logan, 'Introduction' in *Illustrations of Political Economy: Selected Tales*, ed. Deborah Logan (Peterborough, ON: Broadview, 2004), pp. 39–40.

Bibliography

'A Life's Assize'. *The Times*, 14 January 1871, p. 4.

'A Statistical Vindication of the City of London'. *The Athenaeum* 2058 (6 April 1867), pp. 445–6.

'Adulteration, and its Remedy'. *The Cornhill Magazine* 2, no. 7 (July 1860), pp. 86–96.

'Adulteration of Credit'. *The Leader* 6, no. 287 (22 September 1855), pp. 911–12.

'The Adulteration of Food'. *The London Review* 13, no. 326 (29 September 1866), pp. 342–3.

'Adulteration of Food and Drugs." *The Westminster Review* 35, no. 1 (January 1869), pp. 185–206.

'Adulteration of Food, Drinks, and Drugs'. *The British Quarterly Review* 23, no. 45 (January 1856), pp. 288–90.

Agathocleous, Tanya. *Urban Realism and the Cosmopolitan Imagination in the Nineteenth Century*. Cambridge: Cambridge University Press, 2011.

Aho, James. *Confession and Bookkeeping: the Religious, Moral and Rhetorical Roots of Accounting*. Albany: State University of New York Press, 2005.

Alexander James W. and others. *The Man of Business Considered in Six Aspects. A Book for Young Men*. 1864. Edinburgh: William P. Nimmo, 1872.

Allen William Ferneley. *The Corporation of London: Its Rights and Privileges*, 1858, http://www.gutenberg.org/cache/epub/5609/pg5609.html, last accessed 22 April 2015.

Anderson, Amanda. *Tainted Souls and Painted Faces: The Rhetoric of Fallenness in Victorian Culture*. Ithaca, N.Y.: Cornell University Press, 1993.

———. *The Way We Argue Now: A Study in the Culture of Theory*. Princeton: Princeton University Press, 2006.

Anderson, Geraint. *City Boy: Beer and Loathing in the Square Mile*. London: Headline, 2010.

———. *Just Business*. London: Headline, 2011.

Anon. *Business Life: Experiences of a London Tradesman with practical advice and directions for avoiding many of the evils connected with our present commercial system and state of society*. London: Houlston and Wright, 1861.

Arnold, Matthew. *Culture and Anarchy and Other Writings*, ed. Stefan Collini. Cambridge: Cambridge University Press, 1993.

Arthur, William. *The Successful Merchant: Sketches of the Life of Mr. Samuel Budgett*. 1852. New York: Carlton & Porter, 1857.

Assmann, Aleida. 'Canon and Archive'. *Cultural and Memory Studies: An Interdisciplinary Handbook*, ed. Astrid Erll and Ansgar Nünning. Berlin: Walter de Gruyter, 2008, pp. 97–107.

'Austin Friars'. *The Graphic* 27 (4 June 1870), p. 635.

'Austin Friars'. *The Saturday Review* 29, no. 762 (4 June 1879), p. 748.

Bagehot, Walter. 'Mr. Macaulay'. 1856. *The Collected Works of Walter Bagehot*, vol. 1, *The Literary Essays*, ed. Norman St John-Stevas. London: The Economist, 1965, pp. 397–431.

———. *Lombard Street*. 1873. *The Collected Works of Walter Bagehot*, vol. 9, *The Economic Essays*, ed. Norman St John-Stevas, London: The Economist, 1978.

———. *Economic Studies*. 1880. *The Collected Works of Walter Bagehot*, vol. 11, *The Economic Essays*, ed. Norman St John-Stevas. London: The Economist, 1978.

Bailey, Peter. 'White Collars, Grey Lives? The Lower Middle Class Revisited'. *Journal of British Studies* 38 (July 1999), pp. 273–90.

Bakhtin, Michail. 'The *Bildungsroman* and Its Significance in the History of Realism: (Toward a Historical Typology of the Novel)'. *Speech Genres and Other Late Essays*, trans. Vern W. McGee, Austin: University of Texas Press, 1986, pp. 10–59.

Ball Michael and David Sunderland. *An Economic History of London, 1800–1914*. London: Routledge, 2001.

'Bankruptcy'. *The Saturday Review* 27, no. 712 (19 July 1879), pp. 69–70.

Bauman, Zygmunt. *City of Fears, City of Hope*. London: Goldsmith, 2003.

Beer, Gillian. *Open Fields: Science in Cultural Encounters*. Oxford: Clarendon Press, 1996.

'Belles Lettres'. *The Westminster Review* 30, no. 2 (October 1866), pp. 524–38.

Bending, Lucy. *The Representation of Bodily Pain in Late Nineteenth Century English Culture*. Oxford: Oxford University Press, 2000.

Berman, Marshall. *All that is Solid Melts into Air: the Experience of Modernity*. London: Penguin, 1988.

Biagini, Eugenio F. *Liberty, Retrenchment and Reform: Popular Liberalism in the Age of Gladstone, 1860–1880*. Cambridge: Cambridge University Press, 1992.

Bivona, Daniel and Roger B. Henkle. *The Imagination of Class: Masculinity and the Victorian Urban Poor*. Columbus: Ohio State University Press, 2006.

Black, Helen C. 'Mrs. Riddell'. *Notable Women Authors of the Day*. London: Maclaren and Company, 1906, pp. 11–25.

Blackstone, William. *Commentaries on the Laws of England, A New Edition with the Last Corrections of the Author*. London: William Reed, 1811.

Blake, Kathleen. *Pleasures of Benthamism: Victorian Literature, Utility, Political Economy*. Oxford: Oxford University Press, 2009.

[Blathwayt, Raymond]. 'Lady Novelists – A Chat with Mrs. J.H. Riddell'. *The Pall Mall Gazette*. 18 February 1890, p. 3.

Bleiler, E.F., ed. *The Collected Ghost Stories of Mrs. J.H. Riddell*. New York: Dover Publications, 1977.

———. 'Mrs. Riddell, Mid-Victorian Ghosts, and Christmas Annuals'. *The Collected Ghost Stories of Mrs. J.H. Riddell*, pp. v–xxvi.

Bourdieu, Pierre. *The Field of Cultural Production*. Cambridge: Polity Press, 1993.

Bourne, Henry Fox. *English Merchants: Memoirs in Illustration of the Progress of British Commerce*. 2 vols. London: Richard Bentley, 1866.

———. *The Romance of Trade*. London: Cassell, Petter, Galpin & Co, 1876.

———. *Famous London Merchants; A Book for Boys*. London: James Hogg & Son, 1869.

Braddon, Mary Elizabeth. *The Doctor's Wife*. 1864. Oxford: Oxford University Press, 1988.

Brake, Laurel and Marysa Demoor, eds. *Dictionary of Nineteenth-Century Journalism in Great Britain and Ireland*. Gent and London: Academia Press, 2009.

Brantlinger, Patrick. *Fictions of State: Culture and Credit in Britain, 1694–1994*. Ithaca: Cornell University Press, 1996.

Brewer, Henry. 'The Demolition of City Churches'. *The Academy* 100 (4 April 1874), pp. 371–2.

Brontë, Charlotte. *Villette*. 1853. Oxford: Oxford University Press, 1990.

Brown, Rev. Baldwin. *The Young Man's Entrance upon Life and Commencement of Business*. London: John F. Shaw, 1855.

Brown, Richard. *A History of Accounting and Accountants, edited and partly written by Richard Brown*. 1905. London: Frank Cassel & Co., 1968.

Bunce, Michael. *The Countryside Ideal. Anglo-American Images of Landscape*. London: Routledge, 2005.

Burchardt, Jeremy. *Paradise Lost: Rural Idyll and Social Change in England since 1800*. London: I.B. Tauris Publishers, 2002.

'Business'. *The Leisure Hour* 705, (1 July 1865), pp. 404–6.

'Business and Leisure'. *The Chambers's Edinburgh Journal* 375 (6 April 1839), pp. 81–2.

Cain, Peter. 'Radicalism, Gladstone and the Liberal Critique of Disraelian Imperialism'. *Victorian Visions of Global Order: Empire and Relations in Nineteenth-Century Political Thought*, ed. Duncan Bell. Cambridge: Cambridge University Press, 2007, pp. 215–38.

Carlisle, Janice. *Common Scents: Comparative Encounters in High-Victorian Fiction*. Oxford: Oxford University Press, 2004.

Carlyle, Thomas. *Past and Present*. 1843. *Carlyle's Complete Works. The Sterling Edition*. vol. XII, Boston: Estes and Lauriat, 1885.

Carruthers, Bruce and Espeland, Wendy Nelson. 'Accounting for Rationality: Double-Entry Bookkeeping and the Rhetoric of Economic Rationality'. *The American Journal of Sociology*, 97, no. 1, July 1991, pp. 31–69.

Cartwright, Justine. *Other People's Money*. London: Bloomsbury, 2011.

Caruth, Cathy. *Unclaimed Experience: Trauma, Narrative and History*. Baltimore: The Johns Hopkins University Press, 1996.

Chandler, Alfred D. *Scale and Scope: the Dynamics of Industrial Capitalism*. Cambridge, Mass.: Belknap Press, 1990.

'Charlotte Riddell' in *Orlando: Women's Writing in the British Isle from the Beginnings to the present*, http://orlando.cambridge.org/ last accessed May 2014.

Charters, David. *No Tears: Tales from the Square Mile*. London: Elliott and Thompson, 2010.

Chiapello, Eve. 'Accounting and the Birth of Capitalism'. *Critical Perspectives on Accounting* 18 (2007), pp. 263–96.

Colli, Andrea. *The History of Family Business, 1750–2000*. Cambridge: Cambridge University Press, 2003.

Collinson v. Riddell, Riddell, Routledge Brothers, and Whiffin. C92 (1873). British National Archives C16/852 C92 C588778.

[Collyer, Robert]. 'Novels of the Week' (Rev. of *Austin Friars*), *The Athenaeum* 2222 (28 May 1870), pp. 707–8.

'Commercial Literature'. *The Economist* 19, no. 927 (1 June 1861), p. 597.

Cowell, Ben. *The Heritage Obsession: The Battle for England's Past*. Chalford: Tempus, 2008.

Cox, Michael and R.A. Gilbert eds. 'Introduction' in *Victorian Ghost Stories: An Oxford Anthology*. Oxford: Oxford University Press, 1992, pp. ix–xx.

Craik, Dinah Muloch. *A Woman's Thoughts about Women*. London: Hurst and Blackett, 1858.

Crespi, Alfred. 'Trades and Professions'. *New Monthly Magazine* 7, no. 48 (June 1879), pp. 644–61.

Cross, Launcelot. 'Leaves from Life. No. IV, Business'. *New Monthly Magazine* 90 (June 1879), pp. 639–54.

———. 'Leaves from Life. No. V. Business – (Continued)'. *New Monthly Magazine* 116 (July 1879), pp. 764–81.

———. 'The Man of Business – Absolute'. *New Monthly Magazine* 117 (January 1880), pp. 591–613.

Crossick Geoffrey and Heinz-Gerhard Haupt. *The Petit Bourgeoisie in Europe, 1780–1914*. London: Routledge, 1995.

Crosthwaite, Paul. 'Is Financial Crisis a Trauma?' *Cultural Critique* 82 (fall 2013), pp. 34–67.

Dalley, Lana L. and Jill Rappoport, eds. *Economic Women: Essays on Desire and Dispossession in Nineteenth-Century British Culture*. Columbus: The Ohio State University Press, 2013.

Dames, Nicholas. *The Physiology of the Novel: Reading, Neural Science, and the Form of Victorian Fiction*. Oxford: Oxford University Press, 2007.

Dannenberg, P. Hilary. *Coincidences and Counterfactuality: Plotting Time and Space in Narrative Fiction*. Lincoln: University of Nebraska Press, 2008.

Decker, Ina. *Mrs J.H. Riddells Londoner Stadtromane, 1860–1881*. PhD *Dissertation*, Aachen, Germany 1993.

Dickens, Charles. *Bleak House*, 1852–1853. Harmondsworth: Penguin, 1994.

———. *The Uncommercial Traveller*. 1861. London: Chapman & Hall, 1895.

Dolin, Kieran. *Fiction and the Law: Legal Discourse in Victorian and Modernist Literature*. Cambridge University Press, Cambridge: 1999.

Donovan, Elisabeth. *William Morris and the Society for the Protection of Ancient Buildings*. London: Routledge, 2008.

Douglas, Mary. *Purity and Danger. An Analysis of Concepts of Pollution and Taboo*. 1966. London: Routledge, 2001.

Earl, John. 'London government: a record of custodianship'. In *Preserving the Past*, ed. Michael Hunter. Stroud: Alan Sutton, 1996, pp. 57–76.

Earle, Peter. *The Making of the English Middle Class: Business, Society and Family Life in London, 1660–1730*. Berkeley: University of California Press, 1989.

Eco, Umberto. *La vertigine della lista*. Milano: Bompiani, 2009.

Edmundson, Melissa. 'The "Uncomfortable Houses" of Charlotte Riddell and Margaret Oliphant'. *Gothic Studies* 12, no. 1 (2010), pp. 51–67.

Ellis, Stuart M. *Wilkie Collins, Le Fanu, and Others*. 1934. London: Constable 1951.

Escott, Thomas H.S. *England: Its People, Polity and Pursuits*. 1879. London: Cassell, 1881.

Esty, Jed. *Unseasonable Youth: Modernism, Colonialism, and the Fiction of Development*. Oxford: Oxford University Press, 2012.

Evans, David Morier. *City Men and City Manners: The City, or, The Physiology of London Business; with Sketches on 'Change, and at the Coffee Houses*. London: Groombridhe & Sons, 1852.

———. *The Commercial Crisis, 1847–48: Being Facts and Figures Illustrative of the Events of That Important Period Considered in Relation to the Three Epochs of the Railway Mania, the Food and Money Panic, and the French Revolution.* London: Letts, Sons and Steer, 1849.

———. *The History of the Commercial Crisis, 1857–58, and The Stock Exchange Panic of 1859.* London: Groombridge and Sons, 1859.

———. *Facts, Failures, and Frauds: Revelations Financial, Mercantile, Criminal.* London: Groombridge and Sons, 1859.

———. *Speculative Notes and Notes on Speculation.* London, Groombridge and Sons, 1864.

'The Experience of a London Tradesman'. *The London Review* 2, no. 38 (23 March 1861), pp. 335–6.

Fisher, Philip. *The Vehement Passions.* Princeton University Press: Princeton, 2002.

Flower, Michael. 'The Charlotte Riddell Website'. http://www.charlotteriddell.co.uk last accessed 12 March 2015.

'Flowers in the City'. *The Penny Illustrated Paper*, 10 June 1876, p. 388.

Foreman-Peck, James, ed. *New perspectives on the late Victorian economy: Essays in quantitative economic history, 1860–1914.* Cambridge: Cambridge University Press, 1991.

Fortunes Made in Business, Biographical and Anecdotic from the Recent History of Industry and Commerce, by Various Writers. 2 vols. London: Sampson Low, Marston, Searle & Rivington, 1884.

'Fortunes Made in Business'. *The Athenaeum* 2944 (March 1884), pp. 401–2.

'Fortunes Made in Business'. *The Saturday Review* 57, no. 1488 (13 May 1884), pp. 580–82.

Foster, Benjamin Franklin. *Double Entry Elucidated.* London: Bell & Daldy, 1858.

Foucault, Michel. *The Archaeology of Knowledge.* London: Routledge, 2008.

Freedley, Edwin T. *A Practical Treatise on Business, with an inquiry into the chances of success and causes of failure.* London: George Routledge and Co, 1853.

Freytag, Gustav. *Debit and Credit. A Novel by Gustav Freytag from the Original, with the Sanction of the Author, by Mrs Malcom.* London: Richard Bentley, 1857.

Furniss, Henry. *Some Victorian Women – Good, Bad and Indifferent.* London: John Lane, 1923.

Garcha, Amanpal. *From Sketch to Novel: the Development of Victorian Fiction.* Cambridge: Cambridge University Press, 2009.

Genette, Gerard. *Narrative Discourse: An Essay in Method.* Ithaca: Cornell University Press, 1980.

'George Geith'. *The Fortnightly Review* 1 (1 June 1865), pp. 254–5.

'George Geith'. *The Morning Post,* 30 December 1864, p. 2.

'George Geith'. *The Reader* 5, no. 108 (21 January 1865), p. 66.

'George Geith'. *The Saturday Review* 19, no. 489 (11 March 1865), pp. 290–91.

Gilbert, Pamela. 'Ouida and the Canon: Recovering, Reconsidering, and Revisioning the Popular'. In *Ouida and Victorian Popular Culture,* ed. Andrew King and Jane Jordan. Burlington: Ashgate, 2013, pp. 37–51.

Gillooly, Eileen. *Smiles of Discontent: Humor, Gender, and Nineteenth-Century British Fiction.* Chicago: The University of Chicago Press, 1999.

Girard, René. *Deceit, Desire and the Novel. Self and Other in Literary Structure.* Baltimore: The Johns Hopkins University Press, 1965.

Goodlad, Lauren. *Victorian Literature and the Victorian State: Character and Governance in a Liberal Society.* Baltimore: The Johns Hopkins University Press, 2003.

Grey, W.R. *Business Manners and Business Matters or Friendly Hints on Every-Day Affairs*. London: William Kent & Co., 1862.

Habermas, Jürgen. *The Structural Transformation of the Public Sphere: An Inquiry into a Category of Bourgeois Society*. 1962. Cambridge, Mass: The MIT Press, 1989.

Hadley, Elaine. *Living Liberalism: Practical Citizenship in Mid-Victorian Britain*. Chicago: The University of Chicago Press, 2010.

Hager, Kelly. *Dickens and the Rise of Divorce: The Failed-Marriage Plot and the Novel Tradition*. Farnham: Ashgate, 2010.

Haining, Peter, ed. *The Mammoth Book of Haunted House Stories*. New York: Carrol & Graf, 2000.

Hansen, Adam. 'Exhibiting Vagrancy, 1851: Victorian London and the "Vagabond Savage"'. In *A Mighty Mass of Brick and Smoke: Victorian and Edwardian Representations of London*, ed. Lawrence Phillips, Amsterdam: Rodopoi, 2007, pp. 61–84.

Harris, Robert. *The Fear Index*. London: Hutchinson, 2011.

Hartman, Geoffrey. 'On Traumatic Knowledge and Literary Studies'. *New Literary History* 26, no. 3 (Summer 1995), pp. 537–63.

Hassall, Arthur Hill, M.D. *Food and its Adulterations*. London: Longman, Brown, Green, Longmans, and Roberts, 1855.

———. *Adulterations Detected; or, Plain Instructions for the Discovery of Frauds in Food and Medicine*. 1857. London: Longman, Brown, Green, Longmans, and Roberts, 1861.

Hatton, Joseph. 'England's Commercial decline.' *The Tinsley's Magazine* 24 (March 1879), pp. 256–65.

Hawkins Ann R. and Maura Ives, ed. *Women Writers and the Artifacts of Celebrity in the Long Nineteenth Century*. Farnham: Ashgate, 2012.

Hazlitt, William. *Table Talk, Second Series*. New York: Wiley and Putnam, 1846.

Helps, Arthur. *Essays Written in the Intervals of Business*. London: William Pickering, 1843.

Henry, Nancy. '"Ladies do it?": Victorian Women Investors in Fact and Fiction'. In *Victorian Literature and Finance*, ed. Francis O'Gorman. Oxford: Oxford University Press, 2007, pp. 111–34.

———. '"Rushing into Eternity": Suicide and Finance in Victorian Fiction'. In *Victorian Investments: New Perspectives on Finance and Culture*, ed. Nancy Henry and Cannon Schmitt. Bloomington: Indiana University Press, 2009, pp. 161–81.

———. '"Charlotte Riddell: Novelist of the 'City'". In *Economic Women: Essays on Desire and Dispossession in Nineteenth-Century British Culture*, eds Lana Dalley and Jill Rappoport, Columbus: The Ohio State University Press, 2013, pp. 193–205.

———. 'Economic Exhaustion and Literary Energy: Charlotte Riddell'. Paper presented at the annual conference of the Interdisciplinary Nineteenth-Century Studies (INCS), Houston, Texas, 27–30 March 2014.

———. '2008 and All That: Economics and Victorian Literature', *Victorian Literature and Culture* 43 (2015), pp. 217–22.

Herbert, Christopher. 'Filthy Lucre: Victorian Ideas of Money'. *Victorian Studies* 44, no. 2 (Winter 2002), pp. 185–213.

Herman, David, et al. *Narrative Theory: Core Concepts and Critical Debates*. Columbus: The Ohio State University Press, 2012.

'Holiday Scenes – No. 1'. *The Penny Illustrated Paper,* 30 April 1870, pp. 284–5.

Hollingshead, John. *Under Bow Bells, a City Book for All Readers*. London: Goombridge & Sons, 1859.

Hoppen, Theodore. *The Mid-Victorian Generation, 1840–1886*. Oxford: Oxford University Press, 1998.

Hopwood Anthony & Peter Miller, eds. *Accounting as Social Institutional Practice*. Cambridge: Cambridge University Press, 1994.

Houston, Gail Turley. *From Dickens to* Dracula: *Gothic, Economics, and Victorian Fiction*. Cambridge: Cambridge University Press, 2005.

Hume, Robert D. *Reconstructing Contexts: the Aims and Principles of Archeo-Historicism*. Oxford: Oxford University press, 1999.

Hunt, Aeron. *Personal Business: Character and Commerce in Victorian Literature and Culture*. Charlottesville: University of Virginia Press, 2014.

Hunt, Freeman. *Worth and Wealth. A Collection of Maxims, Morals and Miscellanies for Merchants and Men of Business*. New York: Stringer and Townsend, 1856.

Hunter, Leeann. 'Communities Built from Ruins: Social Economics in Victorian Novels of Bankruptcy'. *Women's Studies Quarterly* 39, no. 3 & 4 (Fall/Winter 2011), pp. 137–52.

Hunter, Michael ed. *Preserving the Past: The Rise of Heritage in Modern Britain*. Stroud: Alan Sutton, 1996.

Jaffe, Audrey. *The Affective Life of the Average Man: The Victorian Novel and the Stock-Market Graph*. Columbus: Ohio University Press, 2010.

Jameson, Fredric. *The Antinomies of Realism*. London: Verso, 2013.

[Jewsbury, Geraldine]. 'New Novels' (Rev. of *Too Much Alone*). *The Athenaeum* 1690 (17 March 1860), p. 373.

———. 'New Novels' (Rev. of *City and Suburb*). *The Athenaeum* 1752 (25 May 1861), p. 692.

———. 'George Geith of Fen Court'. *The Athenaeum* 1947 (18 February 1865), p. 233.

[Jones, Henry Arthur]. 'Religion and the Stage'. *Nineteenth Century* 17, no. 95 (January 1885), pp. 154–69.

Joyce, Patrick. *Visions of the People: Industrial England and the Question of Class*. Cambridge: Cambridge University Press, 1991.

———. *Democratic Subjects: The Self and the Social in Nineteenth-Century England*. Cambridge: Cambridge University Press, 1991.

[Kegan, Paul C]. 'The Proper Use of City Churches'. *Nineteenth Century* 7, no. 37 (March 1880), pp. 486–92.

Kelleher, Margaret. 'Charlotte Riddell's *A Struggle for Fame*: The Field of Women's Literary production'. *Colby Quarterly* 36 (2000), pp. 116–31.

King, Andrew. *The London Journal, 1845–83: Periodicals, Production and Gender*. Aldershot: Ashgate, 2004.

Kopytoff, Igor. 'The cultural biography of things: commoditization as a process'. In *The social life of things: Commodities in cultural perspective*, ed. Appadurai Arjun. Cambridge University Press: Cambridge, 1986, pp. 64–91.

Kornbluh, Anna. *Realizing Capital: Financial and Psychic Economies in Victorian Form*. New York: Fordham University Press, 2014.

Koselleck, Reinhart. *Futures Past: On the Semantics of Historical Time*. New York: Columbia University Press, 2004.

Kreisel, Deanna K. *Economic Woman: Demand, Gender and Narrative Closure in Eliot and Hardy*. Toronto: University of Toronto Press, 2012.

Kynaston, David. *The City of London. A World of its Own, 1815–1890*. London: Pimlico, 1996.

Lamb, Charles. 'Imperfect Sympathies'. 1821. In *The Essays of Elia*. London: The Walter Scott Press, n.d, pp. 91–9.

Lanser, Susan Sniader. *Fictions of Authority: Women Writers and Narrative Voice*. Ithaca and London: Cornell University Press, 1992.

Leckie, Barbara. *Culture and Adultery: The Novel, The Newspaper, and the Law, 1857–1914*. Philadelphia: University of Pennsylvania Press, 1999.

Lester, Markham V. *Victorian Insolvency: Bankruptcy, Imprisonment for Debt, and Company Winding-Up in Nineteenth-Century England*. Oxford: Oxford University Press, 1995.

Levine Caroline and Mario Ortiz-Robles, eds. *Narrative Middles: Navigating the Nineteenth-Century British Novel*. Columbus: Ohio State University Press 2011.

Liggins, Emma. 'Introduction'. *Weird Stories by Charlotte Riddell*. London: Victorian Secrets, 2009.

'Literature' (Rev. of *George Geith*). *The Sporting Gazette, Limited*, 21 January 1865, p. 45.

'Literature', *The Sporting Gazette, Limited*, 13 May 1868, pp. 402–3.

'Literature and Business'. *The Saturday Review* 29, no. 745 (5 February 1870), pp. 176–8.

Logan, Deborah. 'Introduction'. *Illustrations of Political Economy: Selected Tales*, ed. Deborah Logan. Peterborough, ON: Broadview, 2004, pp. 9–50.

'London Correspondence'. *The Belfast News-Letter*, 6 January 1865, p. 3.

Luftig, Victor. *Seeing Together. Friendship Between the Sexes in English Writing, from Mill to Woolf*. Stanford: Stanford University Press, 1993.

Lukàcs, Georg. 'Narrate or Describe?'. 1970. In *Writer and Critic and other Essays*. Lincoln, NE: Authors Guild Backinprint 2005, pp. 110–48.

Lyndall, Joseph. *Business: As it Is, and As It Might Be*. London: Walton and Maberly, 1854.

Macdougal, Duncan. *A Complete System of Bookkeeping; or Single and Double Entry Familiarly Explained*. Manchester: Published for the author, Stationers' Hall, 1862.

Macleod, Christine. *Heroes of Invention: Technology, Liberalism and British Identity, 1750–1914*. Cambridge: Cambridge University Press 2007.

MacWilliam, Rohan. 'Liberalism Lite?', *Victorian Studies* 48, no.1 (Autumn 2005), pp. 103–11.

Marshall, Alfred. 'The Social Possibilities of Economic Chivalry'. *The Economic Journal* 17, no. 65 (March 1907), pp. 7–29.

Martin, Felix. *Money: The Unauthorized Biography*. New York: Alfred A. Knops, 2013.

Marvin, Charles. 'English Merchants and German Traders'. *Time* 16 (February 1887), pp. 136–41.

Matz, Aaron. *Satire in an Age of Realism*. Cambridge: Cambridge University Press, 2010.

Maunder, Andrew. 'Charlotte Eliza Lawson Riddell'. In *Nineteenth-Century British Women Writers*, ed. Abigail Bloom. London: Aldywch Press, 2000, pp. 323–7.

McCloskey, David. 'Did Victorian Britain fail?'. In *Trade and Enterprise in Victorian Britain: Essays in Historical Economics*. London: Allen and Unwin, 1981, pp. 98–136.

McCloskey, Deirdre. *The Bourgeois Virtues: Ethics for an Age of Commerce*. Chicago: The University of Chicago Press, 2006.

McKendrick, Neil. ' "Gentlemen and Players" revisited: the gentlemanly ideal, the business ideal and the professional ideal in English literary culture'. In *Business Life and Public Policy. Essays in honour of D.C. Coleman*, ed. Neil McKendrick and R.B. Outhwhite. Cambridge: Cambridge University Press, 1986.

M'Crea, James 'The Queen as a Woman of Business'. *Time* 1 (April 1879), pp. 40–47.

———. 'The Prince as a Man of Business'. *Time* 1 (May 1879), pp. 153–8.

McVeagh, John. *Tradefull Merchants: The Portrayal of the Capitalist in Literature*. London: Routledge & Kegan Paul, 1981.

'The Metaphysics of Business'. *The Chambers's Edinburgh Journal* 74 (31 May 1845), pp. 338–9.

Michie, Elsie. *The Vulgar Question of Money: Heiresses, Materialism and the Novels of Manners from Jane Austen to Henry James*. Baltimore: The Johns Hopkins University Press, 2011.

Michie, Ranald, ed. *The Development of London as a Financial Centre. Vol. 2: 1850–1914*. London: I.B.Tauris Publishers, 2000.

——. *Guilty Money: The City of London in Victorian and Edwardian Culture, 1815–1914*. London: Pickering & Chatto, 2009.

Middleton, R. Dwight. 'Emotional Style: The Cultural Ordering of Emotions'. *Ethos* 17, no. 2 (Jan. 1989), pp. 187–201.

Mill, John Stuart. *On Liberty and other Writings*. 1859. Cambridge: Cambridge University Press, 1989.

Miller, Andrew. 'Lives Unlead in Realist Fiction'. *Representations* 98, no. 1 (Spring 2007), pp. 118–34.

Miller, Peter. 'Accounting as Social and Institutional Practice: An Introduction'. In *Accounting as Social and Institutional Practice*, ed. Anthony G. Hopwood and Peter Miller. Cambridge: Cambridge University Press, 1994, pp. 1–39.

Mitchell, Charlotte. 'Riddell, Charlotte Eliza Lawson (1832–1906)'. *Oxford Dictionary of National Biography*, http://www.oxforddnb.com/view/article/35748?docPos=3 – last accessed 3 April 2015.

Mitford, Mary Russell. *Our Village*. 1819. London: Macmillan, 1900.

Monk, Leland. *Standard Deviations: Chance and the Modern British Novel*. Stanford: Stanford University Press, 1993.

Moretti, Franco, *The Way of the World: The Bildungroman in European Culture*, London, Verso, 1996.

——. *The Bourgeois Between History and Literature*. London: Verso, 2013.

Morgan, H.E. 'The Dignity of Business'. *Review of Reviews* 47, no. 277 (January 1913), pp. 21–3.

——. 'The Dignity of Business. Creating a Common Meeting Ground'. *Review of Reviews* 47, no. 278 (February 1913), pp. 137–40.

[Morley, Henry]. 'Justice to Chicory'. *Household Words* 6 (13 November 1852), pp. 208–10.

'Mortomley Estate'. *The Saturday Review* 38, no. 989 (10 October 1874), pp. 481–2.

'The Mortomley's Estate'. *The Spectator* 2422 (17 October 1874), p. 23.

'Mrs Riddell's New Novel' (Rev. of *The Senior Partner*). *The Pall Mall Gazette*, 11 January 1882, p. 5.

Murphy, James H. *Irish Novelists & the Victorian Age*. Oxford: Oxford University Press, 2011.

Nead, Lynda. *Victorian Babylon: People, Streets and Images in Nineteenth-Century London*. New Haven: Yale University Press, 2005.

'The New Bankruptcy Act'. *The Economist* 27, no. 1372 (11 December 1869), pp. 1457–8.

'New Novels' (Rev. of *George Geith*), *The London Review* 10, no. 241 (11 February 1865), pp. 181–2.

'New Novels' (Rev. of *The Senior Partner*). *The London Standard*, 27 January 1882, p. 1.

'New Novels' (Rev. of *The Senior Partner*), *The Graphic*, 11 March 1882, p. 254.

'New Novels' (Rev. of *Mitre Court*). *The Graphic*, 19 December 1885, p. 26.

[Noble, John Ashcroft] 'New Novels', *The Academy* 709 (5 December 1885), pp. 371–2.

'Noblemen in Business'. *London Society* 33, no.195 (March 1878), pp. 214–22.

'Non-Thinkers'. *The St. James's Magazine* 6 (October 1870), pp. 405–8.

Novak, Daniel. *Realism, Photography and Nineteenth-Century Fiction*. Cambridge: Cambridge University Press, 2008.

'Novels of the Week' (Rev. of *Mitre Court*). *The Athenaeum* 3033 (12 December 1885), pp. 765–6.

'Occasional Notes'. *The Pall Mall Gazette*, 24 April 1884, p. 2.

O'Gorman, Francis, ed. *Victorian Literature and Finance*. Oxford: Oxford University Press, 2007.

'On Mercantile Biography'. *The Athenaeum* 24 (December 1808), pp. 495–6.

Osteen, Mark and Martha Woodmansee, eds. *The New Economic Criticism: Studies at the Intersection of Literature and Economics*. London: Routledge, 1999.

Ott Julia and William Milberg, 'Capitalism Studies: A Manifesto' *Public Seminar Review* 1, no. 2 (Summer 2014) http://www.publicseminar.org/2014/04/capitalism-studies-a-manifesto/#.VVRp0dqqqkp last accessed 5 May 2015.

'Our Bankruptcy Law'. *The Examiner* 3687 (28 September 1878), pp. 1226–7.

Page, H.A. 'A Captain of Industry'. *Good Words* 13 (January 1872), pp. 490–5.

'Panic in the City'. *The Saturday Review* 21, no. 550 (12 May 1866), pp. 547–8.

Parry, Jonathan. *The Rise and Fall of Liberal Government In Victorian Britain*. New Haven: Yale University Press, 1993.

Parsons, Wayne. *The Power of the Financial Press: Journalism and Economic Opinion in Britain and America*. Aldershot: Edward Elgar, 1989.

[Patterson, Robert Hogarth]. 'The City of Gold'. *Blackwood's Edinburgh Magazine* 96, no. 587 (September 1864), pp. 367–84.

'Paying Daughters'. *The National Magazine* 2, no. 7 (May 1857), p. 31.

Payn, James. 'The Literary Calling and its Future'. *Nineteenth-Century* 6, no. 34 (December 1879), pp. 985–98.

Perkins, Harold. *Origins of Modern English Society*. London: Ark Paperbacks 1985.

Peterson, Linda. *Becoming a Woman of Letters. Myths of Authorship and Facts of the Victorian Market*. Princeton: Princeton University Press, 2009.

Phelan James and Peter J. Rabinowitz. 'Time, Plot, Progression'. In *Narrative Theory: Core Concepts and Critical Debates*, ed. David Herman and others. Columbus: The Ohio State University Press, 2012, pp. 5–70.

Pollard, Arthur, ed. *The Representation of Business in English Literature*. London: IAE, 2000.

Poovey, Mary. *Uneven Developments: The Ideological Work of Gender in Mid-Victorian England*. Chicago: The University of Chicago Press, 1988.

———. *Genres of the Credit Economy. Mediating Value in Eighteenth- and Nineteenth Century Britain*. Chicago: The University of Chicago Press, 2008.

Pratt, Stephanie. *American Indians in British Art, 1700–1840*. Norman: The University of Oklahoma Press, 2005.

Preda, Alex. *Framing Finance: The Boundaries of Markets and Modern Capitalism*. Chicago: The University of Chicago press, 2009.

Preston, Alex. *This Bleeding City*. London: Faber & Faber, 2011.

Prince, Gerald. *Narrative as Theme: Studies in French Fiction*. Lincoln: University of Nebraska Press, 1992.

———. 'The Disnarrated'. In *Routledge Encyclopedia of Narrative Theory*, ed. David Herman, Manfred Jahn and Marie-Laure Ryan. Abingdon: Routledge, 2005, p. 118.

Puckett, Kent. *Bad Form: Social Mistakes and the Nineteenth-Century Novel*. Oxford: Oxford University Press, 2008.

Pullaos, Chris. 'Professionalisation'. In *The Routledge Companion to Accounting History*, ed. John Richard Edwards and Stephen P. Walker. London: Routledge, pp. 247–73.

'The Race for Wealth'. *The Saturday Review* 22, no. 567 (8 September 1866), pp. 306–8.
'The Race for Wealth'. *The Morning Post* 14 September 1866, p. 3.
'The Race for Wealth'. *The Daily News* 14 November 1866, p. 3.
Rappoport, Jill. *Giving Women: Alliance and Exchange in Victorian Culture.* Oxford: Oxford University Press, 2012.
Raven, James. 'British History and Enterprise Culture'. *Past and Present* 123 (1989), pp. 178–204.
Reddy, William M. *The Navigation of Feeling.* Cambridge: Cambridge University Press, 2001.
Reed, John. 'A Friend to Mammon: Speculation in Victorian Literature'. *Victorian Studies* 27, no. 2 (1984), pp. 179–202.
Reeve, Wybert. *George Geith, or Romance of a City Life. A Drama in Four Acts and a Tableau Founded on Mrs Riddell's Celebrated Novel.* 1877. London and New York: Samuel French Publisher, 1880.
Reid, Stuart ed. *Memoirs of Sir Wemyss Reid.* London: Cassel and Co., 1905.
Richards, Thomas. *The Commodity Culture of Victorian England: Advertising and Spectacle, 1851–1914.* Stanford: Stanford University Press, 1990.
Riddell, Charlotte. *Too Much Alone.* 1860. London: Hutchinson & Co, n.d.
———. *City and Suburb.* 1861. London: Hutchinson & Co, n.d.
———. *George Geith of Fen Court.* 1864. London: Hutchinson & Co. n.d.
———. *The Race for Wealth.* Leipzig: Bernard Tauchnitz, 1866.
———. *Far Above Rubies.* 1867. London: Hutchinson & Co, n.d.
———. *Austin Friars.* 1870. London: Hutchinson & Co, n.d.
———. *Mortomley's Estate.* 1874. London: Hutchinson & Co. n.d.
———. *Frank Sinclair's Wife and Forewarned, Forearmed.* 1874. London: Hutchinson & Co., n.d.
———. *The Senior Partner.* London: Richard Bentley, 1881.
———. *A Struggle for Fame.* 1883. Dublin: The Tramp Press, 2014.
———. *Weird Stories.* 1883. London: Victorian Secrets, 2009.
———. *Mitre Court: a Tale of the Great City.* London: Richard Bentley, 1885.
Riddell v. Riddell and Smith. R133 (1871). British National Archives C16/747.
Rindisbacher, Hans J. *The Smell of Books: A Cultural-Historical Study of Olfactory Perception in Literature.* Ann Arbor: The University of Michigan Press, 1992.
Ritchie, Anne Thackeray. 'Heroines and Their Grandmothers'. *The Cornhill Magazine* 11, no. 65 (May 1865), pp. 630–40.
Robb, George. *White-Collar Crime in Modern England. Financial Fraud and Business Morality, 1845–1929.* Cambridge: Cambridge University Press, 1992.
'Romance in Business'. *Blackwood's Edinburgh Magazine* 131, no. 796 (February 1882), pp. 221–45.
Rose, Mary B. 'The family firm in British business, 1780–1914'. In *Business enterprise in modern Britain from the eighteenth to the twentieth century,* ed. Maurice Kirby and Mary B. Rose. London: Routledge, 1994, pp. 61–87.
———. 'Beyond Buddenbrooks: the family firm and the management of succession in nineteenth-century Britain'. In *Entrepreneurship, Networks, and Modern Business,* ed. Jonathan Brown and Mary B. Rose. Manchester: Manchester University Press, 1993, pp. 127–43.
Rothberg, Michael. *Traumatic Realism: The Demands of Holocaust Representation.* Minneapolis: University of Minnesota Press, 2000.

Rubinstein, W.D. 'Cultural Explanations for Britain's Economic Decline: How True?' In *British Culture and Economic Decline*, ed. Bruce Collins and Keith Robbins. Weidenfeld and Nicolson: London, 1990, pp. 59–90.

Ruskin, John. *The Seven Lamps of Architecture*. 1849. Leipzig: Bernhard Tauchnitz, 1907.

———. *Modern Painters*. 1860. vol. 5. London: Smith, Elders and Co., 1873.

Russell, Norman. *The Novelist and Mammon: Literary Responses to the World of Commerce in the Nineteenth Century*. Oxford: Clarendon Press, 1986.

Ryan, Marie-Laure. *Narrative as Virtual Reality: Immersion and Interactivity in Literature and Electronic Media*. Baltimore and London: The Johns Hopkins University Press, 2001.

S., Suzana. *Confessions of a City Girl*. London: Virgin Books, 2009

Sala, George Augustus. *Gaslight and Daylight: With Some London Scenes They Shine Upon*. London: Chapman & Hall, 1859.

'Santiago!'. *Punch, or the London Charivari*, 11 April 1868, p. 157.

Schelstraete, Jasper. 'Idle Employment and Dickens's Uncommercial Ruse: The Narratorial Entity in "The Uncommercial Traveller"'. *Victorian Periodicals Review* 47, no. 1 (Spring 2014), pp. 50–65.

Scott, Benjamin. *A Statistical Vindication of the City of London*. 1867. London: Longman, Greens and Co., 1877.

Searle, Geoffrey Russell. *Morality and the Market in Victorian Britain*. Oxford: Clarendon Press, 1998.

Sedgwick, Eve Kosofky. *Between Men: English Literature and Male Homosocial Desire*. New York: Columbia University Press, 1985.

'Self-Help'. *The Fraser's Magazine for Town and Country* 61, no. 366 (June 1860), pp. 778–86.

Shaw, Harry. *Narrating Reality: Austen, Scott, Eliot*. Ithaca: Cornell University Press, 1999.

Smiles, Samuel. *Self-Help With Illustrations of Character, Conduct, and Perseverance*. 1859. Oxford: Oxford University Press, 2002.

Smith Mrs. Adolphe. 'An American Woman of Business'. *The Tinsley's Magazine* 29 (November 1881), pp. 490–93.

Smith, Henry MD. *High-Pressure Business Life, its Evils, Physical and Moral*. London: J.A. Brook and Co., 1876.

'Soll und Haben: Roman in sechs Büchern'. *The British Quarterly Review* 27, no. 53 (January 1858), pp. 152–72.

Solomons, David and Stephen A. Zeff, *Accounting Research, 1948–1958: Selected Articles on Accounting History*. New York: Garland, 1996.

Sparks, Tabitha. 'Fiction Becomes Her: Representations of Female Character in Mary Elizabeth Braddon's *The Doctor's Wife*'. In *Beyond Sensation: Mary Elizabeth Braddon in Context*, ed. Marlene Tromp, Pamela K. Gilbert, Aeron Haynie. New York: State University of New York Press, 2000, pp. 187–210.

Srebrnik, Patricia. 'Mrs. Riddell and the Reviewers: A Case Study in Victorian Popular Fiction'. *Women's Studies* 23 (1994), pp. 69–84.

'The St. James's Magazine'. *The Morning Post*, 9 April 1868, p. 6.

Stark, Susanne. 'Dickens in German Guise? Anglo-German Cross-Currents in the Nineteenth-Century Reception of Gustav Freytag's *Soll und Haben*'. In *The Novel in Anglo-German Context. Cultural Cross Currents and Affinities*, ed. Susanne Stark. Amsterdam: Rodopi, 2000, pp. 157–72.

Stedman, Gesa. *Stemming the Torrent. Expression and Control in the Victorian Discourses on the Emotions, 1830–1872*. Aldershot: Ashgate, 2002.

Stern, Rebecca. *Home Economics. Domestic Fraud in Victorian England*. Columbus: The Ohio State University Press, 2008.

Stewart, Garrett. *Dear Reader: The Conscripted Audience in Nineteenth-Century British Fiction*. Baltimore and London: The Johns Hopkins University Press, 1996.

'The Successful Merchant'. *The Chambers's Edinburgh Journal* 429 (20 March 1852), pp. 188–90.

The Successful Merchant'. *The Tait's Edinburgh Magazine* 19, no. 219 (March 1852), pp. 189–91.

Sussman, Herbert. *Victorian Masculinities: Manhood and Masculine Poetics in Early Victorian Literature and Art*. Cambridge: Cambridge University Press, 1995.

Sutherland, John, ed. *The Stanford Companion to Victorian Fiction*. Stanford: Stanford University Press, 1989.

Sutton, Henry. *Get Me Out of Here*. London: Harvey Secker, 2010.

Taylor, James. *Creating Capitalism: Joint-Stock Enterprise in British Politics and Culture, 1800–1870*. Woodbridge: The Boydell Press, 2006.

———. *Boardroom Scandal: The Criminalization of Company Fraud in Nineteenth-Century Britain*. Oxford: Oxford University Press, 2013.

'Theatrical Gossip'. *The Era*, 28 October 1877, p. 6.

Thomas, David Wayne. *Cultivating Victorians: Liberal Culture and the Aesthetic*. Philadelphia: University of Pennsylvania Press, 2004.

Thompson, F.M.L. *Gentrification and the Enterprise Culture. Britain 1870–1980*. Oxford: Oxford University Press, 2001.

Thompson, Venetia. *Gross Misconduct: My Year of Excess in the City*. London: Pocket Books, 2010.

'Three Novels' (Rev. of *Mitre Court*). *The Saturday Review* 61, no. 1577 (16 January 1886), pp. 96–7.

Tinsley, William. *Random Recollections of an Old Publisher*. London: Simpkin, Marshall, Hamilton, Kent & Co., 1900.

Todd, Janet ed. *British Women Writers: A Critical Reference Guide*. New York: Continuum, 1989.

Toms, Steven. 'Capitalism'. In *The Routledge Companion to Accounting History*, ed. John Richards Edwards and Stephen P. Walker. London. Routledge, 2009, pp. 341–51.

Trollope, Anthony. *Framley Parsonage*. 1861. Oxford: Oxford University Press, 1980.

———. *An Autobiography*. 1883. Oxford: Oxford University Press, 1987.

Trotter, David. *Cooking with Mud: The Idea of Mess in Nineteenth-Century Art and Fiction*. Oxford: Oxford University Press, 2000.

———. 'Household Clearances in Victorian Fiction'. *19: Interdisciplinary Studies in the Long Nineteenth Century* 6 (2008), pp. 1–19, www.19.bbk.ac.uk. Last accessed 3 March 2014.

Turner, Charles C. 'Living London'. 1903. In *The Development of London as a Financial Centre*, vol. 2: 1850–1914, ed. Ranald C. Michie. London: I.B. Tauris, pp. 33–57.

'Union of Literary and Business Habits'. *The Chambers's Edinburgh Journal* 229 (18 June 1836), pp. 163–4.

Vernon, James. 'What Was Liberalism and Who Was Its Subject?; Or, Will the Real Liberal Subject Please Stand Up?' *Victorian Studies* 53, no. 2 (2011), pp. 303–10.

Wagner, Peter, *Modernity: Understanding the Present*, Cambridge: Polity Press, 2012,

———. *Modernity as Experience and Interpretation*. London: Polity Press, 2008.

Wagner, Tamara. *Financial Speculation in Victorian Fiction. Plotting Money and the Novel Genre, 1815–1901*. Columbus: The Ohio State University Press, 2010.

Warhol, Robyn. *Gendered Interventions: Narrative Discourse in the Victorian Novel*. New Brunswick: Rutgers University Press, 1989.

Weber, Max. *The Protestant Ethic and the Spirit of Capitalism*. London: Routledge, 2001.

Weiner, Martin J. *English Culture and the Decline of the Industrial Spirit, 1850–1980*. Cambridge: Cambridge University Press, 1981.

Weiss, Barbara. *The Hell of the English: Bankruptcy and the Victorian Novel*. Lewisburg: Bucknell University Press, 1986.

Weiss, Richard. *The American Myth of Success: From Horatio Alger to Norman Vincent Pealie*. Urbana: University of Illinois Press, 1988.

Wells, Samuel Robert. *How to do Business: A Pocket Manual of Practical Affairs, and a Guide to Success in Life*. New York and London: Fowler and Wells Publishers, 1857.

Whelan, Lana Baker. *Class, Culture and Suburban Anxieties in the Victorian Era*. London: Routledge, 2010.

Williams, Raymond. *Keywords: A Vocabulary of Culture and Society*, 1976. Oxford: Oxford University Press, 1983.

———. *The Country and the City*. Oxford: Oxford University Press, 1975.

Williams, Susan ed. *The Penguin Book of Classic Fantasy by Women*. Harmondsworth: Penguin, 1995.

Woloch, Alex. *The One vs the Many: Minor Characters and the Space of the Protagonist in the Novel*. Princeton: Princeton University Press, 2003.

'Women of Business'. *The Tait's Edinburgh Magazine* 1, no. 9 (October 1834), pp. 596–7.

Worthington, Beresford. *Professional Accountants: An Historical Sketch*. London: Gee & Co., 1895.

Yeazell, Ruth. 'Do It or Dorrit'. *NOVEL: a Forum on Fiction* 25, no.1 (Autumn 1991), pp. 33–49.

Young, Linda. *Middle-Class Culture in the Nineteenth Century: America, Australia and Britain*. Basingstoke: Palgrave Macmillann, 1988.

Young, Paul. *Globalization and the Great Exhibition: The Victorian New World Order*. Basingstoke: Palgrave Macmillan, 2009.

Ziegler, Garrett. 'The City of London, Real and Unreal'. *Victorian Studies* 49, no. 3 (Spring 2007), pp. 431–55.

Zimmerman, Virginia. '"The Weird Message from the Past": Material Epistemologies of Past, Present, and Future in the *Nineteenth Century*', *Victorian Periodicals Review* 42, no. 2 (Summer 2009), pp. 114–35.

Zlotnick, Susan. *Women, Writing, and the Industrial Revolution*. Baltimore: The Johns Hopkins University Press, 1998.

Index

Riddell's novels are indexed alphabetically by title. Novels by other authors are listed under the author's name.

For Product Safety Concerns and Information please contact our
EU representative GPSR@taylorandfrancis.com Taylor & Francis
Verlag GmbH, Kaufingerstraße 24, 80331 München, Germany